Children with Audiological Needs:
From Identification to Aural Rehabilitation

Kate E. Reynolds, Ph.D.

Cynthia McCormick Richburg, Ph.D.

Diane Heller Klein, Ph.D.

Michelle Parfitt, M.A.

Illustrated by
Paul Malbrough, Jr.

Butte Publications, Inc.
Hillsboro, OR, U.S.A.

Children with Audiological Needs:
From Identification to Aural Rehabilitation

Kate E. Reynolds, Ph.D.
Cynthia McCormick Richburg, Ph.D.
Diane Heller Klein, Ph.D.
Michelle Parfitt, M.A.

Editor: Ellen Todras
Design and Layout: Anita Jones, Another Jones Graphics

Butte Publications, Inc.
P. O. Box 1328
Hillsboro, OR 97123-1328
U.S.A.

ISBN: 978-1-939349-06-4

Acknowledgments

Kate

With the publication of this text, one of my dreams has finally been realized. Writing a text such as this has been on my "to-do" list for longer than I care to remember. It goes without saying that I could never have completed this task without the knowledge, skills, and humor of many others. I owe a debt of gratitude to Dee, Cindy, and Michelle, my co-authors; to Paul, our illustrator; to Ellen, our editor; Anita, our layout designer; and of course to our publisher, Matt. They were the best writing partners and friends I could have had. Diane (Dee) Klein's ability to successfully herd cats (that is us, the other authors) was nothing less than miraculous. Her part in my dogsled accident is forever forgiven.

Much appreciation is due my brother, who graciously made it possible for me to work on this text during vacations he planned for us across the globe. You rock, Tom! I also want to thank my amazing students at the University of New Orleans (UNO). Many thanks go to my graduate assistants and rising stars, Christian Gentile and Mimi Burlet-Kinler. While they have moved on to bigger and better things (Mimi into a classroom of lucky children and Christian to an Au.D. program), their input and ability to free me from mundane, time-stealing, yet necessary, tasks was invaluable to getting my work on this text completed. I also offer my sincerest appreciation to the students who saw me begin this project, Evora Baker, Rachelle Feinland, Melissa Barnes, Elizabeth Cash, and Katie Dunn among others, and to those who saw me finish it and then used the text in its draft form for their class. You folks have provided us with invaluable feedback, so thank you Laura Stahl, Jennifer Vollenweider, LaVerne Traylor, Laurie Foreman, and Ashley Argrave. Thank you, thank you, thank you all!

Cindy

I'd like to thank my friend and colleague, Dee Klein, who not only talked me into writing "just one more book," but who literally got us through this process. We couldn't (and wouldn't) have done it without you, Dee. And thanks, too, for introducing me to Kate and Michelle and for putting "the team" together. I also need to thank Ashley Irwin, my graduate assistant, who helped me with the technological aspects of putting my figures and tables together—thank goodness for this tech-savvy younger generation! Finally, I'm grateful to Matt Brink and the folks at Butte for putting up with us through all of our surgeries, family issues, and car wrecks! Hopefully the wait was worth it.

Dee

Without students, there is no need for clear and concise textbooks. I want to sincerely thank the marvelous students from the Deaf Education programs at Indiana University of Pennsylvania (IUP) and the University of New Orleans (UNO) who worked with me over the last several years and had major impact on the content and style of this book. The following students in particular provided not only fabulous feedback, but much needed "warm-fuzzy" emotional support as well: from IUP—Jennifer Jackson, Lauren Jones, and colleagues Annah Hill and Nancy Yost; from UNO—Evora Baker, Melissa Barnes, Rachelle Feinland, Mimi Kinler, and Jennifer Vollenweider.

Sometimes you receive insightful help from the most unexpected sources. Many thanks to my 88-year-old dad, Daniel Heller, who patiently listened to me read this book to him and pointed out a number of terms and concepts that required additional explanation.

Of course, a book can never come to fruition without the unwavering support of the writing team, the publisher, and his personnel! There are few words to explain the joy I find in writing on a team of knowledgeable, expressive, brilliant professionals who not only really know their stuff but continue to teach me more of that stuff every single day. Kate, Cindy, and Michelle have made me one of the most joy-filled people around! Many thanks to Matt Brink for understanding that there is this thing called "life and family" and sometimes they just get in the way of meeting deadlines! Without you, Matt, there would be no book! One cannot overestimate the value of the most extraordinary editor, Ellen Todras. We have officially mind-melded and her thoughts about writing are now my own. Thank you for teaching me so much about this process and making this book one that all can read with ease and eagerness. Last, but not least, our fantastic layout designer Anita Jones gave us our "sparklies" and just the right amount of white space to ensure that our readers could flow through the text seamlessly and learn some rather daunting material. Thank you all for making this text a reality.

Michelle

I'd like to thank Dee, Kate, and Cindy for inviting me to be a part of this book writing team. Thanks to our publisher, Matt, and editor, Ellen, for their teamwork and expertise. I need to give extra thanks to Dee for having patience with my many questions and guiding me through the process. I'd also like to thank Debbie Johnston, who has always been available to consult with me on all matters related to audiology. Many thanks to the staff, students, and families at DePaul School for Hearing and Speech, who have taught me so much about the bright futures available to children with hearing loss.

Dedications

<u>Kate</u>

To the most important women in my life, my mother, Harriet Grosman, and my daughter, Margaret Reynolds; I hope I have made you as proud of me as I am of the two of you. Thank you for your encouragement and love throughout my life. Three generations still going strong! I also dedicate this to my good friend Ava Hines Hamilton in hopes that there is a hereafter, and if so, people read there. I miss your unconditional friendship and laughter, Ava.

<u>Cindy</u>

To my husband, Jim, who put up with me again as I got another book written. Thanks for your patience and willingness to cover for me all those times I was away working. And to my sons, James and Gavin, who will one day hopefully read this book and think it was all worthwhile having Mommy out of the house all those evenings!

<u>Diane</u>

To my husband, Eddie, for his indefatigable conviction, support, and love; as always, I couldn't have done this without you!

<u>Michelle</u>

To my husband, Tony, and my daughters, Julia and Gina, who keep me going with an endless supply of love, support, laughter, and smiles.

Contents

Introduction

This text was written for the individual who is *not* an audiologist but is a professional who either works with, or will work with, deaf and hard of hearing children or adults in some other capacity. While preservice teachers of students who are deaf or hard of hearing (d/hh) are a natural fit for our reading audience, other individuals, such as speech-language pathologists who want a basic review of their knowledge base, physical and occupational therapists, interpreters, school nurses, general educators, administrators, and parents will benefit from the information contained in this text. And while you, our reader, may not fall into any of the above categories, if you are interested in learning more about the biology and physics of hearing, teaching techniques for auditory development, and assistive hearing technology on a practical, functional, and fundamental level, this is the book for you. Though intended for use as a textbook, *Children with Audiological Needs: From Identification to Aural Rehabilitation* can also be used as a reference book. Readers may decide to focus their attention on only those chapters that pertain to their immediate situations. For students in an audiology course in a program that prepares teachers to work with deaf and hard of hearing students, we (the authors) have attempted to write this text in such a way that you can apply its information to situations you encounter, or will encounter, in your own classrooms.

Of necessity, there is much technical and scientific information in the chapters that follow this introduction. This can't be avoided. (And why would we want to, anyway?) That is the nature of studying the field of audiology. However, we have attempted to do three things to help the reader more easily digest the material and make it more relevant to "real life." First, we have carefully selected specific concepts and information from the very wide and deep knowledge base in the field of audiology. We believe that what we present in this text in expanded detail is only the most essential information and concepts a non-audiologist should understand. Thus, there are many audiological concepts not discussed in this text because they are not relevant to the needs of our targeted readership. Second, for information that is quite technical in nature, we have, whenever possible, used real-life and practical examples to present and apply the information in a memorable way. And finally, we think that laughter in response to just the right amount of humor in our text is desirable; after all, the use of humor is supported by research on learning and retention (Berk, 2002). Humor enhances the pleasure of reading a text like ours and cements the concepts we present in a unique and effective way. And to that end, your authors (please consider us as yours for as long as you use this text) sincerely hope that when you turn the last page of this book and close the back cover, you will exclaim, "Wow, I haven't read something so well written and content-filled since (*insert your favorite novel's name here*)!"

Seriously though, we strongly recommend this text for a university program that prepares teachers to work with deaf students. *Children with Audiological Needs* fits well into a course that covers the following major facets of hearing and audiology: (1) overview of professionals in the field of deafness and their responsibilities and affiliations, as well as legal precedents for educating deaf and hard of hearing students, (2) hearing science (physics of sound), (3) the anatomy and physiology of the hearing mechanism, (4) etiologies of hearing loss, (5) hearing assessment, (6) amplification and other hearing technology, and (7) auditory training/aural (re)habilitation. And although this may come as no surprise, those seven areas listed above correspond to our text's seven chapters!

Each chapter follows a structural roadmap:

1. Chapters open with a realistic scenario that one of the authors or author's colleagues has encountered. These scenarios conclude by asking the reader to be able to do something related to the scenario by the end of the chapter in each chapter's Food for Thought section. Think of this request as a creative way to present the learning objective for the chapter. Also, we strive to assure that each scenario highlights the information presented in the chapter in a relatable manner. This should help the reader remember the more technical information presented in the chapter and how, on a daily basis, professionals working with individuals with hearing loss can use that information.

2. Next comes a vocabulary list of key words that the reader will encounter in the chapter. These words will be boldfaced at first use in the text. Supplemental definitions of many of these key vocabulary terms are presented in the glossary at the end of the text.

3. After the vocabulary listing, we take the plunge and present the content of the chapter. There will be narrative material, tables, charts, and figures; there will be some humor; and there will be application and/or functional examples. We believe that these examples are a mainstay of this text. Your authors have taught courses throughout the years and have found that grounding the more esoteric information in real-life situations is invaluable for (1) keeping the reader focused and interested, and (2) keeping the material relevant. Our intent, once again, is to link the narrative and graphic material to situations and decisions made daily by teachers of the deaf (TODs), speech-language pathologists (SLPs), parents, general education teachers, d/hh students and adults, and school administrators.

4. Chapters usually contain one or perhaps many sidebars. Sidebars focus upon items of interest related to, but not always essential to, the main material. Some sidebars will be found in the side margin, but larger sidebars are embedded in the main text. So, below are the two sidebars for this introductory chapter. While these two sidebars present examples of the structure of our text's sidebars, they also explain some of the language conventions we employ throughout the chapters.

Deaf or deaf?

Usually, when referring to the audiological measure of deafness, the authors use (and suggest you also use) the lowercase *d* to describe hearing status. When referring to individuals who share a common language, American Sign Language [ASL], a common history, and who do *not* view themselves as disabled but merely different from people who hear, it is preferred to use the capital letter *D*. This is more commonly referred to as the "big D Deaf." It is also acceptable to refer to those persons who consider themselves culturally **D**eaf in tandem with those who are audiologically **d**eaf by using the written convention, d/Deaf. As usual, there is one exception… we don't mess with the rules of grammar. So, unless you wish to bring the wrath of your former English teacher down upon you, use the capital *D* at the beginning of *all* sentences, because, in these cases, it really doesn't matter if you meant **D**eaf or **d**eaf: the laws of grammar are not meant to be broken!

There are a few other language conventions we use in this text. The only time you will see the term *hearing impaired (HI)* is in a direct quote. This is in deference to big D Deaf people who complain that the term *hearing impaired* is offensive. Some Deaf folks suggest with a sense of irony that the term *HI* be used only to describe those unfortunate hearing people who must listen to unwanted sound and noise (see the definition of *noise* in Chapter 2). Thus, hearing people's listening ability is "impaired" by noise pollution and unwanted sound/voices. (So, yes, hearing reader, you can count your great-aunt Bertha's nonstop ramblings as noise.) There are also language no-no's we'd like to present. The terms *deaf and dumb* (shudder), *deaf and mute*, and *deef*—/dif/—(an old southern United States pronunciation)—are also unacceptable. And please do not tell anyone that you are in a "death education" program. *Death* Education instead of *Deaf* Education is just plain morbid unless you really are studying death and dying, which may still be slightly morbid in your authors' most humble opinion.

5. Each chapter concludes with a summary. And, although counterintuitive to many, we suggest reading this section *before* you start the chapter. Doing this is a great study technique and will help you focus on the chapter's most important ideas.

6. The final page of each chapter contains a section with questions and discussion items called Food for Thought. We always start the Food for Thought section by referring back to our opening scenario. All questions are open-ended and either come directly from the main content of the chapter or offer the reader opportunities to take chapter content and don critical thinking caps to move beyond the facts.

Gender Identification

You can be anything you say you are. We have no reason or desire to doubt you. But with regard to gender, in this text we will interchange the terms *he/she*, *him/her*, and *his/her(s)*. We do, however, promise to be consistent within a sentence so we don't unintentionally confuse you, not that we'd ever want to intentionally confuse you in the first place! Male and female pronouns are alternated from chapter to chapter for gender equity.

At the end of this text, you will find an In Conclusion section summarizing the major concepts developed in the text. You will also find a glossary with definitions for many key vocabulary terms, and a subject index. We use current APA format throughout, as this is the standard for materials in the field of education.

It's time to begin your learning journey: Happy reading!

Chapter 1

Who Works with the Kids and Why:
Legal Foundations and Professional Practitioners

Scenario

Juan and Maria Garcia were so overwhelmed. They understood and accepted the fact that their two-year-old daughter, Gabriella, lost her hearing from a recent bout of meningitis. They were having a difficult time understanding who all the professionals were that were suddenly calling their home to offer services to Gabriella. They were also not certain about the services she was entitled to receive as a newly diagnosed child with a significant hearing loss. They didn't know where to turn or who to turn to for honest guidance.

When you finish reading Chapter 1, you should be able to offer assistance to the Garcias.

Key Vocabulary

American Board of Audiology (ABA)	early intervention (EI)	interdisciplinary collaboration
American Speech-Language-Hearing Association (ASHA)	early interventionist (EI)	interpreter
	Education of All Handicapped Act of 1975 (Public Law 94-142)	itinerant teacher
Americans with Disabilities Act (ADA)		least restrictive environment (LRE)
amplification device	educational benefit	multidisciplinary collaboration
audiologist	Educational Interpreter Performance Assessment (EIPA)	National Association of the Deaf (NAD)
certificate of clinical competence (CCC)		National Interpreter Certification (NIC)
child of deaf adults (CODA)	free appropriate public education (FAPE)	pediatric audiologist
clinical fellowship year (CFY)	general education (gen-ed)	pullout
collaboration	hearing aid dealer	push-in
Communication Access Realtime Translation (CART)	inclusion	Registry of Interpreters for the Deaf (RID)
Cued Speech	Individualized Family Service Plan (IFSP)	related service
Doctor of Education (EdD)	Individuals with Disabilities Education Act (IDEA; Public Law 101-476)	resource room
Doctor of Philosophy (Ph.D.)		self-contained classroom
Doctor of Audiology (Au.D.)		speech-language pathologist (SLP)
due process	Individuals with Disabilities Education Improvement Act (IDEIA; Public Law 108-446)	transdisciplinary collaboration
ear, nose, and throat physician (ENT)		transliterator

Legal Foundations

Going Back to Basics

Having a sound understanding of special education law is important for individuals wanting to learn more about audiology and its impact on children who are deaf/hard of hearing (d/hh). Knowing how special education law came to provide services for these children facilitates an appreciation for how far our educational system in the United States has come to accommodate the needs of children with disabilities.

Until the 1950s and 1960s, federal legislation in support of quality education for school-age children with disabilities was, in essence, absent in this country. Something as basic as captioned films was not even provided to individuals with hearing loss until the Captioned Films Act, PL 85-905, was enacted in 1958. It took three more years for the Teachers of the Deaf Act of 1961 (PL 87-276) to become one of the first acts to focus on the educational needs of persons with hearing loss. This act provided grant funding to institutions of higher education to prepare teachers to educate children who were d/hh. In the mid-1960s, education for individuals with deafness was further expanded with the establishment of the National Technical Institute for the Deaf (PL 89-36) in 1965 and the Model Secondary School for the Deaf at Gallaudet College (PL 89-694) in 1966. These two laws strengthened the services being provided to children with special needs by funding the education and training of a critical mass of professionals going into the fields.

> **Numbering a Law: PL 94-142**
>
> *PL* stands for a US-Congress-passed **P**ublic **L**aw. The first number represents the two-year congressional seating during which the law was passed; for example, *94* means the 94th Congress passed this particular law. The last numbers of the title, in this case, 142, is the consecutive number of the law that passed in that seating of Congress. Thus, PL 94-142 was the 142nd bill passed by the 94th Congress, which sat during the years 1975–1977.

The 1970s were more productive with federal legislation providing resources necessary for better educating children with all disabilities, not just hearing loss. Three federal laws discussed frequently and highlighted in many textbooks include **Section 504 of the Rehabilitation Act of 1973** (aka 504); the **Education for All Handicapped Children Act of 1975** (PL 94-142, later reauthorized as IDEA and IDEIA); and the **Americans with Disabilities Act of 1990** (aka ADA and reauthorized in 2008). These federal laws provide the necessary tools with which children who are d/hh can access a free, appropriate public education without discrimination and with reasonable accommodations. They also provide the foundation for audiology as it is practiced with school-age children in the educational environment. Let's take a closer look at these three laws as they relate to our students who are d/hh.

Section 504. Section 504 of the Rehabilitation Act of 1973 originated as a civil rights law. With the passing of several amendments, this act now protects the rights of individuals with disabilities (visible and not visible) in employment and academic settings that receive federal funding (such as hospitals, human service programs, public schools, and institutions of higher education).

Section 504 Subpart D mandates that schools receiving federal funding provide students with disabilities appropriate educational services designed to meet the student's individual needs. These services are supposed to meet students with disabilities' needs as adequately as the needs of nondisabled students are met. Some appropriate accommodations for a student who is d/hh would include hearing assistance technology, preferential seating, or captioning for video materials. This law is designed to accommodate the needs of students who do not meet the federal definitions of exceptionality as defined in IDEA.

What Happens during Reauthorization

When PL 94-142 was reauthorized in 1990 and became PL 101-476 (IDEA), important changes were made. The Individuals with Disabilities Education Act (IDEA) dropped the word *handicapped* and promoted person-first language (i.e., person with a disability instead of a disabled person). In addition, two new classes of people with disabilities (Traumatic Brain Injury [TBI] and Autism) were added to the law. During the reauthorization in 2004, the name of the act was further modified to the Individuals with Disabilities Education Improvement Act (IDEIA). As an interesting aside, if no changes occur during a scheduled reauthorization, then there is no change in the bill's name or number.

Public Law 94-142. The Education for All Handicapped Children Act (PL 94-142; 1975) mandated that all students with handicapping conditions between the ages of 6 and 21 years be provided with a *free, appropriate, public education* **(FAPE).** This act offered additional key concepts and terminology used with students who are d/hh, such as Individualized Education Programs (IEPs), education in the *least restrictive environment* **(LRE),** and parental participation in their children's education. In addition, nondiscriminatory assessment, zero reject, and procedural **due process** were introduced as basic principles of this law. These principles of PL 94-142 have remained the same throughout all of the reauthorizations.

The first time audiology was referenced in federal legislation was in PL 94-142 (1975). The law described audiology as a **related service** for special education. This related service was defined as a supportive service designed to enable a child with a disability to receive FAPE as designated in the child's IEP. In summary, the services falling under the purview of audiology included:

(1) identification of children with hearing loss
(2) determination of the range, nature, and degree of hearing loss, including referral for medical or other professional attention for the habilitation of hearing
(3) provision of habilitation activities, such as language habilitation, auditory training, speech reading (lipreading), hearing evaluation, and speech conservation

(4) creation and administration of programs for prevention of hearing loss

(5) counseling and guidance of pupils, parents, and teachers regarding hearing loss, and

(6) determination of the child's need for group and individual amplification, selecting and fitting an appropriate aid, and evaluating the effectiveness of amplification. (CFR 300.12[b])

Reauthorizations of PL 94-142

IDEA. PL 101-476 (1990) promoted the idea that children with hearing loss could be educated in their *local* public schools, not just residential schools or separate schools for the D/deaf. The advantage to this was that children did not have to live away from home, sometimes many miles away from their families. With IDEA and its push for educating children with hearing loss in their local schools, the concept of **inclusion**, or the inclusion movement, came into existence. The inclusion of students with disabilities into **general education** classrooms was a direct result of (1) parents, educators, and other advocacy groups becoming concerned that students with disabilities were being segregated into specialized, **self-contained classrooms**, and (2) the IDEA provision calling for students with disabilities to be educated alongside students without disabilities in their neighborhood schools (Roeser & Downs, 2004, p. 11).

IDEA continued the concept of FAPE and added the concepts of assistive technology, transition services, and person-first language. The term *hearing impaired students* was replaced with *students with hearing impairment*. Additionally, the law mandated services to include students between the ages of 3–21 years.

IDE/A (2004). The latest reauthorization of IDEA changed the name a third time to the **Individuals with Disabilities Education *Improvement* Act** (PL 108-446; 2004). Some literature and some state agencies, such as the state of Indiana, refer to the 2004 reauthorization as "IDEIA" (http://www.in.gov/ipas/2411.htm), while other agencies such as the U.S. Department of Education (http://idea.ed.gov/explore/home) kept the original form of the acronym because IDEA is easier to remember. Therefore, you may see IDEA frequently, even when sources are referring to the 2004 and later reauthorizations. For the purposes of

Person First, Always?

While the law embraces the intent of "person-first" language, many professionals who work in the field of deafness, as well as many people who are D/deaf or hard of hearing, do not always use person-first language when speaking about d/hh individuals. This is well documented and an accepted exception to the rule. Many culturally Deaf people would agree that saying, "I am a person who is deaf" is not unlike changing the lyrics to the song, "I am Woman. Hear me roar" to "I am a person who is a woman. Hear me roar." The intent of that song was to highlight a strong pride in being a woman; changing the lyrics greatly dilutes that intent. Similarly, this is the intent of many in the Deaf community when they say, "I am Deaf." It is a point of pride and how members of the Deaf community self-identify. Additionally, saying "Deaf person" is very much a reflection of the grammatical structure of American Sign Language (ASL). So when you read terms such as *deaf educator*, *teacher of the deaf*, *deaf kid*, and *deaf school*, there is no disrespect intended. It is in deference to Deaf culture mores.

this text, we will use IDEA (often actually spoken as the word *idea*) when we discuss either the 1990 or 2004 reauthorizations of PL 94-142.

Previous versions of IDEA contained language that held public agencies (e.g., schools) responsible for ensuring that hearing aids worn in school by children with hearing impairments were functioning properly. The 2004 reauthorization continued this requirement for these devices but changed the wording from *shall ensure* to *must ensure*. The consequences of this wording change were that schools must now have plans for checking **amplification devices** *and* documenting the function of those devices. If the devices are not working, then schools must document what must happen next (i.e., the **audiologist** is to be contacted, the parent is to be contacted, the device is to be sent off for repair, and so on).

Other changes in IDEA resulted in limitations being set on related services for medical devices that are surgically implanted (such as cochlear implants and osseo-integrated, or bone-anchored, devices). The new language stated that schools are not responsible for cochlear implant mapping, maintaining surgically implanted devices, or replacing those devices. However, the law is clear that students with surgically implanted devices are to receive *related services* that are deemed necessary in the student's IEP in order to provide FAPE. For example, speech-language therapy services might be added to meet FAPE. Also, the law clearly states the school is responsible for routine checking of an external component of a surgically implanted device to make sure it is functioning properly. This aligns with the school's responsibility for ensuring that all hearing assistance devices are functioning properly. This very specific information concerning hearing aids and cochlear implants is important, as you will see later, when we discuss case law and cases that concern children who are d/hh.

By 2013, special education law had been amended *six* times since PL 94-142 was initially enacted. Keeping up with the names and numbers can be daunting, but each reauthorization or amendment creates changes in terminology and newer mandates for concepts that are considered necessary and essential for improving the educational process for students with disabilities.

Americans with Disabilities Act of 1990 (ADA)

The 1990s began with the enactment of the Americans with Disabilities Act of 1990, or ADA. This act is viewed by many as the most comprehensive and progressive piece of legislation enacted since the Rehabilitation Act of 1973 and PL 94-142. For instance, this act as well as IDEA (1990) replaced the previously used term of *handicapped* with *disability*. The ADA defines persons who are covered by its protections and prohibits discrimination in all public and private employment, education, and recreational settings. Most importantly, unlike the mandates of Section 504, these accommodations must be made regardless of whether or not they receive federal funding. In a nutshell, for a child who may not qualify for services under IDEA, the

ADA requires employers and school districts to take the necessary steps to ensure that people with deafness and/or hearing loss have access to services and facilities in the same manner as those without hearing loss. For a more complete description of special education law as it applies specifically to audiology services for students who are d/hh, we recommend that you read Richburg and Smiley (2012), Johnson and Seaton (2012), and Martin, Martin, & Terman (1996).

Cases Impacting D/HH Students

To understand the application of special education law as it relates specifically to students who are d/hh, we will now review pivotal court cases and resulting decisions from pertinent case law established in recent years. There have been many local, district, and U.S. Supreme Court cases heard, but we will examine some of the most relevant cases for our students.

The 1960s through the 1980s saw an excessive number of lawsuits in which parents and disability rights groups sued school districts and states for specific rights for students with disabilities. At that time, the courts tended to rule in favor of families over school districts (e.g., *Pennsylvania Association for Retarded Citizens (PARC) v. Commonwealth of Pennsylvania, Mills v. Board of Education of the District of Columbia, Hoenig v. Doe*). The following four cases provide a good historical representation of suits directly impacting services for students who are d/hh.

Board of Education of the Hendrich Hudson Central School District v. Amy Rowley.

The case of *Board of Education of the Hendrich Hudson Central School District v. Amy Rowley* (458 US 176, 200 [1982]), which was initially heard in Westchester County, New York, directly affected students with hearing loss and was the crucial and surprising point at which the tides changed on litigation in special education. It is sometimes referred to as the "Chevy versus Cadillac" case that challenged the legislative mandate of FAPE. The outcome of this case was the basis for the nationwide decree that "some **educational benefit**" was all that a school district had to provide.

In 1977, Amy Rowley, a student with a bilateral profound hearing loss, entered kindergarten in a school in the Hendrich Hudson School District. She was evaluated and deemed eligible for services under PL 94-142 as a d/hh student. She was provided with an FM auditory trainer and received the services of a **speech-language pathologist (SLP)** on a regular basis. Her classroom placement was the general education classroom, in which typically hearing children Amy's age attended. In her classes, Amy was a student making acceptable passing grades. There was no dissention on Amy's placement or use of the FM trainer. However, when Amy's parents asked for an **interpreter**, the school denied the request. After several attempts to resolve the issue on the local level, the Rowleys asked for a due process hearing, which was within their rights, as provided in the due process clause of PL 94-142.

The school district's position was that Amy made passing grades with the modifications in her IEP and, therefore, needed no additional supports. The Rowleys argued that Amy was capable of making As, not the Cs and Bs she was earning, and that the interpreter would make the difference between passing grades and allowing Amy to reach her full potential. The lower courts ruled against the parents, citing that the school district had met the educational intent of FAPE as defined in PL 94-142. This decision set the stage for the appeal process in the Supreme Court. In 1982, the Supreme Court upheld the lower court ruling in favor of the school district. Thus, Amy Rowley was not provided an interpreter.

The issue in this case was the term and application of the concept *educational benefit*. The school district, supported by the lower courts and ultimately the Supreme Court, interpreted this to mean that if a student with a disability is learning and meeting her IEP goals of passing grade-level performance, then the school district has met its obligation under the law. The plaintiffs, Amy Rowley and her parents, contended that she was capable of performing academically at a much higher level, given additional services that would potentially enable her to do so.

To many observers, this seemed like a no-brainer. Give Amy an interpreter. She was deaf and communicated through sign language, as well as speech and hearing. But, to the Supreme Court judges who heard the arguments in Washington, DC, in March of 1982, what mattered most was the educational benefit component of the law, which stated that "school districts were required [only] to provide services to children so that they received educational benefit from their schooling"—no more, no less. The Supreme Court judges determined that Amy Rowley was clearly getting benefit from what the school provided, as evidenced by her acceptable passing grades.

Thus, our opening automobile analogy becomes clear. Because the Hendrich Hudson School District had provided Amy with a basic Chevy (the SLP and FM system), it was not required to upgrade Amy to the fancier Cadillac (educational interpreter). Her basic Chevy was "good enough."

Amy Rowley Update

Amy Rowley's parents, Cliff and Nancy Rowley, also had hearing losses. They wanted their child to attend local public schools. Upon registering her in school, they asked for Amy to be provided with sign language interpreters.

After the Supreme Court sided with the Hendrich Hudson School District, Amy's grades began to fall. Within a short period of time, Amy's parents decided to move their family to New Jersey, where Amy was enrolled in the local school and given related services, *including* a sign language interpreter. Amy is now an adult and a professional in the field of deafness. She has a daughter who has a hearing loss. As of 2013, Ms. Rowley was an assistant professor in the Modern Languages and Literatures Department of California State University East Bay Campus, where "...her research interests... [pertain] to children in special education litigation; systemic and hierarchal structure of American Sign Language programs in postsecondary institutions; and relationships between students/ interpreters and the Deaf community."

Additional Cases. Three more recent court cases address the same issue of educational benefit. They concern the provision of Real Time Captioning (**Communication Access Real-time Translation, aka CART**) services to d/hh students (K–16) who have cochlear implants and/or do not use sign language. These cases are very similar in scope: *K.M. v. Tustin Unified School District* (reference 1), *D.H. v. Poway United School District* (reference 2), and *Argenyi v. Creighton University* (reference 3). In each of these cases, the plaintiff requested CART services and was denied by the defendant, the school entity. In every case, the defendant used the Amy Rowley verdict as the primary defense for denying the service request.

Of particular note in the 2012 *K.M. v. Tustin* case was the fact that legal representation was provided by a leading organization in the field of deafness, the Alexander Graham Bell Association for the Deaf and Hard of Hearing, and was also supported by the Department of Justice. They sued as a civil rights violation under ADA because K.M. was denied access to the same educational information as her peers, regardless of receiving educational benefit. The lower courts sided with the school district/university in all three cases. Because of their similarities, the *K.M. v. Tustin* and *D.H. v. Poway* cases were consolidated and appealed to the next jurisdictional level. All of these cases were resolved in the plaintiff's favor. In August 2013, the 9th U.S. Circuit Court of Appeals ruled in favor of the plaintiff (K.M.) in *K.M. v. Tustin Unified School District*. The landmark decision was groundbreaking from several perspectives. First, it gave students who are deaf or hard of hearing access to CART services as an accommodation in mainstream K–12 classrooms. Secondly, it supported the contention that the ADA requirement of equal access for deaf and hard of hearing students in K–12 classrooms supersedes IDEA. And finally, this ruling means that public schools can no longer use the IDEA concept of basic educational benefit to deny a service that a student needs in order to have equal access in the classroom. In addition, the 8th U.S. Circuit Court of Appeals ruled in favor of Michael Argenyi in *Argenyi v. Creighton University*, indicating that at the university level, ADA provisions support the use of CART services to accommodate a deaf or hard of hearing student's access to oral instruction. For a thorough review of case law in the area of students who are d/hh, see Kreisman and John (2010) and Johnson (2010).

What This Means in Today's Terms. The reason for our looking at these cases is that there are still unresolved issues regarding reasonable accommodations for students who have hearing loss. IDEIA, Section 504, and ADA have loopholes in their language regarding the needs of our students. Even though the educational benefit part of IDEA was weakened by the 2013 court rulings, a student who is d/hh can potentially still be denied a number of hearing-related services if she receives educational benefit from a current placement and accommodations.

The four court cases and legislation described previously help to illustrate the importance for the professionals working with students who are d/hh to know about legislation and case law, since this knowledge can help them to collaborate and share their expertise and skills with each other in order to benefit students who are d/hh.

The second part of this chapter will identify the "players" you may encounter as you seek services for children who have hearing loss. The following sections stress the importance of seamless teamwork and demonstrate the alliances built around serving this very special population of students.

Professional Practitioners

Collaborative Efforts as the Model for "Best Practice"

For as long as you can remember, you have probably been told to "play nicely" and "share your toys." These concepts should not only apply to those of us who play in sandboxes! These concepts should apply to everyone, especially professionals who are working with children who are d/hh.

Collaboration among professionals typically refers to the sharing of expertise, knowledge, and skills. It also includes reliance on other professionals, for both short time frames and on a continuing basis. Collaboration implies that individuals with differing expertise and skill levels (1) work together to maximize each other's strengths, (2) build on each other's knowledge, (3) minimize weaknesses that may prohibit them from providing high-quality services, and (4) co-construct plans of action. Any description of collaboration that applies to professionals working with children who are d/hh should include something about "being of benefit" to those children and allowing the children to obtain the best services possible (whether that is in a medical setting, in the school, or in the child's home). Finally, collaboration has three general purposes: (1) to prevent duplication of services being provided to a student, (2) to improve services that have already been established for a student, and (3) to establish channels of open communication to be used as soon as an issue needing resolution occurs.

Terms Used to Describe Collaboration. There are three terms customarily used to describe collaborative efforts among professionals working with children who are d/hh. These terms are interdisciplinary, multidisciplinary, and transdisciplinary. **Interdisciplinary collaboration** can be described as a group of professionals sharing responsibility for service delivery, but each individual professional remains responsible for her own discipline's service. **Multidisciplinary collaboration** can be described as professionals recognizing the significance and offerings of the other professionals' disciplines, but the service provided by each individual professional remains independent. Lastly, **transdisciplinary collaboration** can be described as professionals committing to providing services across several disciplines; their goals are to plan and provide integrated services for children who are d/hh. Multidisciplinary efforts have the least amount of collaboration, and transdisciplinary efforts have the greatest amount of collaboration. We want you to understand that articles and textbooks written on collaboration may distinguish between collaboration and teamwork. However, many people will use the terms *collaboration* and *teamwork* interchangeably.

Benefits and Barriers to Those Who Collaborate. Collaboration has the potential of being very valuable to all involved individuals. It can lead to the collaborators being more productive, more informed, less fatigued, more creative, and professionally supported. In addition, professional collaboration in schools or the community can make service provision less redundant, thus more cost-effective (and administrators *like* that!). With collaboration of service delivery, the child ultimately gets more out of the learning experience, and the professionals may even walk away with new knowledge or a new set of skills.

Although professionals, students, and family members benefit from collaborative efforts, collaboration is often not stressed or well managed, no matter how much the players want to collaborate with each other. Montgomery (1990) described several reasons why professionals are not able to collaborate easily. Reasons included the idea that collaboration may be new and different to one or more of the professionals involved, thus making it uncomfortable for the professionals to collaborate. Along these same lines, a professional may be unwilling or unmotivated to change the way she has always done something. Some professionals do not feel that they need assistance, knowledge, or skills from other professionals. Some administrators may see collaboration as being too intrusive, too expensive, and/or having the possibility for mismanagement of funds. (This does not bode well for the micromanager.)

In combination with the human characteristics that block collaboration from occurring, scheduling conflicts, location concerns, lack of resources, and lack of time can decrease collaborative efforts as well. It is difficult for multiple professionals from multiple practice settings, or offices, to schedule available time at the *same* time during the work week. Additionally, funding restrictions or policies for technology use within a work setting may not allow for therapy and instructional materials, computers, or other equipment to be used in a different work setting or location.

Overcoming the Obstacles. There are several ways in which professionals can overcome the barriers mentioned above. Some methods will be easier than others, and some may or may not be needed in every situation. One of the most important ways to remove the barriers to collaboration includes fostering *respect* and *equality* among professionals. Respecting colleagues and the educational training they have had, remaining open-minded about other professionals' viewpoints and experiences, and firmly believing that each collaborator is equally valuable to the service delivery of a child who is d/hh is imperative for forming collaborative relationships. (Remember that these matters should also include the students, parents, and caregivers, if appropriate.) Additionally, maintaining the viewpoint that there is no superior-subordinate relationship must exist among members in any collaborative effort. All responsibilities should be equally shared. Shared responsibility for decision making helps the collaborators identify mutual goals.

At the end of the day, the most difficult barriers to overcome with respect to collaboration are *lack of time* and *lack of support* needed for developing collaborative relationships. Although it is always easier to talk about collaborating than actually doing it, making collaboration a high priority is really the most effective way of dealing with these two obstacles.

So What's So Great About Collaboration? You may be wondering why we are emphasizing teamwork and collaboration so much. Well, we believe that many people learning about audiology get confused by all the different professionals who work with d/hh children. By the time children reach the magic first-grade age of six years, the number and types of professionals these children have seen is staggering. When a teacher of the deaf/hard of hearing (TOD), an early interventionist (EI), or a **hearing aid dealer** is mentioned, people tend to have fuzzy ideas about the roles and responsibilities of these professionals. Therefore, sorting out these professionals' specializations can be a real chore. Additionally, the letters behind the names of these professionals can be confusing. You may wonder, who is this CCC-A, or **ENT**, or Au.D., or SLP person, and what does that alphabet soup assortment of initials mean? You may ask yourself, "Does the ENT work well with the interpreter, or do the TOD, SLP, and **pediatric audiologist** who see my child/student have to have any special qualifications?"

Lastly, not everyone is aware of how all these professionals work together in certain teams, such as the cochlear implant team, the evaluation team, or the IEP team. Obviously, different professionals will have different roles and responsibilities, depending on which team they are playing on or in which setting they are functioning. Let us describe for you the players and the teams, so that you'll feel more comfortable knowing who is working with children who are d/hh.

Professional Practitioners and Their Qualifications

Table 1.1 shows that there are a multitude of professionals who provide services to children who are d/hh. Many of these professionals are educated or trained specifically to work with these children, while others are not. Some professionals work in the school setting, some work with children prior to reaching school age, and some practice in hospital or clinic settings. Some of these professionals work together on a team in-house (in the same practice setting), while other professionals work together on a team but cross into other practice settings for that collaboration. The core group of professionals who work with students who are d/hh include audiologists, speech-language pathologists (SLP), teachers of deaf/hard of hearing children (TOD), and general (also called regular) educators. Collaboration among these professionals should be regular and consistent; however, in reality, this is not always the case.

There are also additional professionals, or paraprofessionals, who have contact with children who are d/hh; these include interpreters, social workers, school psychologists, counselors, aides/assistants, special education teachers, administrators, school nurses, and physicians/pediatricians. In ideal situations, these professionals should be involved in the collaborative process as much as the core professionals.

Table 1.1. Professional Practitioners and Their Qualifications

Professional/ Paraprofessional	Minimum Educational Requirement	Possible Degrees	Certification	Some points to note/Comment section
SCHOOL-BASED PERSONNEL				
Teacher of the Deaf (TOD) • TOD - Self-Contained • TOD - Resource Room • TOD - Itinerant	Bachelor's degree	BA BS M.Ed. MAT Ph.D. EdD	SEA[1] Deaf Education / Hearing Impaired Certification	This person is specifically trained to teach children who are d/hh. This person focuses on academic subjects, speech-language development, auditory skill development, self-advocacy skills, and successful inclusion practices with children who are d/hh. Self-contained TODs teach children who spend all day in their own classroom. Resource room TODs follow a "pullout" model, and children come to them from the general education classroom for specific-area instruction for a specified period of time. Itinerant TODs move from school to school and provide support for the general education teacher. In inclusion classrooms, the TOD works collaboratively with that teacher.
• Educational Interpreter • Cued Speech Transliterator	Varies by state	Varies by state	Varies by state; RID, EIPA, NAD	This person is *not* a teacher, tutor, or para-educator. This person is trained to facilitate communication in the student's preferred mode/language between the student and her teacher and peers.
General Education Teacher	Bachelor's degree	BA BS M.Ed. MAT Ph.D. EdD	SEA certification in grade level or content area	This teacher may or may not have experience with children who are d/hh. This teacher should work closely with TODs, SLPs, and educational audiologists to provide appropriate services.
Special Education Teacher	Bachelor's degree	BA BS B.S.Ed. M.Ed. MAT Ph.D. EdD	SEA certification in specific area of special education	This teacher is generally certified in a very specialized area (i.e., LD, emotional disturbance, autism, developmental disabilities, etc.), and this varies widely from state to state. It should be noted that this teacher does not receive specific training for working with sensory disabilities.
Special Education Administrator	Master's degree	M.Ed. MAT Ph.D. EdD	SEA certification in supervision or in educational administration	This person oversees all special education related programs and services. This person monitors programs for compliance with state and national regulations. Not every administrator will have specific knowledge of children who are d/hh.

1 SEA: state education agency

Professional/ Paraprofessional	Minimum Educational Requirement	Possible Degrees	Certification	Some points to note/Comment section
SCHOOL-BASED PERSONNEL, cont.				
Building Level Principal	Master's degree	M.Ed. Ph.D. EdD Ed.S. Ph.D.	SEA principal certification	This person may have little to no experience with children who are d/hh. Parents and other professionals may need to educate this person on special education laws and protocols.
Classroom Paraprofessional (TSS)	High school diploma		Varies by state	This person may have no training with children who are d/hh. This person should not be replacing a teacher or interpreter in the schools. This person should have assistant-type responsibilities.
School Nurse	Associate's degree or vocational degree	LPN RN	National Council of State Boards of Nursing	This person may be in charge of the hearing screenings in some states.
Adaptive Physical Educator (APE)	Bachelor's degree	BA BS MA MS M.Ed.	CAPE	This person may have no specialized training for working with children who are d/hh. This person has training for working with children who have mobility problems.
Speech-Language Pathologist	Master's degree	MA MS M.Ed. Ph.D.	CCC-SLP	This person may work with children who are d/hh on speech and language skills. This person may provide auditory training or aural (re)habilitation therapy for children who are d/hh. This person is not trained to provide academic services to children who are d/hh in the schools or private clinic setting.
Speech Assistant/ Speech Aide	Bachelor's degree	BS	Varies by state	This person works under the supervision of an SLP. This person follows instructions given by the SLP for therapy and service delivery. In some states, the term *speech assistant* refers to a bachelor-level practitioner with an undergraduate degree in communication sciences and disorders.
Auditory-Verbal Therapist (AVT)	Bachelor's degree	BA BS MA MS Ph.D. EdD	LSLS AV.Ed. AVT	This person is most likely also an SLP or teacher of the deaf. This person could be an early educator or an audiologist, as well. This professional has specialized training in the development of the d/hh child's listening and speaking skills. The AVT may be in private practice but could be employed by a school district.
Educational Audiologist	Master's or doctoral degree	MA MS M.Ed. Au.D. Ph.D. EdD	CCC-A or ABA	This audiologist works full-time or part-time for a school district or local education agency (LEA). This audiologist deals with aspects of hearing/hearing loss in the educational setting.
Audiology Assistant/ Audiology Aide	Bachelor's degree	BA BS	Varies by state	This person works under the supervision of an audiologist (cleaning hearing aids, changing tubing, troubleshooting devices, and so on).

Professional/ Paraprofessional	Minimum Educational Requirement	Possible Degrees	Certification	Some points to note/Comment section
EARLY INTERVENTION PERSONNEL				
Early Interventionist (EI)	Bachelor's degree or associate's degree	AA BA BS M.Ed.	Varies by state	This person is not necessarily an educator; however, some EIs have training in fields of education and child development. Some states have school-based professionals working with an EI. This person does not necessarily have experience working with children who are d/hh.
Case Manager (for a child's Individual Family Service Plan)	Varies by state	Varies by state	Varies by state	This person may have some specialty training but is in a managerial position, supervising the multiple services being provided to children who are d/hh.
MEDICAL PERSONNEL				
Pediatric Audiologist	Master's or doctoral degree	MA MS M.Ed. Au.D. Ph.D. EdD	CCC-A or ABA	This audiologist works specifically with the pediatric population in a hospital or clinical setting. This audiologist typically fits hearing aids on children and possibly maps cochlear implants.
Clinical Audiologist	Master's or doctoral degree	MA MS M.Ed. Au.D. Ph.D. EdD	CCC-A or ABA	This audiologist works with clients of any age. This audiologist can also fit hearing aids and/or map cochlear implants.
Psychiatrist	Medical degree	MD/DO/OD plus residency in psychiatry	ABPN	This professional may assist people who are d/hh with their mental health concerns. A psychiatrist is able to prescribe medications.
Pediatrician	Medical degree	MD DO	Certified in specialty area; multiple designators[2]	This doctor has no specialty training in hearing/hearing loss. Although this doctor works with children, hearing loss may not be uppermost on his mind.
Otolaryngologist (ENT)	Medical degree	MD DO	Certified in specialty area; multiple designators[2]	This doctor specializes in disorders of the ear, nose, and throat. This doctor's office may employ an audiologist, but not in all cases are hearing assessments performed by audiologists.
Otologist	Medical degree	MD DO	Certified in specialty area; multiple designators[2]	This doctor specializes in the ear. This doctor's office may employ an audiologist, but not in all cases are hearing assessments performed by audiologists.
Primary Care Doctor/General Practitioner	Medical degree	MD DO	Certified; multiple designators[2]	Although this doctor works with children, hearing loss may not be uppermost on his mind. This doctor has no specialty training in hearing/hearing loss.

2 Refer to http://www.sandiegobizmart.com/tools/t3_acronym_glossary.htm#D for a complete listing of all degree designators for medical doctors.

Professional/ Paraprofessional	Minimum Educational Requirement	Possible Degrees	Certification	Some points to note/Comment section
ADDITIONAL PROFESSIONALS YOU MAY ENCOUNTER				
Hearing Aid Dispenser/Dealer	High school and sponsorship		NBC-HIS	This person is *not* an audiologist. This person has a short training period with hearing devices and likely has no university training in an audiology program.
Social Worker	Bachelor degree	BSW MSW	LCSW LSW NCC	This person may or may not have experience with children who are d/hh. Some areas of the country have social workers who are specifically trained to work with people who are d/hh to help them gain access to community resources.
Mental Health Professional (e.g., mental health social worker, psychologist, licensed professional counselor)	Master's degree	MA MS MSW Psy.D. Ph.D.	LPC LCSW LMHC	This person may or may not have experience with children who are d/hh. Some areas of the country have mental health professionals who are specifically trained to work with people who are d/hh in a counseling capacity.
Communication Access Real-Time Translation (CART) translator	High school and specialized training	AA Specialized vocational training in court reporting	CCP- NCRA Varies by state	This person is a trained operator who provides real-time transcription to convert speech to text at remote locations or at nonbroadcast settings, such as classrooms, churches, and meetings. CART professionals have qualifications for added expertise (speed and accuracy) as compared to court reporters and other stenographers. (See sidebar "Amy Rowley Update")
Occupational Therapist (OT)	Master's degree or doctoral degree	MA MS MOT OTD Ph.D.	Certification: The American Occupational Therapy Association (AOTA), The National Board for Certification in Occupational Therapy, Inc. (NBCOT); Licensure varies by state	This person may work with children and adults who exhibit fine motor deficits caused by injuries or disease, or that have been present since birth. Rarely do you find an OT who specializes in working with clients who are d/hh. This person is not trained to provide academic services to children who are d/hh in the schools or private clinic setting.
Physical Therapist (PT)	Master's degree or doctoral degree	MA MSD MPT DPT MSPT DScPT Ph.D.	Certification: American Board of Physical Therapy (ABPT), Licensure varies by state	This person may work with children and adults who exhibit gross motor deficits present at birth or caused by injuries or disease. Rarely do you find a PT who specializes in working with clients who are d/hh. This person is not trained to provide academic services to children who are d/hh in the schools or private clinic setting.

Note: The reader needs to understand that roles of professionals/paraprofessionals vary from state to state and district to district. These authors are providing some commentary related to currently accepted best practices for these service providers. Services a professional or paraprofessional can or cannot provide should be regulated by his professional organization's Code of Ethics, service delivery models, and best practices guidelines.

Some of these additional professionals are involved in the collaborative process because of their roles on specific teams. For instance, the physician/surgeon may be a member of the cochlear implant team. However, once that device is implanted, that physician will very likely have nothing further to do with the child. At that point, the implant audiologist, the school-based audiologist and SLP, the teachers, the interpreters, and other school officials will become members of the IEP team, and that will be the "team of interest" for the student and her family.

> ### Know the Lingo
>
> Trained, licensed interpreters often refer to themselves simply as "terps," and when speaking about general education, most folks shorten it to "gen ed." Similarly, special education often is shortened to "sped."

Collaboration and progress is more easily made when we know the scope of the responsibilities of each of the individuals involved with students who are d/hh. It is important to know what professionals can and cannot do and what training or education they have had in order to do their work. So, in conjunction with Table 1.1, here is a rundown of some of the professionals a d/hh child might encounter, including some information about the educational degrees and letters attached to their names and the organizations involved in certifying these individuals.

A **Is for Audiologist.** The field of audiology is a well-established and regulated profession. Audiologists, although *not* physicians, may be called "Doctor" if they hold a clinical (**Au.D.**) or research (**Ph.D.**) doctorate. Not all audiologists hold a doctorate; many hold a master's degree. Therefore, those audiologists would be referred to as "Mr." or "Ms."

Audiologists come in a variety of "flavors," meaning they have varying levels of expertise and practice in multiple settings. Audiologists can work in their own private practices, in hospitals, in otolaryngology (ear, nose, and throat) clinics, in speech and hearing clinics, in schools, in universities or research centers, and in hearing instrument manufacturing. Even this list is not all-inclusive. Regardless of where they practice, all audiologists must have, at a minimum, a master's degree in audiology, and many will have a doctoral degree (Au.D. or Ph.D.). Audiologists must have graduated from an accredited university program; they must have passed a national competency exam (called PRAXIS or NESPA); and if they practice in a state that requires licensing, they must be granted licensure from their state board. Audiologists may also elect to complete the requirements for the **American Speech-Language-Hearing Association (ASHA)** certification or the **American Board of Audiology (ABA)** certification. When you see the signature of an audiologist and it reads, for example, "E. Arlene Earl, MS, CCC-A," it means that Arlene has completed a master's degree in an accredited program in audiology, passed her national competency exam, and has interned under an ASHA-certified mentor during her **clinical fellowship year (CFY).** The "Cs" stand for the **Certificate of Clinical Competence** from ASHA. When you see "E. Arlene Earl, MS, ABA," it means that Arlene has elected to be certified by the American Board of Audiology instead of ASHA. Note that if Arlene had obtained her clinical doctorate and also received ASHA certification, she would then sign her name, "E. Arlene Earl, Au.D., CCC-A." In the case of audiologists who have completed the Au.D., there is no need for a CFY because the final year of the Au.D. program is spent completing an externship (residency) out of the university classroom working in a clinical setting.

Historically, a master's degree was the entrance-level degree for practicing audiology. As of 2007, however, individuals who desire to become audiologists in the United States no longer have the option of obtaining a master's degree. Nationwide, universities closed their master's programs in audiology and developed programs that met the new standards for a doctorate in audiology—issuing the newly designed degree called an "Au.D." The Au.D. is a clinical degree that can be earned by enrolling in a three- or four-year postbaccalaureate program. (The Au.D. is akin to the training requirements for the nonmedical degree of optometrist or Pharm.D.) It should be noted that not all universities grant Au.D. degrees, however. Some universities offer **EdD** or Sc.D. or D.Sc., but no matter what designator is used, the audiologist would still be called "Doctor."

The Pediatric Audiologist. This is an audiologist who specializes in working with children and youth, birth to 18 years of age. This audiologist would be licensed to practice audiology within her state (again, assuming the state requires licensing). She may also hold certification from ASHA or the ABA. Until recently, there has been no *required*, formal assessment tool or accrediting organization for pediatric audiologists. Individual audiologists decided to focus their careers in the area of pediatrics and, therefore, self-identified as a pediatric audiologists. However, the ABA recently established the Pediatric Audiology Specialty Certification. An audiologist holding this certification has "demonstrated the ability to pass a rigorous examination in pediatric audiology and has a minimum of two years of audiological practice" (http://www.americanboardofaudiology.org/specialty/pediatric.html).

The primary tasks of a pediatric audiologist include hearing assessments on the birth to 18-year-old population, hearing aid evaluations and fittings, and evaluations for cochlear implantation. In fact, a pediatric audiologist may also have elected to obtain the ABA's Cochlear Implants Specialty Certification. You will usually find a pediatric audiologist working in a children's hospital, an audiology clinic, or a healthcare facility. For more information on the specialty certifications in pediatric audiology and cochlear implantation, go to the Board of Audiology website at http://www.americanboardofaudiology.org.

The Educational Audiologist. Unfortunately for many students who are d/hh, the educational audiologist is a rarely seen school-based audiologist. Few school systems employ any type of audiologist. Educational audiologists are educated and degreed like other audiologists. However, an audiologist working in a school system may or may not hold state licensure (depending on state licensure regulations), and she may or may not hold certification from ASHA or the ABA; it really depends on the state education agency's (SEA) certification requirements. In a few states, educational audiologists must also apply for a separate certification from the state's SEA. Some SEA certification offices will only grant certificates to work in the schools to those audiologists who are ASHA-certified; others will certify anyone with the appropriate degree and/or state license in audiology regardless of ASHA affiliation.

What's the Difference?

Both audiologists and speech-language pathologists are capable of obtaining certification and/or licensing in order to practice their professions. Certification and licensure are different and should not be confused, although they are often mistakenly lumped together or used as if they were interchangeable. First of all, certification is voluntary and exhibits a certain commitment on the part of the professional to meet rigorous academic and professional standards, which are above and beyond the minimum requirements for state licensure. Certification shows a professional's commitment to obtain and maintain knowledge and skills needed for providing high-quality services to her clients. Standards for certification are established by audiologists and speech-language pathologists who are members of the American Speech-Language-Hearing Association's (ASHA) Council for Clinical Certification in Audiology and Speech-Language Pathology (CFCC). Certificate holders are expected to uphold these standards and abide by ASHA's Code of Ethics. In addition to ASHA's certification, audiologists also have a choice of being certified by the American Board of Audiology (ABA). An audiologist can choose to hold certification from both certifying bodies, only one certifying body, or neither certifying body.

State licensure, on the other hand, is not voluntary. An audiologist or SLP is *required* to hold licensure within the state in which she is practicing, assuming the state has a licensing board for audiologists and SLPs. A state licensing board's purpose for granting licensure is to safeguard the welfare of the general public within that state from unethical and unprofessional practices. The board looks into claims of improper conduct from audiologists and SLPs, and it has the ability to deny, issue, revoke, suspend, or renew a professional's license. Anyone practicing audiology or speech-language pathology without a state license sets herself up for ethics charges and possible criminal liability.

Just to throw a monkey wrench into the mix, TODs do not have state licensure requirements, but they may use the terms *certification* and *license* interchangeably. For example, a TOD may say that she has a special certification in reading, but she may also say she is licensed in reading. However, TODs are expected to obtain certification from their respective SEA, and this certification indicates that they are qualified to teach in the public schools.

Educational audiologists focus their work in school settings and concentrate their expertise to the areas of classroom acoustics, limited diagnostic assessments, fitting personal and classroom hearing assistance technologies (HAT), completing and/or supervising hearing screenings, and maintenance of HAT. An educational audiologist may also assist the TOD or SLP with creating and implementing a school-based auditory (re)habilitation program. Although educational audiologists also work with children, they are different from pediatric audiologists because of the roles and responsibilities they possess that are specific to the educational setting. For a complete list of the roles and responsibilities of an educational, or school-based, audiologist, see the position statements of the Educational Audiology Association (http://www.edaud.org).

S Is for Speech-Language Pathologist. The field of speech-language pathology, like audiology, is a well-established and regulated profession. Like audiologists, SLPs will also be found in a variety of practice settings. Speech-language pathologists must have graduated from an accredited master's-level university program; they must have passed a national competency exam (PRAXIS or NESPA); and if they practice in a state that requires licensing, they must be granted licensure from their state board. SLPs may also elect to complete the requirements for ASHA certification; however, the "ASHA Cs" are highly recommended for SLPs in most practice settings. There is no other accrediting body certifying SLPs at this time.

If an SLP chooses to work in a school system, then she may need to apply to the state's SEA for a standard or specialized teaching certificate to be hired by a local school district. Like an audiologist, if the SLP signs her name, "R. Tick, MS, CCC-SLP," it means she earned ASHA certification by graduating from an accredited graduate program, passed the national examination, and completed a mentored clinical fellowship year (CFY).

Why Can't My SpellCheck Find the Term *Habilitation*?

Most often we refer to REhabilitation. This indicates that an individual had skills that she lost. Habilitation denotes that the individual never had those skills. Therefore, habilitation means adding abilities or skills that the individual(s) in question never possessed. This is most often the case with children and youth who are d/hh. However, often the term *re*habilitation is used to include services delivered to individuals who are first developing skills, as well as individuals needing to *re*develop skills. This is what we meant when we included the term *rehabilitation* in the title of our text. This more accurate term (although a little awkward) best describes both types of skill development. Therefore, it is a more general term, and it is used when the concept does not require a distinction between the timing or acquisition of skill development.

Speech-language pathologists work with individuals of all ages and disabilities involving the production of speech, receptive and expressive language, and the disorders involving the articulators (i.e., mouth, tongue, larynx). An SLP's professional background includes coursework and clinical practice in the areas of articulation, fluency (stuttering, cluttering), and voice disorders, as well as language development, delays, and disorders. ASHA certification requirements are based on demonstrated knowledge and skill areas. Current applicants for certification must complete 375 clinical hours in direct client contact during their master's program; however, those hours do not have area specifications or requirements. In terms of specific areas of education (i.e., fluency, hearing impairment), the ASHA website states that:

> The standards do not specify a particular number of hours in different categories. Programs may determine the number of hours they will require and licensure boards may require a specific number of hours in different categories. Students must be aware of the various requirements so that they will be

able to meet the standards of these various entities. (http://www.asha.org/Certification/2014-Speech-Language-Pathology-Certification-Standards)

The reader should know that SLPs employed in school systems may or may not have had clinical experience with children who are d/hh. However, master's-level SLPs usually have excellent training that can transfer to working with this population. SLPs who work in schools for the D/deaf typically have a greater desire to work specifically with children who are d/hh. They also tend to have a different skill set from SLPs who work in local public schools, where only a handful of children who are d/hh may be on their caseloads. The SLP's knowledge and skills can be enhanced through collaboration with a TOD (and vice versa), because it is through this type of collaboration that the most positive results for the student will occur. It is also important for the reader to understand that SLPs are not certified to teach content-area material in classrooms. In other words, the SLP should not be asked to teach d/hh students math, reading, social studies, and other educational courses. However, they can and do support the d/hh students' understanding and use of what they learn in their classrooms.

In addition to master's-level SLPs, there are other speech professionals who work in the public schools. Due to a paucity of master's-level SLPs working in school settings, on occasion, non-master's-level individuals functioning in the role of "speech therapist" have been employed. While these people may be called speech therapists, or even speech-language pathologists in some locations, their training is very different from a master's-level SLP, especially one that holds ASHA certification. Educationally, the best trained of these non-master's level professionals working at the school district level are individuals with bachelor's degrees in communication disorders. They can usually design and implement therapy programs for the students they serve. This professional may work under the auspices of a certified master's-level SLP. However, in some school systems, there is limited direct supervision because the bachelor's-level speech pathologist holds SEA certification, has had the appropriate initial training, and may have had many years working with children.

Finally, some school systems employ speech assistants. Speech assistants (titles vary by state) are non-speech-language trained bachelor- or associate-level degreed personnel who are hired to implement speech-language therapy plans designed and closely monitored by a master's-level SLP. Unlike a bachelor-level professional, a speech assistant should not be allowed to develop therapy plans for students.

Because there are so many different levels of training and experience with working with d/hh students, it is important to ascertain the skill set of the individual offering speech and language services. Collaboration is especially crucial when the child who is deaf communicates through the use of sign language (American Sign Language [ASL] or Manually Coded English [MCE]), in which the SLP may not be proficient. Only through collaboration will the speech and language needs of these students be met. For a complete list of the roles and responsibilities of a school-based SLP, go to the ASHA website (http://www.asha.org/slp/schools/prof-consult/guidelines/).

_T_ Is for Teacher of the Deaf. Teaching deaf/hard of hearing students is a long-established and varied profession. TODs embrace a variety of philosophies about what is best in terms of communication and instruction for a child who is d/hh. Depending upon state teacher certification requirements, the TOD may receive her training from either an undergraduate or graduate-level education program. The TOD may also be required to hold certification in a general education discipline such as elementary education, secondary English, and so on. The Council on the Education of the Deaf (CED) also offers certification to individuals who graduated from CED-accredited programs. While this form of certification is not routinely required by SEAs, many state schools for the deaf do require or prefer their teachers to have CED certification as well as state certification. In addition, to qualify for state teaching certification, the TOD must pass a standardized examination selected by the SEA. There is no other professional—be it an interpreter, an SLP, an audiologist, or an auditory-verbal therapist (AVT)—who has the focused education and the set of skills that a TOD has in her instructional repertoire.

> **So Multifaceted**
>
> Audiologists and speech-language pathologists, in addition to the roles and responsibilities mentioned within the text, have additional roles that do not involve hearing, speech, or language. That means, not all audiologists evaluate hearing or fit hearing aids, and not all SLPs evaluate speech and language skills. Instead, some audiologists test the vestibular, or balance, system and manage balance problems for individuals who are experiencing vertigo or dizziness. Likewise, some SLPs evaluate swallowing and work with individuals who may need to modify their diet due to an inability to swallow adequately (dysphagia).

The reauthorizations of PL 94-142 and the renewed emphasis on LRE changed the direction of instructional delivery from teaching all content areas full-time in a self-contained classroom to itinerant models of instruction in inclusive environments (i.e., the neighborhood schools.) The TOD was then tasked with teaching targeted areas such as English, language arts, auditory skill development, Deaf culture, self-advocacy, and communication skill development in both spoken and sign languages. This means that the role of TODs has broadened and their responsibilities have become more diversified, allowing them to perform successfully in their roles as collaborators, consultants, and providers of direct instruction to the d/hh student.

> **Least Restrictive Environment (LRE) and Kids with Hearing Loss: Why Is This an Issue?**
>
> Over the years, LRE has come to be synonymous with the general education classroom in the student's local school. However, in the late 1980s, the federal government convened a commission, The Commission on Education of the Deaf, to explore why students who were d/hh were doing so poorly in schools. One of the issues that rose to the top during this committee's investigations was LRE. The investigators saw that in some cases, the local public school general education setting was actually more restrictive than other possible settings. Why?!
>
> _cont._

The answer can be summed up in two words: language accessibility. Since language development is the crux of the problem that deaf students face (especially those with hearing parents), placement into a classroom where language exposure and interaction is limited cannot be the child's LRE. In its final report, entitled "Toward Equality: Education of the Deaf," presented to the President and Congress in February 1988, the commission tackled the issue of LRE. They stated, "The least restrictive environment concept has not been appropriately applied by federal, state, and local educational agencies for many children who are deaf." (http://archive.gao.gov/t2pbat17/135760. pdf, p. 24) The report indicated that factors such as language exposure and access, culture, and parental desires must be considered, and an Individual Educational Plan (IEP) must be written addressing these issues *before* LRE is determined. And, unlike other students who may be best served in the general education classroom, deaf (and especially culturally Deaf) students may not get an appropriate education in that setting. By assuming that the local general education classroom is the optimal placement for a d/Deaf child, her LRE determination would not be met. It may be that a TOD and the educational interpreter are the only individuals in a child's school environment who can communicate directly with the student. They reiterated the oft-forgotten fact that the IEP determines a student's placement. In short, if a child cannot freely communicate with her peers, that educational environment is more restrictive than perhaps a school for deaf children, where fluent communication is readily available.

The following sections explore the different responsibilities and roles and placement settings in which various TODs work with d/hh students. While there may not be separate certification requirements for these three types of TODs, they have many distinct roles and responsibilities and they work in different settings.

Teacher of the Deaf in a Self-Contained Setting. In the self-contained setting, the TOD is responsible for delivering instruction in all academic areas as specified on the students' IEPs. She follows closely the grade-level expectations in terms of curricular goals established by the district for that age child. In addition, it is incumbent upon the TOD in this setting to perform daily hearing aid/cochlear implant checks and to arrange her room to provide the optimal auditory environment possible. Self-contained TODs also may incorporate separate times for aural habilitation and spoken language exercises, or the TOD may consciously incorporate them into daily activities.

Teacher of the Deaf in a Resource Room Setting. TODs in resource rooms work individually or in small groups with students who are d/hh and are placed for the majority of the school day in a general education classroom (mainstreamed). Usually, the student will have a regularly scheduled **pullout** time to spend with the TOD in order to work on targeted subject matter. The amount of time is dictated by the student's IEP and also varies from student to student. The responsibilities of the **resource room** TOD include orienting the general education teacher and the d/hh hearing child's peers to the dimensions of deafness in general, as well as to the specific audiological, speech, language, and learning needs of the mainstreamed child. The resource room TOD is most often the professional who is the "air traffic controller" for d/hh students. In addition, the TOD makes sure that the child has a schedule that maximizes her time in resource room instruction, coordinates with related service providers' schedules, and allows enough time for individual instruction in the resource room for preteaching content, auditory skills and spoken language /ASL development, and academic remediation. All this must be accomplished while simultaneously ensuring the student does not miss important information in the general education (gen-ed) classroom.

Teacher of the Deaf Who Is Itinerant. Itinerant TODs have become the mainstay of many public schools' programming for students who are d/hh. Since d/hh students are a low incidence population, there may be only one or two students at each school that the TOD visits, and it is entirely possible for an itinerant TOD in a rural school district to travel great distances to serve multi-age students in a number of different schools. The itinerant TOD may or may not have a home-base school. Obviously a driver's license is a requirement of the **itinerant teacher**'s position!

PUSH-IN vs. PULLOUT Instruction

The itinerant teacher has two ways to provide direct instruction to the d/hh student. She can take the student to a separate room in the school to work on materials. This is known as pullout instruction. Or, the itinerant TOD can work directly with the student within the general education classroom. This is known as push-in instruction. An increasingly common function of an itinerant TOD is to work directly with the student using the push-in model of instruction. The itinerant TOD may take the general education teacher's lesson plans and develop and implement "parallel" lessons, or she may simply parallel-teach the same lesson at the same time, providing the necessary modifications or accommodations. She can differentiate the material and alter teaching methods to meet the needs of the d/hh student. These are two excellent ways to work on auditory and communication skills simultaneously.

The itinerant TOD student's full-time placement is in the general education classroom. The itinerant TOD travels from school to school to meet her students for the times dictated by the IEP. Her caseload and travel schedule can change from semester to semester, and like the resource room TOD, for the itinerant TOD, scheduling is a major responsibility. In terms of scheduling, there are times the itinerant teacher may have to alter part or all of her weekly schedule to accommodate a single student's schedule change.

Also like the resource room TOD, the itinerant TOD may serve the d/hh student in several capacities. The itinerant TOD may provide direct services to the student in either a pullout or a **push-in** model of instructional delivery, with the latter becoming more prevalent. Additionally, many itinerant TODs provide indirect services to d/hh students. That means the itinerant TOD functions as a consultant to the gen-ed teacher. In this capacity, the itinerant TOD conducts regular meetings with the d/hh student's teacher(s) and provides information, suggests specialized teaching techniques, and monitors the student's progress without actually providing direct services (pullout or push-in) to the student (Luckner, Slike, & Johnson, 2012). Because the itinerant model of delivery has become the preferred mode of instruction, it is important to understand the itinerant TOD's roles and responsibilities in more detail than provided here. For an excellent source of information on itinerant teaching for the deaf, read *The Itinerant Teacher's Handbook* by Carolyn Bullard and John Luckner, 2nd edition (2013).

I Is for Interpreter. The field of interpreting has become a well-established and regulated profession. Like audiologists, interpreters can work in a variety of settings and capacities (e.g., medical interpreting, legal interpreting, educational interpreting, community interpreting). Interpreters also have a variety of backgrounds, including formal two- or four-year educational training in an interpreter-training program, or they may be **children of deaf adults (CODAs)** whose native language is American Sign Language (ASL).

Historically, the two major organizations in the United States certifying interpreters have been the **National Association of the Deaf (NAD)** and the **Registry of Interpreters for the Deaf (RID)**. Although they had offered separate certification avenues and assessments, in 2005, the organizations combined efforts to develop and disseminate a single set of competencies for interpreters and a single assessment instrument for certification. This instrument is the **National Interpreter Certification (NIC)** Knowledge Test. However, many interpreters working in educational settings have instead taken The Boys Town National Research Hospital's **Educational Interpreter Performance Assessment (EIPA)** and may not hold combined NAD-RID national certification. State educational agencies usually set the standards for interpreters employed in their school districts. There is a strong national movement toward adopting the EIPA certification as a requirement for employment in schools. To date, nearly 50 percent of US states use the EIPA to assess interpreters working in elementary and secondary settings (http://www.classroominterpreting.org/Admin/legal_rights.asp).

In some cases the d/hh student might use a system called Cued Speech. **Cued Speech** is a non-sign system that clarifies hard to speech read and confusing sounds. It uses a variety of hand placements and configurations to distinguish between sounds such as /p/ and /b/, or /k/ and /g/, which look identical on the lips. **Transliterators** may be certified by passing one of three assessments: the Cued Language Transliterator National Certification Examination (CLTNCE), the Cued Language Transliterator State Level Assessment (CLTSLA) (both administrated by The National Cued Speech Association), or the Cued Speech version of the EIPA (EIPA-CS).

Finally, some students who rely on spoken language but still require the assistance of an interpreter may need an oral interpreter. Since a d/hh student may use one of a variety of communication modes to understand and express language (e.g., ASL, MCE, Cued Speech, Oral/Aural language), interpreters/transliterators should be hired who are proficient in that child's form of communication.

The educational interpreter is there to be the conduit of language between the d/hh student and the hearing people in the environment. Educational interpreters are not trained as teachers or SLPs and should not assume a primarily instructional role. However, in some school districts, educational interpreters do assist the TOD, SLP, educational audiologist, and general education teacher by providing some one-on-one support to the d/hh students when there is time for additional practice in skill development. Should this occur, it is always done under the direct supervision of the one of the above listed professionals. In addition, although not trained to troubleshoot hearing assistive technology products, it is not unusual for the educational interpreter to identify problems that may occur and bring them to the attention of the TOD or general educator.

Let's Talk Teamwork

The TOD, general education teacher, audiologist, and SLP are the core "players" working with students who are d/hh. However, as noted earlier, Table 1.1 includes many other professionals and paraprofessionals who work with these students as well. Some of these other professionals and paraprofessionals will perform their services in a school or educational environment, while others will provide their services and interact with d/hh students outside the educational environment. These academic teams include the **early intervention (EI)** team, the preschool team, and the school-age team. You should be aware that these teams exist and are available to provide a variety of services for our students. As we noted in the previous general discussion on collaboration, what is ideal and what actually exists in reality are often two different things. Not every school has teams that contain all of these professionals, and some "teams" may actually be a single individual.

Early Intervention (EI) Team. The Early Intervention (EI) Team is a family-centered team that serves children with special needs from birth to three years of age. Members of the EI team who serve a child with hearing loss include, at the very least, early interventionists, audiologists, SLPs, TODs, and parents or guardians. Each child is also assigned an EI service coordinator/case manager. Different states will use different terms for early interventionists, such as developmental therapists or intervention specialists. Also, some professions have added EI to their title descriptions, such as "SLP–Early Intervention ," "Occupational Therapist (OT)–Early Intervention," or " Physical Therapist (PT) – Early Intervention," indicating that those professionals specialize in the birth to three population within their field. In some states, special birth-to-five certification is also required for the TOD.

To be a member of the EI team, one should have a bachelor's or higher degree in any of the following fields: education, early childhood education, deaf education, special education, psychology, social work, sociology, physical therapy, occupational therapy, speech-language pathology, audiology, nursing, dietetics, nutrition, public policy, communications, economics, legal studies, political science, health policy, behavioral science, history, ethnic studies, child development, or applied behavioral analysis. In some states, an early interventionist may have to take and pass a civil service examination. As you can see, an **early interventionist** could be someone with a varied knowledge base or area of expertise but not necessarily someone educated about hearing loss specifically.

The early interventionist is responsible for a multitude of tasks. She is primarily responsible for developing and implementing early intervention programs as defined in the **individualized family service plan (IFSP)** process. This plan is similar to an IEP because it explicitly defines developmental goals and the appropriate strategies needed for the child to meet the defined goals. The EI plans and conducts individual and group early intervention in natural environments that include home and community-based settings. She provides consultation and education to families, staff, and other professionals regarding EI. She also provides comprehensive service coordination, including maintaining files, following up with other professionals, identifying community resources for families, coordinating transition activities, and maintaining all required state and LEA documentation. An early interventionist may review and approve provider applications to participate in the EI program. She may administer and coordinate due process procedures or provide training to local governments, providers, and parents regarding state and federal laws, regulations, and policies pertaining to the program. Although not an exhaustive list of responsibilities, this gives you an idea about what an early interventionist may do for a child newly identified with hearing loss.

Not all states have well-established early intervention services, but some states (e.g., New York) have very detailed and multi-tiered systems of EI. In general, the belief behind the EI team's involvement with children in this age range is that the earlier a child is identified, amplified, managed, provided early exposure to accessible language, and provided with needed services, the better the outcomes for that child will be. Also, EI allows a child to move more effortlessly into the preschool and school settings.

Preschool Team. The Preschool Team serves children from three to five years of age with known or suspected hearing loss. Members of this team include the audiologist, SLP, TOD, preschool classroom teacher, parents or guardians, and any professional who would be included on the preschool IEP team. These professionals provide the services for which they are trained but also help with a smooth transition from the preschool years to the school years. Again, the idea behind having a preschool team is to identify and begin management for a d/hh child as early as possible to improve outcomes. Also, the preschool years can be focused more accordingly to meet the needs of these children when speech, language, auditory training, and individualized education can be emphasized.

School-Age Team. The School-Age Team serves children from 5 to 21 years of age with known hearing loss who have IEPs and are in kindergarten through twelfth grade. The core members of this team include the TOD, audiologist, SLP, general education classroom teacher, and parents or guardians. Depending upon the student's global needs, other professionals may be involved on these teams if a specific child has other learning, behavioral, or medical problems. That is, professionals such as pediatricians, nurses, social workers, physical and occupational therapists, behavioral therapists, and educational psychologists may also be on this team if a child's diagnosis involves more than a hearing loss. These professionals focus on the specific needs of the d/hh student and utilize the specially designed instruction necessary to facilitate student learning. In addition, once the student reaches the transition age of 14 years, she is also expected to become a member of her own team and contribute toward her own transitional activities in school.

Collaboration among the Teams. As we noted previously, collaboration is very important when providing services for students who are d/hh. Not only do individual professionals have to work together for a specific child, but the teams of professionals must work in synchrony as well to ensure that the child is properly diagnosed, followed, and transitioned from the early intervention years through the school-age years. As soon as a d/hh student "ages out" of one service level, the team of professionals from the subsequent level should be ready to step in and facilitate a smooth transition to the next level.

Collaboration can be challenging. It is often difficult for the various professionals to find the same time to meet and share information. Parents are often very busy with their home routines and responsibilities. Collaboration among professionals and teams is the best possible plan of action for students who are d/hh. By recognizing and meeting those challenges, team members engage in processes that are clearly focused on providing the student the best possible learning opportunities. When all team members contribute and share the successes and needs of the student on a regular basis, positive outcomes are more likely for everyone.

Joint ASHA/CED Communication Policy

Speech Language Pathologists and TODs often have different roles on collaborative teams, yet, in some instances, their roles overlap. In 2002, a joint commission was formed by representatives of CED and ASHA. The 10 members of the Joint Committee of ASHA/CED developed a draft policy entitled "Roles of Speech-Language Pathologists and Teachers of Children Who Are Deaf and Hard of Hearing in the Development of Communicative and Linguistic Competence." This document was broken into the following sections:
- Specialized roles of speech-language pathologists
- Specialized roles of teachers of children who are deaf and hard of hearing
- Collaborative responsibilities
- Service delivery models
- Recommendations
- References

By 2003, the draft policy was approved by the executive boards of CED and ASHA. One of the intentions of policy writers was to revisit the policy as roles expanded and technology for d/hh children evolved (M. Sass-Lehrer, personal communication). When you review the policy at the ASHA website, consider how the roles of SLPs and TODs have changed in the past decade (especially in relation to spoken language and auditory development for d/hh children) and how the educational audiologist may also figure more prominently into the equation of the collaborative team (ASHA, 2004).

Summary

In this chapter we discussed the legal foundations upon which audiological and educational services for d/hh children were based. The various pieces of federal legislation that promoted free and appropriate public education for all children with disabilities were outlined, and the federal civil rights laws that supported the needs of individuals with disabilities were also discussed. We focused attention on the importance of collaboration, discussing the various forms of collaboration as well as some of the issues that can impact successful collaborative efforts. The core professionals who work with d/hh children were identified and described, as were the three teams that typically work with d/hh children. Finally, we reinforced the critical importance of teamwork and collaboration at all levels of work with d/hh students, noting that the greatest opportunity for successful outcomes for these children lies in the work that team members do to ultimately support the individual needs of the child and family.

Chapter 1 Food for Thought

1. Read the opening scenario again. What would you do first to assist the Garcias with their issues and concerns?

2. Compare and contrast the features of the three laws most impacting d/hh students: Section 504, IDEA, and ADA.

3. If you are involved in the IEP process for a d/hh student, you already know that the IEP team is mandated by IDEA. This team is only required to develop and implement the goals, objectives, and related services delineated on the signed IEP. Assume you are an itinerant TOD for a d/hh student who does *not* have an ongoing team that meets both to provide direction and for support. How would you assemble and develop a collaborative team for this student that could be convened at times other than the official IEP meeting?

4. What makes a TOD different than all the other professionals in a school setting that serve d/hh students? Develop a list of attributes, roles, skills, and responsibilities unique to the TOD that are not performed by these other professionals.

5. Recently your authors, who spend a great deal of time in local school districts across the country, noticed a disturbing trend. It started several years ago in mostly rural districts with only a handful of d/hh students on their rolls. Instead of hiring a TOD, districts were taking the "low-cost option" of hiring interpreters and forgoing the employment of a TOD. More recently, this trend expanded to the point that some districts justify not hiring TODs because they say that their general special education teachers and SLPs can

meet the needs of the student as well, if not better, than a TOD. Districts particularly argue this in cases where the child has a cochlear implant because, most likely, they see these children as hearing children or "fixed/cured deaf kids."

How would you frame your response if asked why the TOD is a necessary part of the instructional team for the d/hh student?

Chapter 2

Curves: The Physics of Sound

Scenario

"Mommy, why does it feel funny when I stand next to the big drum? You know, the floor feels shaky when Tommy hits it." Abigail, who has a bilateral profound hearing loss, looked at her mother with curious eyes and a furrowed brow.

Mom pursed her lips and tapped her forehead in thought. "Well, Abby, there is something called vibration. That means that when Tommy hits the drum, it makes a sound and moves the air around you, and you can feel it move. With the bass drum, the sound is going through the wood on the floor and that is why you can feel it move!"

"Does it happen with every drum?" asked Abby.

"Yep, it sure does." said Mom.

When you finish reading Chapter 2, you should be able to explain this entire process to Abigail.

Key Vocabulary

acoustics	inertia	receptor
amplitude	intensity	reference tone
aperiodic	International Phonetic Alphabet	reflected
audiogram	(IPA)	refracted
audiologist	linear scale	residual hearing
audiometer	logarithmic scale	reverberated
auditory cortex	longitudinal wave	second formant (F_2)
cancellation	loudness	simple harmonic motion (SHM)
complex signal	medium	sound level meter
compression	mels	sound pressure
cycles per second	noise	sound pressure level
dampened	nonlinear system	sound propagation
dB hearing level (dBHL)	object	sound wave
dB sensation level (dBSL)	perception	speed of sound
dB sound pressure level (dBSPL)	periodic	threshold
decibel (dB)	phase	timing
elasticity	phons	transverse wave
energy source (force)	physical concepts	vibration
equal loudness contours	pitch	vocal energy
first formant (F_1)	pressure (dynes/cm^2)	vocal tract
formant	psychoacoustics	voicing
frequency	psychophysical concepts	vowel
hearing scientist	pure tones	
hertz (Hz)	rarefaction	

Sound and Its Characteristics

What Is Sound?

We are sure you have heard the old adage "If a tree falls in the woods and no one is there to hear it, does it make a sound?" Well, the answer is "yes." Why? Because even without a human's ear or auditory system in the woods to detect and perceive the sound, the falling tree will make a disturbance in the air as it hits the ground underneath it. That disturbance will create vibrations that, in turn, move the air molecules closest to where the tree strikes the ground, and the vibrations will create areas of **compressions** and **rarefactions** as **sound waves**. However, because the definition of sound involves having a receptor (such as an ear) detect, perceive, and interpret those sound waves, the adage leaves us with the conundrum of not having that receptor. But anyone who really thinks through this conundrum will know that there are many receptors in those woods, because all the deer, squirrels, porcupines, birds, and other living creatures have ears to detect, perceive, and interpret that tree falling. Thus, a tree falling in the woods *does* make a sound.

But before we get too far ahead of ourselves, let's back up a bit. In order for sound to occur, several things must happen in sequence. We can think of them as steps. First of all, there has to be an **energy source**, or a force. In the case of sound, an energy source would be something like a finger plucking a string on a banjo, a mallet striking a key on a xylophone, or the force of air being expelled from the lungs to pass over the vocal folds to produce speech sounds. Figure 2.1 is one representation of the steps involved in **sound propagation**. An energy source by itself will not produce sound. The energy source has to be applied to an object. Therefore, the second thing needed for sound to occur is an **object**. But that object can't be just any object; it has to be an object that has the ability to vibrate. Therefore, vibration of an object must occur for sound to be present. So, a finger plucking the banjo is the energy source and the banjo string is the object.

Figure 2.1. Steps of Sound Propagation

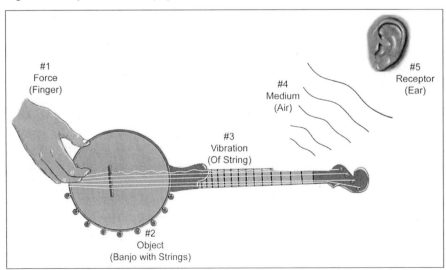

The third thing to happen in this sequence of sound is **vibration**. Vibration is simply the back-and-forth manner in which an object moves around its original resting position—like that banjo string mentioned earlier. In order for an object to be able to move back and forth in this manner, it must have certain physical properties. These physical properties are known as **elasticity** and **inertia**. Elasticity is considered to be a restoring force, which means the object has the ability to return to its original position once the force has been removed. Inertia, on the other hand, is the tendency of an object to remain in motion once it is set in motion, or to remain at rest if it is left undisturbed. As can be seen in Figure 2.1, the vibrating banjo string gets plucked (by a force), and the string is moved away from its resting position (1). Then the string moves back and forth from two different positions (2 and 3) because of the elasticity and inertia contained within the string. **Hearing scientists** would say that inertia and elasticity act to oppose each other, so that when elasticity is high, inertia is low, and vice versa. This motion is the vibration, and the string is the object being set into vibration.

So, we have a vibration occurring, but how does that vibration then get to a person's ear to be heard? Well, this is where a **medium** (and that **receptor** that was mentioned earlier) comes in. The medium is something through which the vibration can travel, such as air, liquids, or solids. The receptor is the ear, which is capable of receiving and interpreting the sound. For us to hear another person talking, sound has to travel through the air. Therefore, the fourth and fifth steps in this sequence of sound are the medium and the receptor. In order for the vibrating object to be heard, the medium must *propagate* sound, or transmit sound from the source to the ear.

How Does Sound Travel?

This idea of sound propagation (or sound travel) takes us back to the beginning when we first mentioned vibration producing areas of compressions and rarefactions. Although sound can travel through water or steel or wood, the most common manner in which sound travels for communication purposes is through air. Air consists of millions of tiny molecules (gases). When sound is propagated through air from the source (Person A's mouth) to the receptor (Person B's ear), the air molecules are compressed together in some areas and separated apart in other areas. These compressed (condensed) and rarefied (expanded) areas of molecules make sound travel out and away from the source. Note that the air molecules themselves do not travel, but the sound waves created by the movement travel. An example of this process involves a tuning fork that has its tines moving in and out after the tuning fork is struck on a table or hard surface. As the tines move out, the air molecules around the tuning fork compress. Then, as expected from the concepts contained within vibrations, the air molecules rarefy, or spread out again. These areas of compression and rarefaction create the sound waves. So, the air molecules are being displaced back and forth, and their movement produces areas of compression and rarefaction. Figure 2.2 shows the tuning fork example of how sound propagates from a source (the tuning fork) and the molecules compress and rarefy creating the vibration.

Figure 2.2. Sound Compression and Rarefaction

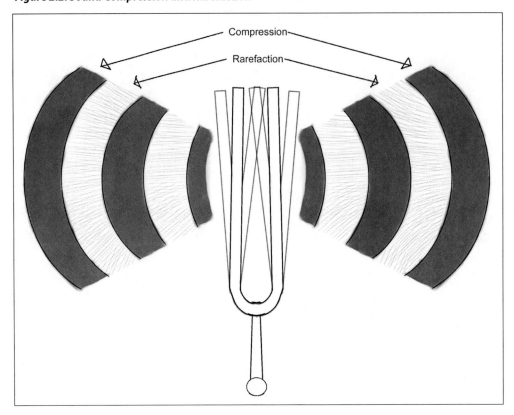

For ease in understanding sound propagation, let's describe the concept of **simple harmonic motion (SHM)**. Like the guitar string described earlier, vibrations consist of back-and-forth motion. That guitar string moves over and over in a similar pattern each time, and that similar, rhythmic pattern is called SHM. Sounds that are the product of SHM are called **pure tones**, meaning they have a tonal quality to them. **Audiologists** use pure tones for calibrating equipment and testing the hearing of their clients. However, pure tones are not encountered by most people on an everyday basis. Most sounds that we hear in life are **complex signals**. That is, most sounds are made up of more than one vibrating source, and the vibrating sources do not move in a simple back-and-forth motion. Speech, for example, is a complex wave.

In addition to being simple or complex, vibrations can be described as **periodic** or **aperiodic**. This means the motion of the vibrating body is either going to be predictable and repetitive (periodic) or it is going to be unpredictable and nonrepetitive (aperiodic). So, most sounds we encounter daily are either *complex periodic* or *complex aperiodic*. A complex periodic vibration is periodic (like SHM) in that it produces a waveform that repeats itself over and over again in time, but it produces multiple tones. Speech would also be an excellent example of a complex periodic sound. But sound that is produced by complex aperiodic vibrations is simply known best as **noise**. An aperiodic signal, such as noise, is not characterized by a waveform with any repeating pattern. It is most easily represented spectrographically, as seen in Figure 2.3.

Both speech and noise can propagate through a medium to get to a person's ear. Figure 2.3 provides examples of each of the sound waves discussed above.

Figure 2.3. Four Types of Sound Waves

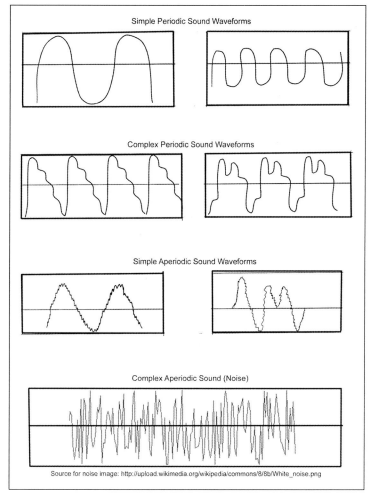

The description above is a very simple description of sound and its propagation from source to receptor. Suffice it to say that vibrations, or sound waves, are pressure waves, and these pressure waves can travel in more than one direction. As described earlier, air molecules do not actually travel themselves. They just bump up against one another and push the sound wave along. The air molecules actually move parallel or perpendicular to the direction of the sound wave motion. That means they can travel

Advanced Physics Concepts

Explanations for several physics concepts (period, wavelength, mass, displacement, and velocity) and hearing science concepts (sine wave, dampening, and resonance) have been left out of this chapter for a few reasons: (1) to minimize confusion, (2) to keep this chapter at a reasonable length, and (3) because TODs, SLPs, and other professionals who work with children who are d/hh don't need an in-depth understanding of these terms. For the audiologist, these are important concepts. If you are interested in reading a more detailed description of sound and sound propagation, we recommend you read any of the following excellent books: DeBonis and Donohue (2008), Hall (2014), Martin and Clark (2012), and Speaks (1999).

longitudinally or transversely. Therefore, the motion of sound has been described as traveling the way a field of wheat waving in the wind would move in the same direction as the wind (**longitudinal waves**), or the way a pebble thrown into water creates swells and troughs of circular motion around the area where the pebble entered the water (**transverse waves**). Because sound can travel in more than just one direction, we can hear many different things, even when distance and location play a factor in what we are hearing. And because of distance, location, and objects around us, things in our listening environments get in the way and interfere with sound propagation. Sound waves can be **cancelled** (silenced) or **reinforced** (made louder). They can also be **dampened, reflected, refracted**, and **reverberated** by objects (such as walls, beams, trees, buildings) in our environments. This means sounds are made softer and bounce off the objects in our surroundings. The actual **speed of sound** is influenced by such things as air temperature, moisture or humidity, and barometric pressure. Sound speeds up as temperature, humidity, and/or barometric pressure increase. It is probably an understatement to say that sound is not a simple, uncomplicated concept. But the understanding of fundamental aspects of sound and sound propagation is extremely important to developing a good grasp of the concepts of audiology, hearing loss, and the impact that this has on children who are deaf and hard of hearing.

That being said, sound propagation is only one aspect of sound as it relates to sending messages from one person to another. All sound vibrations (periodic, aperiodic, simple, and complex) can be described in terms of **amplitude, frequency**, and **phase** (time). Therefore, a more thorough discussion of amplitude, frequency, and phase is needed before we move on. In a book about audiology and auditory concepts, we would be remiss if we did not define these concepts and describe how they relate to the sensations of **loudness, pitch**, and **timing** (or **voicing**). It is these concepts that will allow us to describe and detail certain aspects of voice production, hearing loss, and how hearing is evaluated and recorded by audiologists.

Acoustics and Psychoacoustics

When that infamous tree mentioned earlier hit the ground, it produced a great deal of pressure. The human ear would perceive that pressure as being very loud and having a very low, thudding pitch. But if the receptor in our example had been a device known as a **sound level meter** (see Figure 2.4), that device would have measured the intensity and frequency range of that sound pressure. **Intensity** is the physical measure of what we perceive as the loudness of a sound. It is technically different from amplitude, which was the concept used when describing sound characteristics earlier. **Amplitude** is the term used when describing the displacement of the string's vibration (for the guitar example used earlier), which results in the intensity of the sound that is being produced. There is a subtle difference between these two terms, but it is beyond the scope of this book to dwell on these differences. Therefore, since audiologists use the **audiogram** and their tests to describe intensity of sounds, then the term *intensity* will be used from here on.

Figure 2.4. Sound Level Meters

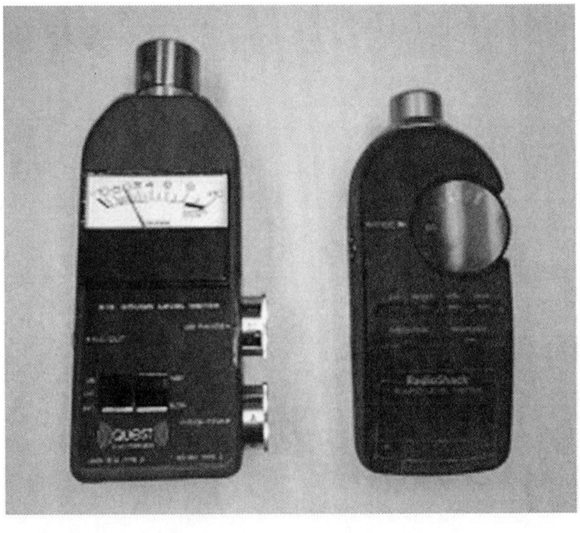

So, if the ear hears "loudness" and "pitch," and a device measures "intensity" and "frequency," what is going on here? Why can't we use the same terms for both? Well, this is best described with the concepts of **physical** and **psychophysical** terminology.

Physical versus Psychophysical Terminology

When describing these concepts to an Introduction to Audiology class, we sometimes get the legendary "deer in headlights" look from the students. If something is loud, then why do we have to talk about intensity? If something has a high pitch, then why do we have to talk about frequency? This is best answered with the idea that the human brain and a sound level meter are two very different things (not hard to grasp this fact, right?). And because they are very different, we have to describe how they measure sound differently.

Let's begin with the concepts of acoustics and psychoacoustics. **Acoustics** is the study of sound as a physical event, and **psychoacoustics** is how we describe sound as a psychological event. So, sound must be measured with devices (sound level meters or sound level meter apps on smart phones) as a physical unit, while the brain takes those physical units and *perceives* them as **psychophysical** phenomena. The **perception** made by the brain is what brings into play this "psycho," or "self," concept. Think of this as the brain being a living, functioning device that perceives psychophysical events, whereas a sound level meter is a nonliving, inert device that is only capable of measuring (not perceiving) the physical properties of sound. Believe it or not, but no two people perceive sound in exactly the same way, even when their hearing sensitivity is perfectly normal (typical). So let's see how this plays into the concepts of intensity, loudness, frequency, pitch, and lastly, phase or timing.

Intensity and Loudness

Loudness is the perceptual correlate, or perceptual link, to intensity. The physical characteristic of the intensity of a sound determines the psychological sensation of loudness. That is, the higher the intensity of a sound, the greater the perceived loudness. Intensity is the physical event (measured with a device), and loudness is the perceptual event (measured with an ear).

When an audiologist measures a person's hearing, earphones are placed over the person's ears and a device, known as an **audiometer**, is used to generate pure tone signals (as described previously) of varying intensities. The person is instructed to respond (usually by raising her hand or pressing a button) to the pure tones. The tones typically start off being comfortably loud to the individual, and then the audiologist decreases the intensity of the signal until the person can just barely detect it (so the intensity decreases and the person perceives the tone as getting softer). The audiologist is interested in obtaining the lowest level at which the person can still just hear the tone (this is known as the **threshold**). The intensity of the tones is measured on the audiogram in units called **decibels (dB)**.

Audiologist vs. Hearing Scientist Vernacular

Hearing scientists (who are different from audiologists and do not tend to work with children who are d/hh in a clinical manner) measure people's perception of loudness in units called phons. A **phon** can be defined as the special unit for loudness level. So, decibel is the unit for intensity, and phon is the unit for loudness. Audiologists plot the intensity of a person's responses to hearing tones on the audiogram in dB hearing level (dBHL), but a hearing scientist plots a person's phons for comparison with the **equal loudness contours** (sometimes referred to as Fletcher Munson curves [Fletcher & Munson, 1933]). Audiologists rarely think about phons or do anything with them. All of the equipment that audiologists use to test hearing and fit amplification use decibels as the unit of measure, not phons. So, even though an audiologist may ask a person to tell him how loud or soft the sounds are coming through a hearing aid, the audiologist is really not thinking about the perceptual side of sound.

Audiologists and hearing scientists also look at and measure the concept of pitch or frequency differently. Audiologists measure frequency in hertz, Hz, and hearing scientists measure people's perception of pitch in units called mels. So, the **mel** can be defined as the unit for pitch, and the Hz can be defined as the unit for frequency. Mels are measured on a mel scale, and a listener is asked to describe what she is hearing as half the pitch of a **reference tone**, as twice the pitch of a reference tone, as three times the pitch of a reference tone, and so on. Audiologists plot the hearing thresholds described previously at each individual frequency on the audiogram. Rarely does an audiologist use mels in the clinical practice of audiology.

Frequency and Pitch

Pitch is the perceptual correlate to frequency. The physical characteristic of the frequency of a sound determines the psychological sensation of pitch. That is, the higher the frequency of a sound, the higher the perceived pitch. Frequency is the physical event (measured with a device), and pitch is the perceptual event (measured with an ear).

When an audiologist measures a person's hearing with the same pure tones, same earphones, and same audiometer described previously, the audiologist typically starts off testing the tones in the middle range, or the mid-frequencies (e.g., 1000 Hz). Testing starts in the mid-frequencies because that is where the human ear is most sensitive. The audiologist then moves into the higher frequencies (towards 8000 Hz) before testing the lower frequencies (125 to 500 Hz). The frequencies of the tones are measured on the audiogram in units called **hertz (Hz)**. Like the unit of the decibel, which got its name from honoring Alexander Graham Bell, the unit of hertz got its name from honoring Heinrich Hertz, a German physicist.

Another term used to explain frequencies or hertz is **cycles per second (cps)**. This relates to how many complete waveforms occur over a one-second period of time. The simple harmonic waveform discussed previously is usually plotted over a time period of one cycle. So, the cycle of the guitar string mentioned earlier would be represented by the movement of the string away from the resting point and the return movement to the same point going in the same direction. Like a circle, a cycle can be described in 360 degrees. Lower frequencies have longer cycles per second because it takes the wave a longer time to complete one cycle. Higher frequencies have shorter cycles per second because the cycle is completed faster, or in a shorter time frame. Cycles per second can be used to describe the number of times an object vibrates, by which a lower number of cycles per second produces a lower frequency sound and a higher number of cycles per second produces a higher frequency of sound. For example, the lowest frequency produced by a tuba is 45 Hz (cps), and the highest frequency produced by a flute is about 2,200 Hz (cps).

The last characteristic of sound to discuss is the phase. It is also the least utilized concept by an audiologist or a TOD. Phase is thought of simply as the timing of a pure tone. That is, the phase of a pure tone is the point at which the wave begins. Like the cycle concept, phase is described in degrees. A complete cycle is 360 degrees of phase. A wave can start at 0 degrees, at 90 degrees, at 270 degrees, or at any point in between. The reason phase is least thought about in audiology is because there is nothing on the audiogram that represents phase the way intensity and frequency are used to represent auditory thresholds. Audiologists typically think about the phase of a sound only if there is any risk of having the phase of one sound cancel out, or decrease, a second sound, as would be the case if one starting phase was 0 degrees and the other starting phase was 360 degrees. For example, due to the nature of pure tones, when an audiologist puts a person in the booth in order to test that person's hearing aids, the audiologist has to remember that pure tones may hit the booth's walls in such a manner that the waves might reflect off other walls and cancel each other out. Therefore, an audiologist must know to manipulate the pure tone while testing to avoid the phase issue of sounds canceling each other out. Figure 2.5 shows examples of sound waves out of phase, and Figure 2.6 shows sound wave **cancellation**.

Figure 2.5. Sound Waves Out of Phase

Now that we have described the three characteristics of sound as intensity, frequency, and phase, let's go further into detail on one more very important concept in the field of audiology—the decibel. By going into more detail, we will have to introduce the concepts of **logarithmic scales** and **nonlinear systems**. Don't throw your hands up just yet—we will make this as painless as possible.

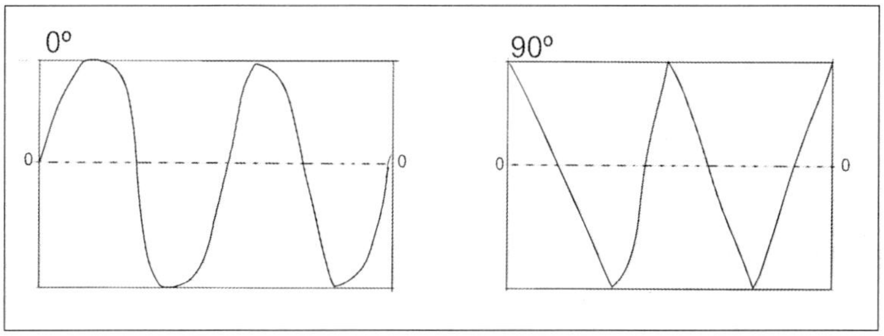

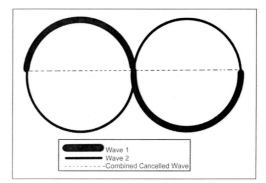

Figure 2.6. Sound Wave Cancellation

Decibel: A Relative Term

As mentioned previously, the decibel (dB) is used to measure the intensity of sound. However, more importantly, the decibel is a measure of **sound pressure** (just like the pressure we mentioned with that tree falling in the forest), and it is a logarithmic scale. If we did not use decibels to describe human hearing, we'd be dealing with some very large units of **pressure** (or dynes/cm^2). Deutsch and Richards (1979) gave a great perspective on this by stating that the softest sound heard by humans is about 0.0002 dynes/cm^2, while the loudest sound heard without causing pain would be about 2000 dynes/cm^2. That means that the loud sound would be 10 million times the intensity of the soft sound; and if we used these measurements to describe people's hearing, we'd have to describe a patient as having a hearing loss of 5 million dynes/cm^2. This massive concept explains why audiologists have had to resort to more clinically feasible terminology for audiograms and hearing loss. It is basically the reason why the logarithmic scale and decibel are used by audiologists.

In a logarithmic scale (log scale), each unit in the scale is larger than the preceding unit. This is not like the common **linear scale** many of us are used to seeing, where all the units are the same size (e.g., mile 1 to mile 2 on a map is exactly the same distance as mile 20 to mile 21). But in order to "pack in more punch," the larger units of a log scale allow us to fit more in. That is, the use of a log scale for hearing "avoids very large numbers and allows us to describe the entire range of human hearing (10 million-fold in linear terms) as 0 dB to 140 dB" (Deutsch & Richards, 1979, p. 27).

So, what do the concepts of logarithmic scales and nonlinear hearing mean for many of us? Basically, it means that hearing concepts are grounded on the decibel, a unit that is based on a logarithmic scale rather than a linear scale. Therefore, each successive unit on the decibel scale represents a greater increase in intensity than the previous unit. Anatomically and physiologically, this means that hearing is very sensitive and has many active properties to it that are only just now beginning to be discovered.

But it also means that hearing and sound measurement are grounded on a relative scale, which must have an arbitrary reference, zero point. The decibel is not an absolute measurement. This means that there is an arbitrary zero (0) reference point, and sound has to be referenced in decibels depending on what is being measured. For example, on an audiogram, 0 dB does not mean that there is no sound. Rather, it is a statistical reference point of the softest intensity that a person with normal hearing would hear a pure tone. So even at 0 dB, there is sound. The decibel, being a logarithmic ratio of one intensity measure to a reference intensity (which is usually a reference pressure of 0.0002 dynes/cm^2), can be measured by referencing it to many other terms, such as **sound pressure level (SPL), hearing level (HL),** and **sensation level (SL)**. There are many more references (for example, dBnHL, dBA, dBC, and so on), but again, this is not the textbook to go into those concepts. We just want our readers to understand that they will hear an audiologist talk about dBSPL and **dBHL**, and they will read audiograms and hearing aid specification sheets that have terms such as "re: dBHL" and "output SPL dB" on them. It is only necessary to know that dBSPL is how intensity levels of sound will be measured by equipment, such as sound level meters or microphones. But SPL is often referenced to the ear, or human hearing, in dBHL. Therefore, an audiogram and audiometer will have

"dBHL" on them, and this term indicates that all intensities are being referenced back to human hearing. Figure 2.7 is a great chart showing the conversion of dBSPL into dBHL for the audiogram. As can be seen in the top graph, human hearing is more sensitive in the middle frequencies (1000, 2000, and 4000 Hz range) than it is in the very low or very high frequency ranges. It takes more sound pressure at 250 Hz (26.5 dB) and 8000 Hz (13.0 dB) for the typical hearing person to hear than it does for that person to hear at 1000 Hz (only 7.5 dB). This creates a curve, where the lower and higher frequencies in dBSPL are greater than the middle frequencies. This curve is known as the minimum audibility curve. For clinical purposes (and to make it easier for audiologists to graph hearing loss), the curve is flattened out into a straight line and called audiometric zero. Audiometric zero is the sound pressure level at which the threshold of audibility occurs in average normal-hearing listeners. Therefore, if the standard sound pressure level is applied at each individual frequency, and the threshold for the average normal listener is designated as 0 dBHL for each of those frequencies, then the curve has been straightened out. The straightened line, or audiometric zero line, can be seen in the middle graph of Figure 2.7. But, because typical responses of average normal listeners vary by as many as 10 decibels around audiometric zero, the flattened line at the bottom of the graph in the middle of Figure 2.7 gets moved up to the top of the graph

Figure 2.7. Conversion of dBSPL to dBHL

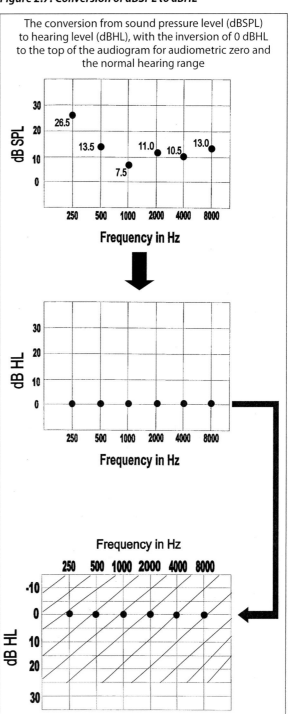

(as can be seen in the lowest graph of Figure 2.7) and becomes an **audiogram**. The normal hearing range on most audiograms range from -10 dBHL to +25 dBHL, and the normal range is represented at the top of the audiogram so that hearing "loss" can be represented in a lower area, or lower range, of the graph. More will be said about the audiogram and hearing loss in Chapter 5. Just knowing that dBSPL is changed to dBHL for audiometric testing purposes should help the reader to understand why some decibels are referred to as "dBSPL" and some are referred to as "dBHL." It really depends on what is measuring the sound or what the measurements are being used for (i.e., levels of sound from the environment or levels of hearing from a person's auditory system).

Now that we have described sound as it travels from a source to the ear and we've described how sound relates to physical and psychophysical aspects of hearing, we need to describe how sound impacts speech production. Speech, language, and hearing must go hand-in-hand.

Formants

Identifying Characteristics

Understanding the physics of sound allows us to more fully grasp the difficulties children with hearing loss have in their ability to receive and process all sounds, especially speech. One particular area of interest for us in this regard is **formants**.

Formants occur during speech production. They are formed along the vocal tract (larynx, pharynx, oral and nasal cavities) as **vowels** are being produced and the shape of the oral cavity changes in response to the speech sounds being articulated. Formants are defined as a "frequency region, for vowels and resonant consonants, in which a relatively high degree of acoustic energy is concentrated" (Nicolosi, Harriman, & Kresheck, 2004, p. 131). In other words, sounds have bands of energy that concentrate at different frequencies, and we call these formants. This energy occurs across time and helps to distinguish among and between vowel sounds. Each band is labeled from F_1, F_2, and so on. English vowels are interesting because the **first formant**, or F_1, is virtually the same for all of the vowels. The range for the first formant is in the low frequencies from 250–730 Hz. This is helpful for us to know because many of our students have **residual hearing** in the low frequencies, which means that they can hear this part of the vowel sound. It is the **second formant**, F_2, with the frequency range of 850–2290 Hz that is critical for vowel discrimination. The vast majority of our students have hearing loss in the mid to upper frequencies. This is why students often have difficulty discriminating vowels through hearing alone. To hear these high frequency sounds, the individual must use a device such as a hearing aid, that transforms or shifts the sounds downward into frequencies they can perceive. The successful use of a cochlear implant also allows the individual to access these frequencies through the stimulation of neural fibers by the implanted electrode array. We discuss both hearing aids and cochlear implants in Chapter 6.

There are several ways to explain formants. Using visualizations is often helpful. In addition, knowing the **International Phonetic Alphabet (IPA)** allows readers to understand which sounds are being discussed. Figure 2.8 is a chart that lists all of the IPA symbols along with key words that are representative of each sound. Figure 2.9 (see page 44) is a spectrographic view of the three vowel sounds "e," "oo," "ah" (IPA symbols /i/, /u/, and /a/, respectively). If you look closely, you can see the concentrated **vocal energy**, represented by the heavy black lines; these are formants 1 and 2. Notice that the first formant (F_1) for /i/ and /u/ is in the same frequency range and that F_1 for /a/ is close; all of these vowels have first formants around 500 Hz. Now look at the second, or F_2, formants. The F_2 for /i/ is much higher at 2500 Hz than the F_2 for the other two vowels at 1000 Hz. If you now think about the student with a high frequency hearing loss, you can understand why she may not be able to perceive this part of the vowel sound. If the student cannot perceive sounds beyond 1000 Hz, the /i/ and /u/ vowels will sound the same!

Figure 2.8. IPA Symbols for English Speech Sounds

English	IPA	Key Words
h	/h/	house
wh	/hw/	when
p	/p/	pie/top
t	/t/	tie/hat
k	/k/	kite/sock
f	/f/	fine/if
th[1]	/θ/	thin, mouth
s	/s/	sun, grass
sh	/ʃ/	ship, dish
ch	/tʃ/	chime, match
w-	/w/	win
b	/b/	boy, cab
d	/d/	dog, mad
g	/g/	game/hug
v	/v/	voice, cave
th[2]	/ð/	them, bathe
z	/z/	zoo, buzz
zh	/ʒ/	genre, garage
j	/dʒ/	john, fudge
m	/m/	mop, hum
n	/n/	nose, line
ng	/ŋ/	hanger, hung
l	/l/	laugh, ball
r	/r/	race
y-	/j/	yellow
oo	/u/	boot
-oo-	/ʊ/	hook
aw	/ɔ/	awful
ee	/i/	eat
-i-	/ɪ/	if
-e-	/ɛ/	end
-a-	/æ/	at
-o-	/a/	odd
-u-	/ʌ/	up
-u-	/ə/	above
ur	/ɝ/	earth
a-e	/eɪ/	made
i-e	/aɪ/	high
oa	/o/	boat
oi	/ɔɪ/	coin
u-e	/ju/	use
ou	/aʊ/	out
er	/ɚ/	mother

Figure 2.9. Spectrograph Image of Formants 1 and 2 for the Vowel Sounds /i/, /u/, /a/

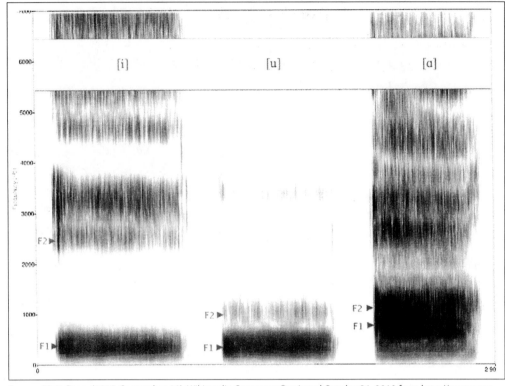

Source: Main Page. (2010, September 18). Wikimedia Commons Retrieved October 31, 2010 from http://commons. wikimedia.org/wiki/File:Spectrogram_-iua.png

Table 2.1 provides a listing of 11 English vowel sounds with their first three formants. Examination of these examples of formants demonstrates that all of the F_1 formants are under 1000 Hz and that there is a large variance among the F_2 formants. Inspection of this data allows you to compare the individual's auditory response information on the audiogram to the numerical values of the vowels used in English.

Table 2.1. Formant Frequencies for 11 English Vowel Sounds

i	ɪ	e	ɛ	æ	ɑ	o	u	ʊ	ə	ɚ
meet	hit	fate	head	at	hot	nose	who	book	above	mother
First formant frequency										
270	390	500	530	660	730	450	390	300	640	490
Second formant frequency										
2290	1990	1880	1840	1720	1100	850	1050	850	1190	1350
Third formant frequency										
3010	2550	2520	2480	2410	2440	2410	2240	2240	2390	1690

These two views (Figure 2.9 and Table 2.1) of formants should help to clarify your understanding of this vocal and acoustic energy. They should also help you understand why people with hearing loss cannot easily discriminate certain speech sounds, and therefore, cannot easily produce certain speech sounds. The next section has even more details that relate this information to spoken language in hearing and d/hh children.

Impact of Formants on Spoken Language

The average person with normal/typical hearing acuity develops speech and language skills, also referred to as spoken language, beginning at birth. This process occurs through a complex exchange of signals that are filtered by the brain. To appreciate the impact that formants have on the development of spoken language, a brief review of speech development is provided here.

The hearing infant hears speech and other acoustic signals from the environment. These signals are transmitted to the brain, passing through various "way stations" (neurons and neural pathways) that allow the baby to perceive differences in the signals. When the sound reaches the **auditory cortex** in the temporal lobe of the brain, it is officially perceived, and cognitive processes allow the infant to determine what the sound represents. Through millions of listening experiences, the infant begins to learn that certain sound combinations represent words that symbolize things in our environment. This phase of development is receptive in nature; that is, the child is constantly receiving acoustic information and learning to understand what those sounds mean.

At the same time, oral motor skills are also developing. Babies begin making oral sounds immediately at birth, beginning with reflexive cries. As the motor skills develop, the types of sounds produced begin to change. Vowels are articulated first; then the consonants that are closely associated with lip and tongue movements used while nursing are articulated next. These consonants produce strong visual and tactile reactions in the baby. This is why *mama, dada,* and *baba* are often identified as the first words a baby says. In reality, these are the first consonant-vowel combinations that occur during babbling. It is not until Mommy and Daddy get excited about hearing these combinations and respond to the baby that the baby begins to make a linguistic connection that these sounds represent these people. Through continuing listening experiences, the baby develops a core vocabulary that is understood. In a child with normal hearing, this increased understanding of spoken language far precedes her ability to produce those same words, phrases, and sentences. With maturation, the spoken representations of these vocabulary words and structures begin to be used; this is speech. For an extensive discussion on normal language development in children, refer to *Language Development* 5th Edition by Erika Hoff (2014).

What happens when a hearing loss is present? First and foremost, there is a reduction in the amount and quality of the auditory input getting to a child's auditory system. Any reduction in audition can have an impact on a child's understanding and use of spoken language. The more severe the loss, the less sound stimulation is experienced.

So, back to formants. Formants impact speech and language in both receptive and expressive ways. From the listening or receptive perspective, speech is *received* in a distorted way when a hearing loss is present. The distortion may occur in the volume of the sound. That is, some speech sounds are produced at a lower volume because of the acoustic nature of the sound. An example might be the word *pat*. This word is a relatively soft word and can easily be misheard as *tat, tap,* or *pap*. The distortion can also occur in the quality of the sound. When a hearing loss involves the cochlea (the major organ for processing sound), the actual hair cells for sound reception are damaged. This damage creates distortion, which in turn, affects the quality of the sound. In some cases, the sound cannot be heard at all. In others, it is heard, but misheard as similar speech sounds. For example, the /f/ as in the word *fin* and /θ/ ("th") as in the word *thin*, are frequently substituted for one another. Acoustically, the words *fun* and *thumb* sound almost the same; to a person with high frequency hearing loss, they might sound exactly the same. An example with the /i/ and /u/ vowels might include the words *team* and *tomb*. Although these words look nothing alike on the lips (and to a hearing person, sound nothing alike), to a person with high frequency hearing loss who can't hear the difference between /i/ and /u/ vowels, these words could sound exactly alike! When you consider just these few examples of receptive distortions, you can imagine how difficult listening to and understanding speech would be for someone with a hearing loss.

Now recall that speech and language have both receptive and expressive elements. Therefore, the ability to learn how to produce speech is also affected by how speech sounds. That is, if you cannot hear the difference among sounds, it is difficult to adjust your articulation and tone of voice to produce speech more accurately. Hearing people routinely use a personal auditory feedback system to self-correct their own speech errors. With the inability to use this system to distinguish among vowel sounds (formants) or other consonant sounds, the spoken message is often distorted as well. There are certain characteristic speech production distortions that are often found in the speech of people with hearing loss. Words that contain the "s," "sh," "ch" (IPA /s/, /ʃ/, /tʃ/, respectively) sounds may sound chopped off, as though a /t/ is being produced instead (e.g., *sun* sounds more like *tun*, or *mash* sounds like *mat*, or *chin* sounds more like *tin*). These distortions occur because the sounds are high frequency and not easily perceived.

The Frequency Playground

The Independent Recording Network website provides an interactive chart that demonstrates a huge variety of frequencies and aids in the understanding of how frequencies impact everything we hear. From the human voice to the piano keyboard and common environmental sounds, you can manipulate and observe the frequencies. Go to this website and have a great time playing and learning! http://www.independentrecording.net/irn/resources/freqchart/main_display.htm

Summary

The objective of this chapter was to give our readers a basic understanding of the science surrounding sound, sound perception, and sound production. We reviewed how sound is made and propagated, how sound is measured, what characteristics of sound are important to audiometric testing and hearing perception, how characteristics of sound are applied to speech reception and production, and how hearing loss impacts speech perception. It should be more easily understood why hearing, speech, and language are so closely tied together.

Chapter 2 Food for Thought

1. Read the opening scenario again. How would you explain the movement that Abby felt while her brother played his drum?

2. Explain the process for sound propagation.

3. Explain the difference between the physical and psychophysical terms used for sound.

4. Does 0 dBHL on an audiogram mean that there is no sound to be heard? Explain.

5. What do formants represent, and why are they important for a TOD and SLP to understand?

Chapter 3

A Symphony in Motion: Anatomy and Physiology of the Hearing Mechanism

Scenario

Jody, who lives by the beach in Florida, is planning to join a scuba diving class. She's always wanted to explore the waters off of the Florida Keys. While she expected to learn how to breathe underwater, how to put on and use the equipment, and how to swim correctly, she finds that in the class before their first venture into the water, the instructor is spending time talking about ears. She knows she hears perfectly and has never had a problem with hearing or her ears. So she thinks, "Why in the world is this instructor spending so much time talking about ears when he should be teaching us how to breathe with our oxygen tanks?"

When you finish Chapter 3, you should be able to answer Jody's question, using anatomical terms she's never heard before and then explaining what they mean in layman's terms.

Key Vocabulary

8th cranial nerve (8 CN)	crus	nasopharynx
ampulla (sing.)/ampullae (pl.)	endolymph	organ of Corti
annular ring/annulus	epitympanic recess	ossicles
anterior	eustachian tube	ossicular chain
anterior/superior canal	external auditory canal	otoscope
antihelix	external auditory meatus	outer ear
antitragus	frontal lobe	outer hair cells
apical end	hearing mechanism	oval window
articulatory facet	helicotrema	pars flaccida
auditory cortex	helix	pars tensa
auditory nerve	horizontal/lateral canal	perilymph
auricle	incus	pinna
basilar end	inferior	posterior
body planes	inner ear	posterior canal
brain hemisphere	inner hair cells	promontory
brainstem	lateral	Reissner's membrane
cerumen	lobule	retrocochlear pathways
cochlea	malleus	round window
cochlear duct	manubrium	saccule
cochlear system	mastoid bone	sagittal/median plane
concha	medial	scala media
cone of light	middle ear	scala tympani
coronal/frontal plane	midline	scala vestibuli *cont.*

Key Vocabulary, cont.		
semicircular canals	stereocilia	tympanic membrane
Shrapnell's membrane	superior	umbo
spiral ganglion	tectorial membrane	utricle
stapedial footplate	tensor tympani	vestibular nerve
stapedial muscle/stapedius	tragus	vestibular system
stapes	transverse plane	vocal folds
	tunnel of Corti	

Chapter Structure

This chapter covers two main topics. The first is the physical structure (anatomy) of our ears. After each anatomical section of the **hearing mechanism** is presented, the function and action (physiology) performed by that section of the hearing mechanism is explained. Then, the final section of this chapter links all of the individual discussions of how the anatomical structures in each section work to describe the complete journey of a sound through the hearing mechanism and on to the brain to be interpreted.

In the previous chapter, you read about the properties of sound. You were introduced to frequency as measured in Hertz (Hz) and intensity measured on two different decibel scales (dbSPL and dbHL). These properties of physics are crucial to understanding the physiology of the hearing mechanism, the production of intelligible speech, the science behind hearing assessment, and the selection of appropriate assistive listening technology. So, if you need to review information on the properties of sound, please refer back to those sections in Chapter 2.

There Is More to the Ear than the Eye Can See

The ear, or more accurately the hearing mechanism, is a complex and well-designed piece of "equipment." It has numerous parts that perform specific actions. When you complete this chapter, you will be as amazed as we are by how effectively the hearing mechanism works. So let's get started. While there are no true anatomical divisions, when we refer to the hearing mechanism, as shown in Table 3.1, we generally break the anatomy into four sections: (1) the outer ear, (2) the middle ear, (3) the inner ear, and (4) the retrocochlear section, which includes the neural pathways and the areas in the brain that interpret what is heard.

Table 3.1. The Segmented Hearing Mechanism: Form and Function

	Outer Ear	**Middle Ear**	**Inner Ear**	**Retrocochlear Portion /Brain**
Image				
Major Structures or Features	Pinna; external auditory meatus/ external auditory canal	Tympanic membrane; Ossicles (malleus, incus, stapes); tensor tympani muscle; stapedial muscle (stapedius); eustachian tube	Vestibular system: semicircular canals; Cochlear system: oval and round windows; cochlea; lymphatic fluids; scala vestibuli; scala media/cochlear duct; scala tympani; organ of Corti; inner and outer hair cells; tectorial membrane	Spiral ganglion; Auditory Nerve (8th Cranial nerve); brainstem; auditory cortex
Function	Capture, conduct, and amplify sound waves to the tympanic membrane to start it vibrating mechanically	Transfer mechanical vibrations through the ossicular chain without loss of frequency and intensity and push and pull on the oval window, creating movement in the lymphatic fluids on the other side	Respond to the hydraulic energy by passing along frequency-specific waves through pressure on the hair cells in the organ of Corti that send electrical impulses when they are bent in direct relation to the force /pressure of, and vibratory cycle of, waves upon specific hair cells. In turn, these bent hair cells send electrical impulses, conveying both frequency and intensity information to the retrocochlear portion of the ear.	Transmit the electrical impulse information of sounds (frequency and intensity) that has been processed in the cochlea through the auditory nerve (8th Cranial Nerve) through the brain stem and various waypoints on the nerves leading to the auditory cortex of the brain. The auditory cortex (one in each hemisphere of the brain) then takes that electrical information and associates it with various sounds, words, or noises, and the listener then receives the transmitted sound/ language.
Type of Energy Transfer	Stage 1 Acoustic energy →	Stage 2 Mechanical energy →	Stage 3 Hydraulic (fluid) energy →	Stage 4 Electrical energy

Anatomical features typically have Latin names and the hearing mechanism is no exception. While some of these anatomical features perform specific functions of which you need to be aware, others are like midpoints on a road map. These features are not actually separate anatomical structures but, rather, important places whose functions will be explained later in the physiology portions of this chapter. There are many additional anatomical structures in the ear that a physician, biologist, or audiologist may have memorized, but for our purposes, you do not need to know their names or functions. The purpose of this particular exploration into learning the names and functions of the anatomical structures of the hearing mechanism is to enable parents and teachers to converse knowledgeably and with confidence with the various professionals who deal with hearing loss. You may also be in a position to explain a particular etiology (cause) of deafness to another person or describe the hearing complaints a student may be experiencing. After reading this chapter, when interacting with a collaborative team, you will be able to do so using shared terminology. Knowing the structures and functions of the system and how they relate to the interpretation of an audiogram will serve you well. We promise, trust us.

Whenever one discusses anatomy, specific terms such as *superior* or *inferior* are used to describe the direction from which you are examining the body or anatomical feature. We use these terms to instruct the reader on how to view and better visualize an illustration or photograph. Table 3.2 presents the terms as opposites (an easier way to remember them), and Figure 3.1 illustrates the various relative body directions presented in the table. (See our superhero models. What is their superpower? If they are cut apart, they can put themselves back together, of course!)

Table 3.2. Anatomical Directional Terms

Term	Meaning	*Is opposite of...*	Term	Meaning
Anterior	In front of, front, forward	➡	Posterior	After, behind, following, toward the rear
Superior	Above, over, higher	➡	Inferior	Below, under, lower
Lateral	Toward the side, away from the midline	➡	Medial	Toward the midline, middle, away from the side
Distal	Farther from the axis/ midline	➡	Proximal	Closer to the axis / midline

We also show structures from different viewpoints. You can think of these as cuts of an anatomical structure. However, they are more appropriately termed **body planes.** To better visualize body planes, imagine you have an Italian salami. You can cut it in three major ways: across into slices (**transverse**), lengthwise into right and left halves (**sagittal**) and lengthwise into front and back halves (**coronal**).

Figure 3.1. Anatomical Directions

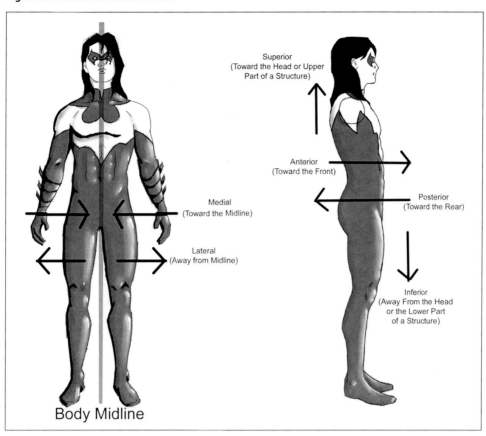

Table 3.3 lists the names of the body planes. Figure 3.2 illustrates the types of cuts using the human body. So, if you visualize the human body standing upright, you can imagine how the body can be divided (like the salami) in several planes. Cutting the body into planes is helpful when viewing structures in the ear. The planes shown in Figure 3.2 can be applied to any anatomical body part. Later in this chapter when you see a segment of a structure of the hearing mechanism, keep in mind the body plane in which it is being shown (Bailey, n.d.).

Table 3.3. Human Anatomical Body Planes

Name of Plane	Alternate Name	Description
Sagittal plane	Median plane	A sagittal cut on a human body separates the body or structure into a right side and a left side. These can be of equal size (midsagittal) or uneven size (parasagittal).
Coronal plane	Frontal plane	A coronal cut on a human body separates the front from the back. A coronal plane cut produces a front (anterior) and a back (posterior) section.
Transverse plane	Horizontal (Axial) plane	A transverse cut on a human body or structure separates it into upper (superior) and lower (inferior) portions. Sometimes, this is referred to as a cross section, especially when several transverse cuts are made. Remember the prefix *trans* means "across" or "cross."

Figure 3.2. Anatomical Body Planes

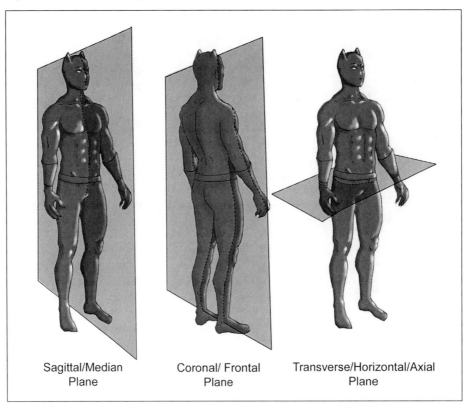

Sagittal/Median Plane

Coronal/ Frontal Plane

Transverse/Horizontal/Axial Plane

The hearing mechanism, broken down in Table 3.1, is put back together as a single organ in Figure 3.3. Referring to Table 3.1 and Figure 3.3 as we move through the anatomy and physiology portions of this chapter will help you remember the four sections and their structures and how they relate to one another.

Figure 3.3. Complete Hearing Mechanism

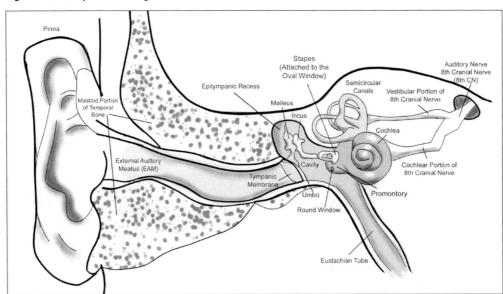

Section 1: The Outer Ear

Outer Ear Anatomy

The **outer ear** has two main sections, the **pinna** or **auricle** (either term is correct) and the **external auditory meatus** (EAM) or **external auditory canal** (EAC) (either term is also correct). Figure 3.4 provides an image of the outer ear sections. The pinna describes the entire portion of the hearing mechanism that can be seen external (**lateral**) to the head. There should be one on either side. In normal conversation, most people would probably mean the pinna when using the word *ear*. According to the online Merriam-Webster dictionary (n.d.), *pinnas* and the more formal Latin *pinnae* are both acceptable terms for the plural of pinna. We present the anatomy of the pinna because some congenital etiologies involve malformations of the pinna, and the structures of the pinna are used when discussing the correct fitting of ear molds. And although the various parts that combine to make the pinna may not be directly connected to hearing, they do collect sound and channel it inwards.

Figure 3.4. The Outer Ear

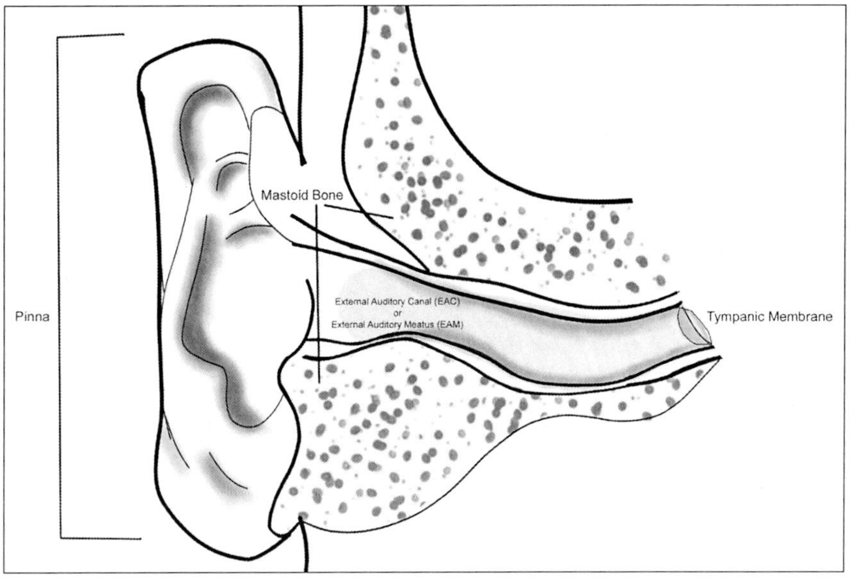

The second major portion of the outer ear, the external auditory meatus (EAM), also called the external auditory canal, not only channels sound to the tympanic membrane and structures beyond, but due to its shape and length, it causes reverberation which in effect boosts low- to mid-frequency sounds by approximately 15 dB.

The following "read and touch" activity will help you identify the pinna's landmarks. Use Figures 3.5 and 3.6 as visual assists. The pinna is shaped like a conch shell. For many mammals, the larger the pinna, the better collector of sound waves it is. The majority of the pinna is made up of cartilage just like the cartilage in the tip of your nose. There are no bones or bony structures in the pinna.

55

Following Figures 3.5 and 3.6, you will see that the outermost edge of the pinna is the **helix** (a-b). Using your finger you can trace the cartilage of the helix from where it begins at the top (a) as it emerges from your head until it stops and you can no longer feel the cartilaginous material (b). Continue to follow the periphery (edge) of the pinna with your finger from there and you will feel

Figure 3.5. Labeled Photo of a Pinna

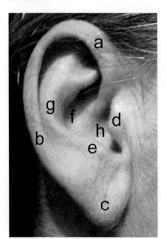

Figure 3.6. Labeled Drawing of a Pinna

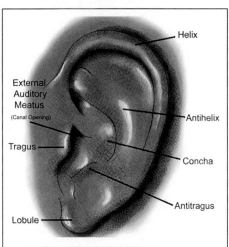

the location of the bottom attachment of the pinna to the head. The soft portion, where the cartilage of the helix ends, is your **lobule** or earlobe (c). Lobules can either be attached or detached. Figures 3.5 and 3.6 illustrate detached or free earlobes. When we discuss the genetics of hearing loss in the next chapter, there is an example that involves attached versus detached earlobes. Whichever you have matters not at all to your ability either to process sound or channel it inwards.

Protect Your Ears the Easy Way

An interesting fact about the tragus is that if you are in a very noisy environment, one that might even cause temporary or permanent harm to your ability to hear, you can push the tragus toward the canal somewhat forcefully (it should not be painful) and occlude the pathway to the rest of the ear (remember, ear and hearing mechanism are interchangeable terms). When you do that, you are decreasing the volume of the sound reaching the other portions of the ear by about 35 decibels (dB). What is a decibel? Well, it is 1/10 of a Bel, which isn't that important to know actually, but decibel is a term that was discussed, at length, back in Chapter 2. So file the word *tragus* away for later use. The important thing to remember here is that you are saving your ears from potential damage by using the tragus to block some harmful sound from going inside.

Continuing along the periphery of the pinna under and around the lobule, you will feel a piece of cartilage that is about ½ inch (1.3 centimeters) wide. It is **medial** to the helix (refer to Table 3.1 for anatomical vocabulary terminology). This structure is the **tragus** (d). If you roll the tip of your finger over the front (**anterior** side) of the tragus and around to the back (**posterior** side), your fingertip should be blocking the external auditory meatus or auditory canal (h) that leads into the unseen portions of the hearing mechanism. If that isn't where you end up, either (1) your ear is very atypical, which is rare but possible, or (2) you haven't followed directions so… go back to the top of this paragraph and start again.

Moving on, directly across from the tragus is the anti-tragus (e). It is a smaller piece of cartilage. If you take your finger and, as you did with the tragus, follow the anti-tragus to its underside, you will find the **concha** (f). The concha is right below the anti-helix (g) and it is the area that gives the pinna its characteristic concave shape. Its shape helps to amplify and send sound waves that are "collected" into the second major structure of the outer ear, the external auditory meatus (EAM) or external auditory canal (EAC). As mentioned earlier, when you speak with an audiologist or person making an ear mold (or earpiece), she may refer to these anatomical landmarks when talking about the fit of the mold (Boys Town National Research Hospital, n.d.).

We now move from the seen to the unseen portions of the hearing mechanism in the outer ear. Behind the tragus is the EAM (*meatus* is the Latin term for a bodily opening). The EAM in adults is shaped like a stretched out *S* lying on its side. It is approximately 2.5–3.5 cm (1") long, 9 mm (3/10") high, and 6.5 mm (1/3") wide (Gelfand, 2009). In children, the *S* shape is more pronounced and it is shorter. The average newborn's EAM is less than 14 mm (1/2") in length, but it grows rapidly, reaching adult lengths at approximately seven years of age (Boys Town National Research Hospital. n.d.). The beginning of the EAM (the aperture) is surrounded by cartilaginous material that soon becomes bone. Two-thirds of the EAM sits within the **mastoid bone**, which is the posterior portion of the temporal bone. The mastoid bone is porous, meaning it has air-filled pockets. This rather unusual bone density assists in regulating the temperature of the brain and supplying fresh air to the living tissues and open cavities of the hearing mechanism. You can feel your mastoid bone if you place your fingers behind your auricle. (Did we just stump you here? Remember, the pinna is also called the auricle!) What you feel is a portion of your mastoid bone.

Fact or Fiction?

Chances are you have been told stories about ears that never stop growing, and you wonder, "How could that be? Do my ears (read *pinna*) continue to grow throughout my lifetime?" You think, "My head stops growing as does my body [height-wise at least] as I get older, so why in the world would my ears continue to grow? If this is true," you wonder, "will my earlobes grow so long that they will hang below my chin when I am 85 years old?" Well, you needn't worry too much. While the answer is "yes" to the first question, it is emphatically "no" to the second. Yes, your pinna does keep growing as you get older. The growth is slow and practically unnoticeable month-to-month so no, your pinnae will not surpass your chin in the human body's fight with gravity. But there are two bright spots in the research on the ever-growing ear. Men's ears grow faster than women's (at least it is a bright spot for your authors who are all women). And ears aren't the only anatomical features that don't stop growing. Your nose doesn't put the brakes on at 16 either. It keeps growing throughout your lifespan. (After rethinking this, maybe that isn't such a bright spot.)

The lining of the EAM is skin or dermal tissue. Small hairs (not unlike those in your nose) grow along the length of the EAM. Finally, there are glands in the first third of the EAM, the cartilaginous portion, that secrete **cerumen** (ear wax) and sebaceous (skin-like) material. The function of these materials will be discussed when we begin to look at the physiology of the hearing mechanism.

The end of the EAM is occluded. It is "closed off" by the eardrum. This is the official ending point of the outer ear. While most texts (including ours) include the eardrum (called the tympanic membrane) in the second section of the hearing mechanism, the **middle ear**, it could as easily be considered an outer ear structure.

Outer Ear Physiology

The main function of the pinna is to collect and then conduct sound waves from the outside into the inside of the ear. Most mammals also have pinnas that look different from ours but function in the same way as the human pinna. There is one difference, though. If you have a cat or a dog, you probably have noticed that their pinnas move to determine the direction and location of a sound in order to decide if a threat is approaching. Most humans do not know how to move their pinnas, possibly because it would serve no purpose. Interestingly, when you read the chapter on hearing aids and assistive listening devices (Chapter 6), you will see that the very first type of hearing aid— the trumpet aid—uses size, direction, and movement to channel sounds into the ear. This mimics anatomical features and function of animals such as the Saharan desert fox, the fennec (the smallest of all canines, but the one that has, proportionally, the largest ears), and the black-tailed jackrabbit of the southwestern United States.

Are You a Wiggler?

Unlike most other mammals that rely heavily on pinna movement for sound localization (think about your sleeping cat), most humans cannot consciously access the specific muscles needed to wiggle their pinnae. A popular explanation is that this ability was lost through evolution. Another suggests that people can train their brains to learn this lost skill, since there are some of us that can somehow locate those muscles and move our ears. Research tells us that twice as many males can voluntarily move their ears than women. While this is a cute party trick, pinna movement is no longer a necessity for human survival.

Now is the time, if you need to do so, to review the portions of Chapter 2 that deal with sound propagation, frequency, and intensity. In addition, you'll also need to remember the terms *vibration, amplitude, Hertz (Hz), loudness, pitch,* and *decibel (dBHL* and *dBSPL),* because understanding these concepts will help you make sense of the action of hearing.

So here is how the outer ear works: You have a mass put into motion; for example, the **vocal folds** (cords) of our person, Ida Speaker. When Ida's vocal folds (our mass in this example) vibrate because her diaphragm is pushing air through them (our force in this example), they make sounds that the structures in the mouth such as the tongue and teeth form into words. In this example, Ida just asked the question, "Can you hear me?" The sound waves produced by the propagation of molecules hitting molecules move in all directions and finally approach the pinna of her friend, Liz Zinner. Liz has a lovely pinna with a well-developed concha. As those waves of sound reach the pinna (Quick quiz…What is the other name for the pinna? Yes, auricle!), they are channeled into the EAM, where the tympanic membrane awaits. The tympanic membrane acts like the plucked banjo string in Chapter 2. The impact of the sound waves causes the tympanic membrane (TM) to vibrate. The sounds that Liz perceives as louder are actually caused by specific sound waves that displace the TM farther on either side. This is what would happen if you pluck that banjo string with more force. The sound would be louder and the string would be displaced on both sides farther from its quiet resting place. Thus, these waves have greater amplitude caused by greater intensity, and they sound louder to your ear.

So, why would some sounds in Ida's sentence have more intensity? Imagine that when Ida spoke the sentence, she took a deep breath before the word *hear* and shouted it. It sounded like this, "Can you HEAR me?" rather than this, "Can you hear me?" So when the sound waves produced by the greater force on the word *hear* impacted Liz's TM, they produced greater displacement from the membrane's resting point, thus more amplitude (perceived as loudness) than had Ida said the word *hear* more quietly.

When the TM is impacted by sound waves, it begins to vibrate. And it vibrates in direct relation to the frequency profile of the sound as well as the sound's intensity. A higher frequency (think, higher pitched) sound will cause faster (aka, more) vibrations each second. A lower frequency (think, lower pitched) one causes fewer per second vibrations. There are areas of the tympanic membrane (discussed later in this chapter) that are frequency-sensitive and assist in the transfer of sound in specific ways to the middle ear.

There is one more question about the outer ear we are often asked: "Why do we need the wax in our ears? It's so messy, and sticky, and yucky." First, cerumen helps keep the skin lining the EAM moist, preventing cracks and potential infections such as swimmer's ear. Second, it is "slimy" enough to push most anything that shouldn't be in the EAM out. What might get into the EAM that shouldn't be there? We'll leave that to your imagination.

Outer Ear: Energy Transfer Dynamics

The source of sound is a force's impact on a mass that vibrates (described in Chapter 2). The vibrations move through the air in the form of sound waves that are collected by the pinna and are channeled down the EAM until they hit the TM, which is then set into vibratory motion, approximately mimicking the frequency (pitch) and intensity (loudness) of the original sound. This is stage 1, where the energy appears in an acoustic form (see Table 3.1). Thus, stage 1 is acoustic energy until it moves the

Cerumen Is Our Friend

Do you want to know more about "ear wax"? Of course you do, who wouldn't? So here are some fascinating facts:

(1) Cerumen comes in two varieties that are associated genetically with different groups of people. Individuals of African or European descent usually produce wet, yellowish-brown cerumen. Grey and flakey earwax is seen most commonly in persons who have Native American or Asian ancestry.

(2) This genetic information has been used by anthropologists to track early human migration.

(3) "The ear scoop of a bodkin [*a thick sewing needle*] was designed to gather earwax for use on sewing thread, to keep the cut ends from unraveling. Women of means could afford bee's wax for this purpose, but earwax was thrifty and readily available—and cleaning out the ears contributed to personal hygiene." (Baudry, 2009, p. 97)

tympanic membrane and becomes mechanical energy (stage 2). See Figure 3.7 for a visual representation of the movement of sound waves in the outer ear.

Figure 3.7. The Outer Ear in Action

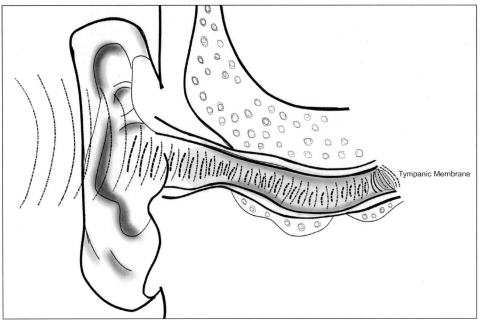

Section 2: The Middle Ear

Middle Ear Anatomy

Figure 3.8. The Middle Ear

The basic middle ear structures, displayed in Figure 3.8, include the tympanic membrane, the ossicles (three small bones), the eustachian tube, the **stapedial muscle** (aka the **stapedius**), the **tensor tympani** muscle, and the oval and the round windows.

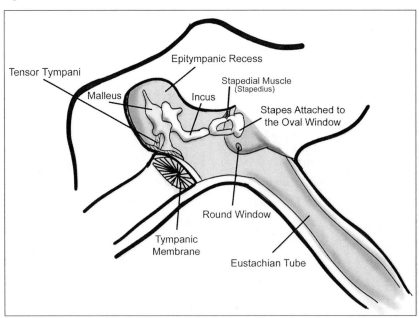

A healthy tympanic membrane blocks the end of the EAM and does not allow anything to enter the middle ear cavity other than sound waves. The TM is made up of three layers of tissue (see Figure 3.9). Think of a sandwich awkwardly balanced on its side. The first piece of bread represents the layer that is seen when one looks down the EAM. This layer of tissue, the outermost layer, is contiguous with the skin that lines the EAM. The middle layer (the "meat" of the sandwich) is fibrous connective tissue, a material that is ideal for con-

Figure 3.9. Three Layers of the Tympanic Membrane

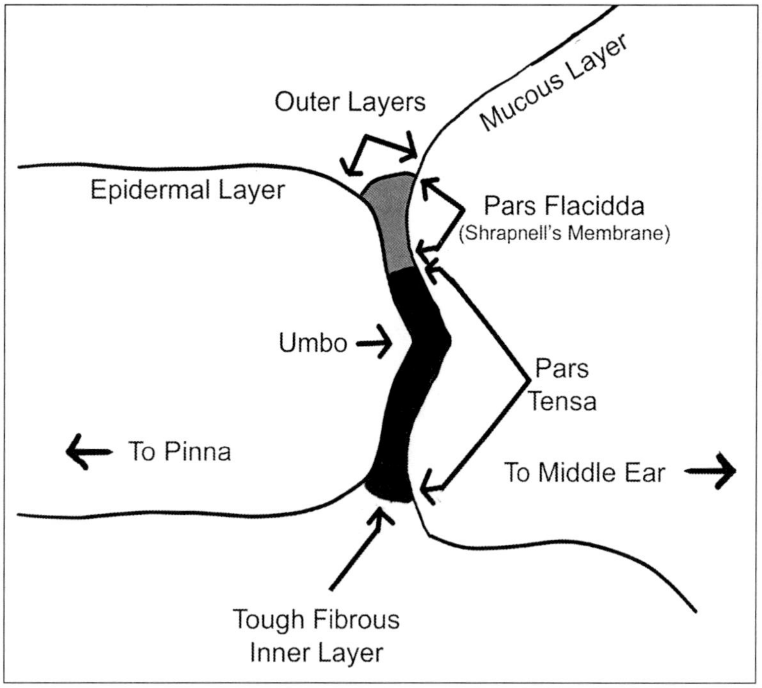

ducting vibrations. The last "piece of bread" is a layer of tissue that is contiguous with the mucous membrane that lines the middle ear cavity.

The tympanic membrane has various areas of tension. Some of the parts of the TM are actually structures; others are places "of interest." Figure 3.10 provides a look at these structures and points of interest. The TM is held in place by its connection to the **annular ring/annulus**. The annular ring is made of tissue, and the slight stretching of the TM across the annulus causes it to be taut. The tautest portion encompasses the majority of the surface of the TM and is called the pars tensa. It has a different vibratory nature than the top of the TM that is

Figure 3.10. Labeled Tympanic Membrane

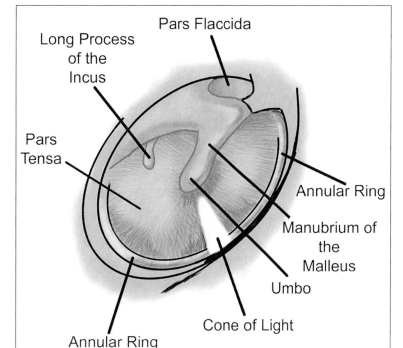

called the **pars flaccida** or **Shrapnell's membrane**. A healthy TM should appear to the observer as a pearly gray color. It should be somewhat translucent, and there should be a bright area where the light from an **otoscope** (the instrument that a physician uses to look into ears) is reflected. This is a triangular area called the **cone of light**, and it only is apparent when light is illuminating the translucent covering of the TM. At the tip of the cone of light is the **umbo**. It also is not an actual structure, but rather, a reference point. It is where the **manubrium**, or handle, of the malleus is connected to the TM. This connection point pulls the TM slightly inward, giving it its characteristic shallow cone shape.

Figure 3.11. Ossicles Compared to a Dime

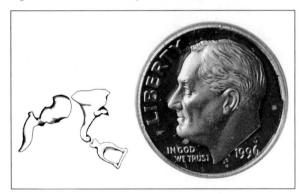

Figure 3.12. The Ossicles (Connected)

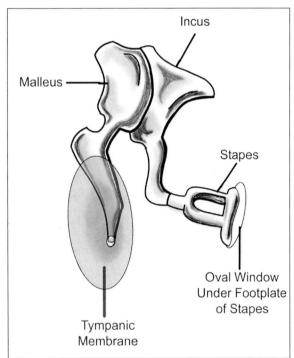

Behind the TM is the middle ear cavity, an air-filled chamber that houses the three smallest bones in our body. These bones are actually smaller than a dime (see Figure 3.11). Collectively, these three bones are called the **ossicular chain** or just the **ossicles** (see Figure 3.12). The term *chain* comes from the fact that they are attached to one another, and although these small bones appear to be floating in the cavity, they are connected and stabilized primarily by two muscular ligaments, the tensor tympani muscle and the stapedial muscle or stapedius. The tensor tympani is a muscle that is attached to the manubrium of the malleus and, by a series of contractions, holds the ossicles in place. As the shortest muscle in the body, the tensor tympani is a little more than 1 mm long (Christensen, 2013; Van de Water & Staecker, 2005). Like the tensor tympani, a second muscle, the stapedius, stabilizes and protects the ossicles by attaching to the stapes and stiffening to dampen the vibration of a loud sound. We suggest that you file away the names and actions of these two middle ear muscles, because they will pop up again when you learn about the acoustic reflex in Chapter 5.

The first bone in the ossicular chain is the **malleus**. Part of the malleus (the manubrium/handle mentioned before) is attached to the TM and appears as a shadow on the far side of the TM when viewed through an otoscope.

In Figure 3.13, you will find a drawing of the malleus. While the manubrium (the longest part of this ossicle) runs along the TM from its top to its tip, it is close to the tip of the manubrium where the actual attachment to the TM occurs. The tension of the ossicles tends to pull the malleus in towards the center of the middle ear cavity, causing the flexible TM to also be pulled inwards slightly. The point of contact of the manubrium is called the umbo. This tension, when viewing the TM from an otoscope, gives it a concave circular appearance.

The second and middle ossicle is the **incus** (Figure 3.14). And the third bone is the **stapes** (Figure 3.15). These three bones are attached to one another in a dynamic relationship, meaning they can move together and, although they are connected, they are not a single bone but three "articulated" bones. The points where they meet one another are called articular facets, and they work very much like a ball-and-joint connection moves (think hip socket and femur bone). In casual conversation, specific ossiclar landmarks (e.g., the anterior **crus** of the stapes) are rarely mentioned. However, when there is a problem with these very fragile bones and they break, we think it is important to be able to read a report and given an anatomical landmark, know where the damage is located and how bad it might be. Thus, we present the most important anatomical landmarks of the ossicles on their respective figures (3.13–3.15) and in Table 3.4.

Come on, Baby: Let's Do the Twitch

You can make your tensor tympani move. Why you might want to do this is anybody's guess, but you can do it and here is how. The tensor tympani moves in a series of twitches/contractions. It can contract between 10–70 times a second (think Hz here—a very low frequency sound). Some people can voluntarily make the tensor tympani contract and can hear the contractions by yawning deeply or contracting all the muscles in the jaw and neck. But you can also do this by making a tight fist and placing the heel of the fist across your pinna, closing the opening to the EAM. Push in and you should hear a rumbling sound. You are listening to the sound of your tensor tympani contracting.

Table 3.4. The Ossicles and Their Anatomical Landmarks

Name of Ossicle	Landmark (1)	Landmark (2)	Landmark (3)	Landmark (4)	Landmark (5)	Landmark (6)	Landmark (7)
Malleus (M)	Manubrium (Handle)	Connection to the tympanic membrane, causing the umbo	Lateral process	Anterior process	Neck	Head	Point of articulation with the incus
Incus (I)	Head	Short process	Point of articulation with the malleus	Long process	Lenticular process	Point of articulation with the stapes	
Stapes (S)	Head	Point of articulation with the incus	Neck	Anterior crus (arm)	Posterior crus (arm)	Base	Connection to the oval window

Figure 3.13. Anatomical Landmarks of the Malleus

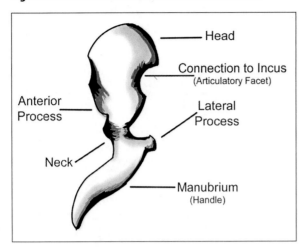

Figure 3.14. Anatomical Landmarks of the Incus

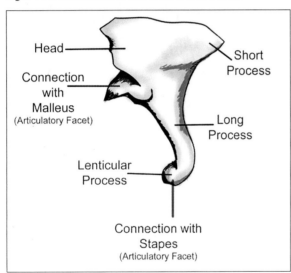

Figure 3.15. Anatomical Landmarks of the Stapes

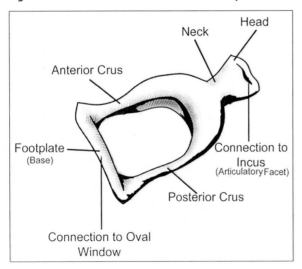

The middle ear or tympanic cavity is filled with air, and it is the job of the **eustachian tube** to be the conduit to keep the fresh air moving in and out in order to keep the mucous tissues in the middle ear healthy. The eustachian tube is located at the bottom of the middle ear cavity and moves downward to an opening in the back of the throat, the area called the **nasopharynx** (that's naso-fair-rinks, *not* naso-fair-rin-nicks). In addition to supplying fresh air to the cavity, the eustachian tube is the structure that functions to assure that the air pressure on the outside of your ear is the same as it is on the inside. If the outside pressure is lower than the pressure in the middle ear cavity, the differential will pull the tympanic membrane into the middle ear cavity. This is what happens when divers do not use techniques to equalize ear pressure. On the flip side, if you are on an elevator zooming up to the 163rd floor of the 2,722-foot-tall (829.8 meters) Burj Khalifa skyscraper in Dubai, United Arab Emirates, and don't use these same types of techniques to equalize pressure (e.g., swallowing, yawning), then when you get to the highest floor, your ears will hurt and sound will also be muffled. This is because you have quickly moved your body to a place where the pressure outside of your middle ear cavity is far less than the pressure inside your middle ear cavity. In this situation, the TM is pulled out into the EAM. In either case, if the eustachian tube does not function to equalize pressure, a person will complain of ear pain and a feeling of having stuffy ears.

In a child, the eustachian tube is about 17–18mm long and sits on a basically horizontal plane (10 percent slope). The adult eustachian tube is approximately double the length and more angled (45 percent slope). No matter the age of the owner of the ear, air is forced into the eustachian tube when a person swallows, yawns, and blows his nose. You can also force outside air into your middle ear by performing the Valsalva maneuver. To do this, close your mouth and pinch both of your nostrils and then blow air into them. Since the air cannot escape through its normal routes, your nose or mouth, it is forced into the eustachian tube and into the middle ear where, hopefully, your ears will "pop," signaling that the pressure on the inside of your middle ear has equalized with the pressure on the outside. A second interesting, though unrelated, use for the Valsalva maneuver is to stop an episode of tachycardia (Merriam-Webster Dictionary, n.d.).

Of note are two additional regions in the middle ear cavity, the **epitympanic recess** (epitympanum), the area in the cavity **superior** to the top of the TM (like an attic space), and the smaller area below the TM that is more pronounced and pouch-like in children (Hill, 2013).

The final structures in the middle ear we'd like to point out are a couple of "windows" separated by a small piece of bone. These windows are not unlike the TM in that they are flexible, made of tissue, are not meant to be penetrated, and are sensitive to vibrations. The **oval window** sits under and is attached to the footplate (base) of the stapes. The **round window** is below (inferior to) the oval window. Between these two windows is a bony structure called the **promontory** that serves to separate the windows. And, like the TM, the oval and round windows are the barrier between two portions of the hearing mechanism—in this case the middle and the inner ear.

Middle Ear Physiology

When the TM begins its vibrations, the ossicular chain (malleus, incus, stapes) also moves because the manubrium (handle) of the malleus is embedded in the TM at the umbo. Thus, the malleus moves in concert with the TM. Remember that the ossicles are like socketed bone joints, or as we usually say, they are articulated. This is why they are called a chain. When one moves, the others must also move since they are connected. Thus, this back-and-forth movement continues as long as the TM is vibrating. Remember that the footplate of the last ossicle,

Did You Know?

(1) The middle ear cavity is no larger than an M&M.
(2) The malleus, incus, and stapes are often called the mallet, anvil, and stirrup. They are so small that all three can fit on the face of a dime.
(3) Unlike your pinna, which continues to grow all your life, when you are born the ossicles are full grown and never change their size throughout your lifespan.
(4) In terms of loudness, a baby's cry is as loud as a car horn (~115dB).
(5) People of the Southern Sudanese African tribe called the Maabans have amazing hearing abilities. These people live in such a quiet environment that they can hear a whisper from across an area the size of a baseball field—and age does not affect this ability.
(6) During World War I, parrots were housed on top of the Eiffel Tower. Because of their acute sense of hearing, they would hear enemy planes long before humans could. They were trained to alert their handlers that planes were approaching.
http://www.sightandhearing.org/news/healthissue/archive/hi_0802.asp
http://www.betterhearing.org/research/factoids.cfm

the stapes, is embedded in the oval window, which is considered to be the beginning of the **inner ear**. When the ossicles pull and push one another, the stapes' footplate must also move, and along with it, the flexible oval window.

Middle Ear: Energy Transfer Dynamics

When sound waves impact the tympanic membrane, they do so in the form of acoustic energy (stage 1). Once the TM is set into vibration by the acoustic energy of the sound waves, the energy can now be seen because it becomes mechanical energy (stage 2). Mechanical energy is like the movement of the gears of a machine. In this case, the machine is the TM, the ossicles, and the oval and round windows. Figure 3.16 represents this movement.

Figure 3.16. The Middle Ear in Action

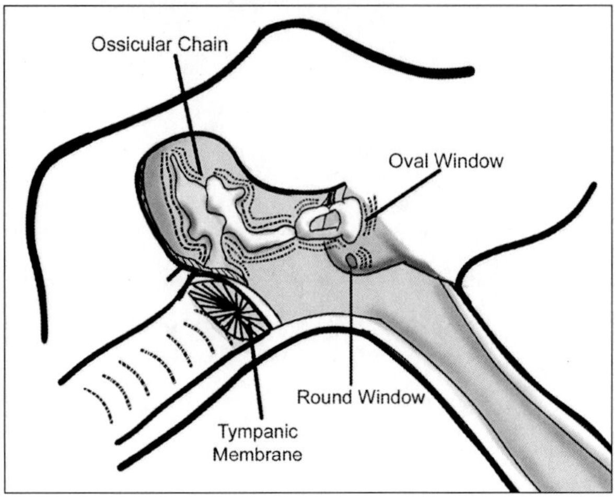

Section 3: The Inner Ear

Inner Ear Anatomy

The inner ear, on the other side of the oval and round windows, is a fluid-filled structure. The

Figure 3.17. The Inner Ear

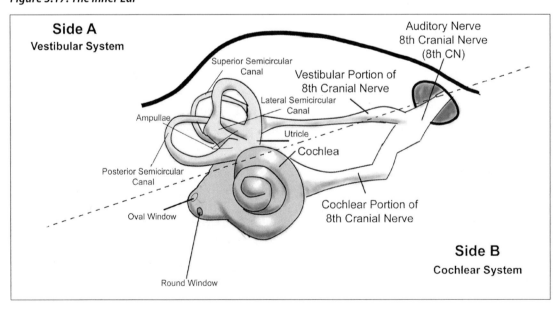

fluids are the lymphatic fluids, **perilymph** and **endolymph**. The inner ear is separated into two sections with two distinct functions, hearing (the **cochlear system**) and balance (the **vestibular system**). Though they are separate structures, they are connected both physically and by the lymphatic fluids they share. Figure 3.17 illustrates the entire inner ear structure that is housed within the temporal bone. Side A (above the dotted line) is the vestibular system, the system responsible for sending messages to your brain to tell it if you are standing still, moving, twirling, and/or dizzy. Side B (below the dotted line) is the cochlear system. It is here, in the cochlear system, where the process of hearing is continued.

The Vestibular System. The vestibular system, while not directly involved with the process of hearing, shares lymphatic fluids with the cochlear or hearing portion of the inner ear. For this reason, on occasion, when there is a problem in the inner ear, hearing or balance may also be affected.

The vestibular system is comprised of three vestibules or semicircular canals (see Figure 3.18). These are (a) the **superior** or **anterior canal**, (b) the **posterior canal**, and (c) the **horizontal** or **lateral canal.** The canals are positioned at right angles to one another. At the base of each canal are ampullae, and inside each bulbous **ampulla** is a flap-like structure called a cupula. There are hair cells (**stereocilia** or just cilia) in each cupula that are connected to the vestibular branch of the **8th cranial nerve (8 CN).** When the endolymphatic fluid in the canal moves, the tiny hair cells are activated, and they send a message to the brain that tells the brain the direction and speed of the head and body's movement. Also within the ampullae, there are two

Figure 3.18. The Semicircular Canals of the Vestibular System

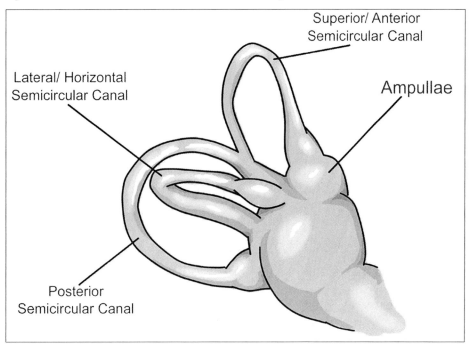

other endolymph-filled sacs called the **utricle** (see Sidebar "Rock and Roll") and the **saccule**. They contain cilia that, when moved by the fluid in particular directions (the utricle detects horizontal acceleration and the saccule detects vertical acceleration), send messages via the neurons connected to the hair cells to the brain. The vestibular cortex receives these electrical messages and analyzes them to determine the information necessary for maintaining balance.

Rock and Roll

Researchers have discovered one of the most common causes of vertigo (dizziness): "ear rocks" rolling around the semicircular canals. The official name is benign paroxysmal positional vertigo, or BPPV. And while this condition is more prevalent in people over 50, it can happen to anyone. The structure called the utricle, in the vestibular portion of the middle ear, contains approximately 1000 calcium carbonate-based crystals. When crystal "rocks" are dislodged, they are free to roam along the semicircular canals. When they do, they stimulate nerves that tell the brain that the body is moving in ways it actually is not. This dissonance causes the person to become dizzy, and this dizziness can be debilitating. It is estimated that dislodged ear rocks cause one in five cases of vertigo. The cure? Well, that is amazingly easy: put the rocks back where they belong through various movements of the head by an audiologist, physician, physical therapist, or the patients themselves. In as little as 15 minutes, many patients are relieved of the sensation of dizziness.

The Cochlear System. The second section of the inner ear is our main focus. It is the hearing portion called the cochlear system, and it is connected to the vestibular system at the base (ampullae) of the **semicircular canals**. Like the vestibular system, the cochlear system is filled with two lymphatic fluids, perilymph and endolymph. The middle ear is connected to the inner ear at the oval window. There is a bone called the promontory that separates the oval window from the round window. Both windows have one side in the middle ear and the other in the inner ear.

Figure 3.19. The Curled Cochlea

The main structure in the inner ear is the **cochlea**. It is a snail or nautilus-shaped structure with three chambers. The next five figures show the cochlea from different points of view. Figure 3.19 shows the cochlea in its natural configuration, curled up upon itself. Figure 3.20 displays a frontal cut in the structure. Notice how the three chambers wind around from the top to the bottom, with fluids flowing first up from the base (**basilar end**) to the tip (apex or **helicotrema**) and then back down again. In Figure 3.20, the chambers are labeled SV (scala vestibuli), CD (cochlear duct), and ST (scala tympani) to assist in your understanding of the illustration. Figure 3.21 shows the "rolled-out" cochlea. While it is actually not possible to roll out the cochlea, we often see it presented this way to show the relationship of the chambers of the cochlea and the movement of the perilymph. If you are having difficulty conceptualizing Figure 3.21 (the rolled-out cochlea), imagine the ever-present birthday party whistle with the rolled-up paper end. It's that party favor that also makes a screechy noise that children seem to adore and adults tolerate only on New Year's Eve. When you blow into it, the paper end inflates and unrolls to show its full length. This is analogous to the rolled-out cochlea.

Figure 3.20. Frontal Cut of the Cochlea

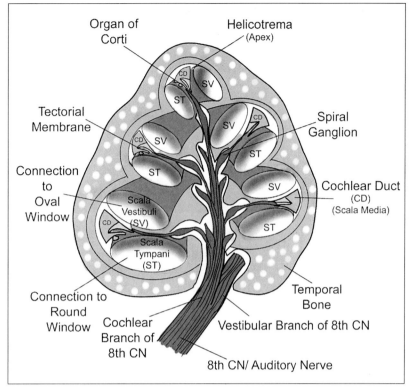

Figure 3.21. Rolled-out Cochlea

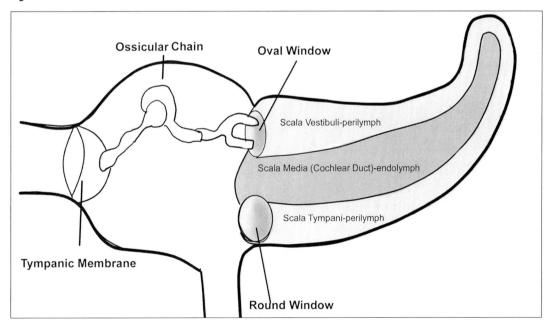

As noted above, there are three chambers in the cochlea. When the cochlea is rolled-out (Figure 3.21), the top chamber is the **scala vestibuli**. The middle chamber is the **scala media** or **cochlear**

duct, and the bottom chamber is the **scala tympani**. Looking at the first chamber, the scala vestibuli, you can see that at the base (basilar end) is the oval window. Following along to the tip, also called the helicotrema or apex (**apical end**), you can see that it turns and becomes the scala tympani. At the other end of scala tympani is the round window just below the oval window. Between the two windows is a piece of bone called the promontory, which the cochlear duct/scala media abuts. The top and the bottom chambers, the scala vestibuli and tympani, are filled with perilymph. The middle chamber, the cochlear duct, is filled with endolymph.

Figure 3.22. Cross Section #1 of the Cochlea

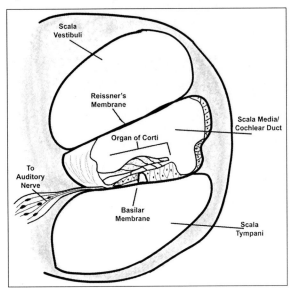

Figure 3.23. Cross Section #2 of the Cochlea

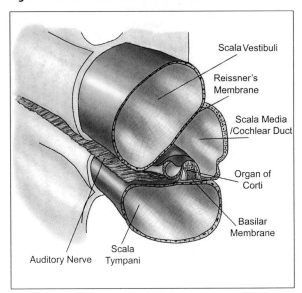

Finally, in this series of figures are two illustrations depicting cross-sectional (horizontal) cuts of the rolled-out cochlea. If you look at Figures 3.22 and 3.23, there are several other structures that are important when we start to talk about the physiology of hearing. First among these structures are the series of membranes that separate the chambers. The membrane that separates the scala vestibuli and the cochlear duct is called **Reissner's membrane**; it is relatively thin and very flexible. The membrane that separates the cochlear duct from the scala tympani is a bit thicker. It is the **basilar membrane.** Referring to these two figures, the cross-sectional images of the cochlea, you can see the relative sizes of the three chambers. The scala vestibuli is the largest, the scala tympani is the middle-sized one, and the cochlear duct is the smallest.

Looking inside the cochlear duct, you will find a small structure attached to the basilar membrane. This is the **organ of Corti** (Figure 3.24). The organ of Corti plays a very important role in the process of hearing. It is within this structure that nerve fibers are stimulated and, in response, send messages to the brain where a sound is "heard." Several parts in the organ of Corti are worth noting. These are the **tectorial membrane** at the top of the structure, the **inner hair cells** towards the medial portion of the structure, and the pillars of Corti that create the **tunnel of Corti**. The tunnel of Corti separates the inner hair cells from **outer hair cells**. These hair cells have delicate stereocilia at the top, and at the bottom are attached to neural fibers that process electrical messages. There is one row of inner hair cells and three rows of outer hair cells in the organ of Corti, and there are approximately 3,500 inner and 12,000 outer hair cells from the beginning or basilar end of the cochlea through to the helicotrema or apical end (Peterson & Bell, 2008). The outer and inner hair cells have different functions. In fact, in 1977, a hearing scientist, David Kemp, discovered that there was sound *produced* by the outer hair cells. It is this discovery that allows us to perform a hearing test commonly used for newborn infant hearing screening called otoacoustic emissions (OAE), which is described in greater detail in Chapter 5. For a complete description of the actions of the inner and outer hair cells and the story of the discovery of the otoacoustic emission phenomenon, go to http://www.oae-ilo.co.uk/downloads/advisories/the%20oae%20story.pdf

The organ of Corti is a complex anatomical structure. Scientists and biologists are still discovering its more intricate workings. Refer back to Figure 3.23, which shows the organ of Corti as it sits in the cochlear duct, and Figure 3.24, which displays the cross section of the organ of Corti in greater detail. While reviewing these figures, moving medially toward the **midline**, you first encounter the outer hair cells. Then, continuing to move medially, you encounter the tunnel of Corti, which separates the outer from the inner hair cells. As mentioned earlier, each hair cell is attached at its base to a neural fiber that combines with other fibers into a grouping of nerve fibers called the **spiral ganglion**. Remember that in the cross-sectional figure, you are only viewing a slice of the whole. The organ of Corti is a long anatomical structure, beginning at the basilar end of the cochlea and lining the cochlear duct to the apical end of the cochlea. While the base of the organ of Corti sits upon the basilar membrane, there is another membrane that is crucial

Figure 3.24. The Organ of Corti (cross section)

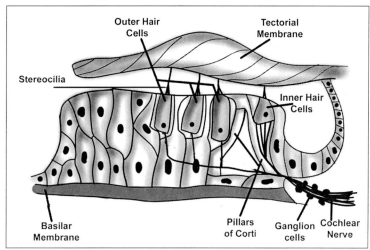

Figure 3.25. The Hair Cells of the Organ of Corti

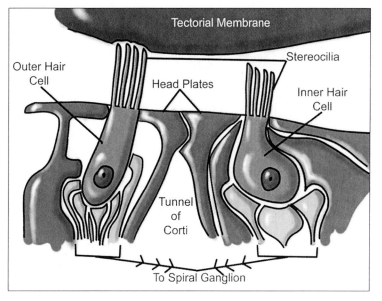

to the functioning of the organ of Corti, the tectorial membrane. It is at the very top of the organ of Corti and it is flexible. The tips of the outer hair cells (stereocilia) are embedded in the tectorial membrane. The stereocilia of the inner hair cells are not embedded in the tectorial membrane (see Figure 3.25).

Inner Ear Physiology

The vibratory motion of the ossicles moves the footplate of the stapes back and forth, and the attached oval window follows suit. It is pulled out slightly and pushed in slightly by the stapes. The perilymph in the scala vestibuli follows the motion of the oval window. The scala vestibuli connects to the scala tympani at the apical end and they share perilymph. So, when the oval window at the base of the scala vestibuli is pushed in, the perilymph is also pushed inward. Like a ripple created by a pebble thrown into a still pond, the fluid wave propagates. When it moves down around the helicotrema and enters the scala tympani, it continues its wave action until it hits the base of that closed chamber, the round window. When it does, something has to give, and what "gives" is the round window. The motion of the fluid pushes the window out slightly. When the stapes pulls the oval window out into the middle ear, the opposite happens and the round window is pulled into the scala tympani to compensate for the motion of the perilymph.

Now our focus moves to the middle chamber of the cochlea, the cochlear duct (Last quick quiz: What is the other name of the cochlea duct? The scala media?... BINGO!) When the perilymph is pushed inwards in the scala vestibuli, the fluid does not move in a straight line. It is a waveform with peaks (compressions) and troughs (rarefactions). As these waves hit the flexible Reissner's membrane, which is the separation between the top and middle chambers, and also the basilar membrane, the separation between the middle and bottom chambers, it sets the endolymphatic fluid that fills the cochlear duct into motion. This motion presses upon the tectorial membrane, which in turn presses on the stereocilia of the hair cells. The stereocilia react by bending, and the motion of the stereocilia excites the nerve fiber in the hair cell that then sends an electrical signal through a grouping of nerve fibers and on to the auditory pathway to the brain.

But the question remains, "How does the cochlea differentiate a variety of frequencies?" It is generally accepted that the hair cells in the organ of Corti are arranged so that they detect different sound wave frequencies at different positions along the organ's length. This has been referred to as the Place Theory of Hearing. Combined with another theory postulated by Bekesy in the1960s called the Traveling Wave Theory, the action of the cochlea has been fairly well determined (Martin & Clark, 2012). According to these two theories, higher frequencies are detected toward the basilar end and lower frequencies at the apical end. This arrangement is referred to as the tonotopic organization of the cochlea. Figure 3.26 illustrates the tonotopic attribute of the organ of Corti and the approximate locations of the hair cells responsible for sending frequency-specific messages to the brain for interpretation.

Figure 3.26. Tonotopic Properties of the Cochlea

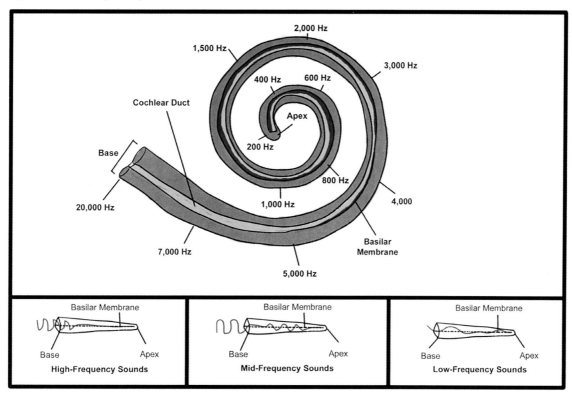

Figure 3.27 illustrates the action of the lymphatic fluids and motion of the hair cells in the organ of Corti in the cochlea in the inner ear.

Figure 3.27. The Inner Ear in Action

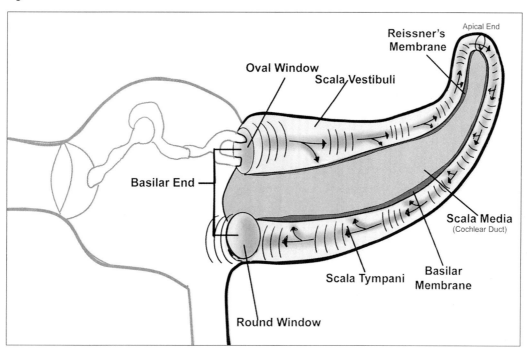

Inner Ear: Energy Transfer Dynamics

Backing up a bit to review, the outer ear is dealing with acoustic energy (stage 1), the middle ear, mechanical energy (stage 2), and now the inner ear, the portion of the hearing mechanism that is fluid-filled, has transformed that energy into hydraulic or fluid energy (stage 3). But there is a slight catch here. Because the inner ear contains nerve fibers that come into play when the stereocilia of the inner and outer hair cells are excited, there is a transfer of energy from hydraulic to electrical energy occurring in the final processing of sound in the inner ear. So while we equate the inner ear with fluid energy, we need to acknowledge that there is also a transformation of hydraulic to electrical energy happening here.

Put on That Thinking Cap!

Use your knowledge of the planes and relative directions when discussing the body to decipher and construct a picture of the following:

Imagine the entire hearing mechanism. Now without using any visual references, follow the directions below to draw a picture of the structures in the ear.

For this exercise, imagine that we have made a coronal cut of the hearing mechanism. The external part or most lateral structure of the ear is the pinna. Medial to the pinna is the external auditory canal followed by the tympanic membrane. The tympanic membrane is the most lateral of all structures in the middle ear. In the middle ear cavity are the three bones called the ossicles. The bulbous portion of the first bone (the most distal of the three bones) is called the head of malleus. It sits in the superior portion of the middle ear cavity called the epitympanic recess. The eustachian tube is located in the anterior inferior part of the middle ear space and provides an airway from the nasopharynx into the middle ear cavity. Medial to the footplate of the stapes is the oval window and on the proximal side of the oval window is the cochlea, which sits within the inner ear. If a transverse cut is made to the cochlea, you will see several iterations of the three fluid-filled canals of the structure. This is because the cochlea is shaped like a snail wrapping itself around an imaginary axis. The superior canal is called the scala vestibuli; the middle canal is the cochlear duct or scala media. The inferior canal is the scala tympani.

Refer to Figure 3.3 to see how close you came to that drawing. If you need to review the anatomical directional terms and/or body planes, take a look at Tables 3.2 and 3.3 and Figures 3.1 and 3.2.

Section 4:
The Retrocochlear Portion of the Hearing Mechanism

Anatomy and Physiology Combined

The retrocochlear portion of the hearing mechanism can be thought of as three connected subsections. (See Figure 3.17.) The first consists of the shared portion with the inner ear, those nerve fibers that are connected to the inner and outer hair cells. Beyond the cochlea itself the nerve fibers group together into bundles to form the spiral ganglion. From there they become the cochlear nerve, or more accurately the cochlear branch of the 8th cranial nerve (8 CN or CNVIII). The cochlear branch then merges with the vestibular branch of the 8th CN to become the *vestibulocochlear nerve* (auditory-**vestibular nerve**), or as it is more commonly referred to, the **auditory nerve** or 8th CN. This begins the second subsection of the retrocochlear part of the hearing mechanism. The 8th CN leaves the area of the cochlear and vestibular systems and, like an electric wire in a wall, runs to the **brainstem** at the base of the back of the skull where your head sits atop your neck. Remember that this is a duplicated system; each ear to this point is completely independent, yet is a mirror image of the other. This is why a normally functioning hearing mechanism is said to be *bi*naural.

It is important to an audiologist or physician to know the numerous names and functions of all segments and structures of the neural pathway to the brain. However, for our purposes, it is only necessary to note that there are way stations from the brainstem to the third subsection of the retrocochlear portion of the hearing mechanism, the auditory cortices of the brain (see Figure 3.28). When you see a report that mentions, for example, the medial geniculate body, if you recognize such a term as a way station to the auditory cortices, you will be able to understand, at a basic but adequate level, the information contained in the report.

Heady Plurals

Sometimes you will read a report or other material that refers to the auditory cortex but is really addressing the auditory cortexes, both the one in the left hemisphere and the one in the right hemisphere of the brain. Since there is no such word as *cortexes*, here is the correct terminology to use when discussing more than one cortex: *cortices*, as in the auditory cortices. Now you've got their attention. You look like you know your stuff, and, actually, you do!

One of the more important things to note is that although the right and left ears' neural pathways are mostly separate as they travel to their respective auditory cortices, there are points at which nerve fibers carrying information on the sounds heard actually cross over. This means that sounds heard by the right ear are processed not only by the right **auditory cortex** in the right hemisphere of the brain but also by the left auditory cortex in the left hemisphere of the brain (and vice versa.) So, if there is a lesion, for example, just before the nerve delivers its sound message to the right auditory cortex, and this lesion prevents the sound from being received by that cortex,

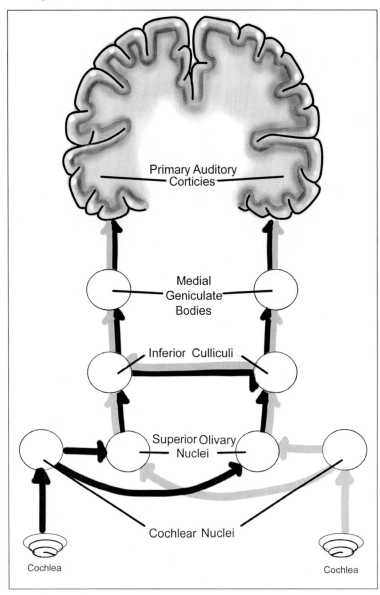

Figure 3.28. Auditory Pathways: Retrocochlear Components of the Hearing Mechanisms

the information processed by the right outer, middle, inner, and retrocochlear portions of the hearing mechanism can be interpreted because the nerve fibers cross over (shaded lines in Figure 3.28) along the neural pathway to the auditory cortices of the brain. Thus, there is a binaural aspect of the retrocochlear portion of the hearing mechanism.

The final structure in the retrocochlear portion of the hearing mechanism is the auditory cortex. The main auditory cortex is located in the temporal lobe of the brain. Its purpose is to receive the electrical impulses that travel along the 8th CN and interpret them. So ideally, if Ida Speaker asks, "How are you doing today?" the speech sounds go through the energy transfer paradigm of the normally functioning hearing mechanism and reach the auditory cortices, where the brain alerts its speech and language processing areas (Wernicke and Broca's areas; see Figure 3.29). They then start processing the language input and possibly create output. In turn, the articulation structures of the larynx and oral and nasal cavities are activated so that Liz Zinner can say, "Well, I'm feeling a bit confused by all these new terms and actions and materials, actually." And in a flash, Ida Speaker says, "Well, study a bit more, check out what's on the Internet, and you'll get it. Trust me." And almost instantaneously, Liz Zinner processes that and responds, "I'll trust you," and off Liz goes to check out the myriad of resources to be found on the Internet.

Figure 3.29. Auditory Functions of the Brain

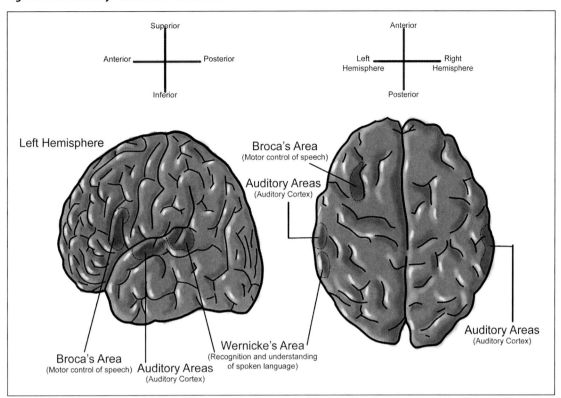

This is such an amazing process that we bet *you* forgot to say the following: "Yup, this is such an amazing process. It is most certainly astounding that humans have this capability. But the real burning question I have is, how do the auditory cortices change the electrical impulses of the words and sounds into something I so quickly understand and to which I can react?" And our response is a resounding, "No one is really sure." Scientists have been trying to answer that question for years. They are continuing to explore how the auditory cortices and associated neural structures (such as the thalamus) process the signals the 8th CN delivers. And even when they can map *where* the myriad of aspects of the signals are processed in the anatomical structures of the brain, the magic of *how* these are all pulled together and then associated with words that form the language that we associate with concepts is still a mystery. And we find that fascinating. Don't you?

A Symphony of Motion: Adult Version

There are many very good animations of the physiology of the hearing mechanisms, from sound source to listener's interpretation. Two of our favorites can be found on YouTube at http://www.youtube.com/watch?v=fHJy0EMCJyQ and http://www.youtube.com/watch?v=stiPMLtjYAw&feature=endscreen (captioned). Another animation that more clearly shows the tonotopic nature of the cochlea is http://www.pennmedicine.org/encyclopedia/em_DisplayAnimation.aspx?gcid=000063&ptid=17. These are great for adults but may be a bit difficult for a child to understand. A simple and fun activity to explain this process, say to a class with a d/hh student enrolled, is described in the next sidebar.

Retrocochlear Portion of the Hearing Mechanism: Energy Transfer Dynamics

This portion of the process involves the transmission of an electrical signal along the auditory neural pathways to the brain. Once the signal is received in the auditory cortex, the language centers take over to decode the message received.

A Symphony of Motion: Kid's Version

For fun, complete the following activity with your students:

Objective: Explain the four parts of the hearing mechanism.

Use the illustrations from this text or find online illustrations. Don't bother with names of the various structures of the major anatomical parts. All you need to introduce is the pinna, EAM, TM, malleus, incus, stapes (the ossicular chain), the oval and round windows, the promontory, the cochlea and its hair cells, the 8th CN, and the brain.

Casting:
- One person raises her arms above her head and curves her body inward, becoming the Pinna.
- Two students face one another about two feet apart, raise both hands, and touch palms. They are the EAM.
- Another student blocks the passage with his front toward the EAM and his back toward the middle ear. He is the tympanic membrane.
- Three students form a line holding hands (they are the ossicular chain). The malleus student places his hand on the tympanic membrane student's back.
- Select three students to stand shoulder to shoulder with the first and the last in this group facing opposite directions. The first student will turn his back toward the ossicles, and the stapes student will place his hand on the back of the first student, who is now the oval window. The middle student has an easy job, since he is the promontory and just stands still. The third student in this group is the round window. (Note: Take this time to show the oval and round window students how to move in opposite directions. When you say "stomachs," they arch their backs and push out their stomachs. When you say "butts," they do the opposite motion.)
- Select four to six students (or more) to be the cochlea. Have them line up, about one foot apart, front to back, behind the oval window student but instead of standing in a straight line, they will mimic the snaillike shape of the cochlea. All students in the cochlea will raise both arms.
- Then five or six more students play the part of the 8th CN (auditory nerve).
- A final student is the auditory cortex of the brain. The 8th CN group and the student playing the brain line up in front-to-back orientation about four feet apart.

***Yes, you need a large space for this activity.**

Action:
- Have all students line up in the correct order as described above.

cont.

- Then you act the part of a sound. First you enter the pinna as acoustic energy and impact the tympanic membrane, taking the person playing the TM by the shoulder and shaking back and forth (gently).
- In turn, the ossicles, who are holding hands, get pulled and pushed by the movement of the tympanic membrane student. The hand (footplate) of the stapes student is on the back of the oval window student. You now say, "Butts, stomachs, butts, stomach, and so on," and the two windows start to move accordingly. When the oval window is in "stomach" position, the arms (stereocilia of the hair cells in the organ of Corti of the cochlea) begin a wave similar to the ones we see happen at football games when the crowd stands up in succession and begins a wave around the stadium.
- This is the movement of the cochlea, and this wave causes the students of the 8th CN to run from their spot and push the next student to do the same until all the 8th CN students have moved sequentially four feet forward.
- The last student tickles the shoulders of the student playing the auditory cortex of the brain.
- The auditory cortex student then proudly announces, "I hear something!"

Variation 1
Perform the same movements but add a sentence to the demonstration. This is like the old game of Telephone. You go through the pinna and EAM and whisper (or discreetly sign—if you have a deaf student who uses sign in the game) the sentence that is then passed, student-to-student, until the brain receives the sentence. One rule is that no student except the student playing the brain can ask for the sentence to be repeated. This is how listening and hearing actually work.

Variation 2
Simulate problems in the hearing mechanism by disconnecting the ossicles, placing something in the EAM that the sound has trouble passing. Have some of the hair cells in the cochlea lie down and not move. This can demonstrate many of the causes of hearing loss that are covered in Chapter 4.

Putting It All Back Together

So far, you've read about the physiology of hearing by learning the function of each section of the hearing mechanism. We separated the process of hearing into sections because it is often easier to analyze a smaller piece of the whole picture than the entire picture at once. So, now let's get the pieces in the right places in relation to one another. What follows is the whole picture, soup to nuts, sound source to auditory perception.

We begin with a force that has put a mass in motion. The motion is vibration and the vibration, in turn, produces sound waves. These sound waves propagate through the air (the medium) and eventually hit the listener's pinna. The pinna, the external portion of the outer ear, is shaped to direct sound waves into and down the external auditory meatus, where the waves strike the tympanic membrane, causing it to vibrate. The membrane vibrates in direct relation to the acoustic wave that has hit it; that is, the frequency (think, pitch) and intensity (think, loudness) are transmitted exactly like the sound wave that sets the tympanic membrane into motion. The energy to this point is acoustic energy.

On the other side of the tympanic membrane in the air-filled middle ear are three tiny bones called the ossicles. The handle or manubrium of the first bone, the malleus, is embedded in the tympanic membrane. The malleus is connected to the incus, and the incus to the stapes. The movement (mechanical energy) of the tympanic membrane pulls and pushes the ossicles, transmitting the vibrations through the three bones to the footplate of the stapes. Again, intensity and frequency dimensions of the sound are maintained during this mechanical energy phase occurring in the middle ear. The stapes' footplate is embedded in the oval window, the barrier between the middle and inner ear. The footplate causes the oval window to move in and out, as it is a flexible membrane.

On the other side of the oval window is the base of the cochlea. The cochlea is the inner ear structure that processes sound, and it has three chambers, each filled with fluid. The top and the bottom chamber, or the scala vestibuli and the scala tympani, are filled with perilymph. These two chambers are actually attached to one another at the apical end of the cochlea. The movement of the oval window causes waves in the fluid in these two chambers. If the sound being transmitted is of high intensity (loud), then the waves' peaks and troughs are greater than if it is of lesser intensity. Similarly, if this sound being transmitted is high frequency in nature, the wave peaks are closer together. The movement of the fluid is in direct relation to the shape (intensity and frequency) of the sound being transmitted. As the fluid moves in the scala vestibuli and scala tympani, it presses on the membranes that separate these two chambers from the middle chamber. The middle chamber, the cochlear duct or scala media, is filled with a different lymphatic fluid, endolymph. Once the membranes of the scala media begin to move, the organ of Corti, a structure that sits on the lower membrane that separates the scala media from the scala tympani, is impacted. The organ of Corti has thousands of small hair cells that react to the movement of the fluid in the inner ear (hydraulic energy).

So, the vibration caused by sound is transferred from the stapes' footplate through the oval window moving the fluids in the three chambers of the cochlea. During this process, the fluid in the scala media pushes against the organ of Corti's (the sound receptor) top membrane, called the tectorial membrane. The hair cells are partially embedded in this membrane, and as the membrane pushes against them, the hair cells send electrical messages that are frequency- and intensity-specific into the retrocochlear portion of the hearing mechanism. Thus, electrical energy is the fourth transformation in the energy transformation continuum.

Once the frequency-specific neural fibers leave the cochlea, they band together into groups and eventually join to form the eighth cranial nerve (8th CN). This is also called the auditory or auditory-vestibular nerve. The 8th CN carries the electrical message containing frequency and intensity information to the auditory cortices in each hemisphere of the brain. At various points on the journey from the brainstem to the auditory cortices of the brain, information from the right ear crosses to the left channel of the nerve and information from the left ear crosses to the right channel of the nerve. This ensures that if there is some sort of damage to one side of the neural transmitter to the brain, information from that side's ear will still be interpreted in the auditory cortex of the other side. From there, the auditory cortices move into action, and while we don't know the exact way our brains make sense of what we have heard, the act of sound transmission has been completed.

Summary

In this chapter we introduced the anatomical structures of the hearing mechanism located within the four sections of the ear: (1) the outer ear, (2) the middle ear, (3) the inner ear, and (4) the retrocochlear portion of the hearing mechanism. These features were described in sufficient detail so you should feel comfortable in discussions with physicians, cochlear implant teams, audiologists, and parents. We also explored the physiology, or the normal function, of these anatomical structures. We explained how the structures work together to channel sound from the outside world to the brain for interpretation. Keep all of this in mind when you read the next chapter, where we will discuss a variety of causes (etiologies) of hearing loss.

Chapter 3 Food for Thought

1. Reread the opening scenario. Explain why Jody's scuba instructor is talking about ears.

2. In the human ear, why don't we refer to the relationship between anatomical structures as *to the right of* or *to the left of* and use instead the terms *medial to* and *lateral to*?

3. What might happen if water filled the middle ear instead of air?

4. Why do people often have balance and hearing problems appearing at the same time?

5. Explain the process of hearing to another adult. When you use anatomic terms, make sure you describe them adequately so that your listener easily understands what you are saying.

6. How do you think the placement of the two ears helps humans determine the location of a sound?

Chapter 4

Stone Soup: Genetics, Environment, and Other Contributions to Hearing Loss

---

Scenario

Natalie, Margaret, and Cassie shared an apartment while attending graduate school. The three women majored in education of deaf and hard of hearing students. Cassie and Margaret are hearing; Natalie has been profoundly deaf from birth. Cassie is from the San Francisco area, Margaret is from New York, and Natalie is from the province of Québec in Canada. During the two years they shared the apartment, the hearing women noticed that Natalie started having problems driving to their night classes. Additionally, there were times that she missed seeing objects that were not in the center of her visual field.

At first, this was just an annoyance. But towards the middle of the second year of graduate school, Natalie had had three minor car accidents. She was also having trouble navigating up and down stairs, and in darkened environments. Even more worrisome, since Natalie used speech reading and spoken language for communication, she was making more mistakes in speech reading as the year went on. Margaret and Cassie were concerned that Natalie might be losing her vision, and they suspected a particular cause. Unfortunately, when they spoke with Natalie, she offered a variety of excuses for her lapses in vision and the car accidents. The hearing roommates were frustrated that Natalie was not ready to admit that there was a problem. Even more so, they were worried that with her declining ability to see and her insistence on driving, she might have an accident that would be much more serious than her earlier fender benders.

When you finish reading Chapter 4, you should be able to make a very educated guess as to the cause of Natalie's vision problem.

Key Vocabulary		
acoustic neuroma	autosomal	carrier
acute otitis media	autosomal dominant	CHARGE syndrome
adventitious hearing loss	autosomal recessive	chromosome
air conduction	bilateral	chronic otitis media
allele	binaural	coloboma
Alport syndrome	bone conduction	conductive loss
anoxia	branchio-oto-renal syndrome	congenital loss
atresia	(BOR)	connexin 26 *cont.*

Key Vocabulary, cont.

cytomegalovirus (CMV)	nonsyndromic	rubella (congentital rubella
dominant transmission	onset	syndrome—CRS)
Down syndrome	ossiculoplasty	sensorineural hearing loss
etiology	otitis media	stapedectomy
erythroblastosis fetalis	otitis media with effusion	stenosis
Fetal Alcohol Syndrome (FAS)	otosclerosis	suppurative otitis media
genetic transmission	ototoxic	syndromic
gene	PE tubes	syphilis
genetics	perforated tympanic membrane	tinnitus
genotype	(TM)	titer
gestational age	perinatal	TORCH(S)
herpes simplex I	phenotype	toxemia
herpes simplex II	postlingual	toxoplasmosis
mastoiditis	postnatal	Treacher Collins syndrome
maternal rubella	pre-auricular tags	trisomy 21
Mendelian inheritance	preeclampsia	tympanoplasty
Ménière's disease	prelingual	tympanostomy
meningitis	prenatal	unilateral
microsia	presbycusis	Usher syndrome
mixed hearing loss	progressive hearing loss	variably expressed trait
monaural	Punnett square	Waardenburg syndrome
myringoplasty	purulent	X-linked transmission
neurofibromatosis	retinitis pigmentosa	
noise-induced loss	Rh factor incompatibility	

Introduction

In this chapter, various causes, or **etiologies,** of hearing loss are discussed. Etiologies are categorized by a number of factors, including when they occurred, called time of **onset**, whether the hearing loss was present at birth or acquired, the type of loss, and the degree of hearing loss. In addition to these factors, deafness can be attributed to a number of causes, including genetic factors, environmental factors, disease, or the natural aging process. In this chapter, when an etiology of hearing loss is presented, if appropriate, typical treatment will also be discussed. However, as you will read, some causes of hearing loss cannot be medically corrected. Also, while we realize that you are not studying medicine, do not plan to be a famous geneticist, nor are you planning (at this point) to become an audiologist, we think understanding genetic inheritance models and knowing the dimensions of a variety of causes of deafness are vital pieces of information to have when working with children who have hearing loss. This is especially true when the cause of the hearing loss is due to either a genetic syndrome or a disease that affects other domains of development and involves nonhearing anatomical features.

Basic Concepts and Terms

One of the first things you will want to determine when looking at a hearing loss is its onset; that is, the point in time that hearing loss began. So, there are three terms we will use when describing particular etiologies in terms of onset of hearing loss. The first is prenatal. When an infant is born with a hearing loss, that hearing loss is considered to have occurred during that child's **prenatal** development. Any hearing loss that is present at birth, no matter the cause, is considered to be a **congenital hearing loss**. And as you will learn later, congenital hearing losses may either have genetic or nongenetic etiologies. A second term you will encounter is a **perinatal** hearing loss. This term is used to describe a hearing loss occurring during the birth process. As a rule, most perinatal hearing losses are caused by an exceedingly difficult delivery or viral transmission occurring during delivery. And finally, the onset of a **postnatal** hearing loss occurs postpartum or after the birth process is completed. Postnatal hearing losses can occur any time in a person's life.

There are three other terms that are important especially to educators, SLP's, and parents. The first term is **prelingual** deafness. When you read that a child is prelingually deafened, you are looking at those years and months before a child begins to gain proficiency interacting with others using spoken language. For the most part, we consider the upper end of this period to be about three years of age. There is one obvious exception to the term *prelingual deafness*. If a child is born with a severe or profound hearing loss to parents who are also Deaf and communicate with their child using American Sign Language (ASL), then even though their baby was without hearing during the period of time when a hearing child acquires spoken language, the Deaf child of Deaf parents will acquire language (ASL) in the same natural manner and on approximately the same timeline as a hearing child learning his native spoken language.

The second term is **postlingual** deafness. This means that the individual has already acquired spoken language and for some reason has lost the ability to hear after that point. This can occur at any time past the prelingual stage. Another name for a hearing loss acquired after birth is an **adventitious hearing loss**. Obviously, the earlier the onset of the hearing loss, the more difficulty the child will have when dealing with spoken language. Keep this fact in mind during the discussion of hearing aids and cochlear implants in Chapter 6 and aural (re)habilitation in Chapter 7.

The third term, and one that is particularly important when planning instruction, is **progressive hearing loss** (also called heteditodegenerative hearing loss). There are numerous causes for progressive hearing loss (usually genetic), but the important thing to note is that this type of hearing loss must be continually monitored to determine how much the child is actually receiving through auditory channels as he ages.

As we begin to discuss a number of etiologies of hearing loss, we present information on the degree of the loss because the severity of the loss directly affects amplification, communication, and instruction. While there is some mild disagreement on the decibel level ranges connected to the degree of hearing loss, most professionals refer to hearing loss, as presented in Table 4.1, as slight, mild, moderate, moderately severe, severe, and profound. Just as the time of onset can give you a clue to the degree of difficulty of spoken language acquisition, so can the severity of the hearing loss. A child who has a moderate postlingual hearing loss will more easily acquire language through audition than a child who has a profound prelingual loss.

Table 4.1. Degree of Hearing Loss

Degree of hearing loss	Decibel range of hearing loss (dBHL)	This person would be considered to have/be (audiologically)
Normal	Less than 15 dB	normal hearing
Normal/Slight*	16–25 dB	normal hearing in adults but may be considered a slight hearing loss in children
Mild	26–40 dB	hard of hearing
Moderate	41–55 dB	hard of hearing
Moderately Severe	56–70 dB	hard of hearing
Severe	71–89 dB	hard of hearing–deaf
Profound	Greater than 90 dB	deaf

* For a screening audiogram, many school systems consider any threshold less than 25 to 30 as normal hearing and do not refer the student on for a full audiological workup.

While discussed in greater depth in Chapter 5, there are three terms that describe the nature or type of hearing loss. First, a hearing loss can be determined to be a conductive hearing loss. A **conductive loss** occurs most commonly in the outer and middle portions of the hearing mechanism. Conductive hearing losses are often **unilateral/monaural**, meaning they occur in one ear but not the other. It is possible, however, that a conductive loss could be **bilateral/ binaural**, involving both ears. With a conductive loss, sound is being prevented from being delivered or conducted to the inner ear. This could be due to a variety of factors discussed later in the chapter. While not mentioned in Chapter 3, which focused upon hearing via **air conduction** (the initial energy transfer process from outer ear acoustic energy to final retro-cochlear brain wave electrical energy), a second, though less effective, way for sound to be processed is called **bone conduction**. With bone conduction hearing, sounds can bypass any problem occurring in the outer or the middle ear. This is because all of the bones in your body react to sound by vibrating, and the skull is no exception. So when sound waves hit the skull, it vibrates, and the frequency-specific vibrations are transferred through the bone directly to the inner ear, thus bypassing any problem existing in the outer or middle ear. This vibratory process causes direct hydraulic movement of the lymphatic fluids in the inner ear and results in a process that is called bone conduction hearing. Again, air and bone conduction transmission of sound will be discussed in greater detail in the next chapter. For our purposes, when looking at etiologies, the rule of thumb is that most conductive hearing losses can be medically and/or surgically corrected. So get ye (or the child with the problem) to a doctor, pronto!

The second term that relates to the nature/type of the hearing loss is a sensorineural hearing loss. A **sensorineural hearing loss** most commonly occurs in the inner ear and retrocochlear portions of the hearing mechanism. As the term indicates, this type of loss affects the hair cells of the cochlea, and nerves (neural fibers) beyond that carry sound to the auditory cortices to be interpreted. If the cause of the hearing loss is sensorineural, bypassing the problem through bone conduction of sound is not possible. If, as is most often the case in a sensorineural hearing loss, there is damage to the cochlea, its stereocilia, the neural fibers, the 8th CN, or the auditory cortices, the vibrations caused by sound impacting the skull cannot be transmitted further along in the system, since one or more of the anatomical structures that the vibrations impact in the cochlea and beyond are not functioning correctly.

The final term, when describing the nature/type of a hearing loss, is a mixed hearing loss. This type of hearing deficit combines features of a conductive loss and a sensorineural hearing loss. While some mixed hearing losses are permanent, it is more likely that a **mixed hearing loss** is caused by a temporary conductive loss on top of a permanent sensorineural hearing loss. You will be shown ways to determine if a hearing loss is mixed, sensorineural, or conductive by looking at a variety of audiograms in the next chapter. If you suspect that a child has a conductive or mixed hearing loss, he should immediately be referred to a medical professional. Left untreated, some causes of conductive hearing loss can escalate into more dangerous, even fatal, medical problems.

> **Identifying a Sudden Onset Conductive Hearing Loss Experienced by a Child with a Sensorineural Hearing Loss**
>
> You need to be aware when dealing with d/hh students who have sensorineural hearing losses that colds and upper respiratory viruses may cause conductive problems. In a practical sense, it is important to be vigilant with young children who are d/hh because there may not be the same behavioral clues that their hearing peers exhibit when they have conductive hearing problems. Commonly, d/hh children will pull at their ears, sneeze, cough, and generally be out of sorts if they are experiencing additional conductive problems. However, unlike hearing children, you may not see a change in listening or speech abilities.

Etiologies of Hearing Loss

Now that you have an understanding of the basic terms and concepts associated with the causes of deafness, we turn your attention to those specific causes. Note that only the most common etiologies will be presented here. It is entirely possible that a particular etiology of the hearing loss of a person you know may not be included. We've always found that an Internet search is a great starting place to research etiologies that are rare and unfamiliar even to us. (And like our readers, we, your authors, know what we know and we know what we don't know, so we too are good friends with search engines.) Table 4.2 classifies the various etiologies of hearing loss presented in this chapter in a number of ways. Each etiology is listed with its time of onset, specific cause if known, nature/type of hearing loss, and degree(s) of hearing loss.

Table 4.2. Most Common Etiologies of Hearing Loss and Additional Sequelae

Etiology	Onset	Agent	(1) Type of hearing loss (2) Possible degree of hearing loss	Possible additional problems (sequelae)
Alport syndrome	Postnatal onset (but prenatal cause)	X-linked and autosomal dominant inheritance	(1) Sensorineural [progressive] (2) Varied degree of hearing loss—from mild to profound with progressive late onset hearing loss	• Kidney disease including blood and high levels of protein in urine • Eye abnormalities
Anoxia (Asphyxiation)	Perinatal	Environmental[1] —Lack of oxygen at birth	(1) Sensorineural (2) Varied degree of hearing loss—from mild to profound	• Visual problems • Cognitive issues
Branchio-oto-renal syndrome (BOR)	Prenatal	Autosomal dominant inheritance with variable expression[2]	(1) Sensorineural, conductive, or mixed (2) Varied degree of hearing loss—from mild to profound	• Ear pits • Neck cysts or fistulas • Altered ear shape • Structural or functional changes in the kidney
CHARGE Originally CHARGE stood for: **Co**loboma of the eye (hole in eyelid), **H**eart defects, **A**tresia of the choanae (nasopharyngeal passages), **R**etardation of growth and/or development, **G**enital and/or urinary abnormalities, **E**ar formation abnormalities and deafness.	Prenatal	Autosomal dominant genetic disorder	(1) Most commonly mixed hearing loss with ossicular malformations causing conductive portion of loss (2) Severe to profound hearing loss (50 percent of individuals with CHARGE have hearing loss and nearly all auditory system structures are affected.)	More than 20 other severe disorders including: • Deaf-Blindness • Visual impairments • Heart defects • Atresia or stenosis of nasal passages • Retardation of growth and/or development • Genital dysfunction • Urinary system problems
Childhood diseases • Chicken pox • Measles [rubiola & rubella] • Mumps	Postnatal	Environmental —Viral	(1) Sensorineural, conductive, or mixed (2) Slight to profound hearing loss	• Cognitive deficits • Learning disabilities • Behavioral problems • Memory difficulty

cont.

Etiology	Onset	Agent	(1) Type of hearing loss (2) Possible degree of hearing loss	Possible additional problems (sequelae)
Connexin 26 (CX26)	Prenatal	Autosomal recessive inheritance	(1) Sensorineural (2) Moderate to profound hearing loss	• No known sequelae
Down syndrome	Prenatal	Mutation of genes (trisomy of 21st chromosome)	(1) Sensorineural, conductive, or mixed (2) Slight to moderate hearing loss	• Cognitive disabilities • Stenosis of EAM • Flattened eustachian tube • Eyes have an upward slant, oblique fissures, epicanthic skin folds on the inner corner, and white spots on the iris • Low muscle tone • Small stature and short neck • Flat nasal bridge • Single, deep creases across the center of the palm • Protruding tongue • Large space between large and second toe • A single flexion furrow of the fifth finger
Fetal Alcohol Syndrome (FAS) or Fetal Alcohol Syndrome Disorder (FASD)	Prenatal	Environmental	(1) Sensorineural, conductive, or mixed (2) Varied degree of hearing loss—from slight to profound	• Short stature • Wide-set eyes • Microcephaly • Various dysmorphic (malformation) features (e.g., craniofacial dysmorphia) • Congenital heart disease • Dysplasia of the skeleton (abnormal development of cells) • Dysplasia of the urogenital system • ADHD/ADD • Cerebral palsy • Epilepsy • Developmental delay • Cognitive disabilities
Influenza	Prenatal and postnatal	Environmental—Viral	(1) Sensorineural, conductive (otitis media), or mixed; also possible idiopathic sudden hearing loss (2) Varied degree of hearing loss—from slight to profound	• Pneumonia • Death
Ménière's disease	Postnatal (usually occurring mid-life to later in life)	There is no single known cause.	(1) Sensorineural (2) Varied degree of hearing loss—from mild to profound (may be inconsistent)	• Tinnitus • Vertigo • Nausea

cont.

Etiology	Onset	Agent	(1) Type of hearing loss (2) Possible degree of hearing loss	Possible additional problems (sequelae)
Meningitis	Postnatal	Viral or bacterial infection (Bacterial meningitis is usual cause of hearing loss.)	(1) Sensorineural (2) Varied degree of hearing loss—from mild to profound	• Learning disabilities • Behavioral problems • Memory difficulty • Brain damage • Gait problems • Seizures • Kidney failure • Shock • Death Note: many problems may resolve over time (usually not hearing loss).
Neurofibro-matosis (NF)	Prenatal with postnatal symptoms developing as tumors compress nerves	Genetic mutation	(1) Sensorineural (2) Varied degree of hearing loss—from mild to profound (sudden onset with gradual progressive loss)	• Tumors (neurofibromas) develop on nerves including auditory nerve (8th CN) • Vestibular problems • Tinnitus • May affect skin, eye, and/or hair pigmentation • Bumps under the skin • Learning disabilities • Behavioral problems • Vision problems • Bone problems • Pressure on spinal nerve roots • Other neurological problems
Otitis media	Postnatal	Environmental; Upper respiratory infection—Viral	(1) Conductive (2) Varied degree of hearing loss—from slight to moderate	• Speech difficulties • Language delay • Recurrent upper respiratory infection
Otosclerosis	Postnatal (Target population—Caucasian women of childbearing years)	Probably genetic, maybe environmental	(1) Conductive (2) Varied degree of hearing loss—from mild to moderately-severe	• Tinnitus • Vestibular disorders (dizziness, balance problems)
Ototoxicity	Postnatal	Environmental	(1) Sensorineural (2) Varied degree of hearing loss—from mild to profound	• Tinnitus • Vestibular disorders (dizziness, balance problems)
Prematurity	Perinatal	Various causes	(1) Sensorineural (2) Varied degree of hearing loss—from mild to profound	Short-term complications: • Increased risk of sudden infant death syndrome (SIDS) • Breathing problems • Heart problems • Brain problems • Temperature control problems • Gastrointestinal problems • Anemia • Metabolic problems • Immune system problems

cont.

Etiology	Onset	Agent	(1) Type of hearing loss (2) Possible degree of hearing loss	Possible additional problems (sequelae)
Prematurity, cont.	Perinatal	Various causes	(1) Sensorineural (2) Varied degree of hearing loss—from mild to profound	Long-term complications: • Cerebral palsy • Impaired cognitive skills • Vision problems: retinopathy of prematurity • Dental problems • Behavioral problems • Psychological problems • Chronic health issues
Presbycusis	Postnatal	Natural aging process	(1) Sensorineural (2) Varied degree of hearing loss—from mild to profound	• No known sequelae
Rh factor incompatibility	Perinatal	Mother and father have different Rh blood factors (Mother is Rh – Father is Rh+… the autosomal dominant blood factor is Rh+); condition manifests with the 2nd birth if mother is untreated	(1) Sensorineural (2) *Varied degree of hearing loss—from mild to profound	*If mother is untreated prenatally with Rhogam: • Hearing loss (complete blood transfusion; hearing loss due to anoxia during transfusion) • Death (if no transfusion)
TORCH(S)[3]				
• **To**xemia (preeclampsia) *or may refer to:* • **To**xoplasmosis	Perinatal	Environmental —may be genetic Environmental — parasite	(1) Sensorineural (2) Varied degree of hearing loss—from mild to profound	• Prematurity • Intrauterine growth restriction • Jaundice • Hepatosplenomegaly (spleen and liver enlargement) • Hydrocephaly • Microcephaly • Myocarditis (heart) • Pneumonitis • Various rashes • Psychomotor deficits • Visual impairment
• **R**ubella/ German Measles (maternal)	Prenatal	Environmental —viral	(1) Sensorineural (2) Varied degree of hearing loss usually severe to profound deafness	• Vision problems • Heart problems • Intellectual disabilities • Growth retardation • Low birth weight • Developmental delays • Learning disabilities • Behavioral problems • Diabetes • Enlarged liver and spleen • Skin lesions

cont.

Etiology	Onset	Agent	(1) Type of hearing loss (2) Possible degree of hearing loss	Possible additional problems (sequelae)
• **C**ytomega-lovirus (CMV)	Prenatal Perinatal	Environmental —viral	(1) Sensorineural (2) Varied degree of hearing loss—from mild to profound	If prenatal: • Jaundice at birth • Low birth weight • Poorly functioning liver • Severe cognitive deficits • Epilepsy • Visual impairments • Prematurity • Encephalitis • Death If perinatal (not congenital—can be acquired by exposure to infected cervical secretions, breast milk, or blood products): • Significant cognitive deficits • Visual impairments • Asymptomatic infection • Acute infection with hepatitis • Fever • Pneumonitis
• **H**erpes Simplex (HSV-1 & HSV-2)	Prenatal Perinatal	Environmental —viral	(1) Sensorineural (2) Varied degree of hearing loss—from mild to profound	• Prematurity • Low birth weight • Significant cognitive disabilities • Seizures • Psychomotor retardation • Blindness • Learning disabilities • Death
• **S**yphilis	Perinatal	Environmental —bacteria	(1) Sensorineural (2) Varied degree of hearing loss—from mild to profound If hearing loss is evident, it is usually caused by problems affecting the 8th CN.	Manifestations of syphilis are classified as early congenital (birth through age 2) and late congenital (after age 2) • Cognitive deficits • Seizures • Visual deficits • Left untreated, the child will manifest all the symptoms of adult syphilis.
Treacher Collins syndrome	Prenatal	Autosomal dominant with variable expression	(1) Conductive (2) Mild to moderate hearing loss	• Downward sloping eye openings • Flattened cheekbones • Malformed or absent outer ears (pinna and EAM) • Small chin • Coloboma of eyelid (hole)
Usher syndrome (II)	Prenatal with additional postnatal onset retinitis pigmentosa (RP)	Autosomal recessive	(1) Sensorineural (2) Varied degree of hearing loss usually severe to profound deafness	• Later onset retinitis pigmentosa (RP)

cont.

Etiology	Onset	Agent	(1) Type of hearing loss (2) Possible degree of hearing loss	Possible additional problems (sequelae)
Waardenburg syndrome	Prenatal	Autosomal dominant with variable expression	(1) Sensorineural (2) Moderate to profound unilateral or bilateral sensorineural hearing loss	• White forelock of hair • Vitiligo (skin depigmentation) • Hypopigmentation • Differently colored or brilliant blue eyes (Type I includes the appearance of widely spaced eyes)

Notes:
1. "Environmental" could be a contagious virus, ingested substance of medicine, bacteria, parasites, and so on, but does not include genetic causes of deafness/other disorders.
2. "Variable expression" means not all additional sequelae may occur. For example in the case of Waardenburg's Syndrome, the affected individual may not have a hearing loss, or may not have a white forelock.
3. "TORCH(S)" is a group of prenatal congenital noninherited causes of hearing loss due to maternal transfer of virus to fetus or newborn by a group of infectious agents (Toxemia has nonviral cause).
4. Information for this table gathered from numerous sources and personal knowledge.

Genetic Transmission/Inheritance

Deafness caused during the fetal development period is called congenital. Congenital losses fall into two basic categories: (1) genetic, and (2) nongenetic. But, before we talk about specific etiologies in these two categories, a review of basic **genetic transmission** is in order. It's very important to understand genetic transmission as it relates to hearing loss because, unlike scientists' earlier suspicions, we now know, for certain, many of the specific genes responsible for the ability to hear or not to hear and we also know that approximately 60 percent of deafness is related to genetic causes (The American Academy of Otolaryngology – Head and Neck Surgery). The completed mapping of the human genetic code opened the door to the ability to learn, in advance, if a child may (or will) have a hearing loss. We believe that the field of **genetics** and genetic engineering, especially as it concerns human embryology, will captivate scientists and moralists throughout the first half of this century. Having a clear understanding of genetic inheritance will allow you to develop a well-supported position in this debate, and, more importantly, will help you field questions you may be asked about the field of genetic counseling. You should also be able to speak with parents and older students who are considering their own chances of having a child or another child with genetically caused deafness. And so, while we explain genetic inheritance, we've done so using simplified examples that you can use with parents and curious young adults who are deaf.

Huge advances have been made in the understanding of the human genome in the late 20th and early 21st centuries. The International Human Genome Sequencing Consortium, led in the United States by the National Human Genome Research Institute (NHGRI) completed its work in 2003, many years earlier than expected. Today, the mapping of the human genome continues to supply scientists with a wealth of information on the biology of human development and the genetics of inheritance (National Human Genome Research Institute, n.d.).

The Human Genome Project

The Human Genome Project or HGP is a collaborative international effort to map the genetic code of human beings. The term *genome* refers to the entire genetic code of a human being; in other words, every gene on every chromosome in the human body would be identified. Funding for the project, the largest biological research study ever undertaken, was granted in 1992. The National Institute of Health's National Human Genome Research Institute (NHGRI) led this international scientific investigation. Researchers across the globe began the massive endeavor to "map" the human genome. It was estimated that it would take at least 15 years to accomplish this task.

On June 26, 2000, years earlier than had originally been thought, President Bill Clinton and UK Prime Minister Tony Blair jointly announced that the rough draft of the human genome had been completed. By mid-2003, the final sequencing of the human genome was completed. The HGP determined that there were about 20,500 genes on the 23 pairs of human chromosomes. These genes determine the blueprint for the development and functioning of humans. By 2006, it was estimated that there were over 400 genetic causes of deafness.

Two scientists involved in the HGP, Kathleen Arnos, the director of the genetics program at Gallaudet University, and Bronya Keats, former chair of the Louisiana State University – Health Science Center's Department of Genetics and currently a professor at the Australian National University (ANU), have been instrumental in the discovery of genetic causes of hearing loss. Keats is considered by some to be the foremost expert in the genetics of Usher syndrome and the other syndromic causes of deafness. Arnos was responsible for the establishment of Gallaudet University Genetics Service Center (GSC) in 1983. The GSC has provided genetic education and counseling services to the deaf community and to parents of children who are deaf and hard of hearing. In addition, Arnos has long been interested in ethical issues in genetic counseling (Arnos, 2002).

Genetic counseling is free of charge at the GSC, which can be contacted at:
Genetics Program
Gallaudet University
Department of Biology
800 Florida Avenue, NE
Washington, DC 20002
Phone: (202) 651-5258
Fax: (202) 651-5179
Video Phone: 866-936-2270

Humans have 23 pairs of **chromosomes**, with a number of genes on each chromosome pair. Chromosome pairs are numbered, and the higher the number, the smaller the actual chromosome pair is in size. The last pair of chromosomes, the 23rd pair, determines the sex of the child. At conception, both the mother and the father contribute a single **gene** from their own pair to the embryo, creating a complete set of genes for the developing fetus. Although you may come across the term *a single gene*, it is more accurately called an allele. An **allele** is one-half of a complete gene pair, and a complete gene is made up of two alleles. Thus, an allele accounts for one-half of the genetic code for a trait. A corresponding allele from the gene pair of the mother and gene pair of the father are matched (or donated) during conception. Eggs and sperm are full of important genetic information! What this means is that every human receives an allele from the mother that is matched with an allele from the father on each gene the new person will carry. This is called a genetic pairing, transmission, or inheritance. Thus, the mother donates one of the alleles and the father donates the other. Some of the alleles in a pair may be dominant, meaning that the traits associated with the gene pair will appear in the new human being, and others are recessive, rendering the trait hidden within the genetic code of the new child. Recessive alleles will only become observable traits if they are matched with another recessive allele in the pairing.

You will also encounter the terms genotype and phenotype. **Genotype** refers to actual genetic makeup of an individual, while **phenotype** indicates the traits or characteristics that an individual displays. So, a person may carry an allele for a disorder or a trait (have the gene), but that trait may not be apparent. In this case, the person is labeled a **carrier** because he has the allele in his genetic makeup but does not "express" (display) the trait. When you hear the word **autosomal** in reference to genetic transmission, it means that the alleles responsible for a trait are located on one of the first 22 pairs of chromosomes. The 23rd pair of chromosomes determines sex as previously indicated. The mother always "donates" the female allele called "X" because she carries only two X alleles (no Ys) on her 23rd chromosome. Therefore, she can only donate an X to the embryo. On the father's 23rd chromosome are both an X and a Y (male) allele, so he can donate either a female X allele or a male Y allele. The Y allele is dominant, so therefore, it is the father who determines the sex of the child. (Mom is always pulling for a girl.)

There are three basic types of simple genetic transmission (this is called **Mendelian inheritance**): **autosomal dominant transmission, autosomal recessive transmission,** and **X-linked transmission**, which is a type of genetic inheritance that can be either dominant or recessive. To make this information clearer, let's use the example referred to earlier in Chapter 3, the attached versus detached (also called free) earlobe, a trait inherited through autosomal dominant transmission. In this type of transmission, a single dominant gene on one of the pairings of alleles from the mother and the father will cause that child to display the trait. Conversely, the allele for an attached earlobe is a recessive allele. If one of the parents donates the dominant allele and the other parent donates the recessive allele for earlobe attachment, the child's earlobes will be… (you, our aspiring geneticists, get a chance to guess here) Yes, detached. If you refer to Figure 4.1, you will see a mother and a father and the possible combinations of genetic pairings that they can transmit to their child for earlobe attachment. This type of chart, called a **Punnett square**, displays genotype inheritance possibilities.

Figure 4.1. Autosomal Dominant Inheritance

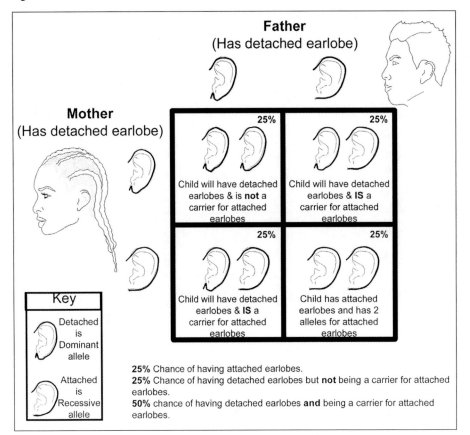

In the Punnett square shown in Figure 4.1, the mother is listed on the left side and the father on the top. What the figure demonstrates is what might occur in the phenotype of any child of this particular union in terms of earlobe attachment. There are four squares, and each square represents a 25 percent chance of getting that particular match of alleles. So in Figure 4.1, Mom and Dad both have detached earlobes, but in this example, both Mom and Dad carry the allele (again, often referred to as a gene) for attached earlobes. In combination 1 (top left square), both Mom and Dad donate an allele for a dominant detached earlobe. If this is the combination the child receives, he will have detached earlobes and be the carrier of two alleles in his gene pair for detached earlobes. In combination 2 (top right square), Mom donates an allele for a detached earlobe and Dad donates an allele for an attached earlobe. This child will have a detached earlobe but he will be a carrier of an allele for an attached earlobe. Combination 3 (lower left square) is identical to combination 2. The difference in this combination is that Mom donates an allele for an attached earlobe while Dad donates an allele for a detached earlobe. Again, if the child receives this genetic pairing, he will have a detached earlobe yet carry an allele for an attached earlobe. The final combination in the fourth square (lower right) occurs when Dad donates an allele for an attached earlobe and Mom also donates an allele for an attached earlobe. This child will definitely have an attached earlobe and will only have alleles for attached earlobes. Figure 4.1 clearly (we hope) illustrates simple autosomal dominant genetic transmission.

Obviously, we do not consider attached earlobes to be normal or abnormal, but if instead of earlobes, we were talking about a particular genetic cause of deafness, we are faced with a different issue. Figure 4.2 depicts autosomal dominant transmission of deafness and illustrates what happens via a Punnett square when a mutated/abnormal allele for deafness is introduced.

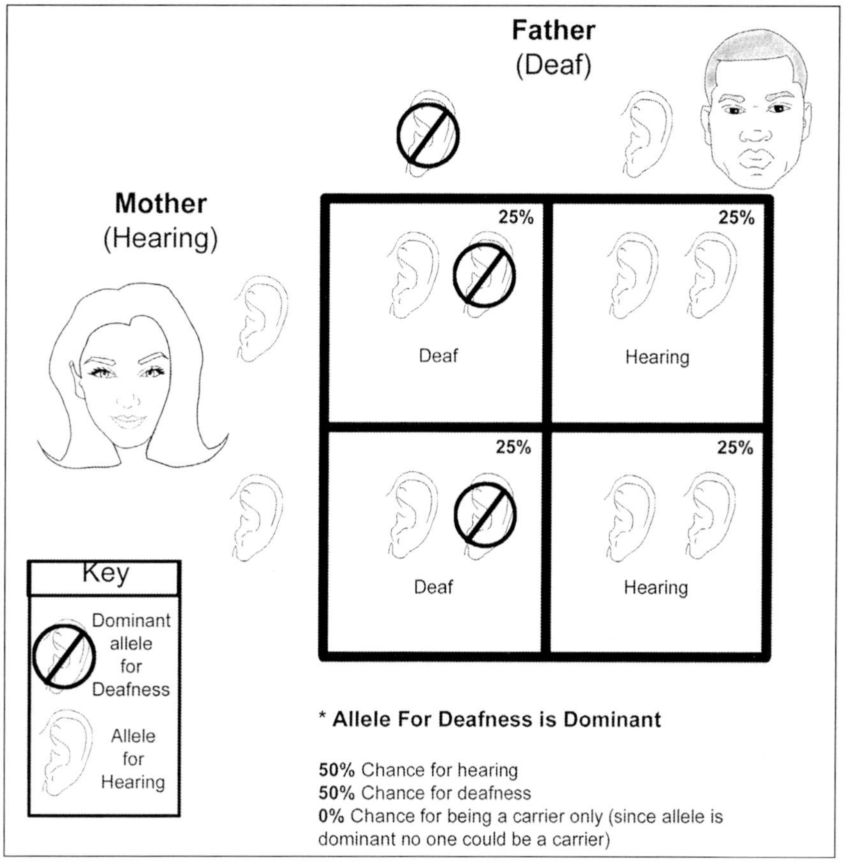

Notice that the mother, who is hearing, has two alleles for hearing. The father, who is deaf, has one allele for deafness and one allele for hearing. Since the allele for deafness is dominant in this type of transmission, any time it shows up in one of the squares, that child will be deaf. So, in this example, there is a 50 percent chance of this couple having a deaf child because, even if the combination is one allele for hearing and one allele for deafness, since the allele for deafness is dominant, the trait (deafness) will manifest itself and the

Figure 4.2. Autosomal Dominant Transmission of Deafness

child will have a hearing loss. This same couple has a 50 percent chance of having a child who is hearing and is not a carrier of the allele for deafness. **Dominant transmission** of deafness occurs in approximately 20–30 percent of the cases of hereditary deafness (Moores, 2000).

Our final Punnett square, Figure 4.3, illustrates simple autosomal recessive genetic transmission of deafness. In autosomal recessive transmission or inheritance, there must be two copies of the recessive gene (in Figure 4.3, the recessive gene is deafness) for the child to display the trait. Both hearing parents in Figure 4.3 are carriers of the recessive trait for deafness. Only when their recessive alleles match up in one of the four sectors of the Punnett square, will the child be deaf. In this type of transmission, two recessive alleles for deafness must be donated to the child in order for the trait to be exhibited. All children with only one recessive gene for deafness will be carriers but will be hearing. This final scenario, where many children are carriers (illustrated in Figure 4.3, see page 98), occurs most commonly in isolated communities where intermarriage between distant (and sometimes close) relatives occurs. Such a situation significantly increases the probability that a greater than average number of deaf children (in this particular case) will be born. This means that in autosomal recessive genetic transmission of deafness, when one parent is deaf (and therefore must have two recessive genes for deafness) and the other parent is hearing with no recessive alleles for that type of deafness, none of the children will be deaf

97

Figure 4.3. Autosomal Recessive Transmission of Deafness

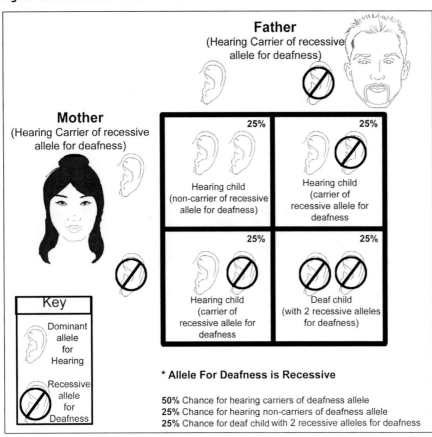

themselves but all of the children will be carriers. The American Academy of Otolaryngology – Head and Neck Surgery (AAO-HNS) estimates that approximately 80 percent of (non-syndromic) genetic hearing loss is due to autosomal recessive genetic transmission (http://www.entnet.org/healthinformation/genes-and-hearing-loss.cfm).

Extra! Extra! Hear All about It: Famous Inventor Claims to Be Able to Eradicate Deafness

The famous inventor, Alexander Graham Bell, was an important and influential figure in the history of deaf education. His father was a teacher of speech in Scotland, and his mother and wife were both deaf. It has been said (and yes, widely questioned) that he invented the telephone accidentally while trying to build the first electronic hearing aid. He did however dabble in genetics. In 1884, he published a manuscript entitled "Upon the formation of a deaf variety of the human race." In it he outlined, with the knowledge of genetics during that time, a theory that said that if deaf people would be prohibited from marrying one another, deafness could be eliminated within a generation or two, thus preventing the establishment of a "deaf race." While other eugenicists "… called for legislation outlawing intermarriage by deaf people," Bell rejected such a ban as impractical. Instead he proposed the following steps: "(1) Determine the causes that promote intermarriages among the deaf and dumb; and (2) remove them." (" Signing, Alexander Graham Bell and the NAD," http://www.pbs.org/weta/throughdeafeyes/deaflife/bell_nad.html)

Immediately after the publication of Bell's manuscript, Gregor Mendel, the father of genetics, was playing around with smooth and wrinkled peas. His work, presented at a conference in what was then Moravia (now the Czech Republic) in 1865, clearly showed A. G. Bell that merely prohibiting deaf people from marrying one another would not eliminate deafness because hearing people could always be carriers of the genetic allele for deafness. (Moores, 2000; Signing, Alexander Graham Bell and the NAD, n.d.)

Sometimes, the rarest genetic causes of deafness are combined with a myriad of additional disabilities and can be traced to the chromosome that determines sex, the 23rd pair of chromosomes. These are not autosomal genetic disorders since they occur on the 23rd chromosome. They are called X-linked genetic disorders. The NIH Medline Plus website describes X-linked genetic transmission well:

> X-linked diseases usually occur in males. Males have only one X chromosome. A single recessive gene on that X chromosome will cause the disease.

The Y chromosome is the other half of the XY gene pair in the male. However, the Y chromosome doesn't contain most of the genes of the X chromosome. It therefore doesn't protect the male. This is seen in diseases such as hemophilia and Duchenne muscular dystrophy. (http://www.nlm.nih.gov/medlineplus/ency/article/002051.htm; U.S. National Library of Medicine, National Institutes of Health, Medline Plus website)

Prenatal Genetic Etiologies of Deafness. Now that you have become a master of the variety of ways that a disorder can be genetically transmitted, we're ready to present the major congenital genetic and nongenetic causes of hearing loss. And since you've just finished the section on genetic transmission, we present those genetically determined etiologies first.

Genetic causes of deafness occur at the moment of conception (if you skipped the previous section, or need a review, return to the section above labeled "Genetic Transmission/Inheritance"). It is estimated that there are over 400 genetic causes of deafness (Smith, Shearer, Hildebrand, & Van Camp, 1999). Many of these causes are fairly obscure, so we will focus on the most common genetic etiologies of hearing loss.

At this point, we must introduce two new terms. While still a genetic hearing loss, a **nonsyndromic** loss has no additional traits associated with the genetic transmission, just hearing loss. This is in contrast to a **syndromic** etiology of hearing loss that, while also genetic in nature, is associated with traits in addition to deafness, such as renal failure, wide-set eyes, and heart defects.

By far, the most common cause of genetic deafness is the recessively transmitted protein-laden gene, **connexin 26 (cx26)**. And while there are at least 400 (and still counting) genetic causes of deafness currently identified, cx26 accounts for one-third of all of those cases (Boys Town Hospital Research Center & The National Institute on Deafness and Other Communication Disorders [NIDCD]). The cx26 gene is generally inherited through autosomal recessive transmission. It is considered a nonsyndromic genetic cause of hearing loss since the only trait associated with cx26 is deafness. Because it is transmitted recessively, there may be no apparent history of hearing loss in the family lineage. Yet, there must be hearing carriers of a recessive cx26 allele. So, when two carriers of the cx26 recessive gene have a child, the chance of that child being deaf is 25 percent, of being a hearing carrier of the cx26 gene like his parents is 50 percent, and being a noncarrier of the cx26 gene is 25 percent. Refer back to Figure 4.3 for a visual representation of this type of genetic transmission. Connexin 26 can cause hearing loss of all degrees, but the most likely degree of hearing loss is in the range of severe to profound. An excellent resource for anyone interested in one family's discovery that the cause of their son's deafness was cx26 can be found at http://www.handsandvoices.org/articles/fam_perspectives/connexin.html (Bernabei, n.d.).

While cx26 has been shown to be the most prevalent cause of nonsyndromic genetic hearing loss, researchers have identified at least 46 other genes responsible for nonsyndromic causes of deafness. For more information on these other etiologies, see the article by Hilgert, Smith, and Van Camp (2009).

There are numerous etiologies of deafness attributed to dominant syndromic genetic transmission. Again, while it is not practical to discuss all of these causes, the major syndromes that include hearing loss as a trait are presented below. Remember that in syndromic genetic transmission, deafness is only one of the traits that is associated with the syndrome. A syndrome may have traits that are all expressed, meaning that all traits or characteristics of the syndrome will be present if the person is affected. However, some syndromes have traits that are variably expressed. In such a case, a person may have some of the traits but not display others. This is true of the first syndrome we present.

Waardenburg syndrome is an autosomal dominant inherited syndrome. While there are many traits of Waardenburg syndrome, they are variably expressed. The major traits associated with Waardenburg syndrome are some degree of hearing loss, a white forelock of hair that can be seen as early as age 12, and exceedingly bright blue eyes or two differently colored eyes (usually blue and green). Other traits include wide-set eyes and a broad nasal bridge. Some people with Waardenburg syndrome may also have skin pigmentation abnormalities, "unibrows," and a hairline that begins low on the forehead. Individuals who have hearing loss will have type I or type II Waardenburg syndrome. These two Waardenburg syndrome subtypes are differentiated by the physical characteristics that a person displays. People who have wide-set eyes have Waardenburg type I, while people who do not display this characteristic have type II Waardenburg syndrome. There is about a 20 percent chance that someone with type I Waardenburg syndrome will have a hearing loss, while people with type II of the syndrome have a 50 percent chance of having a hearing loss. The severity of the hearing loss varies widely among people with Waardenburg syndrome, but the loss always has a major sensorineural component (What is Waardenburg syndrome? http://ghr.nlm.nih.gov/condition/waardenburg-syndrome).

There are three clinical types of the autosomal recessively transmitted syndrome called **Usher syndrome** (Keats & Corey, 1999). Between 6 and 12 percent of all children who have hearing loss are affected by Usher syndrome. There are three major and one minor identified types of Usher syndrome. While each type has its own profile, the common traits they share

are hearing loss and progressive vision loss. The culprit causing visual difficulties is **retinitis pigmentosa**. Retinitis pigmentosa (RP) also exists separately from Usher syndrome. Accordingly, all people with RP do not have hearing loss, but all Usher-syndrome-affected individuals have hearing loss *and* progressive vision loss due to RP. The first symptoms of RP are a decline in the ability to see in darkened environments and a narrowing of the field of vision to the point that the individual has tunnel vision and must move his head right and left and up and down in order to see things within the environment that are not in his central visual field. Table 4.3 presents the basic facts about each type of Usher syndrome. The most common Usher syndrome in the United States and Canada is type 2 (Usher Syndrome, http://www.nidcd.nih.gov/health/hearing/pages/usher.aspx).

Table 4.3. Types of Usher Syndrome

	Type 1	Type 2	Type 3
Hearing	Degree of hearing loss at birth: severe to profound	Degree of hearing loss at birth: moderate to severe	Degree of hearing loss at birth: none apparent; however, progressive hearing loss appears early in life
Vision	RP affects child prior to the age of 10, particularly at night.	RP affects child in late adolescence and early adulthood, with symptoms appearing first with night vision and followed by diminishing field of vision.	RP affects child in late adolescence, with varying levels of severity.
Vestibular function (balance)	Vestibular function at birth: noticeable balance difficulties	Vestibular function at birth: no noticeable problems and no progressive balance problems	Vestibular function at birth: no noticeable problems, though balance deficits may appear later in development

Heredity Matters

In the United States, four of every 100,000 babies born have Usher syndrome, and due to immigration/migration patterns, the Acadian parishes of southern Louisiana have the highest incidence of this syndrome. This is attributed to the fact that the Acadians of Louisiana (Cajuns) were originally French and were initially exiled to the French-speaking areas of Canada and then exiled again to the swamps of French Louisiana. These new Louisianans, and also their French-Canadian relatives, tended to marry within their ethnic communities. The gene for Usher syndrome was prevalent in this population, and due to intermarriage there were many carriers of this gene. It was only a matter of time that Usher gene carriers began to marry one another. Therefore, it's not surprising that the incidence of Usher is so high in these two geographic regions. Due to the high incidence of this disorder in South Louisiana, all children with hearing losses enrolled in schools in the state are screened during their early elementary years for Usher syndrome. (NIDCD)

Conductive hearing loss is one of the traits of the syndromic disorder known as **Treacher Collins**. This autosomal dominant genetic disorder involves the prenatal development of the jaw and the bones of the head in addition to the placement of various anatomical features such as the eyes (wide-set) and the pinnae (appearing more inferior [lower] on the head than usual). Hearing loss is caused by **stenosis** (narrowing), **atresia** (absence), or **microsia** (incomplete fetal development) of the pinna, external auditory meatus, and/or ossicles. People affected by Treacher Collins syndrome are usually small in stature, have underdeveloped jaws and chins, have downward slanting eyes with minimal eyelashes, and may have a cleft palate or lip. It is estimated that 1 in 50,000 individuals is affected by Treacher Collins syndrome, and even though the hearing loss is caused in the outer and/or the middle ear, and is therefore conductive in nature, it cannot be medically alleviated.

Alport syndrome is another genetically acquired cause of hearing loss. "Inheritance is variable and may be either: X-linked dominant (approximately 85%), autosomal recessive (approximately 15%), or autosomal dominant (approximately 1%)" (Willacy, 2011). In addition to progressive kidney disease—and that is certainly the most debilitating of all traits of Alport syndrome—individuals with this genetic disorder often have progressive sensorineural hearing loss that starts during puberty as well. Hearing loss has been traced to components of the organ of Corti, and although there are some correlates of problems with eyes, generally these do not affect visual ability. Because 15 percent of Alport syndrome incidence is linked to a recessive allele located on the X chromosome, it is more common in males than in females. It is estimated that 1 in 50,000 newborns is affected by Alport syndrome.

While not a major trait of the syndrome, conductive mild to moderate hearing loss is common with **Down syndrome,** a syndrome also known as **trisomy 21** because the 21st chromosome pair actually has an extra chromosome. Affected individuals are often said to look like brothers and sisters because of the shape of their heads and placement of the eyes and width of the nose. The conductive hearing loss component of Down syndrome is linked to an inadequately shaped eustachian tube that is prone to malfunction, causing fluids from the respiratory system, especially during colds and other respiratory ailments, to enter the middle ear (Shott, Joseph, & Heithaus, 2001). If your child has Down syndrome or you are working with a child with Down syndrome, you need to be extra-vigilant when it comes to the possibility of middle ear infection. Look for telltale clues that the child is having problems hearing or shows some sign of discomfort in the area near the ears.

Found to be transmitted through autosomal dominant inheritance, the gene for **neurofibromatosis** (type 2) is located on chromosome 22. Neurofibromatosis 2 causes noncancerous tumors (**acoustic neuromas**) to develop along the 8th CN and other nerves in the brain and the spinal column. This is a progressive disorder that may not appear until the teenage years or later. However, some symptoms that tumors are developing include progressively worsening balance problems and **tinnitus** (ringing in the ears). As these tumors enlarge and the individual ages, vision may be affected as well as hearing and motor abilities. Usually, neurofibromatosis causes bilateral sensorineural hearing problems. It is estimated that 1 child in every 25,000 births will be born with this disorder.

Hearing loss in the final two genetic syndromes presented is not the primary disorder in either of the syndromes. Each of these syndromes carries a name that stands for the various components of the syndrome. The first one is **branchio-oto-renal syndrome** or **BOR syndrome**. The first term, *branchio*, relates to the development of tissues in the front and side of the neck; the middle term, *oto*, as you may remember, refers to hearing; and the final term in this syndrome, *renal*, means that there are associated kidney issues. In terms of hearing loss, individuals with BOR will usually have a mixed hearing loss, as there can be some malformation of the pinna and outer ear structures. BOR is also associated with ear tags, more accurately called **pre-auricular tags**. These small pieces of tissue are located anterior to the pinna. Ear tags are a fairly common trait of many genetic syndromes, and when audiologists and physicians try to determine the cause of a hearing loss, one of the first things they will do is look for ear tags.

The final inherited syndrome that involves hearing loss is **CHARGE syndrome**. The CHARGE Syndrome website explains how the acronym came about:

> The name "CHARGE" was a clever way (in 1981) to refer to a newly recognized cluster of features seen in a number of children. Over the years, it has become clear that CHARGE is indeed a syndrome and at least one gene causing CHARGE syndrome has been discovered. The letters in CHARGE stand for: <u>C</u>oloboma of the eye, <u>H</u>eart defects, <u>A</u>tresia of the choanae, <u>R</u>etardation of growth and/or development, <u>G</u>enital and/or urinary abnormalities, and <u>E</u>ar abnormalities and deafness. Those features are no longer used in making a diagnosis of CHARGE syndrome, but we're not changing the name. (The CHARGE Syndrome Foundation. http://www.chargesyndrome.org/about-charge.asp)

While these are the major disorders associated with the syndrome, there are a multitude of minor problems associated with CHARGE. CHARGE is inherited in an autosomal dominant pattern, and it is estimated that it occurs in 1 in 8,500 to 10,000 births. Hearing loss can be mild to profound in degree. Malformations of the outer ear, most notably pinna malformation and both middle and inner ear problems, are caused during prenatal development. Yet, clearly, hearing loss in children with CHARGE syndrome is not the primary disorder. The CHARGE Syndrome Foundation website explains the genesis of the name CHARGE Syndrome and its current meaning.

These are but a handful of nonsyndromic and syndromic genetic disorders that cause hearing loss. For an extensive list and description of a great many of the other 391 known genetic causes of deafness, visit the U.S. National Library of Medicine's website at: http://ghr.nlm.nih.gov/conditionCategory/ear-nose-and-throat.

Prenatal Nongenetic Etiologies of Deafness

Although there are numerous causes for hearing loss acquired during the prenatal period, we discuss the six most common ones. Prenatal nongenetic etiologies of deafness can occur at any time during fetal development but most often occur during the first trimester of pregnancy. At a mere five weeks **gestational age** (calculated as the time lapsed since last menstrual period), rudimentary pinnas appear on the side of a head. And by week 8 the inner ear begins to form. Not surprisingly, other organs, especially the kidney and the heart, are also undergoing major development during this week. Thinking back to genetic syndromes, and given this information, it is understandable why many major syndromes that cause hearing loss are also correlated with kidney and heart disorders. In any case, as you can see, the first trimester of pregnancy is crucially important to the development of the hearing mechanism (Pregnancy week by week, Mayo Clinic website, n.d.). It is in the second trimester, in gestational week 20, that the developing infant has the peripheral structures in place to assure the ability to hear. Researchers Graven and Brown (2008) state:

> The structural parts of the cochlea in the middle ear are well formed by 15 weeks' gestational age and are anatomically functional by 20 weeks' gestation. … [At] 29 weeks' gestational age …the ganglion cells of the spiral nucleus in the cochlea connect inner hair cells to the brain stem and temporal lobe of the cortex (pp. 188–189).

For more information and an animation of the fetal development of the hearing mechanism, go to the University of Pennsylvania Health System's Penn Medicine Medical Animation Library – Fetal Ear Development website at http://www.pennmedicine.org/encyclopedia/em_DisplayAnimation.aspx?gcid=000057&ptid=17.

The first four nongenetic prenatal etiologies of hearing loss have been grouped together under the acronym **TORCH**. The acronym stands for Toxemia, Maternal Rubella, Cytomegalovirus (CMV), and herpes simplex II. These involve diseases that the mother acquires during initial embryonic and later fetal development. The resulting effect upon the fetus depends on a number of things. First, if the **onset** of the disease coincides with a crucial period of auditory fetal stages of development, the passing of the virus or pathogens (germs) through the umbilical cord disturbs the normal development of the hearing mechanism. However, if Mom has acquired these viruses previous to pregnancy and does not have an outbreak during the developmental period, there will usually be no detrimental effect to fetal development. If, on the other hand, the mother first acquires the virus, has a subsequent outbreak of the dormant virus, or if she develops toxemia during a crucial fetal development sequence for ear development, there is a significant chance that the newborn will have, at a minimum, a congenital hearing loss.

Toxemia is the first of the TORCH etiologies. A more accurate name for toxemia is **preeclampsia**. Preeclampsia occurs after the 20th week of gestation and is diagnosed by symptoms that appear suddenly in the pregnant mother. These symptoms include sudden high blood pressure, excessive protein in the urine, headaches, abdominal pain, visual disturbances, nausea, and shortness of breath. Preeclampsia is quite common as compared to other nongenetic prenatal conditions. A significant number of babies born to women who develop preeclampsia during pregnancy are prematurely delivered, and babies of women who develop preeclampsia during pregnancy have a much higher chance of being premature. While the great majority of these babies will experience no postpartum problems related to the condition, we know 20 percent of all premature births are due to this condition, and that preterm infants run a higher risk of being born with disabilities such as hearing loss, cognitive issues, visual and motor problems, and a slew of other disabilities. By far, the most dangerous of all complications of untreated preeclampsia is maternal and fetal death (Bakhshaee et al., 2008; Preeclampsia Foundation, n.d.).

Sometimes you will find that the *TO* in TORCH refers to **toxoplasmosis**. Hearing loss is correlated with maternal exposure to a parasite that can be found in poorly cooked food, the soil, and cat feces. Pregnant women who contract toxoplasmosis may or may not show symptoms, and if the result of exposure is neonatal hearing loss, it may not be immediately apparent during the early months of infant development (Bluestone, Stool, Alper, & Arjmand, 2002).

The second prenatal TORCH etiology of deafness is **maternal rubella**. In 1964–1965, there was an international epidemic of rubella (German measles). German measles are different from regular measles (known as rubeola), so it is possible to be immune to one type of measles yet still be able to contract the other type. Because in the mid-1960s there was no inoculation against the disease, a much greater number of pregnant women at that time would be expected to contract maternal rubella in their first trimester of pregnancy. Usually, these mothers-to-be recognized the characteristic rash and knew that they had German measles. However, there were many subclinical cases during those years. A subclinical case of a disease such as maternal rubella occurs when no external symptoms of the disease appear and, therefore, the affected person has no indication that she is battling the virus. As a result of the 1964–1965 epidemic of maternal rubella, there were 12,500,000 cases of rubella reported in the United States. Of these cases, approximately 20,000 infants were adversely affected during the first trimester of their development when their mothers contracted the disease and the children were subsequently born with **congenital rubella syndrome (CRS)**. Many of these infants had hearing losses, some were born with visual impairments, and others had a multitude of disabilities. Not long after this epidemic, in 1969, the inoculation we know as MMR (measles, mumps, and rubella) was developed and widely administered, thus practically eliminating the possibility of another such epidemic in the United States and other developed nations. By 2006, only 11 cases of rubella were reported in the United States, with only one case of CRS (Baby Center Medical Advisory Board, 2012).

The fourth initial in the acronym TORCH stands for **cytomegalovirus** or **CMV**. It is highly likely that if you have children, or work in a field such as daycare or education, where there are children who are prone to get sick, you have been exposed to CMV without your knowledge. In fact, most people have contracted CMV and do not know it. The symptoms of CMV are flulike, lasting three to five days, and then disappearing. The Centers for Disease Control and Prevention (CDC) estimate that between 50 and 80 percent of all adults over the age of 40 in the United States would test positive for CMV, since after initial exposure, this virus lies dormant in the body. The CDC also estimates that for every 1000 live births, approximately 1 to 2 babies will have prenatal CMV-related deficits (Centers for Disease Control and Prevention, n.d.).

Most people who have experienced CMV are not aware that they have contracted this particular virus, but for a small percentage of people who contract CMV, the viral symptoms linger and can be apparent for a month or longer. These symptoms include low-grade fever, exhaustion, swollen glands, and a general lack of energy. Without a **titer** (the measurement of the concentration of a substance in a solution—antibodies in this case) run for CMV, physicians tend to attribute this cluster of symptoms to chronic fatigue syndrome. There is neither a medical remedy for CMV nor an inoculation available to prevent contracting the virus. The affected patient must just wait until the virus becomes dormant in his system. CMV is part of the Herpesviridae family of viruses. It can be dangerous when the mother-to-be contracts it during the first trimester and transmits the virus to the fetus during a crucial developmental period. Most commonly, CMV acquired by the fetus at this point of development affects not only hearing ability but causes other severe sensory, motor, and cognitive deficits as well. Luckily, the CDC estimates that only about 1 in 750 children in the United States is born with or develops permanent problems due to congenital CMV infection (How many babies, Centers for Disease Control and Prevention, n.d.).

There are at least 25 viruses in the Herpesviridae (herpes) family. Humans can contract eight of these herpes viruses. They include Epstein-Barr, CMV, the herpes zoster viruses (e.g., shingles, chickenpox), and the two most recognized types of herpes, herpes simplex I and herpes simplex II. **Herpes simplex I** is also commonly referred to as cold sores that usually occur close to, or on the lips. Scientists estimate that 50 percent of people have herpes simplex I. Herpes simplex I and **herpes simplex II**, otherwise known as genital herpes, are both spread by physical contact with bodily fluids containing the active (not dormant) virus, and both can have a deleterious effect on the developing fetus. These two types of herpes viruses cannot live long outside of the body, so bodily contact and/or an exchange of fluids is necessary to pass on these viruses. Estimates of the prevalence of herpes simplex II in the general population of the United States range from a high of 33 percent (1 in 3) to 16 percent (1 in 6) of all sexually active adults. Both herpes simplex I and II can be transmitted to the fetus prenatally, but it is herpes simplex II that is the most dangerous, especially during the first trimester of pregnancy. And although it is extremely rare that the fetus will be affected if the mother is not experiencing an initial episode of the herpes simplex II, it is not impossible. The American Social Health Association (also called ASHA) is an excellent resource to learn about the herpes viruses and other sexually transmitted diseases that have the potential to affect the developing fetus and cause hearing loss and other disabilities (Herpes simplex II, http://www.ashasexualhealth.org/std-sti/Herpes.html).

And on the topic of sexually transmitted diseases, you may find the letter *S* on the end of the acronym when reading about the TORCH diseases (TORCH[S]). The *S* is for congenital **syphilis,** a disease that is on the rise in the United States, especially in populations that fall below the poverty level and that have limited access to public health resources. A mother with syphilis can transmit the disease through the placenta to her unborn child. Transmission of untreated syphilis in utero is statistically high (70–100 percent), especially after the fourth month of gestation and when the mother is in the initial stages of the disease, because this is when the virus is most aggressively getting established. There is an early form and a late form of syphilis, and, depending on the form, hearing loss may or may not be apparent at birth. However, after the age of two years, many children affected by syphilis in utero will begin to display symptoms of hearing loss (Bluestone et al., 2002).

Not related to the TORCH group of diseases, **Fetal Alcohol Syndrome (FAS)** or Fetal Alcohol Syndrome Disorder (FASD) can also be a prenatal cause of hearing loss. The Children's Hospital of Philadelphia estimates that 40,000 babies are born with FAS each year in the United States (Fetal alcohol syndrome, CHOP, n.d.). The syndrome, which is nongenetic, has many correlates such as ear malformation, brain and facial abnormalities, defects in numerous organs, and neurodevelopmental abnormalities. While we often associate FAS with mothers who are alcoholic, researchers have determined that no amount of alcohol consumption is safe when it comes to fetal development. Just one alcoholic drink, at precisely the wrong time, may adversely affect whatever process is currently occurring in fetal development. Michael Miller, Ph.D., a long-time researcher in the field of fetal alcohol syndrome, points to days 26 and 27 postconception as particularly crucial days in fetal development. Harrington quotes Miller in a 2007 interview: "This is when stem cells are forming protostructures for the body and mapping out the face," Miller explains. "At this point, alcohol exposure reduces the size of certain cranial nerve nuclei in the brain stem and leads to the craniofacial irregularities characteristic of FAS" (Harrington, p. 14).

Because this is a syndrome, children affected by FAS tend to look alike due to the constellation of similar problems induced by alcohol exposure in utero. Unlike many other prenatal nongenetic causes of hearing loss and significant disabilities, FAS is often said to be completely preventable. A woman wishing to become pregnant should stop drinking prior to conception. Unfortunately, many women do not know that they are pregnant until the damage has been done. And, according to Miller, alcoholism itself may have genetic underpinnings. Once the child with FAS is born to a mother who is an alcoholic, the baby is immediately deprived of the alcohol previously provided by his mother through the umbilical cord. And like anyone who is alcoholic and stops drinking suddenly, the baby will have significant withdrawal symptoms in addition to developmental and physical disabilities (Fetal alcohol syndrome, CHOP, n.d.).

Perinatal Etiologies of Deafness

Perinatal causes of deafness occur during the birth process. Two of the diseases that were discussed as etiologies of deafness in the prenatal developmental period are also implicated in perinatal hearing loss. These are CMV and herpes simplex II. It is important to realize that during the birth process, women who carry these viruses in their dormant stages are at only a slightly higher risk of passing these on to their newborn child. And in fact, in the case of CMV, since so many women have been exposed to the virus well before conception, it is often not a factor of concern to obstetricians and neonatologists. However, it is when these viruses are active and shedding viral cells during delivery that significant problems can develop for the newborn.

A woman who knows she has genital herpes should work with her physician to determine if the virus is in an active stage prior to delivery. This can be done through a blood test or a vaginal swab taken during her weekly visits to the obstetrician prior to her due date. If the herpes virus is active a week or two before delivery, the obstetrician will arrange for cesarean section (C-section) delivery. This prevents the possibility of newborn infection because, for both of these viruses, it is the passing of active viral cells from the vaginal canal and cervix of the mother to the mucous membranes of the infant during the birth process that causes the problem at birth. A newborn has a weak immune system and has not yet developed adequate defenses against the virus. Therefore, viral cells passed from the mother to the newborn infant quickly invade the brain, damaging the anatomical structures needed for hearing, vision, cognition, and motor skills. The real problem occurs when the mother does not know she has an active case of either of these viruses. Without warning, especially in a first episode of genital herpes or a subclinical case of CMV, the obstetrician has no indication that a C-section delivery should be performed.

Another perinatal cause of deafness and often an accompanying visual impairment is a lack of oxygen flowing to the brain, or **anoxia**. By far, the most common cause of anoxia is an umbilical cord wrapped around the newborn's neck, preventing adequate oxygen from reaching the brain and the various structures, such as the hearing mechanism, housed within it. On the flip side, straight oxygen delivered in the perinatal period is also a cause of hearing and vision deficits. Several decades ago, it was common practice to place a newborn in an oxygen-rich environment immediately after birth, especially if that child was premature. This too was found to cause vision and hearing deficits and so the practice was halted.

Infants born prematurely have a much higher chance of having both developmental and physical disabilities such as hearing loss. As they develop, prematurely born children also seem to be more prone to middle ear infections than full-term babies. This is due to the fact that infants' sensory, cognitive, and other anatomical organs were not fully developed upon birth. Depending on how prematurely the child was born, the degree of disability may be mild and disappear as the child ages, or it may be significant and continue to be a problem throughout his life.

The final perinatal etiology of deafness is **Rh factor incompatibility,** also called **erythroblastosis fetalis.** While not a significant cause of hearing loss in the developed world where prenatal care is readily available, Rh factor incompatibility persists in underdeveloped nations and areas of extreme poverty that have limited or no prenatal care available. Years ago, before it was common for pregnant women in the first stages of pregnancy to have their blood typed and Rh factor determined, the incidence of deafness due to Rh factor incompatibility was much higher than it is now. In Rh factor incompatibility, the mother has a negative Rh factor (Rh–) that is a recessive trait, and the father has a positive Rh factor (Rh+), the dominant trait. The woman's first pregnancy, be it full-term or not, is not a problem for the infant. It is in successive pregnancies where the Rh factor incompatibility comes into play.

During the first pregnancy, the mother builds up antibodies against the positive Rh factor of the father that have been inherited by the infant. In essence, the mother's immune system views the Rh+ red blood cells of the fetus as foreign and dangerous and develops antibodies against them. Because this is an initial pregnancy, these antibodies are not well developed enough to harm the newborn. In subsequent pregnancies, however, the Rh+ infant is protected from his mother's angry antibodies while he is directly connected to the blood supply of his Rh– mother, because the buildup of dangerous levels of bilirubin being produced by the infant in response to the Rh factor incompatibility are excreted by the mother. However, during the perinatal period, when the infant separates from his mother and establishes his own independent blood supply, the mother's antibodies activate the production of bilirubin in the baby's circulatory system and without mother to excrete the excess the infant is in danger. In fact, without medical intervention the infant might die. (Rh incompatibility, http://emedicine. medscape.com/article/797150-overview#a0199 , n.d.).

Until the late 1960s, it was routine for the baby to undergo a complete blood transfusion, ridding his circulatory system of his mother's attacking antibodies. While a routine procedure at the time, the total transfusion of blood could deny the brain oxygen, causing a state of anoxia. And, as described before, anoxia can cause hearing, vision, and other deficits. Since 1968, once a woman is determined to be Rh–, her physician will begin a series of injections of a drug with the brand name Rhogam. This drug prevents the mother's antibodies from destroying the blood supply of the newborn and therefore causing the associated disabilities, or even worse, death. So, you can see how essential it is for pregnant women to receive adequate prenatal care and to be followed throughout their pregnancies (Reid & Lomas-Francis, 1997).

Postnatal Etiologies of Deafness

The onset of the final category of etiologies of hearing loss spans a number of years, from the point of birth through the remainder of a person's life. Collectively, hearing losses occurring in this period are called postnatal etiologies; they occur after the birth process is completed. Postnatal etiologies of hearing loss can be further divided into (1) those that cause primarily conductive hearing losses, and (2) those that cause primarily sensorineural hearing losses.

The most common of all causes of hearing loss is a middle ear infection, called **otitis media**. Otitis media may be caused by a number of viruses or bacterial pathogens, and although it is particularly prevalent in children under the age of five, it can occur at any age. Brooks (1994) states that only the common cold is more prevalent in children than otitis media. Researchers at Boston's Children's Hospital estimate that by three years of age, 80 percent of children born in the United States will have experienced an episode of otitis media, and half of them will have had at least three episodes (Otitis media, http://www.childrenshospital.org/health-topics/conditions/otitis-media, n.d.).

In otitis media, fluid from the respiratory system (for example, mucus from a cold or a cough, or saliva) finds its way into the eustachian tube, only to be deposited in the middle ear cavity. This fluid impedes the motion of the tympanic membrane, and if there is enough fluid in the middle ear, also the movement of the ossicles that reside, primarily, in the epitympanic recess. An individual with otitis media may complain of a muffled sound or pain somewhere in the ear. The pain may be emanating from an inequality of air pressure between the middle ear and the outside world, causing painful retraction or bulging of the tympanic membrane. Martin and Clark (2012) have noted a recent and dramatic increase in the incidence of otitis media. They speculate that this is due to the fact that infections are increasingly more resistant to antibiotic treatment. Also, research has shown that some people are predisposed to being affected by otitis media. These include people with poorly developed eustachian tubes and anatomical malformations of middle ear structures. Also age, race, socioeconomic status, access to healthcare, and compromised immune systems are correlated with a higher incidence of otitis media. Martin and Clark (2012) further speculate that it is this latter predisposition, a compromised immune system that accounts for an increase in otitis media in individuals who have AIDS/HIV. Additionally, children exposed to secondhand smoke are four times more likely to develop otitis media than those who are not exposed to secondhand smoke.

There are two stages of otitis media. **Acute otitis media** (AOM) occurs when there is an initial bout with the disease that is cured through medical means and may only infrequently return. **Chronic otitis media** (COM) must last at least eight weeks and returns quickly after the completion of a round of antibiotics. The cycle of treating otitis media with antibiotics, having it return, retreating with antibiotics, and finally placing pressure equalizing tubes, or **PE tubes**, is common in children and indicates chronic otitis media is being experienced. The American Speech-Hearing-Language Association (ASHA) website states, "**Otitis media with effusion (OME)** or fluid in the middle ear without evidence of ear infection is one type of otitis media. [You may also see this called serous otitis media.] OME differs from acute otitis media (AOM), where there is middle ear fluid with rapid onset of one or more signs or symptoms of middle ear inflammation."

Suppurative otitis media occurs when negative pressure in the middle ear cavity causes the tympanic and mucous membranes to become very vascular. The negative pressure pulls mucus and sometimes blood into the fluid sitting in the middle ear. If there is a bacterial organism within the middle ear that happily reproduces in the warm fluid environment, the fluid becomes **purulent** or pus-filled. Characteristically, in this situation, a child may feel fine, showing no symptoms, and then complain about mild symptoms that will quickly turn into a serious infection within several hours of the initial complaint. Left untreated, chronic purulent suppurative otitis media causes **mastoiditis**, a condition that breaks down the mucous membranes and capillaries supplying needed blood for healthy membranes. Eventually, these membranes will die and the infection can invade the mastoid bone and, can, if left untreated, ultimately lead to death.

Otitis media is medically addressed through the administration of antibiotics. If that fails to eliminate the problem, surgical insertion of PE (pressure equalizing or **tympanostomy**) tubes are placed through the tympanic membrane to allow fluid to flow out via the external auditory meatus. These PE tubes are tiny and often look like grommets placed in the lower half of the tympanic membrane. Otitis media rarely produces permanent hearing loss. Rather, during the time that otitis media is active, the individual will experience a temporary conductive mild to moderate hearing loss. In children who are learning language through hearing, this has a deleterious effect, delaying the natural process of spoken language acquisition. For a detailed discussion on insertion and placement of PE tubes, visit the Healio Pediatric website, Infectious diseases in children — Tympanostomy tubes: http://www.healio.com/pediatrics/respiratory-infections/news/print/infectious-diseases-in-children/%7B506b942c-059a-445a-98cd-6ab36428cf77%7D/tympanostomy-tubes-eustachian-tube-bypass-with-imperfections.

A **perforated tympanic membrane (TM)** may be associated with otitis media and, then again, it may not. Rapid change in air pressure; the insertion of a sharp object deep into the EAM, breaking the surface of the tympanic membrane; and severe head trauma can cause a perforation, a hole or a tear in the eardrum. No matter the cause, a slight (in a child) or mild hearing loss may ensue post-perforation. An ENT may wait up to six weeks before suggesting an operation to repair the perforation. This is done when the perforation is small and has a chance of fixing itself. However, if the perforation is larger, the physician may immediately suggest an operation called a **tympanoplasty**, where a piece of tissue is taken from the patient's vein or muscle and is used to close the perforation. Or an ENT may suggest a **myringoplasty**, in which a piece of cigarette paper or gel is placed across the tympanic membrane to encourage healing.

Trauma, such as a car accident or severe fall, may also cause a hearing loss. As mentioned above, trauma may produce a perforated eardrum. It also could cause a disarticulation of the ossicles, meaning the ossicular chain is no longer connected. If the ossicles are disconnected, they cannot transmit sound in the form of mechanical energy to the inner ear. While this condition is rather rare, it does need to be remedied surgically to prevent a mild to moderate conductive hearing loss. Depending on the location and severity of the disarticulation, an operation called an **ossiculoplasty** is performed. A small incision is made posterior to, or behind, the pinna, and the surgeon gains access to the middle ear cavity. The damaged bone or bones are removed, and in their place artificial ossicles, devices that are prosthetic, are inserted and attached where damaged ossicles were located. A number of human or manufactured materials, including the patient's own cartilage or a reshaped stapes, are used to make the ossicular chain function normally.

Otosclerosis, the final conductive postnatal cause of hearing loss we present, is characterized by a bony growth that affixes the stapes to the oval window. The otosclerotic material covers the footplate and the anterior and posterior crus of the stapes, preventing the ossicle from moving the oval window. When the oval window doesn't move, sound cannot be transferred from mechanical to hydraulic energy, and as a result a moderate to severe hearing loss occurs. Otosclerosis seldom affects very young children. The growth develops slowly and is most common in postpubescent Caucasian girls and young women, with an onset associated with pregnancy (Vincent, Oates, & Sperling, 2002). Left untreated, otosclerosis can invade the tympanic cavity and affect all of the ossicles, causing near-complete deafness. Scientists, supported by recent research, speculate that there are genetic factors involved in the development of otosclerosis. Through the years, physicians have tried a number of techniques to alleviate the problem. Some of these procedures worked to free the stapes from the growth, but most ended up destroying the stapes, oval window, and other structures, causing complete deafness. The most common procedure used today is to remove the stapes and clear out the bony growth. Then an artificial stapes, made of materials on which the growth will not adhere, is put into place. This procedure is called a **stapedectomy** and involves folding back the tympanic membrane and operating through the external auditory meatus (Stapedectomy, http://www.surgeryencyclopedia.com/Pa-St/Stapedectomy.html).

The final group of etiologies presented in this chapter has a postnatal onset and is primarily sensorineural in nature. They affect typically hearing individuals and cannot be mediated, to any great extent, by medical intervention. The first of these etiologies is **meningitis**. The most common course of this disease involves a very quick onset of a very high fever. Although it can affect people of all ages, infants, toddlers, preschoolers, and individuals with compromised immune systems are most susceptible to the lingering effects of meningitis.

Meningitis is caused by an infection, bacterial or viral, that inflames the meninges, the covering of the brain and spinal cord. In humans, the meninges is made up of three layers of tissue that protect the brain and its anatomical structures from outside damage. The meninges also assists in regulating the temperature of the brain, the cranial nerves, and the spinal cord. In contagious viral meningitis, symptoms can range from mild to severe but seldom have lasting effects. Bacterial meningitis, on the other hand, is quite dangerous and is also contagious, primarily being transferred through an exchange of bodily fluids (e.g., kissing, sneezing). There isn't one single pathogen/germ that causes meningitis; rather, there are several, including Streptococcus, which is frequently the culprit when young children have meningitis. The onset of symptoms of bacterial meningitis is quite sudden. For a child, a high fever may spike within mere hours of the child feeling quite healthy. The CDC reported 4,100 cases of bacterial meningitis between 2003 and 2007. Of these recorded cases, there were 500 that resulted in death. Because bacterial meningitis is such a serious disease, it is very important to take the affected person to a hospital as soon as possible. In addition to a sudden high fever, the patient may complain of headaches, nausea, vomiting, increased sensitivity to light, and mental confusion (Bacterial meningitis, http://www.cdc.gov/meningitis/bacterial.html). The number of cases of childhood bacterial meningitis has decreased since 1998, indicating that the new vaccines against bacterial meningitis have had their intended effect (Thigpen et al., 2011). Once the fear of death has passed, there are other worries, especially for the parents of young children. These include post-meningitis hearing loss, vision loss, cognitive delay (cognitive and learning disabilities), speech and language deficits, behavioral problems, and motor delay and impairment. Negative long-term effects such as these do not always occur in cases of bacterial meningitis. In fact, many affected individuals have no residual damage to note. In the authors' experiences, while the hearing loss does not improve, other domains such as cognition and motor skills may return to their normal pre-meningitis states. This has been supported in the literature. The Meningitis Centre of Australia estimates that "approximately 25% of people who survive [*meningitis*] … will have less obvious after effects, such as difficulties with coordination, concentration, and memory. These are usually temporary" (Meningitis and septicaemia, p. 4).

There are a number of other viral infections that have been identified as causes of hearing loss during the postnatal period. Mumps, measles (especially rubeola), influenza, pneumonia, and chickenpox can all result in hearing loss. Most of these losses are bilateral, with the exception of those caused by mumps, which tend to be unilateral. Since the introduction of vaccines to control many of these causative factors, a negligible number of cases of hearing loss due to these viral infections is now reported. Unfortunately, a recent laxity in adherence to CDC recommendations on childhood vaccination is causing an uptick in the incidence of these viral infections in children, and the long-term negative effects, including hearing loss, that they may cause.

During the 1950s and early 1960s, it was common practice for physicians to use drugs that we now know are **ototoxic** to combat infection and other acute problems. The American Speech-Hearing-Language Association notes that there are over 200 ototoxic medications on the market. While some ototoxic drugs produce only temporary and mild hearing loss and vertigo, others can have lasting effects on the hearing and vestibular systems. This last group of drugs is seldom used because of the drugs' damaging effects, and therefore they are considered drugs of last resort. Symptoms of ototoxicity include tinnitus, balance difficulties, and temporary or permanent very high-frequency hearing loss. There are guidelines available to physicians considering the use of ototoxic drugs. Hopefully, it goes without saying, that as a consumer of medical services you should be well informed and involved in the decision-making process. Cone et al. (2011) note:

> Ototoxic medications known to cause permanent damage include certain aminoglycoside antibiotics, such as gentamicin (family history may increase susceptibility), and cancer chemotherapy drugs, such as cisplatin and carboplatin. . . .
>
> Drugs known to cause temporary damage include salicylate pain relievers (aspirin, used for pain relief and to treat heart conditions), quinine (to treat malaria), and loop diuretics (to treat certain heart and kidney conditions).

Prescribing physicians resort to known ototoxic medications when the condition is very serious and/or life-threatening. Ototoxic drugs are the choice of last resort.

In 1861, a French physician, Dr. Prosper Ménière, discovered what is now known as **Ménière's disease**. Reported symptoms include sudden bouts of vertigo, nausea, unilateral hearing loss, and low-frequency high-intensity tinnitus. While not all of these symptoms will present themselves in every case, nor will each case of Ménière's disease be equally severe, the disease is described by those who have it as debilitating. Ménière's patients experience sudden and unexpected symptoms, so activities such as driving or performing manual labor may be impossible. There is not one specific cause attributed to Ménière's disease. It may result from cerebral trauma, infection, cochlear degeneration, or tumors. Since the exact physiology of the disease is unknown, there have been many proposed theories attached to this etiology that causes hearing loss and vertigo. Currently, it is thought that there is a problem with the volume and chemical makeup of the fluid in the vestibular and cochlear systems. Treatment includes sedatives and medications such as Antivert. Some patients report relief of some symptoms when using these medications. Coffee (caffeine of any type), alcohol, and smoking tend to exacerbate the symptoms of Ménière's disease (Martin & Clark, 2012).

One of the most preventable postnatal sensorineural causes of hearing loss is continued exposure to noise above 85 dB. The Occupational Safety and Health Administration (OSHA) requires that employers provide hearing protection for workers who are exposed for more than eight hours a day to high noise levels. OSHA recommends that all workers wear hearing protection in noisy environments, no matter how long the exposure, since exposure to noise on a frequent and repetitive basis will destroy the ability to process higher frequency sounds. (When is an employer, https://www.osha.gov/Publications/OSHA3074/osha3074.html). Even a single exposure to an exceedingly loud noise, such as an explosion, can cause permanent hearing loss. Individuals who have noise-induced hearing loss will have similar-looking audiograms (see Chapter 5). **Noise-induced** deafness is not a major factor in school-age children; however, with the use of earphones to listen to music, at especially loud volumes, a temporary or a permanent hearing loss may soon be seen in younger children.

The final (in more than one way) cause of hearing loss is **presbycusis**, or hearing loss due to the process of aging. After the ripe old age of 21 years, many of our anatomical systems begin their downhill tumble. Nowhere is this truer than with the hearing system. For the majority of people, presbycusis starts as a loss of acuity in the high-frequency range. If you think back to the tonotopic arrangement of hair cells in the cochlea (Chapter 3), you should remember that the lower frequencies are stimulated at the farthest end or apex of the cochlea, and the higher frequencies are at the basilar end of the structure. This means that for the entirety of one's life, whenever sound is perceived, be at low or high frequency, the hair cells responsible for receiving high-frequency information must always move, no matter the frequency of the sound. The more often these hair cells are moved by sound, the less flexible and more brittle they become. The hair cells that conduct high-frequency sounds must move when any sound, regardless of frequency range, is processed. Therefore, they are the first hair cells to deteriorate over time. As we age, they are simply worn out. Many an audiologist has had to field a remark (and perhaps a snippy one at that) from a woman who states, "My husband doesn't have a hearing problem. He can hear just perfectly. He can hear all of his buddies, but when I talk to him he just doesn't pay attention." Well, that very well might be true, but it's more likely that he is suffering from hearing loss due to presbycusis. Women's voices generally contain a greater number of high-frequency elements than men's voices. Therefore, yes, he can hear his male friends better than he can hear his wife, but it's not usually because he doesn't want to hear his wife—it's just that the hair cells responsible for high-frequency sound processing are not functioning correctly. As the baby-boomers age, the market for assistive listening devices, such as high-tech hearing aids, will grow accordingly.

What Is Everybody Looking At?

Presbycusis, the loss of hearing sensitivity due to the aging process, starts rather early in life, as evidenced by the following true story:

While in a class in sign language recently, one of your authors noted that all of her younger college students, in unison, started looking around the room. Your author, who is well into her 50s (okay, really early 60s), ignored the incident and kept on lecturing. In the back of her mind, she remembered seeing dogs display the same behavior, perking up their ears and looking around as if something had entered the room, but nothing had.

About 15 minutes later, the younger students in the classroom again all raised their heads in unison and began looking around the room and into pockets and purses. Finally, one of the students reached into her pocket grabbed her cell phone and fiddled with it, and everybody went back to concentrating on the class material.

Your author, now very perplexed and curious, asked the students why they had been looking around the classroom. The students replied that they had heard a very high-pitched sound that they knew was coming from someone's cell phone. With a little more investigation, the author found that no one in the classroom over the age of 30 had heard the sound. Apparently, cell phones, when placed on a certain setting, emit a high-frequency tone that is inaudible to "older" people. So while the 20-something students knew someone's phone was ringing, the older students and your author had no idea what was happening.

Ah, the joys of getting older!

And That's Not All...

There are three terms that, while not presented in the main text, you may come across in your reading or in discussions with parents, physicians, and audiologists.

Auditory Neuropathy: Auditory Neuropathy is a relatively newly diagnosed cause of sensorineural hearing loss. As recently as a quarter-century ago, auditory neuropathy—or as it is more appropriately referred to, auditory neuropathy syndrome disorder (ANSD)—went undiagnosed. Symptoms include problems with sound in noise, and hearing abilities can range from normal hearing to profound hearing loss. Charles Berlin, PhD, arguably the foremost expert on ANSD, describes it as the absence of an acoustic reflex with normal otoacoustic emissions testing (OAE) results and abnormal auditory brainstem testing (ABR) response results (Personal communication, January 1992). Teachers often describe the auditory behavior of children with ANSD as inconsistent. While the site of lesion has not been precisely identified, it is known that the outer hair cells in the cochlea are functioning correctly, so the problem may be occurring within the inner hair cells, the spiral ganglia of the cochlea, and/or the 8th CN fibers leading to the brainstem. For a transcript of a short interview with Dr. Berlin on ANSD, see: http://www.audiology.org/news/Pages/20120809.aspx

cont.

(Central) Auditory Processing Disorder (CAPD or APD): A central auditory processing disorder (CAPD or APD) is not related to a malfunction of the peripheral hearing mechanism. All tests of hearing sensitivity, including patient nonparticipatory hearing assessments such as otoacoustic emissions (OAE) and assessments of the movement of electrical impulses reacting to sound along neural pathways, as measured by auditory brainstem response (ABR), appear normal. Individuals with APD display a deficit in processing and understanding of auditory input. This deficit is related to neural processing of auditory stimuli but is not usually attributed to cognitive deficits. Yet, APD appears to be the culprit in some disorders in some higher order language learning (expressive and receptive) and communication skills.

While researchers understand the effects of APD, there is some discord concerning the acceptance of the actual existence of this disorder. Shemesh (2010) states, "…some professionals [are] still unconvinced that [*auditory processing disorders*] exist[s] as a separate clinical entity, [due to] poor understanding of the boundaries and overlap between APD and language or other developmental disorders, and lack of uniform accepted guidelines regarding testing and management of APD."

Recruitment: "Recruitment causes your perception of sound to be exaggerated. Even though there is only a small increase in the noise levels, sound may seem much louder, and it can distort and cause discomfort. Someone with recruitment can have problems only with specific sounds and frequencies or may have problems with all sound in general. . . . The net effect is that people who have recruitment along with their hearing loss will experience an increasingly narrow [dynamic] range between the softest sound they can hear… and the loudest sound they can comfortably tolerate. It's important to note that the configuration of a hearing aid will be affected when fitting an ear that recruits."

Hearing Loss Association of North Carolina. Retrieved from http.nchearingloss.org/recruit.htm

Summary

A variety of etiologies of hearing loss have been presented in this chapter. Both sensorineural and conductive hearing losses were categorized by their time of onset and the degree of loss. Symptoms and remediation (if appropriate) were discussed. In order to understand the ever-changing field of genetics and hearing, an overview of genetic inheritance was included in this chapter. View this chapter as the beginning, not the end, of your investigation into any specific etiology of deafness. When working with a child who is deafened by a specific etiology, the more you know about the cause and its long-term effects, the better you can serve his—the child's—needs.

Chapter 4 Food for Thought

1. In the scenario at the beginning of this chapter, roommates Margaret and Cassie suspect a specific problem that is causing roommate Natalie to have visual difficulties. What do you think this problem might be, and why would Natalie be reluctant to admit that there is a problem? Finally, what factors in the story are clues to this particular cause of visual difficulties?

2. Now that you know how to develop a Punnett square, can you predict your own chances of having attached or detached earlobes?

3. Draw a Punnett square showing a deaf father who has two recessive alleles for deafness and a hearing mother who is a carrier of that recessive allele for deafness. What are the chances that a child will be a hearing noncarrier of the recessive gene, a hearing carrier of the recessive gene, or deaf?

4. What does it mean when a genetic syndrome is said to be "variably expressed"?

5. Describe how CMV and herpes simplex II can affect the hearing of an infant/and or developing fetus.

6. Explain the disorder called presbycusis to a woman who is complaining that her husband no longer listens to her.

7. Why is it important to be extra vigilant when a child with a sensorineural hearing loss has otitis media?

Chapter 5

Can You Hear Me Now? Hearing Screenings, Testing Procedures, and Basic Interpretation

Scenario

Mrs. Cahill, the school nurse, along with Mr. Montague, the SLP, and Ms. Markup, the TOD, just completed **hearing screenings** *on over 100 children in Center Elementary's kindergarten classes. In front of them was a list of nearly 30 children who failed the screenings! They had not even tested the first and third graders yet! Mrs. Cahill remarked that it is extremely unusual for almost a third of the group to fail the state-mandated hearing screenings. She looked at the data and asked Mr. Montague and Ms. Markup for their thoughts and opinions.*

When you complete reading this chapter, you will be able to offer your own thoughts and opinions about what might be going on in this situation and what needs to happen next.

Key Vocabulary

acoustic immittance	central masking	phonetically balanced word list
acoustic immittance bridge	conditioned play audiometry	pure-tone average (PTA)
acoustic reflex arch	cross hearing	pure-tone threshold
acoustic reflex decay	distortion product otoacoustic	sound booth
acoustic reflex threshold	emissions	speech-in-noise test
air-bone gap	dynamic range	speech audiometry
air-conduction testing (AC)	electroencephalogram (EEG)	speech discrimination score
air-conduction threshold	electrophysiology	speech recognition score
asymmetrical hearing loss	endolymphatic hydrops	speech recognition testing
attenuator dial	hair cell motility	speech recognition threshold
audiogram	Hearing in Noise Test (HINT)	(SRT)
audiometer	hearing screening	speech-spectrum noise
audiometry	hearing threshold	spondee words
auditory brainstem response (ABR)	infrasound	suprathreshold
auditory-evoked potential (AEP)	interaural attenuation	transient-evoked otoacoustic
auditory steady-state response	masking	emissions
test (ASSR)	masking noise	tympanometry
bone-conduction testing	mismatch negativity (MMN)	ultrasound
bone-conduction threshold (BC)	narrow band noise	unaided threshold
bone oscillator	noise-notch audiogram	unilateral hearing loss
broadband noise	nontest ear	visual reinforcement audiometry
calibrated	otoacoustic emissions (OAE)	(VRA)
central auditory processing	otoscope	word recognition score (WRS)
testing (CAP)	P_{300}	

Hearing Sensitivity

The human ear is capable of hearing sounds between the frequencies of 20 Hz and 20,000 Hz. This is an extremely wide range of hearing, but as most people know (especially animal lovers), human hearing is not nearly as sensitive as the hearing of many animals. (See Figure 5.1 for a comparison of human hearing and the hearing of other animals.) Sounds heard below the human range of hearing are called **infrasound,** while sounds heard above the human range of hearing are called ultrasound. To give the reader some perspective, elephants hear and communicate through infrasound and can hear (and feel) frequencies as low as 14 Hz or 15 Hz. This allows them to communicate with each other from as far away as six miles, due to the very long wavelengths (Payne, Langbauer, & Thomas, 1986). Dolphins, whales, and bats hear and communicate through ultrasound and can hear frequencies up to 200,000 Hz. Mice hear some frequencies that humans hear, but they also hear higher frequencies than humans; their frequency range is 10,000 Hz to 70,000 Hz. They do not hear the lower frequencies that humans hear, but they can communicate using high frequency noises (most of which cannot be heard by humans). When a young mouse is in trouble, it can produce a signal that is as high as 40,000 Hz (Sales & Pye, 1974)!

Figure 5.1. Ranges of Human Hearing Compared to That of Other Animals

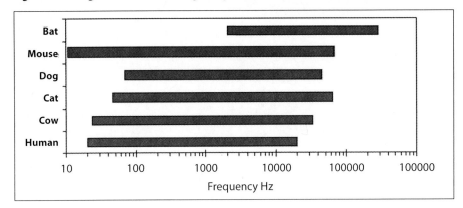

Human hearing is most sensitive to frequencies between 500 Hz and 5000 Hz, which is handy since that is the range where acoustic speech signals have the most relevant information. These frequencies are also the frequencies used during hearing screenings, specifically 500; 1,000; 2,000; and 4,000 Hz. So, although we humans can hear lower and higher frequencies, we do not have to in order to hear what we need to hear. In fact, when we listen on the telephone, we are only hearing a small range of frequencies (approximately 300 Hz to 3,400 Hz), but we can still determine who is talking to us on the other end of the line. We know whether it is our mother, a friend, or a telemarketer whom we've never talked with before.

Since we cannot only think about the frequency range of hearing, we must also discuss the intensity range of human hearing. The human ear is capable of responding to the widest range of stimuli of any of the five senses. The **dynamic range** is the range of hearing from a person's threshold (lowest level at which one can hear) to the threshold of pain. Therefore, the dynamic range of human hearing is roughly 130 to 140 dB (Yost, 2000). Additionally, the dynamic range of speech, which is said to be between 50 and 80 dB, is located in the mid-frequency region of the cochlea. This is not accidental; it is due to evolutionary advancements in which speech and hearing functions have become attuned to each other. Thus, our most sensitive hearing is in the frequency and intensity ranges of speech. We humans were "programmed" to communicate!

Although information about the frequency and intensity ranges of human hearing is interesting, this book is really about hearing *loss*. It is a person's inability to hear those ranges that concerns audiologists and other professionals working with children who have audiological needs. Therefore, this chapter describes how hearing loss is measured.

Hearing can be screened or fully evaluated at any age, from birth to 100+ years. This means that hearing can be partially evaluated to determine if hearing loss may be present, or it can be fully evaluated using several different tests and technologies to diagnose a hearing loss. Screening for hearing loss just allows the tester to determine if hearing loss is present. A hearing screening can be completed by virtually any trained individual. However, a full hearing evaluation should be done by a licensed audiologist with the purpose of determining the degree, type, and cause of the loss. This chapter will describe the equipment and testing procedures used by audiologists. The various types of hearing loss will be explained and illustrated, and the concept of "test battery" will be described. The chapter will end by comparing hearing screenings and full audiometric evaluations.

Basic Hearing Evaluation Methods
Case History

Before any formal testing takes place, an audiologist will ask many questions about a person's hearing. For children, parents and caregivers will be asked questions such as, "Is there any family history of hearing loss?" "Is there any history of ear infections?" or "Were there any pre-, peri-, or postnatal complications during pregnancy?" These answers are important to know prior to initiating any tests. The more information an audiologist can gain prior to beginning the evaluation, the better he will be at selecting the appropriate tests and interpreting the results of those tests. Table 5.1 has a more complete list of case history questions that a person may encounter when having his hearing evaluated.

Table 5.1. Routine Case History Questions

1. Have you noticed any difficulty hearing?
2. Have you noticed any fluctuating hearing loss?
3. Do you ever experience dizziness?
4. Have you noticed any noises in the ear (ringing, chirping)?
5. Do you ever experience pain in the ear?
6. Have you noticed any fullness or stuffiness in the ear?
7. Do you have any history of ear infections?
8. Have you ever been examined by an ear specialist?
9. Have you ever had ear surgery, such as tubes?
10. Have you ever had a head injury and experienced unconsciousness?
11. Have you ever taken mycins, quinine, or express aspirin?
12. Do you participate in noisy hobbies, such as race cars, ATVs, snowmobiles, or woodworking?
13. Do you ever shoot guns? Targets or hunting?
14. Do you currently have a noisy job? Does your employer abide by OSHA regulations for hearing?
15. Are you experiencing a head cold today?
16. Have you ever had measles?
17. Have you ever had mumps?
18. Have you ever had chickenpox?
19. Have you ever had scarlet fever?
20. Have you ever had diphtheria?
21. Is there a history of hearing loss in your family? If yes, who?
22. Have you ever served in the military? If yes, were you exposed to loud noise?
23. Do you use an iPod/MP3 on a daily basis?
24. Do you currently use a hearing aid? Describe.
25. Have you ever been evaluated for a hearing aid?

Figure 5.2. Example of a Handheld, Battery-Operated Otoscope, Common to Many Audiology Clinics

Otoscopy

An **otoscope,** briefly described in earlier chapters, is a device, much like a small flashlight, that is designed to direct light down the ear canal (external auditory canal) to visualize the eardrum, or tympanic membrane (see Figure 5.2). Otoscopy, or an otoscopic inspection, should be completed by the audiologist prior to any other testing. A thorough inspection of the pinna allows the audiologist to determine if any birth defects or unusual markings, such as pits or tags that might indicate a genetic hearing loss, exist. Visual inspection of the ear canal allows the audiologist to determine if any foreign objects, excessive earwax (cerumen), fungus, or infections are evident. If the ear canal is clear enough, otoscopy allows the audiologist to visualize tears (perforations), pressure equalization tubes, or growths on the tympanic membrane. In some cases of otitis media with effusion, tiny air bubbles within the fluid behind the eardrum can even be seen. In general, the audiologist looks for a clear pathway for sound to travel from the environment to the tympanic membrane, and he hopes to see a healthy, intact, pearly membrane with a "cone of light" reflecting the light of the otoscope off of it. That cone of light is a landmark (or as described in Chapter 3, a nonanatomical structure), and it allows the audiologist to know that the otoscope's light is reaching the eardrum and that things are generally in good shape.

Acoustic Immittance Measures

Acoustic immittance measures help an audiologist to identify abnormalities of the auditory system, particularly of the eardrum and middle ear system. However, immittance measures are not measures of hearing. Acoustic immittance measures are often called impedance audiometry or middle ear measurements, but those terms are not entirely accurate. Since the word *immittance* is used as a catch-all term and encompasses the concepts of impedance,

Figure 5.3. Example of an Immittance Bridge Common to Many Audiology Clinics

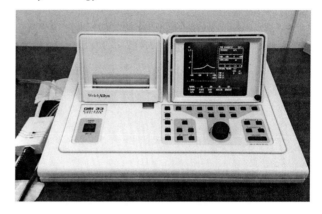

compliance, resistance, reactance, and admittance (all physics terms beyond the scope of this book), an **acoustic immittance bridge,** or meter, takes measurements in the plane of the eardrum with three measures: static acoustic immittance, **tympanometry,** and acoustic reflex. Figure 5.3 illustrates an immittance bridge common to many audiology clinics.

Static Acoustic Immittance. Static acoustic immittance measures the ease of flow of acoustic energy through the middle ear system. This measure is usually recorded in cubic centimeters (cm^3) or milliliters (ml), with low values indicating a stiffening pathology in the middle ear (such as fluid surrounding the ossicles) and abnormally high values indicating an overly mobile system (which could be disarticulation of the ossicular chain or a healed perforation in the eardrum).

Tympanometry. Tympanometry is a measurement of the mobility of the middle ear system when air pressure in the ear canal is varied from +200 daPa to –400 daPa (decapascals; a unit of pressure). A probe is placed into the ear canal, and the equipment has the ability to change the pressure to move the eardrum, produce a tone, and then measure that tone as it "bounces" off the tympanic membrane. Tympanometry can be measured with a single frequency tone (226 Hz or 660 Hz), or it can be measured with multiple frequencies (226 Hz, 339 Hz, 452 Hz, 565 Hz, on up to 1243 Hz). If only a 226 Hz probe tone is used, five predictable patterns will emerge which can be typed as A, B, C, A_s, A_D/A_{DD}, or described as normal, flat, negative, shallow, or deep (see Figure 5.4). Many clinical audiologists rely heavily on these patterns, or graphs, and use the information obtained from the tracings to confirm or negate information seen on other audiometric tests. If multifrequency tympanometry is used, a different set of predictable patterns will emerge. These four patterns are conductance (G_a), admittance (Y_a), susceptance (B_a), and phase angle (φ_a). Although it has been said that multifrequency tympanometry can improve diagnostic capabilities, not many clinicians opt to use it. However, with infants under four months of age, multifrequency tympanometry can be more effective in detecting middle ear fluid. Therefore, a pediatric audiologist is probably more likely to use multifrequency tympanometry than other clinical audiologists.

Figure 5.4 summarizes the information seen from the five tracings obtained with single frequency tympanometry. Tympanometry can tell an audiologist how well a child's eardrum moves and if a child's eustachian tube is opening and closing the way it should. Tympanometry can also tell an audiologist if there is a hole in the eardrum (caused by either a perforation or a pressure equalization tube) or if there is fluid or a mass growing behind the eardrum. However, as we will discuss later in this chapter, audiologists never rely on information from only one test measure.

Figure 5.4. Tympanogram Types and Configurations Seen During Single Frequency Tympanometry

Type	Description	Possible Cause	Tracing
A	Normally shaped peak in the vicinity of 0 daPa	Normal middle ear system; no perforation in eardrum	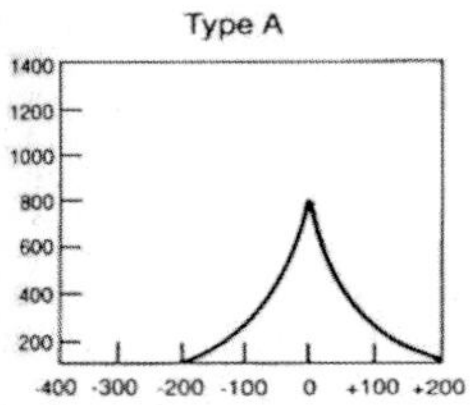
A$_S$	Normal shape, but height is significantly decreased or shallow	• Ossicular chain fixation • Scarred or thickened eardrum • Otosclerosis	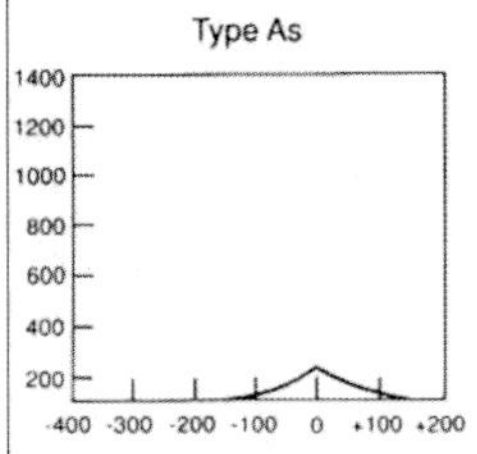
A$_D$ {A$_{DD}$}	Normal shape, but height is significantly increased or deep	Flaccid eardrum {Ossicular discontinuity/disarticulation}	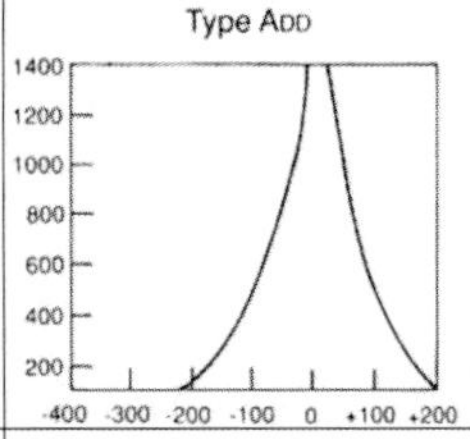
B	Essentially flat, no peak evident, but normal ear canal volume	Otitis media with effusion	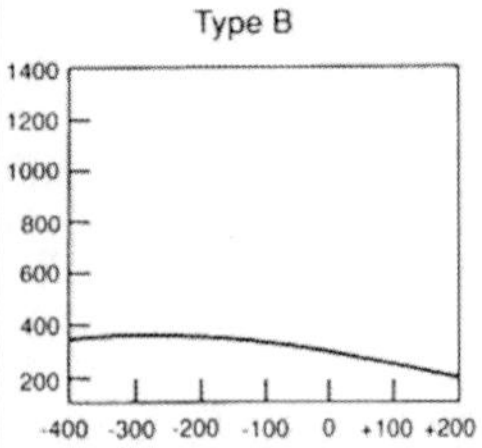
C	Normally shaped peak, but it is located in the substantially negative range ($\geq$ 150 daPa)	• Eustachian tube dysfunction • Immerging or resolving otitis media with effusion	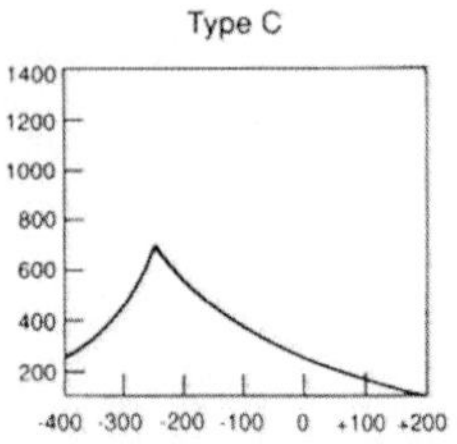

124

Tympanometry should be used with other audiometric tests to "paint the whole picture" for determining the cause of a person's hearing loss.

Acoustic Reflex Testing. The two middle ear muscles introduced in Chapter 3 (the stapedial and tensor tympani muscles) contract in a sonomotor response when relatively intense sounds are heard. The tensor tympani muscle contracts with other head and neck muscles as part of the startle response to high-intensity sound, while the stapedial muscle contracts to high-intensity sound alone and is innervated by the seventh cranial nerve, the facial nerve [CNVII]. Sounds that activate the stapedial muscle contraction are about 70 to 80 dBSL and are usually either **narrow band noises** or tones. This means that if a person hears a 1000 Hz tone around 5 dBHL, then the stapedial muscle will contract around 75 to 85 dBHL. (See Chapter 2 for descriptions of dBSL and dBHL.) The stapedial reflex is frequency-specific, so the muscle contracts at slightly different levels depending on the frequency of the tone. More interesting is the fact that, when sound to one ear elicits an acoustic reflex, the muscle will contract in both that ear and the opposite ear. When the muscle contracts, there is a temporary increase in middle ear impedance, and that increase in impedance can be measured in both ears by the immittance bridge. The contraction is viewed on the screen of the bridge and the printout as a dip in the tracing (see Figure 5.5).

Most immittance bridges will have two modes for testing acoustic reflexes: **acoustic reflex threshold** and **acoustic reflex decay**. The acoustic reflex threshold is simply the lowest level at which the stapedial muscle will contract to the eliciting tone. Thresholds are useful for determining levels of hearing, but in and of themselves, they are not the same as a pure-tone hearing test. The information from the acoustic reflex threshold can be extrapolated, or inferred back, to the level of the auditory threshold to help the audiologist determine if a hearing loss is present. For example, as noted earlier in this section, if the acoustic reflex threshold at 1000 Hz is obtained at 85 dBHL, then the audiologist can estimate that the **pure-tone threshold** at 1000 Hz is normal because it should be in the 0 to 10 dBHL range.

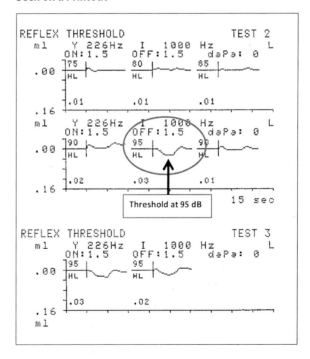

Figure 5.5. Example of the Acoustic Reflex Threshold Seen on a Printout

Audiologists use the information obtained from the threshold tracing (dip) seen on the same side as the ear in which the tone is presented (ipsilateral reflex) and from the tracing seen on the opposite side of the ear in which the tone is presented (contralateral reflex). Because there are anatomical structures and pathways that send the signal up to the level of the brainstem and there are structures and pathways that send the signal back down to the middle ear, these ipsilateral and contralateral reflexes are said to be part of an acoustic reflex arch. The information seen from muscle contractions within the **acoustic reflex arch** helps an audiologist determine if a person has hearing loss, and using the ipsilateral and contralateral pathways also helps the audiologist to determine if a pathology exists in anatomical structures that are in the auditory pathway beyond the cochlea (a retrocochlear pathology).

Information obtained from the reflex arch helps determine retrocochlear pathology, but so does the reflex decay test. Like the reflex threshold test, a loud signal is used to elicit the stapedial muscle contraction; however, the signal for the reflex decay test is presented at a **suprathreshold level.** That is, the signal is presented above the level at which the acoustic reflex was obtained, so it is more intense and perceived as louder than the threshold level. This suprathreshold signal is presented for 10 seconds, and the audiologist watches the dip in the tracing to see if the muscle can stay contracted (see Figure 5.6). You see, in the normal, healthy ear, the reflex will continue to stay contracted for as long as 10 seconds because all the structures and pathways are intact and functioning properly in the reflex arch. So, if the structures in the reflex arch are not healthy, or they have a pathology or disorder, the stapedial muscle will not be able to stay contracted. The muscle will fatigue; see the sidebar "Analogy for Acoustic Reflex Decay" for a good analogy describing this situation. Abnormal findings for the reflex decay test are defined as a decrease of 50 percent or more in the amplitude (depth) of the dip in the tracing during that 10-second time period. A person would be said to have a retrocochlear finding if reflex decay is observed, and that person would be sent immediately to a medical specialist, such as an otologist or otolaryngologist (ear, nose, and throat doctor).

Figure 5.6. The Acoustic Reflex Decay Test Seen on a Printout

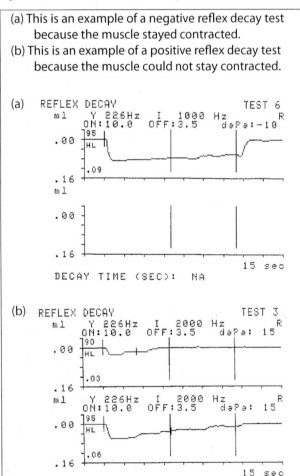

(a) This is an example of a negative reflex decay test because the muscle stayed contracted.
(b) This is an example of a positive reflex decay test because the muscle could not stay contracted.

To summarize, static acoustic immittance and tympanometry tell an audiologist about the integrity of the eardrum and middle ear system. The acoustic reflex tests allow an audiologist to determine how much hearing loss a person may have, what kind of loss that person may have (conductive, sensorineural, or retrocochlear), and if the auditory system up to the level of the brainstem is healthy or disordered. However, even with all this information, an audiologist does not rely on tympanometry and acoustic reflex measures alone.

Audiometric Testing

Before we can go any further, we must take time to describe the equipment on which hearing is measured, the graph on which **hearing thresholds** (and hearing loss) are plotted, and the protocol by which hearing loss is measured. Therefore, we must describe the audiometer, **audiogram**, and audiometry.

Audiometry is the science of measuring hearing acuity, and it involves obtaining hearing thresholds at differing frequencies. Hearing thresholds are the lowest sound levels at which a person can detect a tone approximately 50 percent of the time. These thresholds are plotted out on an audiogram to determine if a person's hearing is normal or disordered. An **audiometer** is the piece of equipment designed to test a person's hearing thresholds. Some audiometers are very basic and have limitations to what they can test. A screening audiometer would be an example of a basic audiometer (see Figure 5.7). Basic/screening audiometers typically have (1) a frequency selector dial, (2) an **attenuator dial** or volume control, (3) an interrupter dial or tone presenter switch, and (4) an output selector dial to determine which earphone is being used. Screening audiometers require some training, but are ultimately very easy to use. Other audiometers are more sophisticated and have the capability of performing more tests and

Analogy for Acoustic Reflex Decay

The concept of acoustic reflex decay is similar to that of a person's arm muscle being required to hold a bucketful of water out to the side for a long period of time. Most people with normal muscle structure and central nervous system capabilities can hold that full bucket out to their sides for at least a 30-second time frame with little or no discomfort, without having the arm fall down to their side. But for a person with a condition such as multiple sclerosis (a degenerative condition of the fatty and protective covering of the nerve fibers of the central nervous system), holding a bucketful of water out to the side for 30 seconds may be impossible; that person's arm muscles will not be able to hold the contraction for that amount of time. Therefore, if the acoustic reflex cannot remain contracted for the 10-second time frame (which would be indicated with positive reflex decay), then a retrocochlear pathology would be suspected, and the audiologist would refer the person to a physician for a complete medical workup.

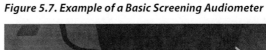

Figure 5.7. Example of a Basic Screening Audiometer

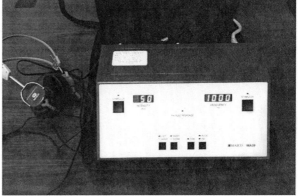

Figure 5.8. Example of a Diagnostic or Clinical Audiometer

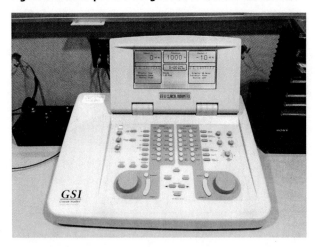

evaluating the two ears simultaneously. A diagnostic audiometer would be an example of a more sophisticated audiometer (see Figure 5.8). This type of audiometer has all the dials and switches listed in the description of a screening audiometer, in addition to speech testing capabilities with two individual channels. Also, diagnostic audiometers can be connected to CD players for recorded voice testing capabilities. Diagnostic audiometers require very specific training for proper use. But whether the audiometer is simple or sophisticated, there are basic components that must exist in order for the audiometer to test hearing. These components include (1) a frequency selector dial to select different frequencies, or tones, for testing, (2) an attenuator dial to increase and decrease the intensity (volume) of the different tones, (3) an interrupter dial to allow the different frequency tones to be presented to the listener, and (4) an output selector dial to determine whether the tones will be presented through the earphone for **air-conduction testing** or through the **bone oscillator** for **bone-conduction testing.** More sophisticated audiometers will have the ability to produce **masking** noise for masking purposes and speech signals for **speech recognition testing.** (These terms and concepts will be described more fully later in this chapter.)

Figure 5.9. Audiometric Sound Booth

The two rooms are separated by a thick wall. One room houses the audiometer and audiologist, the other room houses the patient.

For clinical, diagnostic purposes, a **sound booth** (see Figure 5.9) must be used to obtain threshold measures that are in accordance with American National Standards Institute (ANSI) standards. ANSI standards dictate the background noise levels that are allowable in a testing situation (ANSI, 1991). With the double-insulated walls and door of the sound booth, audiologists are able to test threshold levels accurately and with minimal audible distractions. With a two-room sound booth setup, the audiologist and audiometer are on one side of a window, while the person being tested is seated on the other side of the window in a room in which few external noises are able to be heard during the testing.

Audiogram.

The audiogram is a graph used to record the hearing threshold levels from a person's two ears. In addition to these thresholds, other test results may be recorded (e.g., immittance results, speech recognition thresholds, **word recognition scores**) and written alongside the hearing thresholds so that more

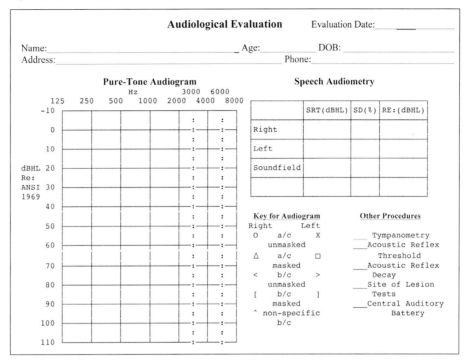

Figure 5.10. Audiogram with Key for Symbols Used during Audiometric Testing

than just the graph will be present on the audiogram. Most audiograms have a key on them with all the symbols depicting the responses from the two ears. Figure 5.10 shows an audiogram with a key depicting symbols recommended for use by the American Speech-Language-Hearing Association (ASHA). The intensity level (in dBHL) of each signal is represented along the left side of the graph and usually ranges from –10 dBHL up to 110 dBHL in 5-dB increments. The frequencies of the tones are represented along the top of the graph and usually range from 125 Hz up to 8000 Hz. There are additional boxes or tables to the right of or underneath this graph in which the other test results are recorded.

Pure-Tone Thresholds.

Pure-tone audiometry is the foundation of any hearing evaluation. Pure tones were described in Chapter 2 as the sound that is created by a single vibrating object and represented with a sinusoid, or sine wave. Pure tones can be transmitted either through air-conduction (a/c or AC) or bone-conduction (b/c or BC) methods. That is, pure tones that are sent from the audiometer through an earphone (either supra-aural earphone

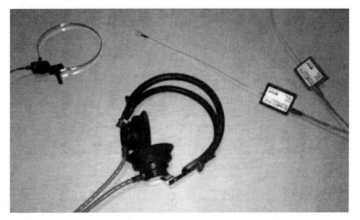

Figure 5.11. Supra-Aural Earphones (center), Insert Earphones (right), and a Bone Oscillator (left)

or insert earphone) are used to obtain **air-conduction thresholds**, and the bone oscillator (or bone vibrator) is used to send the pure tones through the skull to obtain **bone-conduction thresholds** (see Figure 5.11).

As an audiologist tests a person's hearing with earphones, he will record the air-conduction thresholds for the right ear with red Os and for the left ear with blue or black Xs. (An easy pneumonic to remember this is to think of the 3 Rs: red, right, round.) As an audiologist tests a person's hearing with the bone oscillator, he will record the bone-conduction thresholds for the right ear with a < (bracket opening to the right) and a > (bracket opening to the left) for the left ear (see Figure 5.12). It is important to understand the difference between air- and bone-conduction thresholds because they indicate how hearing loss is typed (conductive, sensorineural, or mixed) and to what degree (minimal, mild, moderate, moderately severe, severe, or profound). These concepts will be described in more detail later in this chapter.

Figure 5.12. Audiogram with Air-Conduction Thresholds and Bone-Conduction Thresholds Indicated

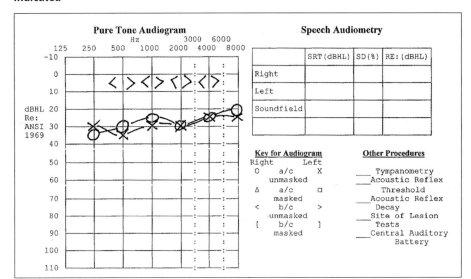

It is easiest to think of air-conduction thresholds by envisioning the lowest levels of hearing plotted onto the audiogram when the signal (tone) has to travel through the outer ear and middle ear to get to the inner ear (specifically the cochlea). The conduction of sound through these three sections of the ear is referred to as air-conduction testing and, if the cause of the hearing loss is found in the outer or middle ears, the loss is said to be conductive in nature. An earphone that fits over the pinna or inserts into the ear canal has to be used to obtain air-conduction thresholds.

Bone-conduction thresholds are the lowest levels of hearing plotted on the audiogram when the signal is presented directly to the cochlea by vibrating the skull that houses the cochlea. The tones do not have to travel through the outer or middle ears; they are picked up directly by the cochlea and are thus referred to as bone-conducted in nature. It takes a special bone oscillator put onto the mastoid bone behind the pinna or strapped to the forehead to produce the vibrations that act on the skull and stimulate the two cochleae directly to obtain bone-conduction thresholds.

130

In addition to air- and bone-conduction threshold symbols, you may see an audiogram with an *A* placed at specific frequencies and intensities. These *A* thresholds are the lowest level at which a person heard those frequencies with one or two hearing aids on his ears, and the testing is done in the sound field with the speakers presenting the tones. Any **unaided threshold** that is obtained in the sound field through the speakers (maybe because the patient refused to wear the earphones) would have the threshold marked with an *SF*. Another symbol seen frequently with the deaf/hard of hearing population is the *NR* or downward pointing arrow dangling off of the X or O (see Figure 5.13). All of these symbols refer to the frequencies in which there was "no response" from the person. So, as you can see, there are many different symbols that represent different thresholds on an audiogram. Now let's go back to describe the two most basic, most readily identifiable thresholds.

Figure 5.13. Audiogram with Air-Conduction Thresholds Indicating a "No Response" from the Higher Frequencies in Both Ears

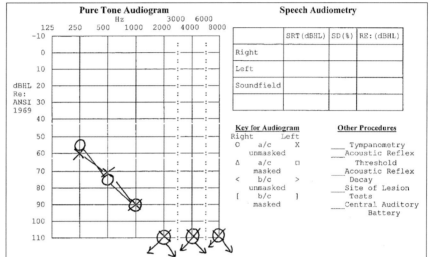

Obtaining Pure-Tone Thresholds. Audiologists follow specific protocols for obtaining pure-tone thresholds, and many may choose to follow the American Speech-Language-Hearing Association's 2005 guidelines (ASHA, 2005). These guidelines recommend the audiologist start the test at 1000 Hz (an easily audible signal for most listeners) by presenting the tone at 30 dBHL. If the person raises his hand (or presses a button or puts a block in a bucket), then the tone must be above the person's threshold and the action (hand raise, button push, or toss of the block) indicates that the tone was heard. If the person does not respond to the tone, the audiologist must raise the intensity of the tone to 50 dBHL and present it at that level. Again, if the person responds, then the audiologist knows that he is above the person's threshold. If the person does not respond, then the audiologist increases the intensity of the signal in 10 dB increments until the person responds.

Once the person has responded to the signal (tone) and the audiologist knows that he is above the person's threshold, the audiologist will begin a "bracketing" approach to obtaining the threshold. That means that the audiologist will decrease the tone by 10 dB increments until the person no longer responds. When the person does not respond (meaning he did not hear the tone), the audiologist will raise the level of the tone by 5 dB. If the person does not respond, the audiologist raises the level of the tone by another 5 dB, and so on. Once the person responds to the tone, the audiologist will decrease the intensity again by 10 dB and the process will begin once more with the audiologist raising the tone in 5 dB increments until the person responds. With this up-and-down (or bracketing) method, the audiologist can obtain the level at which the person responds to the tone at least 50 percent of the time (albeit, in most cases, the person really is responding 33 percent [2 out of 3 times] or 75 percent [3 out of 4 times]), to satisfy the audiologist's criterion for accepting a response as a threshold.

After obtaining the threshold for the 1000 Hz tone, the audiologist will use the bracketing approach (also referred to as the Hughson-Westlake approach) to obtain the thresholds from the middle and higher frequencies, moving next to 2000, 4000, and then 8000 Hz. Depending on the person and the reason for testing, the audiologist may also test 3000 and 6000 Hz at this time. For example, if the audiologist suspects a noise-induced hearing loss, she will test 3000 and 6000 Hz to look for the **"noise notch,"** or dip in hearing thresholds, that is often seen in this higher region of the audiogram when intense sound levels have damaged the cochlea. After testing the higher frequencies, the audiologist will retest the threshold at 1000 Hz (to make sure the person fully understood the directions and the initial threshold was accurate) and then test 500, 250, and, in some cases, 125 Hz. So, once the audiologist has tested all the frequencies and plotted all the thresholds for air-conduction results, there will be X and O symbols plotted along the horizontal lines at each individual frequency represented by the vertical lines (see Figure 5.12).

Usually the audiologist will test the "better" ear first, or the ear that was described by the person during the case history as having the least amount of trouble hearing. Many audiologists will use a pulsing tone instead of a steady tone, because research has shown that patients report an increased awareness of the tone when it is pulsed. In fact, people with tinnitus (ringing or noises in the ears) are able to pick out the test tone from their tinnitus more easily if the tone is pulsed.

Pure-tone testing with the bone oscillator is performed in the same manner when obtaining bone-conduction thresholds. The bracketing approach is used, and the audiologist moves from the middle frequencies up to the high frequencies, then back to the middle frequencies and down to the lowest frequencies (that is, 1000, 2000, 4000, 1000, and 500 Hz only). Once again, the audiologist will have tested all the frequencies and plotted all the thresholds for bone-conduction results, so there will now be < and > symbols plotted along the horizontal lines at each individual frequency represented by the vertical lines, as can be seen in Figure 5.12.

Due to the vibratory constraints of the oscillator and the fact that very intense signals sent through the bone oscillator can be felt instead of heard, only certain frequencies and certain intensity levels can actually be tested for accurate bone-conduction thresholds. At the present, with the audiometers being so technologically advanced, the audiologist rarely has to know all of the testing limitations. The equipment does not allow the attenuator dials to go any higher than the oscillator can function appropriately. However, if unusual (or unlikely) results are being obtained, the audiologist has to have a sound understanding of why the results are not consistent with normal practices.

Although obtaining a threshold for a pure tone is neither magical nor the equivalent of performing brain surgery, obtaining audiometric thresholds is outside the scope of practice for speech-language pathologists and other professionals, and therefore, should not be attempted. Obtaining screening levels for hearing, which will be described more fully at the end of this chapter, is not outside the scope of practice for a speech-language pathologist or teacher of the deaf and can be performed by anyone properly trained to do so.

Speech Recognition Thresholds. Most audiologists will perform **speech audiometry** measures after obtaining pure-tone air-conduction thresholds. They hold off on testing bone-conduction thresholds until after speech testing is completed, because it keeps them from having to go back and forth into the test booth and switching the earphones more than once.

Speech-recognition thresholds, also known as speech-reception thresholds or SRTs, are used with pure-tone thresholds to help the audiologist determine the degree and type of hearing loss a person has. The SRT (because it is a *threshold*) is the intensity level at which a person can identify words 50 percent of the time. This test serves as a means for checking the validity of the pure-tone thresholds, and it helps the audiologist know at which level to test the person's speech-recognition abilities. Because the SRT is derived from speech (words), it should correlate closely to the person's **pure-tone average (PTA)** in the same ear. The pure-tone average is usually a three-frequency average obtained from the thresholds at 500, 1000, and 2000 Hz (see sidebar on obtaining pure-tone average); therefore, it contains most of the frequencies seen in the speech signal. If the SRT and PTA are not within 10 dB of each other, the audiologist would have to question the test results. He would have to determine if he did something wrong, if the person did not understand the testing instructions, if his calculations were wrong, or (more likely) if the person was giving intentionally incorrect responses that suggest a functional, or nonorganic, form of hearing loss. Refer to the sidebar "Why Would a Person Intentionally Respond Incorrectly during a Hearing Evaluation?" for some reasons why people might do this.

Figure 5.14. Lists of Spondees and Monosyllabic Speech Stimuli

Below are examples of spondee (two-syllable, equally-stressed) words used with speech recognition threshold testing and open-ended monosyllabic words used after a carrier phrase to obtain speech recognition scores.

SPONDEE WORDS	MONOSYLLABIC WORDS	
Cowboy	Pick	Jam
Airplane	Base	Poor
Toothbrush	Mess	An
Birthday	Judge	Now
Oatmeal	Ripe	Not
Inkwell	Food	Knee
Armchair	Near	All
Northwest	Perch	Ham
Mushroom	Dodge	Dad
Woodwork	Chair	Thin
Greyhound	Turn	Camp
Hardware	Gin	Bathe
Backbone	Goal	Thing
Headlight	Size	Wire
Outside	Mode	Ate
Cookbook	Met	Flat
Whitewash	Fat	Farm
Pancake	Rain	Bin
Baseball	Witch	Glove
Mousetrap	Back	Three
Sunset	Red	Toy
Shotgun	Lip	Clothes
Cough drop	Bee	Pass
Daylight	See	Hurt
Streetcar	Low	Bead
Bluejay	Choose	Neck
Ashtray	Clown	Own
Dollhouse	Blind	Pond
Downtown	Leave	Grab
Railroad	Way	Rose
Cupcake	Cars	Loud
Hot dog	Tan	Nuts

Speech recognition thresholds are obtained with a list of two-syllable, equally stressed **spondee words**, such as *baseball, cowboy, hot dog,* and *airplane* (see Figure 5.14 for more examples). As with the pure-tone thresholds, the audiologist will decrease the level of her voice in 10 dB increments, using the microphone input of the audiometer and the attenuator dial. She will decrease the intensity of her voice to a level at which the person stops responding to two consecutive words on the list. Then the audiologist will increase the level of her voice in 5 dB increments (or some audiologists prefer 2 dB increments) until the person starts to respond to the words again, indicating that a threshold has been obtained. A similar bracketing approach to obtaining this threshold is used with words, as it was with tones. The detailed description of SRT testing can be found in the ASHA *Guidelines for Determining Threshold Level for Speech* (ASHA, 1988).

Calculating and Obtaining a Pure-Tone Average (PTA)

To obtain a three-frequency pure-tone average, the audiologist adds the patient's thresholds at 500, 1000, and 2000 Hz and then divides that number by 3. That PTA should correlate, or match up with, the patient's speech recognition threshold (SRT) by being within +/-10 dB of the SRT. Therefore, for the audiogram below, the PTA for the left ear would be calculated: 25 + 35 + 45 = 105/3 = 35 dBHL

Because the SRT for the left ear is 30 dBHL, the PTA and SRT are said to match.

If one of the thresholds is very different from the other two (if one is an "outlier"), then a two-frequency PTA should be calculated in order to be more accurate. Therefore, because the right ear has a very different outlier threshold at 2000 Hz (65 dBHL), the PTA for the right ear should use a two-frequency calculation, and the PTA would be calculated: 15 + 20 = 35/2 = 17.5 dBHL

Because the SRT for the right ear is 20 dBHL, the PTA and SRT are said to match.

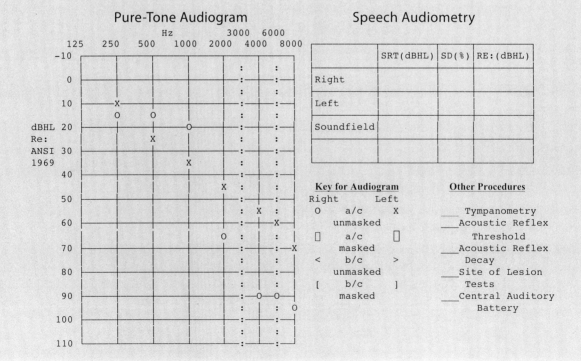

Why Would a Person Intentionally Respond Incorrectly during a Hearing Evaluation?

It may seem odd, but at some point during their careers, audiologists come across individuals who intentionally give incorrect responses on their hearing tests. These people are referred to as malingerers by many audiologists, but because that term implies that the patient is untrustworthy and a liar, it is best to refer to a person who intentionally falsifies her audiometric results as exhibiting a functional, nonorganic, exaggerated, erroneous, or false hearing loss.

There are many reasons why a person falsifies or exaggerates audiologic test results, but those reasons can usually be summed up as being due to (1) wanting attention, and (2) wanting monetary gain. The person has to perceive herself as obtaining something of value for faking the loss. To a child, that may be obtaining Mommy or Daddy's attention or getting better treatment from a teacher. To an adult, that may be obtaining financial gain from a lawsuit or workman's comp case.

Audiologists usually don't have a hard time identifying someone trying to intentionally fake a hearing loss, for a couple of reasons. The first reason includes the "test battery" concept referred to in this chapter. When a person fakes a hearing loss, it is nearly impossible to get results that correlate with each other when several tests are used. No one can accurately give pure-tone results that match the speech recognition thresholds that match the pure-tone average that match the tympanometric results; it is just too difficult.

The second reason audiologists can easily identify someone faking a hearing loss is because many special tests exist for just such a purpose. Any audiologist worth her weight in salt will use special tests such as the Stenger test, the Lombard test, ascending threshold searches, acoustic reflex thresholds, and auditory evoked potentials to help identify a functional or exaggerated loss.

Lastly, because it is quite difficult to consistently know when to raise your hand and when not to respond at a particular frequency at a specific decibel level, most people are not successful at faking audiometric thresholds. If you get a chance to take a hearing test, and you actually have normal hearing, tell the audiologist that you're going to try to fake a hearing loss and you'll find how difficult this really is.

Speech Recognition Scores. Speech recognition scores, also known as **speech discrimination scores** (SDS) or word recognition scores (WRS), are used to help the audiologist determine the person's ability to recognize or discriminate words in a quiet listening environment. Unlike the SRT, the speech recognition score uses **phonetically balanced word lists** presented at a suprathreshold level. That means, the audiologist presents the list of words at a level above the person's threshold level so that the words are easily heard. In fact, the speech recognition testing is typically done 30 dBSL or 40 dBSL above the person's SRT. Therefore, if the audiologist obtained a SRT for the right ear at 35 dBHL, then he will add either 30 or 40 dBSL to that level to present the list of words at a level of 65 dBHL or 75 dBHL. That sensation level is plenty loud for a person to be able to repeat back words without having the intensity of the signal creating a problem with hearing.

The speech recognition scores are given in percentages (%), unlike the SRTs, which were thresholds (dBHL). For speech recognition testing, the audiologist presents a 25- or 50-word list of short, one-syllable words (such as *pick, list, my,* or *puff*) following the carrier phrase, "Say the word _____" or "You will say _____." The carrier phrase alerts the person to the fact that a word is coming up and he must repeat the word back to the audiologist. A complete list of 50 words is said to be "phonetically balanced," meaning (1) each list of 50 words has all the speech sounds contained within the English language, and (2) these sounds occur in the same proportions as the phonemes heard in everyday conversations. The words are presented as an open set, meaning that there is equal probability of any single-syllable word in the English language coming up next on the list and that there is no way a person can simply guess what word is going to be presented next (see Figure 5.14). There are many word lists that can be used by audiologists to test speech recognition abilities. Some of these lists include the Northwestern University Auditory Test #6 (NU6), the Central Institute for the Deaf – Word List 22 (CID-W22), and the Phonetically Balanced–Kindergarten (PB-K) word list. Each audiologist decides for himself if he is going to test patients using "live voice" or "recorded" techniques. There are arguments for the use of each presentation format, but ultimately it is the audiologist's own preference that determines which format of presentation is used. Whether the audiologist uses recorded or live voice methods, a simple percentage score is obtained for each of the patient's ears. That is, if a person's right ear is given a list of 50 words and he is able to repeat 30 of those 50 words correctly back to the audiologist, then the score for that ear would be 60 percent (30/50). Likewise, if only a half list of 25 words were given to the left ear, and the patient was able to repeat back all but 4 of them correctly, then the score for that ear would be 84 percent (21/25).

As with pure-tone thresholds, obtaining SRTs and speech reception scores is outside the scope of practice for the speech-language pathologist and other professionals. Audiologists are trained to ensure that the speech testing is **calibrated** appropriately, and if a live-voice format is used, the audiologist has been taught how to monitor the volume unit (VU) meter appropriately to ensure accuracy of the test results. These considerations, along with proper training for providing instructions to patients, all factor into the reliability of speech recognition test results.

Speech-in-Noise Testing. When audiometric testing is being performed with the intent of properly fitting amplification or hearing aids, the audiologist will also put the patient through a **speech-in-noise test,** such as SIN, QuickSIN, or **HINT** (Killion, Niquette, Gudmundsen, Revit, & Banerjee, 2004; Nillson, Soli, & Sullivan, 1994). These tests are used because people with hearing loss almost always report problems hearing in background noise. They rarely report having a problem listening in a quiet environment or when only one speaker is conversing with them in a quiet setting. Speech-in-noise tests allow the audiologist to manipulate the signal-to-noise ratio and obtain a patient's speech recognition scores in more realistic listening conditions, such as everyday listening environments. The tests are recorded materials that use background noise (such as **broadband noise** or **speech-spectrum noise**) and include most frequencies heard in speech; or the materials may be more complex, such as recorded cafeteria noise or multi-talker babble. Information gained by the audiologist during this additional testing is very useful for fitting amplification and determining management strategies. These tests also help the audiologist decide whether or not additional diagnostic testing (such as **central auditory processing testing**) is warranted.

Masking. It is beyond the scope of this textbook to go into detail about the procedures and theories behind masking; however, we must discuss this concept from the standpoint of (1) the symbols one may see on an audiogram, and (2) the fact that without the use of masking in cases of asymmetrical or **unilateral hearing loss,** pure tone and speech thresholds would not be accurate. Suffice it to say that masking procedures are complicated and require a working knowledge of such concepts as **interaural attenuation, cross hearing,** and **central masking.** Most audiology textbooks have entire chapters covering the masking procedures, and masking is a concept that many audiology graduate students have spent sleepless nights trying to fully grasp and prepare themselves for when seeing patients with unilateral hearing loss. But for our purposes, we will simply describe what masking is, why it is used, and how it shows up on an audiogram.

First of all, **masking noise** is used by audiologists to prevent the **nontest ear** (meaning the better-hearing ear) from hearing the tones that are being presented to the test ear, or the poorer ear. One unusual, but interesting, fact about bone-conduction testing and the cochlea is that vibrations of the skull result in bone-conducted stimulation of both inner ears. This means that without masking, the audiologist does not know which cochlea is responding to the signal during bone-conduction testing.

Masking noise is usually a narrow band of noise (which sounds a lot like the white noise described in Chapter 2) or speech noise (which contains only the frequencies found in speech). The noise is presented to the nontest ear to ensure that it is not hearing for the other ear and contributing to the patient's responses. The need for masking is based on two important facts. If an intense signal is presented to one ear via an earphone, that signal may cross to the opposite ear by vibrating the skull (bone conduction) or by traveling around the head to the other ear (air conduction). Also, bone-conducted signals can stimulate both cochleae at the same time, even at low intensity levels, so neither ear is free from the possibility of hearing a bone-conducted signal from the other side of the head. Therefore, using masking noise elevates the threshold of the nontest ear and eliminates the problems mentioned earlier by keeping the nontest ear from participating in the test.

If masking is used during testing, the audiologist will indicate this by changing the air- and/or bone-conduction threshold symbols. That is, if masking is used when air-conduction thresholds are being obtained, then the X and O for the unmasked thresholds will be changed to a

□ and Δ, respectively, to indicate that the other ear had masking noise placed in it while the threshold was being obtained. Also, the masked bone-conduction symbols would be changed from the < and > to [and], respectively. The changing of symbols allows anyone reading the audiogram on a later date to feel confident that the threshold for that ear was obtained without the possibility of the sensitivity of the other ear crossing over the head and chipping in to make the person respond inaccurately. You may be thinking to yourself that if you were hearing a tone in one ear, you would know exactly which ear you were hearing it in. You may think that there is no way an audiologist could be testing one ear and you would be responding as if you heard it from the other ear, but you would be mistaken in both cases. Unilateral and **asymmetrical hearing loss,** especially when the signal is loud enough to vibrate the skull, creates very odd sensations and variable responses in people. Masking must be used to obtain accurate threshold results in these cases. The sidebar "Why Is Masking So Important?" further explains the value of masking during a hearing test.

Why Is Masking So Important?

There would be nothing worse for an audiologist than to record inaccurate thresholds on an audiogram for a patient who has unilateral or asymmetrical hearing loss. Doing so would be equivalent to the situation in which a radiologist provided ultrasound results for his patient's right breast or lung, when in reality the results were from the left breast or lung. Ultimately, a surgeon might decide to remove the affected breast or lung, even though it was the body part from the other side that needed to be removed! Therefore, an audiologist always needs to provide accurate information from the two ears because the audiometric results may lead to amplification or surgery for the wrong ear.

How Pure-Tone Thresholds Are Used to Describe Hearing Loss. Now that we have discussed the concepts of pure tone air-conduction and bone-conduction thresholds, and we have introduced you to the symbols used to depict those forms of testing, we need to describe how hearing loss is presented on an audiogram and how the thresholds allow us to determine the degree of hearing loss and whether a loss is conductive, sensorineural, or mixed. In Figure 5.10, you saw the symbols mentioned earlier for both air- and bone-conduction testing. All good audiograms should have a key that presents all of the possible symbols used for testing purposes, so that memorizing the symbols is not necessarily mandatory. Being very familiar with the symbols will help to read an audiogram efficiently, however.

First of all, to determine the degree, or amount, of hearing loss, one must realize that the left side of the audiogram displays the intensity level in decibels hearing level (dBHL). There are six categories of hearing loss for adults and seven categories of hearing loss for children. The six categories for adults are: normal, mild, moderate, moderately severe, severe, and profound. A seventh category is added for children between the normal and mild categories, and this category is referred to as slight or minimal hearing loss. Table 5.2 lists the classifications of hearing loss for both adults and children and describes the effects on speech recognition caused by those degrees of loss.

Table 5.2. Hearing Loss Classifications for Adults and Children Shown in Relation to Speech Recognition Abilities

ADULT		
Range of Thresholds	**Classification of Hearing**	**Speech Recognition Abilities**
-10–25 dBHL	Normal/Typical	No significant problems hearing faint speech
26–40 dBHL	Mild loss	Problems hearing faint speech only
41–55 dBHL	Moderate loss	Daily problems hearing speech at normal conversational levels
56–70 dBHL	Moderately severe loss	Daily problems hearing speech at loud levels
71–89 dBHL	Severe loss	Can only understand shouted or amplified speech
≥90 dBHL	Profound loss	Obtains little understanding from even amplified speech

CHILD		
Range of Thresholds	**Classification of Hearing**	**Speech Recognition Abilities**
-10–15 dBHL	Normal/Typical	No significant problems for hearing faint speech or developing language
16–25 dBHL	Minimal/Slight loss	• Some problems hearing faint speech (unvoiced consonants) • Possible auditory inattention and language delays
26–40 dBHL	Mild loss	• Problems hearing faint speech • Auditory inattention and learning dysfunction • Mild speech & language delays
41–55 dBHL	Moderate loss	• Daily problems hearing speech at conversational levels • Auditory inattention and learning dysfunction • Speech & language delays
56–70 dBHL	Moderately severe loss	• Difficulty hearing normal conversational speech • Learning dysfunction • Severe speech and language delays
71–89 dBHL	Severe loss	• Can only understand shouted or amplified speech • Learning dysfunction • Severe speech and language delays
≥90 dBHL	Profound loss	• Obtains little understanding from even amplified speech • May not rely on auditory input, speech, or language

So, if the left side of the audiogram represents the intensity level of the tones and allows audiologists to classify the degree of hearing, then the frequencies are represented at the top of the audiogram and go from low frequency at the far left of the graph to high frequency at the far right (see Figure 5.10). Therefore, the degree is based on where the threshold falls in relation to the left axis of the audiogram, and the frequency range (or location of the loss, such as low, middle, or high) is based on where the threshold falls in relation to the top axis of the audiogram.

Figure 5.15 is an audiogram representing normal hearing, with air- and bone-conduction thresholds in the normal range. As you can tell, all thresholds at all of the frequencies fall within the -10 to 25 dBHL range (normal). There is no significant gap or space between the air-conduction symbols and the bone-conduction symbols; therefore, there is no **air-bone gap.** The thresholds on this audiogram are telling us that when the signal is sent through the

Figure 5.15. Audiogram Representing Normal Hearing, with Normal Air- and Bone-Conduction Thresholds for Both Ears

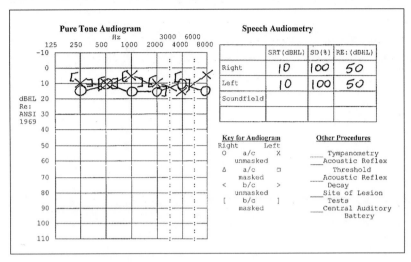

earphones (air-conduction testing), down the ear canals, and then across the tympanic membranes and into the middle ears, nothing is blocking or obstructing the sound from reaching the cochleae. Likewise, when the signal is sent through the bone oscillator (bone-conduction testing) and vibrates the skull directly, the vibrations stimulate the cochleae, which are healthy and show no damaged hearing. If an audiologist obtained these results while testing an adult or child, the results of the testing would indicate normal hearing sensitivity. (However, recall that no audiologist will rely on just one test. Although the pure-tone thresholds may be normal, the patient may still be reporting problems that would be detected only with additional testing. A person may have fair or poor speech recognition scores, which would be incongruent with the pure-tone results. A complete audiometric test battery would be indicated in such an instance.)

Figure 5.16 illustrates an audiogram with a mild conductive hearing loss. The air-conduction thresholds are indicating hearing loss, while the bone-conduction thresholds are indicating normal hearing. Therefore, there is an air-bone gap on this audiogram. These thresholds are telling us that when the signal is sent through the earphones (air-conduction testing), down the ear canals, and then across the tympanic membranes and into the middle ears, something is blocking or obstructing the sound from reaching the cochleae, so the person does not hear the signal very well. In contrast, when the signal is sent through the bone oscillator (bone-conduction testing) and vibrates the skull directly, the vibrations stimulate the cochleae, which are healthy and show no damage. Because healthy, intact cochleae will vibrate

Figure 5.16. Audiogram Representing a Mild Conductive Hearing Loss with an Air-Bone Gap Seen in Both Ears

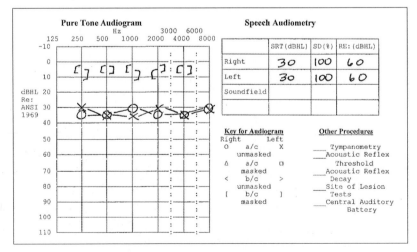

together and hear the signal at essentially the same time with bone-conduction testing, masking has to be used to ensure each ear is being tested independently. This is why you will see masked bone-conduction thresholds more often than unmasked bone-conduction thresholds on audiograms. If an audiologist obtained the results in Figure 5.16 while testing an adult or child, the results of the testing would indicate a mild, relatively flat *conductive* hearing loss in both ears.

Figure 5.17 illustrates an audiogram with a mild sloping to moderately severe sensorineural hearing loss. The air-conduction thresholds are indicating hearing loss along with the bone-conduction thresholds. Therefore, there is no air-bone gap on this audiogram, but there is loss, especially in the higher frequencies. These thresholds are telling us that when the

Figure 5.17. Audiogram Representing a Mild Sloping to Moderately Severe Sensorineural Hearing Loss in Both Ears

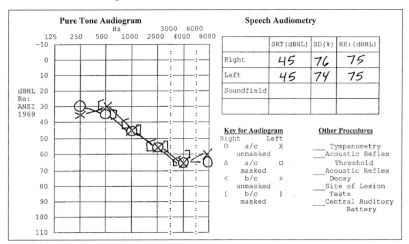

signal is sent through the earphones, down the ear canals, and then across the tympanic membranes and into the middle ears, nothing is blocking or obstructing the sound from reaching the cochleae. Similarly, when the signal is sent through the bone oscillator and vibrates the skull directly, the vibrations stimulate the cochleae. Because the cochlea is damaged, the thresholds will be similar to the air-conduction thresholds. If an audiologist obtained the results in Figure 5.17 while testing an adult or child, the results of the testing would indicate a mild sloping to moderately severe *sensorineural* hearing loss in both ears. There would be no way to determine if the loss was coming only from the cochlea's hair cells (the "sensori" part of the term) or from retrocochlear structures beyond the cochlea (the "neural" part of the term).

Figure 5.18 illustrates an audiogram with a mixed hearing loss. The air-conduction thresholds are indicating hearing loss, and the bone-conduction thresholds are indicting hearing loss; however, there is still a conductive component (air-bone gap) present with this type of hearing loss. The thresholds on this audiogram are telling us that when the signal is sent through the earphones, down the ear canals, and then across the tympanic membranes and into the middle ears, something is blocking or obstructing the sound from reaching the cochleae. In addition, when the signal is sent through the bone oscillator to vibrate the skull, the results are indicating that the cochleae are damaged. Therefore, the audiometric thresholds are showing loss with air- and bone-conduction procedures, but on top of that, there is a gap between the air- and bone-conduction thresholds. If an audiologist obtained the results in Figure 5.18 while

Figure 5.18. Audiogram Representing a Moderate to Severe Mixed Hearing Loss in Both Ears

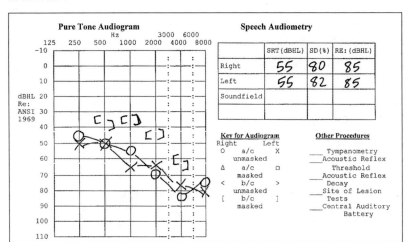

testing an adult or child, the results of the testing would indicate a moderate sloping to severe *mixed* hearing loss in both ears. An example of this kind of hearing loss would occur in a person born with a malformation of the cochleae (sensorineural component), who got a middle ear infection and the fluid created additional hearing loss (conductive component).

Figures 5.15, 5.16, 5.17, and 5.18 give very basic examples of audiograms representing normal hearing and the various types of hearing loss. However, audiograms obtained from the clinic can show differences (or asymmetry) between the two ears and can become more confusing when interpreting. The more practice a person has in reading audiograms, the easier it becomes. And if all else fails, ask an audiologist!

Pattern Recognition and Configurations. Along with determining the degree and type of hearing loss, audiologists will look for a pattern, or configuration, to the loss. There are several configurations that are typical and that always indicate the same findings (see Figure 5.19). For example, high-frequency sensorineural hearing loss that has thresholds dropping off in the highest frequencies is a configuration consistent with presbycusis, or hearing loss caused by the natural aging process (Figure 5.19a). Similarly, a high-frequency sensorineural hearing loss that has thresholds dropping off in the 2000 to 4000 Hz region and then "recovering" in the 6000 and 8000 Hz region is a configuration consistent with noise-induced hearing loss (Figure 5.19b). Intense sound levels damage the cochlea in the 2000 to 4000 Hz region of the basilar membrane; therefore, the majority of the loss is seen in that "notch." Another familiar pattern or configuration is the low-frequency, upward-sloping sensorineural loss, which has thresholds that tend to fluctuate (get better and worse) at times (Figure 5.19c). Most audiologists will agree that this configuration of loss is seen in patients who have a condition known as **endolymphatic hydrops,** or Ménière's disease. With this condition, the damage to the cochlea is seen in the lower frequencies initially: the loss will eventually spread throughout all the frequencies of the audiogram, and the fluctuations will cease, but that is later in the disease process. If the configuration shows a low-frequency, upward-sloping conductive loss, then those thresholds are an indication of a middle ear pathology, especially something such as fluid in the middle ear (Figure 5.19d). Another familiar configuration is known as a cookie-bite configuration (Figure 5.19e). The thresholds on this audiogram would indicate damage or malformation of the cochleae in the mid-frequency regions. People with this configuration are typically born with the loss. Lastly, some people are born with such extensive hearing loss that they exhibit a "corner," or "dog-eared," audiogram. Figure 5.19f shows that hearing thresholds are only seen in the very lowest frequencies on the corner of the audiogram. This is the residual hearing for that person, meaning this is the region in which some lasting or lingering hearing sensitivity remains. This residual hearing rarely helps a person to discriminate or understand speech; however, it can be useful for alerting the person to sounds in the environment.

Figure 5.19. Configurations Commonly Seen during Audiometric Evaluations

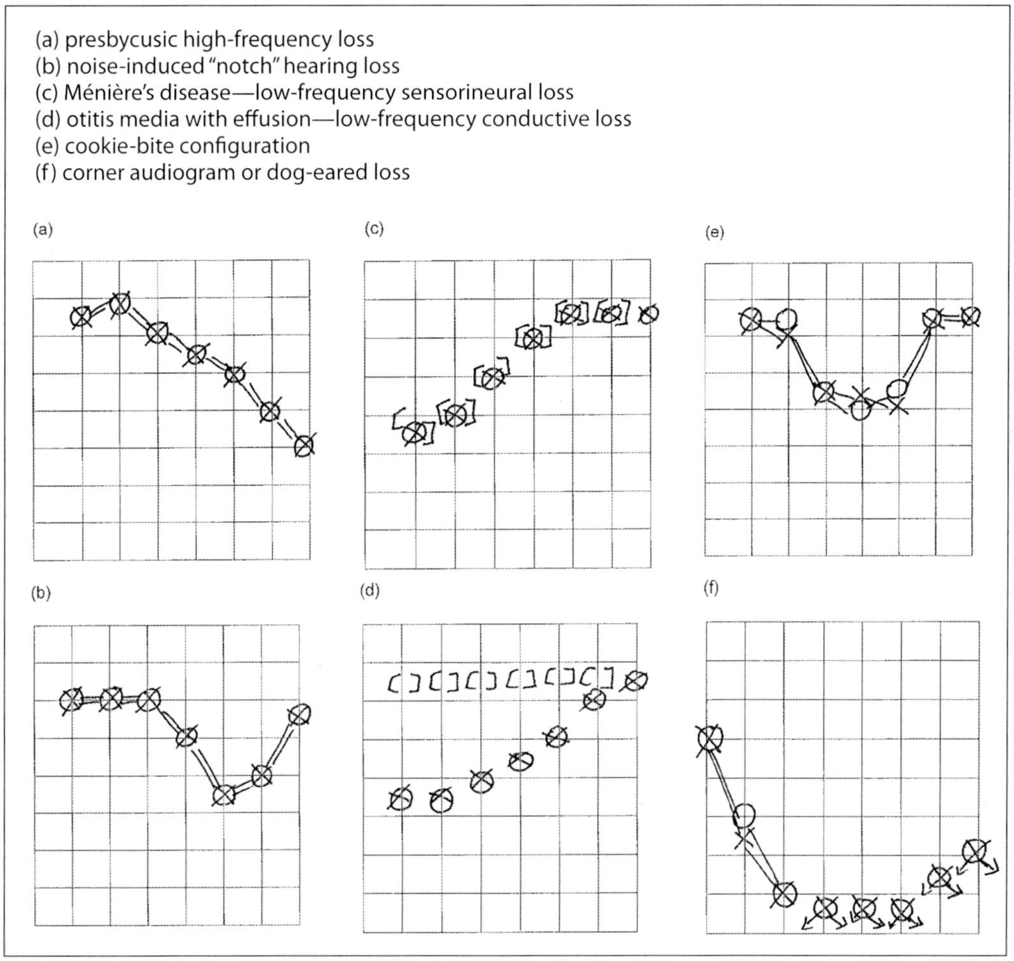

(a) presbycusic high-frequency loss
(b) noise-induced "notch" hearing loss
(c) Ménière's disease—low-frequency sensorineural loss
(d) otitis media with effusion—low-frequency conductive loss
(e) cookie-bite configuration
(f) corner audiogram or dog-eared loss

Although the configuration of hearing loss can tell the audiologist a good deal of information about what might have caused or attributed to the loss, the configurations are not always foolproof. A person can have a high-frequency sensorineural hearing loss that is *not* caused by the aging effect; the loss could have been congenital or it could have been caused by ototoxic medications (that is, caused by drugs that damage hearing). It takes all information (case history report, immittance testing, pure-tone testing, and sometimes additional testing) to determine the nature of a specific hearing loss.

Test Battery Concept. As we mentioned previously, no audiologist would accept the results from a single test as being *the* answers or findings for a patient's hearing loss. Audiologists use multiple tests to give a well-rounded picture of what is going on with a person's hearing. Tympanometry helps the audiologist feel confident about results found during pure-tone air- and bone-conduction testing on the audiogram. Speech recognition thresholds should match closely to the pure-tone average at 500, 1000, and 2000 Hz. When the pure-tone average and the SRT are approximately 10 dB apart from each other, the audiologist knows that the results are accurate and the person is responding appropriately. If the person reports or exhibits problems hearing in background noise, the pure-tone thresholds, the acoustic reflex pattern, and speech-in-noise testing can give a more complete picture of what the person may be experiencing and why. One test alone will never provide enough information for an audiologist to be completely confident about the results and recommendations needed to be given to the patient or other health care professionals. Therefore, an audiological evaluation really consists of multiple tests, not just a pure-tone audiogram.

Advanced Hearing Evaluation Methods

The audiometric testing procedures described to this point are typically referred to as basic audiometric procedures. That doesn't mean that they are not difficult to perform or that they don't reveal detailed information about hearing loss. It simply means that these are the procedures most often performed in the audiological evaluation. However, basic audiometric procedures only scratch the tip of the iceberg in some cases, and more thorough evaluation techniques sometimes have to be completed in order to help the audiologist get a complete picture of what is going on in the patient's ears.

Electroacoustic Measures. Another form of audiometric testing falls into the category of electroacoustic measures along with acoustic immittance measures (which were described earlier when we wrote about tympanometry and acoustic reflex testing). **Otoacoustic emissions (OAEs)** are low intensity sounds (0–15 dB SPL) that are the product of movement (or motility) within inner ear structures (specifically the hair cells in the organ of Corti). These sounds are measured by a probe microphone that is placed into the ear canal; they are elicited, or brought about by, various testing techniques and equipment. There are four different methods for testing OAEs (spontaneous, **transient-evoked, distortion product,** and stimulus-frequency), but only two forms of the testing are clinically feasible and used routinely by audiologists. These two forms of OAEs are the transient-evoked (TEOAE) and distortion product (DPOAE) forms. In a nutshell, both of these tests use an evoking stimulus (such as a click in the case of TEOAEs or a pair of pure tones [f_1 and f_2] in the case of DPOAEs) to create the movement of the cochlear structures. OAE recordings are representations of the energy associated with outer **hair cell motility** that makes its way from the cochlea, through the middle ear, spreading outward into the external ear canal, to be picked up and recorded by the equipment. OAEs are only so useful, however, because their presence or absence has limited value for distinguishing between normal hearing and impaired hearing. That is, a person can have a mild amount of hearing loss (approximately 30 to 40 dBHL of hearing loss) and still produce OAEs. This does help an audiologist to determine if any significant inner ear abnormalities may be present, but it limits the ability to use OAEs the same way pure-tone thresholds are used. With that said, OAEs have become an indispensable, evidence-based part of the audiometric test battery, and they are most useful in the pediatric population due to the speed with which testing can be completed (they take only seconds per ear). Current clinical applications of OAEs in-

Figure 5.20. Transient-Evoked Otoacoustic Emission Results (a) and Distortion Product Otoacoustic Emission Results (b)

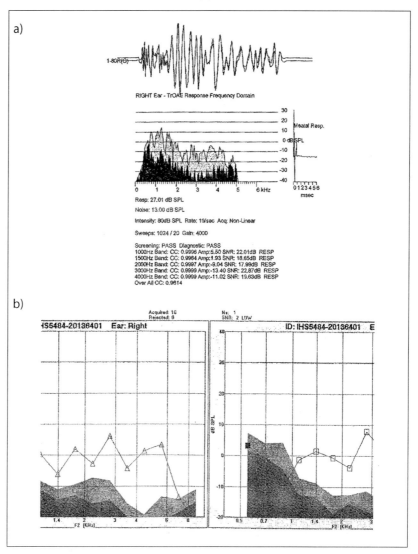

clude hearing screenings for newborns and early detection of inner ear pathologies associated with a variety of causes, including hearing loss caused by excessive noise exposure, ototoxic medications, and/or the aging process. Figure 5.20 shows example TEOAE and DPOAE results, and Figure 5.21 shows screening and diagnostic testing equipment for OAEs.

Figure 5.21. Otoacoustic Emission Diagnostic Equipment (a) and Hand-Held Screening Equipment (b)

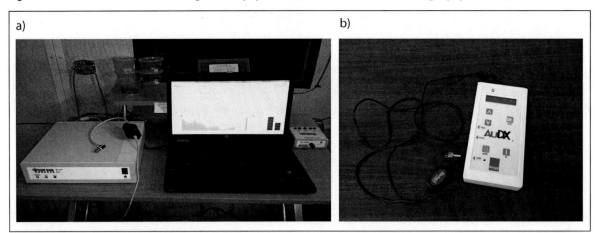

Electrophysiological Measures. Since the 1970s, waveforms obtained from the brain and elicited from auditory signals sent through the central auditory nervous system have become a popular means for assessing the auditory pathways in people of all ages. **Electrophysiology,** or **auditory-evoked potentials,** refers to a series of testing methodologies in which the neural structures along the auditory pathways are evaluated to determine if hearing loss is present. Because random neural activity (recorded with the **electroencephalogram,** or EEG) is always present in the brain, recording methods using electrodes placed on the scalp have been devised to evoke specific waveforms from the EEG. Those waveforms allow an audiologist to determine if the evoking stimulus (which can be a click, a pip, a tone burst, a phoneme, or even a short word) was detected and heard in the central auditory nervous system.

Auditory Brainstem Response (ABR). The most common auditory evoked potential is the **auditory brainstem response** (ABR: see sidebar "An ABR by Any Other Name"). This waveform (evoked by clicks, pips, or tone bursts) consists of seven waves, of which five are used clinically. The waves are labeled with Roman numerals (I, II, III, IV, and V), and the amplitude and latency measurements of the waves help an audiologist determine if a problem exists in a portion of the auditory nerve (CN VIII) and several brainstem structures (see sidebar "Why Are the Brainstem Structures Important to Hearing?" on page 148). Figure 5.22 is an example of what the ABR waveform looks like for a person with normal hearing and no neurological pathology. Audiologists use the amplitude and latency information of Waves I, III, and V of the ABR to obtain threshold information about hearing capabilities or to identify neurological problems. ABR testing is used for multiple purposes: (a) to screen newborns' hearing, (b) to

An ABR by Any Other Name….

Auditory brainstem response (ABR) testing goes by several names. In addition to ABR, you may see BSER (brainstem-evoked response) and BAER (brainstem auditory evoked response) when reading about this form of testing. Physicians use the terms more often than audiologists. But it is important to know that they are all referring to the same test. So, don't be confused by the alphabet soup; these acronyms are just different ways of referring to the same auditory-evoked potential.

evaluate the hard-to-test population, (c) to determine thresholds and types of hearing loss in all ages, (d) to determine if a neurological diagnosis is present, and (e) to perform intraoperative monitoring (IOM) of the VII and VIII cranial nerves during surgical procedures.

ABR can be used in children too young to be tested with traditional audiometric testing techniques. The use of electrodes taped to the head and earlobes eliminates the need for active participation on the part of the child (such as raising a hand or putting a block in a bucket each time a tone is presented). The brainwaves obtained during ABR (see Figure 5.22) can be presented in a similar manner to which pure-tone thresholds are tested; that is, the audiologist can start ABR testing by presenting clicks at an intense stimulus level (such as 70 or 75 dBHL) and then decrease in 10 dB increments until the waveform is no longer identifiable or repeatable. Figure 5.23 is an example of a threshold search using ABR.

Figure 5.22. Auditory Brainstem Response (ABR) Waveforms

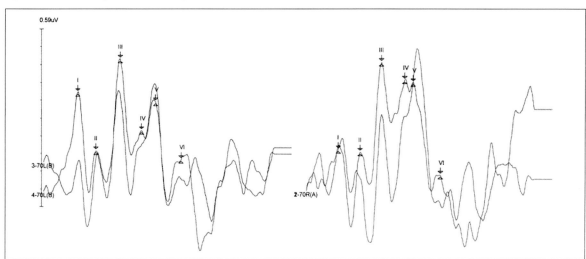

Figure 5.23. Threshold Search Using Auditory Brainstem Response Testing

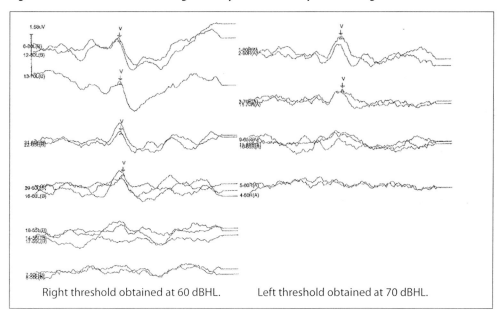

Right threshold obtained at 60 dBHL.   Left threshold obtained at 70 dBHL.

Why Are the Brainstem Structures Important to Hearing?

The anatomical structures contained within the brainstem that are important to hearing and considered to be within the central auditory nervous system pathway are the cochlear nucleus, superior olivary complex, lateral lemniscus, inferior colliculus, and medial geniculate body. Some of these are actual structures (neurons), while some are neural pathways. Auditory signals pass ipsilaterally (same side) and contralaterally (opposite side) through the neural pathways in a very complicated, but exact, manner. The complicated neural structures, networks, and pathways help protect our auditory systems; if one area is damaged, another area usually has enough left over to make up for it! Problems or disorders with auditory brainstem structures lead to changes in the amplitudes and latencies of the waves obtained with auditory brainstem response (ABR) testing. These changes allow the audiologist to compare the results of one person to the results of many others in the same age range (called norms). This comparison allows the audiologist to determine if a problem is present or not.

Auditory Steady-State Response. Similar to ABR testing is a relatively new electrophysiological form of testing hearing: the **Auditory Steady-State Response (ASSR).** The ASSR is an objective test also used for evaluating children too young for traditional audiometric testing. Results are obtained by recording brain activity while the child listens to tones of varying frequency (pitch) and intensity (loudness). As with the ABR, the ASSR records brain waves using electrodes taped on the forehead and behind each ear. The results are detected objectively, using statistical formulas that determine the presence or absence of a true response. Similar to traditional audiometric testing, the ASSR threshold is determined as the lowest level at each of four frequencies (500, 1000, 2000, and 4000 Hz) at which a response is present. Therefore, ASSR provides an accurate, frequency-specific estimate of the behavioral pure-tone audiogram. Many pediatric audiology clinics have supplemented their ABR testing with ASSR testing in the recent years. The sidebar "Similarities and Differences between Auditory Brainstem Response and Auditory Steady-State Response Testing Techniques" compares these two measurements.

Additional Auditory-Evoked Potentials. There are other forms of auditory-evoked potentials that use different stimuli and different testing parameters to determine if hearing loss is present or if neurological dysfunction is suspected. The middle latency response (MLR) and late latency response (LLR), along with the **mismatch negativity (MMN)** and P_{300} (which are evoked by an oddball stimulus using speech stimuli instead of clicks or tone bursts), are not used clinically as often as ABR is used, but they are available for assessing higher-level auditory functions, such as differentiating and processing acoustic stimuli. As with ABR, electrodes are attached to the surface of the scalp and/or earlobes, but the waveforms picked up by the electrodes are representations of neural activity much higher up in the auditory nervous system, well above the brainstem structures. For the purposes of this textbook, it is not our desire to go deeply into these forms of testing. Instead, it is our desire to inform the reader of these additional methods available to the audiologist and to allow the reader to get a better perspective of the more advanced techniques that can be used to evaluate hearing, especially in the very young and school-age populations. At the present time, no child should go without an accurate diagnosis, including degree and type of hearing loss, for very long. If less invasive, more subjective forms of audiometric testing can be obtained accurately, an audiologist will stick with those forms of testing. However, if a child's age, behavior, and/or other medical conditions prohibit traditional forms of testing, then an audiologist can resort to electroacoustical and electrophysiological measures to obtain information about a child's hearing.

Similarities and Differences between Auditory Brainstem Response and Auditory Steady-State Response Testing Techniques

Both of these tests are used for testing very young children to determine if hearing loss is present.

Similarities:
- Both tests deliver an auditory stimulus to the patient's ears.
- Both tests stimulate the patient's auditory system.
- Both tests are used to record bioelectric responses from the auditory system using electrodes attached to the patient's scalp and/or earlobes.
- Neither test protocol requires the patient to respond voluntarily.

Differences:
- The ABR stimulus is usually a click or a tone burst (one tone and one ear at a time) presented at a slower rate, whereas ASSR stimuli are amplitude or frequency-modulated sounds (four frequencies and both ears simultaneously) presented at a rapid rate.
- ABR relies on a relatively subjective analysis of amplitude versus latency, whereas ASSR relies on a statistical analysis of the probability of a response, usually at a 95 percent confidence level.
- The ABR response is measured in millionths of a volt (microvolts), and the ASSR is measured in billionths of a volt (nanovolts).

Pediatric Evaluation versus Adult Evaluation

Up to this point, we have mainly focused on the testing equipment and techniques routinely used to assess hearing. We have said nothing about the fact that pediatric testing techniques are usually very different from adult testing techniques. All of the tests and methods described throughout this chapter can be used on both populations of patients; however, there are different forms, or different protocols, for use with infants and small children. Once again, it would take an entire chapter (or even an entire book) to fully cover all of the testing procedures used with small children, but we would like to point out that **Visual Reinforcement Audiometry (VRA)** and play audiometry techniques are routinely used to evaluate young children.

Figure 5.24. Visual Reinforcement Audiometry (VRA) Smoked-Glass Box, with Moveable Toy Animal Inside

Visual Reinforcement Audiometry

Visual Reinforcement Audiometry, or VRA, is used on infants and toddlers from the age of 6 to 24 months, and can be used for other children with developmental delays. VRA relies on the audiologist's ability to condition a child to respond to an auditory stimulus by reinforcing the response with something visual, such as a light or a toy contained inside a lighted box. (See Figure 5.24 for an example of VRA.) By pairing the auditory stimulus with the visual stimulus, the child can be conditioned to orient to the light or lighted box when the auditory stimulus alone is perceived. Therefore, the child will be seated inside the sound booth on a parent's lap with or without headphones, and the audiologist will use the speakers (located to the front and side of the child) or headphones to present tones or speech to the child's ears. As the child turns his head to look for the stimulus, a smoke-glassed box containing a toy will light up and reinforce the child's behavior (head turn) each time the tone or audiologist's voice is heard. (Some more modern facilities use computer screens in the corners of the sound booth instead of smoke-glassed boxes containing moveable animals.) The audiologist will lower the level of the stimulus until a threshold is obtained for speech and/or tones. The main advantage to VRA is that the child does not have to provide a voluntary motor task (hand raise or button push) to the auditory stimulus.

Play Audiometry

Play audiometry, or **conditioned play audiometry,** is used to assess the hearing of three- and four-year-olds. Instead of relying on a head turn or a hand raise, the audiologist will condition the child to "put the block in the bucket" or "put the peg in the board" each time the child hears a tone. Therefore, the response to the auditory stimulus is the play action, and the child does not have to even be aware that his hearing is being tested. Again, the child can be under headphones or listening to the speakers in the sound booth (which gives very different results to the audiologist, but may be the best method for testing some children initially). The audiologist will demonstrate and play with the child for a while to make sure the child understands the concept of "doing something when he hears something." So, when the audiologist presents the tone, the child who puts a block in the bucket, a peg into a board, a ring on a stick, and so on is said to have given a response, and the level of the tone is lowered until the child stops responding. The lowest level at which the child responds with the play action is the threshold level. For a thorough description of these tests and other methodologies used for assessing hearing in young children, refer to Roeser and Downs (2004) or Northern and Downs (2001).

Hearing Screenings versus Full Audiological Evaluations

Screening for Hearing Loss

Hearing screenings are used for quickly identifying infants and children (and even adults!) who are at risk for (or suspected of) having a hearing loss. Because between one and six out of every 1,000 children is born with a hearing loss, and because nearly 10 to 15 percent of people will acquire a hearing loss during their childhood (Cunningham & Cox, 2003; Kemper & Downs, 2000; Niskar et al., 2001), the need for hearing screenings is well justified. Newborn and school-age hearing screenings are designed to identify hearing loss early in a child, thus permitting audiologists and other professionals mentioned in Chapter 1 to intervene at an early age and quickly manage the loss. Early identification and management have the ability to reduce the effects hearing loss can have on speech and language development, education, psychosocial development, and more. Additionally, school hearing screenings should result in recommendations for rescreenings, full audiologic testing, or referrals for additional assessment and/or treatment. If hearing screenings are to be performed on every child at birth, and then at regular intervals throughout their school years, the hearing screening process needs to be easy, quick, relatively painless, and effective at identifying children who are at risk for hearing loss. The following sections describe the different methods and measures for screening hearing in infants and school-age children.

Screening Measures and Methodology

The American Speech-Language-Hearing Association (ASHA) has clear guidelines for screening hearing abilities in all age groups—the *Guidelines for Audiologic Screening* (ASHA, 1997). The document is very specific about what tests can be used, how they are to be used, in what testing environments they are to be used, who is able to use the tests, and what constitutes a "pass" or "refer" on the tests. Although the current guidelines are more than 10 years old, they continue to apply for audiologists and speech-language pathologists today. Other professionals and volunteer hearing screeners are not bound by the American Speech-Language-Hearing Association's Code of Ethics; however, the ASHA guidelines are well written and backed with evidence-based practices for performing accurate and trustworthy hearing screenings. New ASHA guidelines are currently being written and are expected to be published in the near future. These new guidelines will refer to the most current and clinically available screening methods being used. Due to the thoroughness with which the ASHA guidelines address screenings for all ages, it is recommended that the reader refer to www. asha.org/policy to review the information provided there.

Newborn Hearing Screenings. Since 1993, hospitals throughout the United States have embraced the National Institutes of Health (NIH) Consensus Development Conference Statement on universal newborn hearing screening. In 1999, Congress passed the Newborn and Infant Hearing Screening and Intervention Act, which provided for funding to help with coordination of statewide programs. As of 2013, hearing screenings are being completed in hospitals on all newborns prior to the infants leaving the hospital in nearly all (43/50) states. Every state has an Early Hearing Detection and Intervention (EDHI) system in place, but many lack sufficient funding and have difficulties tracking and following up with infants identified with hearing loss and their families. The Early Childhood Hearing Outreach (ECHO) Initiative, a part of the National Center for Hearing Assessment and Management (NCHAM) at Utah State University, focuses on the continued screening of hearing for children from birth to three years of age in many health and educational settings. They work with EDHI and Head Start programs to get as many children screened and identified as possible. For more detailed information on hearing screenings in infants and the birth to three population, go to www. infanthearing.org.

Currently, when technology has advanced to a fairly high level, newborn hearing screenings are performed with one of two forms of technology: otoacoustic emissions (OAE) or auditory brainstem response (ABR). Each of these forms of testing was described earlier in this chapter. In some instances, if an infant fails the OAE screening, then an ABR screening may be performed. If both an OAE and ABR screening are failed, then the infant would be referred on for a full, diagnostic ABR, specifically looking for a threshold and possibly bone-conduction ABR responses.

Both forms of technology have the ability to be shortened regarding the length of time it takes to administer the screening and can be automated so that an untrained volunteer or hospital employee can perform the screening without knowing much about hearing loss or the equipment's capabilities. Screening OAEs can take as little as 30 seconds per ear, and a screening, or automated, ABR can take as little as 10 minutes from placement of electrodes through completion of testing in a cooperative (sleeping) infant.

For the reader who is a parent of a child with hearing loss, you were possibly contacted by an audiologist or nurse in the hospital prior to going home with your newborn. For the reader who is a healthcare provider or school-based professional, the children with hearing loss with whom you work were probably screened for hearing loss prior to leaving the hospital as newborns. Whether or not any hearing loss was detected at the newborn screening depends on the etiology of the hearing loss. Some causes of progressive hearing loss will not be present when the newborn hearing screening is completed, but sometime after that screening, the loss will occur and hopefully be identified during a checkup at the pediatrician's office or a school hearing screening.

Hearing Screenings in Schools. Screenings of school-age children have been occurring, in mass or independently, for years. (Some of you older readers may remember having to raise your hand when you heard a "beep" sitting at your desk in elementary school!) The ASHA *Guidelines for Audiologic Screening* (1997) "Section 5 Guidelines for Screening for Hearing Impairment—School-Age Children, 5 through 18 Years" recommend that school-age children obtain a hearing screening when they initially enroll in school (this is often done in a pediatrician's office), then again in kindergarten, 1st, 2nd, 3rd, 7th, and 11th grades. Wording in the document also states that school-age children should be screened "as needed, requested, or mandated" (p. 42). Therefore, if a parent or guardian, healthcare provider, teacher, or other school professional expresses concern about a child's hearing, speech, language, or learning abilities, then a hearing screening should be conducted. Unlike other assessments that are specific to a particular child in order to determine a disability, the Individuals with Disabilities Education Improvement Act (IDEIA) allows school systems to proceed with hearing screening (and also vision screening) without parental notification and permission because it is school board policy for all children. Additionally, a hearing screening should be scheduled if a student is already enrolled in a special education program, has to repeat a grade, or enters a new school system. However, students who already receive audiologic or otologic management from an audiologist or otolaryngologist (due to a previously diagnosed loss or ear disease) are not expected to participate in the school screening process.

Conventional or play audiometry are the screening procedures of choice for this population; however, tympanometry and otoacoustic emission screening are acceptable options. The ASHA guidelines recommend using supra-aural earphones for screening pure tones of 1000, 2000, and 4000 Hz at 20 dBHL in a quiet environment with limited visual and auditory distractions (ASHA, 1997). The ambient noise levels in the screening environment should abide by American National Standards Institute standards for pure-tone threshold testing adjusted for the 20 dBHL screening level (ANSI, 1991). That means that, as of this printing, ambient noise levels in the screening area should not exceed 49.5 dBSPL at 1000 Hz, 54.5 dBSPL at 2000 Hz, or 62 dBSPL at 4000 Hz when measured using a sound level meter with octave-band filters centered on the screening frequencies. Because newer ASHA guidelines are forthcoming, it is anticipated that any new ANSI standards for ambient noise levels for test rooms replace the current ANSI standards recommendation.

Not only should the screening environment meet ANSI standards, but the screening audiometers should also meet ANSI S3.6-1996 requirements. They should be calibrated annually to meet those same specifications, and a daily listening check should be conducted by the person completing the screenings to determine that no equipment problems exist (that is, intermittency, crosstalk, or distortion in the earphones).

153

In truth, ANSI standards are very hard to adhere to when testing in a preschool or school environment. Therefore, the standards are not adhered to in many screening situations; however, the tester must keep these ambient background noise levels in mind and perform screenings in areas in which background noise is kept to a minimum.

If a student does not respond (hand raise or block in bucket) to the criterion intensity level (20 dBHL) at any one of the three frequencies (1000, 2000, or 4000 Hz) in either ear, the audiologist should: (1) reinstruct to ensure that the child understands the screening instructions, (2) reposition the earphones over the child's ears, and (3) rescreen the child within the same screening session. If the student responds during this rescreening session, then he would pass the screening. If the student does not respond during the rescreening session, then he would fail the screening and be referred for a complete audiological evaluation. (Note: audiologists do not like to say a child "failed" a hearing screening. The word *refer* is used to eliminate the stigma and negative context of the word *fail*.)

Although hearing screenings are not full audiometric evaluations, one should not consider them to be less important in the quest to identify hearing loss. If a hearing loss is missed during a hearing screening, it may be months or years before a child is diagnosed with the loss. That time period can make a huge difference in a child's ability to develop speech and language, perform well in the educational environment, develop lasting relationships, and become a successful adult capable of dealing with the daily challenges of life.

Summary

In this chapter, we discussed the sensitivity of human hearing in order to describe more clearly how hearing loss is measured. We distinguished the differences between screening for hearing loss and fully evaluating hearing loss. A description of the typical audiological evaluation process was given, starting with collecting answers to a case history questionnaire, completing an otoscopic examination, evaluating the middle ear systems with tympanometric measures, obtaining pure-tone air- and bone-conduction thresholds, and finishing up with speech measures (speech recognition thresholds and scores). The audiogram was described, and placement of threshold symbols on the graph was used to describe hearing loss. The varying types of hearing loss (conductive, sensorineural, mixed) were described, along with the concepts of configuration and pattern recognition. In order to stress the concept of identifying hearing loss with a test battery approach, and in order to distinguish between a screening method and a diagnostic method, more advanced audiological tests and protocol were described (electroacoustic measures, eletrophysiological measures, masking, speech-in-noise testing, play audiometry). The objective of this chapter was to give our readers a better understanding of the "neat toys" audiologists have in their repertoire as a means for providing accurate and complete audiometric evaluations. Hopefully, our readers are more comfortable looking at an audiogram and understanding what the symbols mean with respect to a child's hearing sensitivity.

Chapter 5 Food for Thought

1. What is the first thing that Mrs. Cahill, Mr. Montague, and Ms. Markup should do as they troubleshoot the cause of the over-referrals? How can they make sure the remaining grades do not have such a high referral rate?

2. A child was born with atresia of the external auditory meatus. What audiological tests would be available to assess that child's hearing? What limitations would be placed on the equipment and testing methods used to obtain a diagnosis? How could the audiologist get around these limitations and obtain reliable results on this child's hearing?

3. Where is the office for EDHI services and programs located in your state? What rates are reported for universal hearing screenings in your area? Are they better or worse than other state rates of screening?

4. What screening level and frequencies are recommended by the ASHA Guidelines (1997) for school-age hearing screenings? Why are that intensity level and those frequencies recommended?

5. If a mother of an 18-month-old became concerned about her child's responses to sounds, what options are available for her to pursue with her local audiologist?

6. Obtain an audiogram or draw one yourself. Insert the air- and bone-conduction thresholds that would be seen on the graph if a person had a "moderate gently sloping to profound sensorineural hearing loss in the right ear" and a "moderately severe sloping to profound mixed hearing loss in the left ear." What types of tympanograms would you expect to obtain if you tested each ear with a single-frequency probe tone during immittance testing?

Chapter 6

Watson, Come Hear! Hearing Devices

Scenario

Caleigh was working her usual shift at the Urgicare, the television broadcasting the latest news on CNN, when an older man came through the door. She watched him closely because he seemed to be looking around a bit disoriented. "Can I help you, sir?" asked Caleigh. The man didn't answer. She noticed that he was wearing a hearing aid and repeated a bit more loudly, "Sir, can I help you with something?" Again, he did not answer. She thought to herself, "What is the issue here? I can see he is wearing hearing aids and I talked louder, now what?" One final time she stood at her desk and nearly shouted, "Excuse me, sir, are you ill?"

When you complete this chapter, you will be able to help Caleigh respond to the gentleman's issues.

Key Vocabulary

American Sign Language (ASL)	frequency modulation (FM)	peak clipping
amplification	gain	personal amplification device
Aural-Oral therapy model	hearing aids	Phonak Roger system
Auditory-Verbal Therapy (AVT)	hearing assistance technology	receiver
Bilingual/Bicultural (Bi-Bi)	(HAT)	receiver-in-canal aid (RIC)
bone-anchored hearing aid	induction loop system	sign language
(Baha)	infrared system (IR)	SoundBite in-the-mouth aid
behind-the-ear aid (BTE)	input compression	Soundbridge vibrating ossicular
brainstem implant	in-the-canal aid (ITC)	prosthesis system (VORP)
cochlear implant	in-the-ear aid (ITE)	signal-to-noise ratio (S/N or SNR)
completely-in-the-canal aid	kneepoint	sound-field amplification system
(CIC)	mapping	speech processor
compression limiting	maximum output	telecoil
Cued Speech/Language	microphone	transducer
digital modulation (DM)	middle ear implant	transmitter
digital noise reduction	omnidirectional microphone	wide dynamic range
directional microphone	open fitting	compression
ear mold	osseointegrated aid	
electrode array	output compression	

History of Hearing Aids

Did you know that the concept of a hearing aid is not new? The original **hearing aid**, a device that helps a person hear sounds louder, was used as far back as 1588. In 1551, Girolamo Cardano discovered that he could conduct or transmit sound to his ear via the shaft of a spear being held between his teeth. Soon afterward, other devices were invented to bring sound to the ears. Speaking tubes, horns, funnels, listening thrones, and ear trumpets made from animal horns, and later of various metals, were the original types of hearing aid used throughout Europe and in the early Americas. The first recorded commercial manufacturer of hearing aids was Frederick C. Rein, who established F. C. Rein and Son in London. This company remained in business until 1963. The first manufacturer in the United States was E. B. Meyrowitz, a company established in New York City in 1873. They began the company as opticians and shortly began manufacturing hearing aids as well (Washington University School of Medicine, 2009). Figure 6.1 is a representative sample of the hearing devices commonly used during the 16th–19th centuries.

Figure 6.1. Listening Devices Used During the 16th–19th Centuries

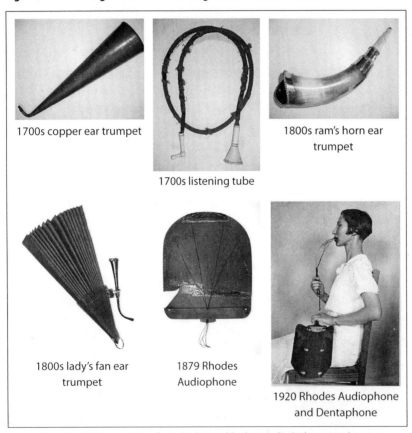

1700s copper ear trumpet

1700s listening tube

1800s ram's horn ear trumpet

1800s lady's fan ear trumpet

1879 Rhodes Audiophone

1920 Rhodes Audiophone and Dentaphone

Source: Reprinted with permission from the Bernard Becker Medical Library, Washington University School of Medicine. The Central Institute for the Deaf–Max A. Goldstein Historic Devices for Hearing Collection.

The 20th century brought the development of batteries and other electronic forms of auditory stimulation to the production of hearing aid devices. After Alexander Graham Bell invented the telephone in 1876, electronics were introduced to hearing aids. The first electric hearing aid was created in 1898 by Miller Reese Hutchison using a carbon transmitter. His aid, called the Akouphone, was portable, allowing an individual to carry a device that electrically amplified sounds. The first electronic aid using vacuum tubes, the Vactuphone, was patented in 1920 by Earl C. Hanson, a naval engineer.

The Vactuphone was lightweight enough to be carried. In the 1920s and 1930s, vacuum tubes were reduced in size, eventually making these **amplification** devices small enough to be worn; however, they were extremely bulky. Then, as now, the purpose of each of these tools was to conduct sound through the outer and middle ears and on towards the cochlea.

Personal Amplification Devices

The electronic revolution brought consumers the transistor, which had a major impact on the development of hearing aids (also known as **personal amplification devices**). Prior to electronic manipulation of sound, people who had hearing loss were dependent upon an unmodified environmental signal being channeled to the ear. After the development of transistors, sound could be electronically manipulated and amplified to truly make the sound more accessible to the listener. Figures 6.2 and 6.3 display representative examples of 20th century hearing aids.

Figure 6.2. 20th Century Hearing Aids: Carbon to Vacuum Tube

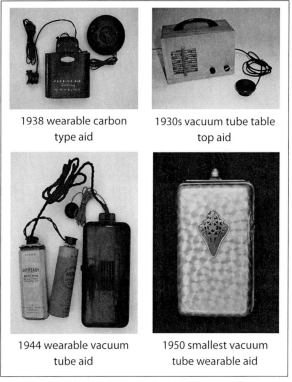

1938 wearable carbon type aid

1930s vacuum tube table top aid

1944 wearable vacuum tube aid

1950 smallest vacuum tube wearable aid

Source: Reprinted with permission from the Bernard Becker Medical Library, Washington University School of Medicine. The Central Institute for the Deaf–Max A. Goldstein Historic Devices for Hearing Collection.

The first electronic hearing aids were known as analog aids. As described in Klein (2011):

> Hearing aids from the 1940s through the 1990s primarily utilized analog technology. In this form of amplification, the acoustic sound pressure is analogous to the electric current or voltage being produced in the aid. When the pressure of an acoustic signal increases, so does the voltage required to produce that signal. Analog technology is less precise and is more likely to allow for various types of sound distortion to occur in the amplified sound that is transmitted to the ear. (p. 51)

Current hearing aid technology rarely incorporates analog signals. Instead, digital signals are now used to program and produce amplified sound.

> A special converter in the hearing aid is used to change the analog electrical signal into a series of number strings. Digital signals are comprised of a combination of 1s and 0s. Sounds are mathematically converted to these numerical signals, and no information regarding the sound is lost. This makes digital technology far superior to analog because the information regarding the sound is accurate. In addition, digital hearing aids

allow the audiologist to manipulate the sound signal to provide a sound that is best suited to the listening needs of the individual user. Sounds that would normally be too loud can be compressed to make them more accessible and comfortable to the listener. Speech signals can be enhanced to make them more accessible to the listener as well. Digital hearing aids became available in the 1990s. This technology is currently the "gold standard" for hearing aids. The quality of the sound production has made a significant difference for the users of digital hearing aids. Although the initial cost of digital hearing aids was prohibitive for many, like other forms of technology, the cost has come down, making these hearing aids affordable for virtually anyone who wants one. Babies identified with hearing loss at birth are now routinely fitted with the state-of-the-art BTE digital hearing aids. (Klein, 2011, pp. 51–52)

Figure 6.3. 20th Century Hearing Aids: Transistor

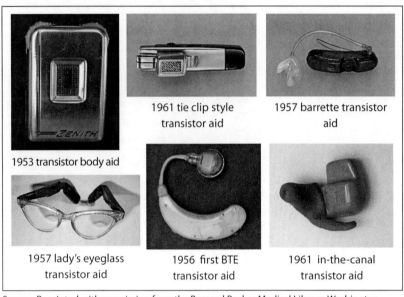

1953 transistor body aid

1961 tie clip style transistor aid

1957 barrette transistor aid

1957 lady's eyeglass transistor aid

1956 first BTE transistor aid

1961 in-the-canal transistor aid

Source: Reprinted with permission from the Bernard Becker Medical Library, Washington University School of Medicine. The Central Institute for the Deaf–Max A. Goldstein Historic Devices for Hearing Collection.

Traditional Hearing Aids

More Hearing Aid History

The Washington University School of Medicine–Bernard Becker Medical Library has a website, "Deafness in Disguise," that provides outstanding bits of information on the timeline of hearing aids and deaf education. It is filled with other resources as well. Visit the site to browse and learn a bit more in depth about these topics. http://beckerexhibits.wustl.edu/did/index.htm

Although hearing aids can be discussed in several ways, we will explain them from the perspective of placement on the head and type of hearing loss. All hearing aids have certain components in common. They all have a case that houses the working parts (i.e., **microphone/transducer**, amplifier, and receiver/transmitter), some form of control switch for volume and power, and all hearing aids require a battery as a power source. Hearing aids that send sound through the ear canal have some form of **ear mold** that channels the amplified sound down the ear canal. Other hearing aids that transmit the sounds in alternate ways will be discussed later.

The most common style of hearing aid used with children is the **behind-the-ear (BTE) hearing aid.** This aid consists of a small case that sits behind the ear against the mastoid bone. There is a short plastic tube that attaches to the case on one end and connects to an ear mold on the other end. An ear mold is made for each ear by casting impressions and then creating a mold that is explicitly designed (customized) for the individual user. For the child with a severe to profound hearing loss, the BTE is the most appropriate type of hearing aid for several reasons. Typically, this style of hearing aid is the most powerful and can provide a significant amount of acoustic **gain** (loudness) to the user's ear. In addition, it is a very sturdy model that can accommodate rough handling and rough play, and it attaches to (couples with) an ear mold, which can be changed out regularly (and inexpensively) as a child's head and ear canal grows. Figure 6.4 provides examples of some of the most common behind-the-ear hearing aids used with children.

A recent addition to the BTE family is the **receiver-in-canal (RIC)** type of hearing aid. This hearing aid looks like a traditional BTE aid with one exception: the **receiver** compo-

Figure 6.4. 21st Century Hearing Aids: Digital BTE

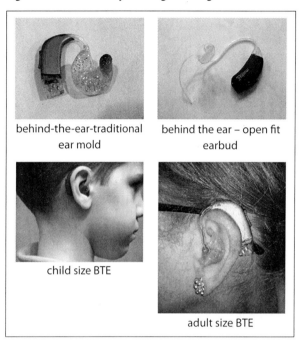

behind-the-ear-traditional ear mold

behind the ear – open fit earbud

child size BTE

adult size BTE

nent is at the end of the tubing and located directly in the ear canal rather than in the case that fits behind the ear. **Open fit** style earbuds are typically used in this type of aid. The RIC aids are available in several sizes and colors. The RIC aid is intended for those with mild to severe hearing losses. The benefit of this hearing aid is that the sound from the receiver goes directly into the ear canal rather than through the tubing and ear mold. There is less chance for distortion or reduction in gain.

Another style of hearing aid actually fits inside the ear canal. There are three types that match this description. These include the **in-the ear (ITE)**, **in-the-canal (ITC)**, and the **completely-in-the-canal (CIC) aids**. As named, each of these aids is progressively smaller and fits more snugly into the ear canal. These aids were originally developed for cosmetic reasons; adults wanted to hide the use of a hearing aid and these canal models are discreet and not visually obvious to the casual observer. In essence, they are ear molds that contain all the working parts of a hearing aid. The canal style of hearing aid is typically not as powerful as the behind-the-ear style because of acoustic feedback, or "squeal" issues. When a microphone and speaker get too close together, acoustic feedback can occur. The microphone and receiver in these aids are very close together by virtue of the size of the instrument. Therefore, if there is too much gain (loudness) coming from the hearing aid and the aid is not snugly fit into the ear canal, sound can leak around from the microphone to the receiver, which causes this feed-

Figure 6.5. In-the-Canal Style Hearing Aid

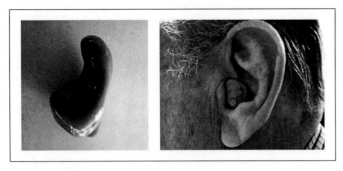

back. These hearing aids are more appropriate for teens or adults who have less severe losses. Figure 6.5 provides images of the ITC type of hearing aid.

These styles of hearing aids channel sound from the environment through the ear canal (outer ear) to transmit sound waves to the tympanic membrane, where the amplified vibrations will continue to travel through the middle ear to reach the cochlea (inner ear). These traditional styles of hearing aids (in which all of the unit is said to be located externally) function very differently from the newer styles of hearing aids described next.

Implantable Hearing Aids

Two newer types of hearing aids now on the market are implanted directly into the skull (osseointegrated auditory device) or into the middle ear (**middle ear implant**). These aids eliminate the outer ear altogether and transmit sound directly to the cochlea.

A hearing aid that is implanted into the skull is called an osseointegrated auditory device, or **bone-anchored hearing aid (Baha)**. Whenever a person has an anatomical problem with the outer or middle ear, such as atresia (closed or absent ear canal), stenosis (extremely narrowed ear canal), or problems with the ossicles (fixated, disjointed/disarticulated middle ear bones), an **osseointegrated aid** could be an appropriate choice for amplifying sound. Therefore, these aids are used for people who have conductive hearing loss, mixed hearing loss, or single-sided deafness. This style of aid has a small plastic case that contains a microphone and amplifier that can be worn in two ways. A young child may wear a headband with the Baha attached and held in place over the mastoid bone of the skull. For an older child (five

Figure 6.6. Osseointegrated Auditory Device: Baha 4 Hearing Aid Components

to six years and older) or adult, a surgical grade snap is placed in the mastoid bone and the case snaps tightly onto the implanted connection. The microphone picks up the sound and then transmits it through the mastoid bone of the skull. Therefore, amplified sounds go directly to the cochlea, bypassing the damaged outer and middle ear systems. See Figure 6.6 for an example of an osseointegrated auditory device.

Images courtesy of Cochlear Americas ©2013.

Another middle ear implant, MED-EL's VIBRANT **Soundbridge**, includes a unit that is placed directly into the middle ear space. These devices are used for people who have sensorineural hearing losses, and at the time of writing are being studied in a clinical trial for mixed and conductive hearing loss indications. There are external and internal components to this style of hearing aid. The external component is an Audio Processor (AP), which contains a microphone, a digital signal processor, and a battery. It is worn externally on a person's head, often under hair. The digital signal processor sends electrical information to the internal components. The internal components include the Vibrating Ossicular Prosthesis **(VORP)** and the Floating Mass Transducer (FMT). The FMT is attached to the ossicles. The vibrations are sent directly to the middle ear, bypassing the outer ear completely. The components of the Soundbridge System are pictured in Figure 6.7.

Figure 6.7. MED-EL VIBRANT Soundbridge Middle Ear Implant System

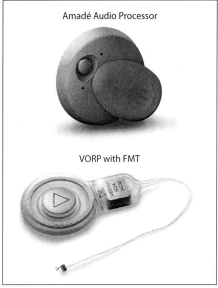

Images provided courtesy of MED-EL Corporation, USA.

A very recent addition to the hearing aid family (brought to market in 2012 and FDA-approved) is the **Sonitus Medical SoundBite**™ Hearing System, or SoundBite™. This is an in-the-mouth hearing prosthetic that works on the principle of bone conduction. The sound vibrations are transferred through the molars (via jawbones) to the cochlea. Sonitus Medical™ explains how the prosthetic works:

> It is intended to help patients who are essentially deaf in one ear regain spatial hearing ability.... Nearly invisible when worn, the SoundBite system consists of an easy-to-insert and remove ITM (in-the-mouth) hearing device—which is custom-made to fit around the upper, left or right, back teeth—and a small BTE (behind-the-ear) microphone unit. No modifications to the teeth are required. As long as one cochlea is functional, SoundBite Hearing System allows sound to travel via the teeth, through the bones, to the functioning cochlea, bypassing the middle and outer ear entirely. The ITM is easily inserted and removed by the wearer. It contains electronics; a sealed, flat, rechargeable battery; wireless capability that picks up sound transmissions from the BTE; and a small actuator that converts those signals into vibratory energy. All of these miniaturized components are hermetically sealed inside a dental grade acrylic that has been safely used for making dental appliances for many years. (2013)

Figure 6.8 provides images of the SoundBite™ hearing prosthetic.

163

Figure 6.8. Sonitus Medical SoundBite™ Hearing Prosthetic

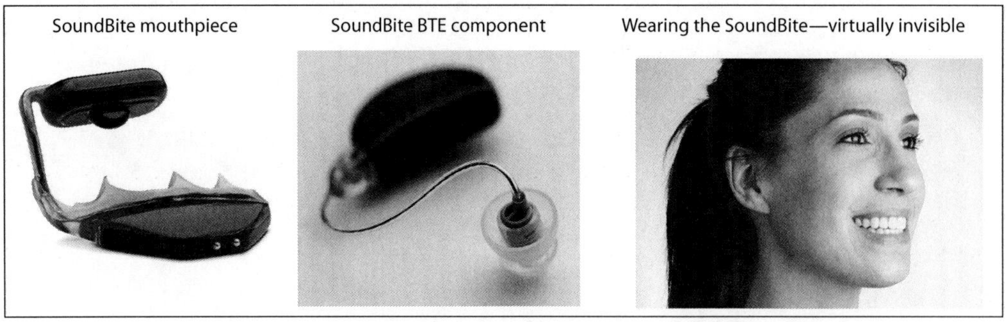

SoundBite mouthpiece   SoundBite BTE component   Wearing the SoundBite—virtually invisible

Images provided courtesy of Sonitus Medical ™.

Design and Function of Hearing Aids

How Does a Hearing Aid Work? The Mechanics

A hearing aid functions much like a public address system. In general, it takes a signal and intensifies it to make it louder. The hearing aid has a tiny microphone that captures the speech and environmental sounds near the listener. It takes these speech and environmental sounds and encodes them, using digital technology (digital processor).

This digital technology enables hearing aid manufacturers to do truly amazing things with both incoming and outgoing sound signals. The digital process allows sounds to be manipulated in a variety of ways. Audiologists manipulate sound by programming a hearing aid to accommodate an individual's specific hearing loss.

Non-audiologists working with children who wear hearing aids should be familiar with the following terms and what they mean to hearing aid users. You never know when you might be a member of the team asked to explain these words or concepts. For a detailed explanation of these terms, read *Digital Hearing Aids* by James M. Kates (2008).

As an audiologist considers the best options for a patient's hearing aid fitting, one area of interest is the **maximum output** of a hearing aid. Maximum output refers to the maximum intensity (loudness) that a hearing aid can produce regardless of the intensity of the input. The maximum output can be different at different frequencies. For example, one hearing aid may have a maximum output of 120 dBSPL at 500 Hz but only 110 dBSPL at 2000 Hz.

Along with the concept of maximum output comes the concept of gain. Gain represents the amount (in decibels) that an output level exceeds the input level. For example, speech is typically produced at about 60 dBSPL (input level), and a hearing aid that has 45 dBSPL of gain will make the output level 105 dBSPL. This output falls within the hearing aid's maximum output capacity of our example aid noted above. Audiologists need to know the maximum output of the hearing aid(s) they are fitting on their clients so that they can ensure the amount of sound being produced is tolerable for each individual.

There are many methods with which an audiologist can meet the listening needs of a hearing aid wearer by adjusting sound input and output. These methods include peak clipping, compression, and noise reduction. Some of these functions are hardwired into the hearing aid at the manufacturer, and some are able to be manipulated or adjusted by the audiologist in the office.

Peak clipping is a form of sound manipulation that limits the maximum output intensity of targeted frequencies by removing alternating amplitude peaks at a fixed level. In other words, if you think of the highest point (greatest amplitude) of a sound wave, the top part of every other wave is cut off at a specific level (height of the wave). Figure 6.9 shows what peak clipping looks like in a simple drawing. Peak clipping allows sound to be enhanced individually for each frequency without it becoming too loud or uncomfortable for the listener at any one frequency.

Figure 6.9. Manipulating Sound Output through Peak Clipping

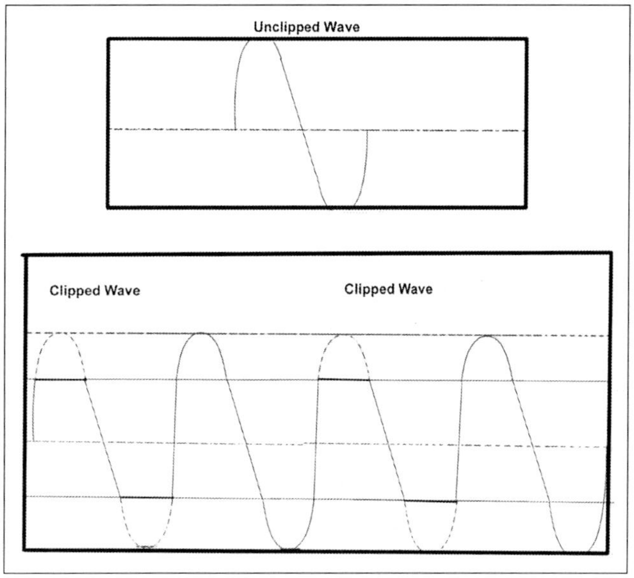

Compression limiting is another method for manipulating sound. Audiologists sometimes find compression limiting preferable to peak clipping, but this will usually depend on the individual's hearing loss. With compression methods, signals can be compressed on the input end of the process (**input compression**) or on the output end of the process (**output compression**). During output compression limiting, the outgoing signal is compressed into the person's dynamic range (see Chapter 5) by changing the amount of gain as the input signal changes; the volume control on the hearing aid affects the gain but not the maximum output of the aid. During input compression limiting, however, the incoming signal is compressed into the dynamic range and the volume control does impact the gain, as well as the maximum output. Input compression is used with mild to moderate hearing losses, and output compression is used with severe hearing losses in which the person also exhibits a reduced dynamic range. So, this means that sounds that would normally become too loud for a person to tolerate are digitally squeezed down so that the hearing aid wearer still has access to sounds without their becoming too loud to tolerate. This is important because too much output can damage a person's residual hearing (see Chapter 5) and it can also make listening difficult or

How Loud?

There are two additional terms associated with dynamic range. They are uncomfortable loudness level and most comfortable loudness level and can be defined as follows:

Most comfortable loudness level (MCL): This is the point that a person will identify, in dBHL, as the most comfortable for listening to speech. The speech signal is not too loud, nor is it too soft, but comfortable for long-term listening.

Uncomfortable loudness level (UCL): This term refers to the point, measured in dBHL, that is a sound (usually speech) too loud for comfortable listening. This can occur when there is too much gain for the person to tolerate while listening to speech.

The audiologist takes this into consideration when determining the dynamic range needed to optimize listening for each individual listener.

painful, which defeats the purpose of wearing the hearing aid in the first place.

Wide dynamic range compression is yet another form of compression. When talking about compression, the term **kneepoint** is used to describe the "point at which compression is activated" (Stach, 1997, p. 113). With wide dynamic range compression, the kneepoints are lower than in other forms of compression and the degree of compression is less. This type of compression is used to increase gain for soft sounds rather than protect a person from loud sounds. This is important to understand because the soft high-frequency sounds (consonants) are a large part of the English language and using this form of compression is helpful to the listener in understanding speech.

Finally, some hearing aids use wide dynamic range hearing compression and compression limiting together. Soft sounds are amplified based on the lower kneepoints and loud sounds are prevented from becoming too loud (DeBonis and Donohue, 2008). Figure 6.10 provides a graphic example of output compression.

Another function important for manipulating sound output is **digital noise reduction**. This type of technology allows the hearing aid to monitor incoming sounds and determine whether the input is noise or speech. When this technology detects noise, the aid automatically reduces the amplitude of the noise. This allows the speech signal to sound louder to the listener, thereby improving the listener's ability to hear speech in noisy environments.

Figure 6.10. Sound Compression (Output)

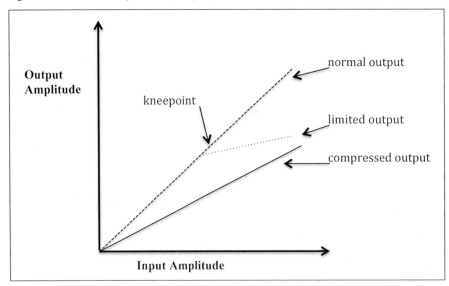

Microphones

In addition to the methods for manipulating sound mentioned earlier, a hearing aid has different components that allow it to function in a manner that assists a person's hearing abilities. For instance, different microphones and layouts of microphones can be used to help a person hear better. Omnidirectional and directional microphones are the two types most often used. **Omnidirectional microphones** pick up sound from all directions with approximately the same sensitivity. In other words, sounds are picked up from all directions and amplified equally. This can present a problem in noisy environments because the noise can be amplified as much as the desired signal (e.g., speech), and that makes it difficult to hear the speech above the noise. This problem is referred to as a poor **signal-to-noise ratio (S/N or SNR)**. For good speech perception, an audiologist wants the hearing aid(s) to increase the signal (speech) to be louder than the environmental sounds (noise). **Directional microphones** can assist in improving SNR because they are arranged so that they pick up sounds from one direction, typically the sounds coming from the front of the listener (usually where a speaker is talking). The speech information is therefore amplified more than the surrounding environmental sounds; it becomes easier for the listener to hear, and therefore discriminate, over the noise. Directional microphones can improve SNR by 6 dB (DeBonis and Donohue, 2008), which can be a significant difference when hearing the spoken message over the background noise.

Ear Molds

There are two ways to deliver amplified sound from a BTE hearing aid to the auditory canal. Sound can be sent through an ear mold or through an open fit earbud. The traditional mode of delivery is the ear mold. The audiologist makes an impression of the client's ear canal and concha, using a material that molds to and replicates the shape and size of the ear. This impression is then sent to a lab, which takes the impression and creates a custom ear mold for the individual. This ear mold can be made of any number of FDA-approved materials (plastic, acrylic,

How Do Noise-Cancelling Headphones Work?

Did you ever wonder how headphones can cancel noise so that you can listen more comfortably to music or a movie on an airplane? This is done by manipulating the *phase* of sounds (recall from Chapter 2). There is a microphone that picks up the incoming sound frequencies (the environmental noise), takes the sounds, and digitally produces sounds that are the complete opposite phase of the incoming noise. Those opposite phase sounds cancel out the incoming sounds! This allows the listener to hear only what is being fed through the headphones themselves, that is, the music on your iPod, the dialogue from your in-flight movie, or your narrator from your e-reader.

Listening to Noise through a Hearing Aid

Have you ever wondered what it sounds like to listen to speech through a hearing aid? How about listening to noise and speech simultaneously? It is a real challenge to try to hear a speech signal when there is a lot of noise. Visit this YouTube video for an excellent simulation: http://www.youtube.com/watch?v=1I37IzLIgQU

For all different types of simulations, visit the Supporting Success for Children with Hearing Loss website: http://successforkidswithhearingloss.com/demonstrations

silicone, Lucite, vinyl). The ear mold is then returned to the audiologist, who makes sure it fits properly and is capable of coupling (connecting) the hearing aid to the client's ear.

The **open fit** type of delivery, or coupling, system is relatively new and very popular. It is an aesthetically pleasing system because the tube and earbud are virtually invisible. The sound travels from a small BTE aid through a tiny thin tube that hooks over the ear and is attached to a small earbud that fits in the canal. The receiver is actually fit into the earbud, so sound is sent from the hearing aid directly into the ear canal. The earbuds come in various sizes to accommodate the different sizes of ear canals. There are several advantages to this type of delivery system: (1) no ear mold impression is needed, so the hearing aid can be used immediately on the day it is fit, (2) the ear canal remains open since there is no occlusion effect (stopped-up feeling) from a full ear mold, (3) the listener is able to receive sounds from the environment in addition to the amplified sounds from the hearing aid, which improves a person's listening abilities, and (4) most of the hearing aids using this delivery system have directional microphones, which increase the SNR and improve speech reception. In addition, it is reported that the open fittings are more comfortable in the ear, less itchy or irritating, and seem to reduce dampness in the canal from perspiration (personal communication, P. Surloff, August 12, 2013).

> **Learn More about Ear Molds**
>
> Remember that ear molds can be used for things *other* than hearing aids! Remember the old earplugs that you used for swimming? How would you like a custom set of ear molds to listen to your mp3? A very good website that provides a lot of information about all different kinds of ear molds can be found at Earmold Concepts, Inc.: http://earmoldconceptsinc.com/Home_Page.php. You may find a set that meets *your* needs!

Care and Maintenance of Hearing Aids and Ear Molds

Hearing aids require a major investment of money and time. One cannot simply place a hearing aid on a client and expect the person to use it without any training. In addition, a person needs to learn how to *listen* using a hearing aid. A hearing aid user is taught how to listen with aural habilitation and rehabilitation methods; such tasks and activities are described in Chapter 7 of this book.

Aside from this training, the hearing aid user must know how to take care of this expensive piece of equipment. Typically, the audiologist or hearing aid dealer provides the new user with a care kit. This kit may include a case to store the aid, some desiccant material to help dry out an aid if it gets damp, a blower to blow moisture out of the ear mold tubing, and a wax removal tool to remove earwax from the receiver tubing. Some kits also contain additional batteries and cleaning fluid in a spray bottle for the ear molds. Hearing aid users should get into a daily habit of hearing aid maintenance by (1) keeping the aid in a dry, easy-to-remember location, (2) check the batteries every day and replace them when needed, (3) wipe off the aid and the ear mold daily, (4) check for and remove earwax lodged in the ear mold or earbud daily, or as needed, (5) check the tubing for flexibility and replace when it becomes less flexible (around three months), and (6) check the toggle switches (if there are any) to ensure they are working correctly. If the wearer determines that there is a problem with the aid, the hearing aid dealer or audiologist should be contacted to locate and repair the problem.

A major problem for hearing aids, due to their electronics, is perspiration. Dampness, in general, can cause the hearing aid to malfunction, and excessive perspiration is the sort of dampness that creates problems for hearing aids. It is a good idea to have some dehumidifying or desiccant products available, especially if the hearing aid wearer plays sports or works out at a gym, works outdoors, or lives in a part of the country in which high humidity is a problem. Putting an aid into this material dries it out. Another way to dry out a damp hearing aid is by using a blow dryer and gently streaming warm air back and forth across the aid. The ear mold and tubing must also be dry on the inside. A bulb-style blower that has a small insertion point at the end is a good tool for drying out an ear mold and tubing. As a reminder, hearing aids are not generally waterproof and should not be worn in a shower, when swimming, or in a sauna or steam room. Exposure to these forms of dampness can ruin a hearing aid.

Another problem for hearing aids is earwax (cerumen). Everyone produces earwax, which in itself is usually not a problem. This becomes a problem, however, when the wax clogs an ear mold or receiver to the point at which sound is unable to get through. A variety of tools are available (e.g., brush, pick, loop) to remove the wax from the ear mold or receiver. The tubing and receiver should be checked every day to ensure that there is no wax buildup in the ear mold. Figure 6.11 shows various tools that assist in hearing aid maintenance.

Figure 6.11. Tools for Hearing Aid Maintenance

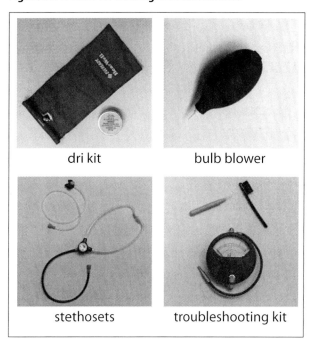

dri kit

bulb blower

stethosets

troubleshooting kit

The tubing that attaches the hearing aid body to the ear mold can also present a problem. The tubing is made of a flexible material that can lose its malleability over time. This loss of malleability can be caused by the tubing drying out or by ultraviolet rays from the sun damaging the material. When this happens, the tubing turns yellow and can crack or get holes in it. This can cause the sound to leak out, which creates a high-pitched squeal called feedback. Because of this, the tubing should be replaced every three months or so to keep such problems from occurring.

If a hearing aid is dropped against a hard surface (e.g., countertop or floor), the impact can damage internal and external parts of the aid. A hearing aid has delicate circuitry and internal components that cannot handle hard shocks. In addition, the hearing aid case can crack and toggle switches can break or stop functioning. It is important to thoroughly evaluate the hearing aid if it has been dropped and return it to the dealer or audiologist for repair if it is malfunctioning.

Last, but certainly not least, the hearing aid user must always carry spare batteries. If you work with young children who wear hearing aids, you may want to carry spare batteries with you. In order to preserve a battery's life and keep it working for as long as possible, it is a good idea to open the battery door at the end of each day to interrupt the battery's contact with the aid. It is also important for a hearing aid user to check the battery strength each day before wearing the aids to make sure they will function properly. In some cases, the hearing aid comes with a rechargeable battery that regains its power when placed back into its case each night. This type of battery also needs to be checked for replacement periodically. In all cases, no battery power = no hearing aid.

Figure 6.12. Visual Representation of a Hearing Loss and Hearing Aid Function

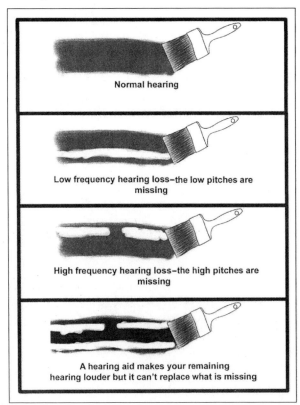

Normal hearing

Low frequency hearing loss—the low pitches are missing

High frequency hearing loss—the high pitches are missing

A hearing aid makes your remaining hearing louder but it can't replace what is missing

What a Hearing Aid Cannot Do

It is not uncommon for people to have misperceptions about the capabilities of the hearing aid. Hearing aids can make sound louder, but they cannot make sounds clearer. They cannot replace sounds that are missing as a result of the hearing loss. Figure 6.12 is a visual representation of this concept. Consider your hearing as a broad brushstroke of sound. When the brush is full of paint, you get a complete stroke with no missing elements. Hearing works the same way. When your cochlea and its hair cells are functioning properly, you get a full range of sounds that you are able to hear. If the brush does not have a full load of paint, the stroke shows gaps, it is an incomplete stroke, and a part of the picture is missing. In similar fashion, when there is damage to the cochlea and the tiny hair cells inside are injured or destroyed, the sound signal is missing a portion of its range. In the visual image, you can try to fill in the missing elements, but it will not look the same. In the ear, you cannot replace the damaged hair cells and those sounds are now permanently missing from your hearing. Even the best digital hearing aid cannot replace what is permanently missing. The best the aid can do is take sounds from the environment and make them louder. This can help the person wearing the hearing aid to cognitively fill in the blanks as much as possible, but it is not replacing the person's hearing sensitivity.

Cochlear Implants

A number of books have been written describing all aspects of **cochlear implants** (CIs), from the history of CI development, to the strategies for mapping the devices, to the types of instructional strategies best utilized with children who have CIs. Klein's (2011) concise yet thorough description in *Spoken Communication for Students Who Are Deaf or Hard of Hearing: A Multidisciplinary Approach* (2nd edition), is presented in the following sections of this chapter.

History of Cochlear Implants

Interest in stimulating the auditory nerve directly began back in the late 1700s when Allesandro Volta inserted metallic probes into his own ears and applied an electrical current. He reported hearing loud booms and crackling sounds. Throughout the 1800s, other doctors and scientists attempted to stimulate hearing using direct electrical currents but were unsuccessful. In the 1900s, doctors and scientists grew in their understanding of how hearing actually takes place and began to focus their efforts directly on the cochlea.

Figure 6.13. Cochlear Americas Nucleus 6 Cochlear Implant Products

In the 1960s and 1970s, Dr. William F. House at the House Ear Institute in California led the field in working on what we know today as a cochlear implant. Initially he implanted a single-channel unit into a postlingually deafened adult with a focus to bypass damaged hair cells and electrically stimulate remaining neural parts of the cochlea. Early single-channel users were able to detect environmental sounds and a variety of sound-related signals or tones. They could not understand speech.

The FDA approved the use of the single-channel implant for postlingually deafened adults in 1982. This opened up the opportunity to investigate the use of cochlear implants with children. In the meantime, Dr. Graeme Clark (Cochlear), Dr. Ingeborg Hochmair (MED-EL), and other researchers in Australia and Europe were

Image courtesy of Cochlear Americas ©2013.

working on the development of multichannel implants. It was believed that multichannel implants would provide more information to the cochlea so that speech could be understood. The first company to develop multichannel cochlear implants approved by the FDA was the Cochlear Corporation in Australia. In the 1980s, this device was tested in the United States and was FDA-approved for use in postlingually deafened adults in 1986. Pediatric trials began and the Nucleus-22 was FDA-approved for children in 1990.

Other companies were developing cochlear implants and applied to conduct clinical trials in the United States. Two companies in addition to Cochlear Americas received FDA approval in the mid-1990s to provide their cochlear implants to children and adults in the United States. They are Advanced Bionics and MED-EL. Figures 6.13, 6.14, and 6.15 show the latest implants produced by each of these companies. There are other CI makers in Europe and Asia, but their products have not yet been FDA-approved for use in the United States.

The rapid development and improvement of cochlear implant devices continues. There are new hardware cases that streamline the size and shape of the implant, making it more comfortable and aesthetically appealing (particularly for children). There are new internal processing systems that continue to advance how well the CI enables its user to understand speech, and there are new speech processing models that also enhance the user's ability to understand and use spoken language (Ertmer, 2005; Chute & Nevins, 2006).

Figure 6.14. Advanced Bionics Harmony, Naída CI Q70, and Neptune Cochlear Implant Products

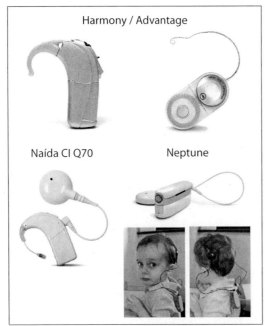

Implant images provided courtesy of Advanced Bionics, LLC; child image provided courtesy of DePaul School for Hearing and Speech.

Figure 6.15. MED-EL Cochlear Implant Products

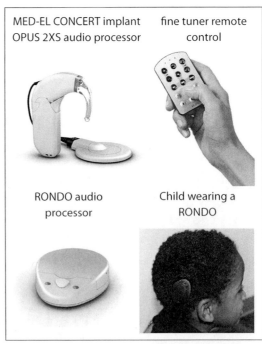

Implant images provided courtesy of MED-EL Corporation, USA; image of child provided courtesy of DePaul School for Hearing and Speech.

This was just a brief outline of the cochlear implant's history. For a more detailed history, Niparko (2009) is an excellent resource.

What Is a Cochlear Implant and How Does It Work?

The CI is composed of both external and internal parts. The external parts include a **microphone,** a **speech processor,** control switches, and a **transmitter**. The internal parts include the **receiver/stimulator** and the **electrode array.** Like hearing aids, cochlear implants require batteries to work.

Initially, CIs had large boxlike speech processors that were worn on the body using a halter-type device. Now, CIs are small, self-contained units. They look like a typical BTE hearing aid.

The case that fits behind the ear contains the battery compartment, the microphone, and the speech processor. A short cord attaches the case to the transmitter, which is a piece of circular plastic and contains a small magnet that allows it to attach to the scalp. The receiver is an internal component that contains an antenna and is housed in a sealed sterile plastic unit. It is surgically embedded in the mastoid bone behind the ear. It also contains a magnet that allows the transmitter to link the external and internal components through the scalp. Attached to the receiver is the electrode array. It looks like a very fine thread or wire about an inch long that has tiny electrodes placed along its length. This electrode array is inserted into the cochlea in the scala tympani and provides the electrical stimulation to the neural fibers in the cochlea along the basilar membrane.

> ### How a Cochlear Implant Works
>
> We can describe how an implant works, but nothing beats seeing a moving image of the process. You will find this type of example by visiting the MED-EL website:
>
> http://www.medel.com/us/show/index/id/75/titel/How+MAESTRO+Works to view a good video presentation on how a CI works.

When the CI user hears a sound, the microphone on the unit picks it up. The sound is converted to electrical energy and sent to the speech processor. The speech processor takes this energy and digitizes it, based on a specific speech processing program built into the unit. The digitized sound goes to the transmitter, which sends the signal, through the scalp, to the receiver. The receiver converts the digitized signals to electrical energy that is sent to the electrode array. When an electrode is stimulated, it in turn stimulates the corresponding area in the cochlea (low pitches are perceived on the apical end of the cochlea, and high pitches are perceived at the basal end). The nerve fibers that are stimulated then send the electrical impulse through the auditory nerve to the brain, and the brain perceives sound.

It is important to realize that not all of the electrodes fire at once. The speech processor program dictates how the signal will be formulated; the individual's map dictates how the individual electrodes will fire and the amount of energy that goes to each electrode.

How Is a Cochlear Implant Different from a Hearing Aid?

There are distinct differences between hearing aids and cochlear implants. The cost, the hardware and software, the various medical-psychosocial-functional indications for use, and the type of (re)habiliation are some of the major differences. However, the most significant difference is the purpose of the instrument and the way in which it works. The intent of a hearing aid is to make sound louder for the listener. As discussed in the beginning of this chapter, this increased intensity of sound can be manipulated digitally in a manner that best suits the configuration of an individual's hearing loss. Hearing aids do not replace missing sounds and do not fix a hearing loss. Hearing aids facilitate listening with the cochlea as it is.

The cochlear implant, on the other hand, has a completely different intent. The main difference is that a CI does not amplify sound. The electrode array of a CI is inserted into the cochlea and provides electrical stimulation to the neural tissues along the basilar membrane. This allows the nerve to send impulses from a wide range of frequency areas within the cochlea to the brain. The electrode array does not actually replace missing nerve fibers but allows those areas of the cochlea to be stimulated in a way that the brain is able to perceive and respond to the missing frequencies. The listener does not hear sound in the way that a person wearing a hearing aid hears sound. The sound stimulation takes a different form and, therefore, sounds completely different to the wearer. The CI makes sound more accessible to the person with a severe to profound hearing loss, but like the hearing aid, it does not make sound clearer.

Listening through a Cochlear Implant

As we noted in the text (and if you listened to the hearing aid simulation from the sidebar above), listening through a hearing aid is different than what we hear through a cochlear implant. Before you listen to any CI simulation, there is one very important thing to remember: it is the *brain* that perceives sound and decodes messages. The brain is a miraculous organ and it can learn to recognize all different kinds of sounds and make sense of the sounds it perceives. To those of us with normal hearing, the sounds from a CI are just plain horrible—no doubt about it! But, to a brain that has never heard normal speech and has learned to decode the CI signals, this is clear and makes all the sense in the world. Visit the following YouTube site for a simulation of both speech and music: http://www.youtube.com/watch?v=SpKKYBkJ9Hw

With a hearing aid, the brain perceives the same sounds that you and I hear (although they may be distorted or less intense). With a cochlear implant, the brain perceives sound as a series of squeals, clicks, and whooshes. The brain learns how to take those sounds and interpret them to represent speech and other sounds in the environment. However, the CI user has to be taught (through extensive auditory training and aural rehabilitation) how to use the CI to detect sound and perceive useful input from it.

What Cochlear Implants Cannot Do

The cochlear implant is truly a wondrous piece of scientific equipment. It has provided many people with a more viable means of establishing spoken communication skills because it has given them an alternate way to make sound accessible to the auditory system. There remains a caveat, however. A cochlear implant does not fix a hearing loss. The person who uses a cochlear implant is still deaf from a physical and physiological perspective. If anything should happen to the device and it fails to perform correctly, the wearer will not hear sounds at all and will be deaf for all intents and purposes.

What can go wrong? Batteries can die, the map that controls how the sound is processed can be erased, the hardware itself can break or malfunction, any major head trauma could damage internal components of the implant, the wearer can have an allergic reaction to the materials in the implant, and the list can go on. It is a marvelous piece of technological equipment, but any piece of equipment can stop working.

It is important for people working with children who wear CIs to remember this point. More frequently in the future, we will see children who use CIs function like any other hearing children, and that is fantastic. As professional or caregivers, we must also be cognizant of potential problems and how they might impact our implant wearers. We must recognize that a broken CI can potentially result in a breakdown in spoken communication abilities.

Making the Surgical Decision

Cochlear implant surgery has been a hot topic for a long time, especially among members of the Deaf culture. It is extremely difficult for parents to make the decision to implant their children, and because it is impossible to see into the future, it is hard for parents to determine if life will be better or easier after their children undergo implantation. But several factors have to be investigated if successful outcomes are to be obtained from cochlear implantation. Many professionals have to be consulted, and many considerations have to be taken into account from all perspectives.

Assessing the Cochlear Implant Candidate. Not all children are good candidates for cochlear implantation. Determining candidacy requires a team approach. Typically, the family physician, an ENT (ear/nose/throat) surgeon, a radiologist, an audiologist, an SLP, a psychologist or social worker, and an educator of deaf and hard of hearing children (TOD) are all involved in assessing and helping to decide on the appropriateness of CI surgery.

When physicians, audiologists, and radiologists begin the screening process for implantation surgery, they look at several variables. First, they look at the age of the child and the type and degree of hearing loss. Typically, CI surgery takes place after 12 months of age, but in some cases, children are implanted as young as six months of age. Within months of birth, a baby can be fitted with personal hearing aids, if hearing loss is identified early. It is essential for the child to have the opportunity to gain auditory information through the use of hearing aids as early in life as possible. The physician and audiologist want to know if the child has had any success using hearing aids. There are questionnaires and assessments that help to determine how much benefit a child receives from his hearing aids. CIs are designed for people who are at least severely or, more often, profoundly hearing impaired. CI candidates are those who have had minimal to no success with utilizing hearing aids for at least six months.

The surgeon will also want to closely examine the child's physical well-being. Is the anatomical structure of the cochlea capable of accommodating a CI? Does the child have other medical conditions that might interfere with the surgery or the success of the implant? Is the child currently in good health? If the child has poorly developed or absent cochleae, then cochlear implantation is not an option. If the child has retrocochlear lesions or other auditory nerve problems, then cochlear implantation will not work because the signal cannot travel along the neural pathway to the brain.

In addition to examining the physical and audiological factors, the CI implant team completes a thorough evaluation of the child's and family's psychological and social well-being. The child's overall development is evaluated. Are the fine and gross motor skills developing on target? Is the child showing appropriate cognitive and social growth? Do the parents understand the ramifications of the surgical procedure and all that is involved in postsurgical, audiological, and educational follow-up, and are they committed to these requirements? In some cases, the team may determine that the nature of additional conditions may preclude the likelihood of implantation success. For example, a child with severe sensory integration problems may find the implant signal extremely disorienting or disturbing and be unable to adjust to its input. A child with minimal cognitive abilities may not be able to process and make sense of the signal. A child with a severe seizure disorder may be negatively impacted by the electrical stimulation used in a cochlear implant. Therefore, an implant might not be appropriate for these children.

Another area of assessment is communication. The SLP and TOD together can help to provide a picture of the child's current receptive and expressive communication skills. In addition, the TOD is educated in relating auditory skill development to both speech and **sign language** development, as well as understanding hearing loss from an educational and classroom-based perspective. The SLP assesses the quantity and quality of speech sounds produced, as well as the functionality of those sounds. In other words, does the child use sound to gain attention? Does the child use sounds in a differentiated way? Are sounds developing in a normal progression? The TOD is typically skilled in the use of sign language and can help determine the child's responsiveness to sign stimulation. In addition, if parents begin using sign language with their child at birth, the TOD can assist in determining the child's receptive and expressive use of sign language. In general, children who demonstrate significant positive growth in listening and spoken language skills with their hearing aids are often not considered appropriate candidates for an implant.

Finally, cost and insurance coverage may be factors in making a decision about surgery. Recent research (Papsin & Gordon, 2008) indicates that bilateral cochlear implants are more effective than unilateral implants. Bilateral implants can be done simultaneously or in interstage intervals (sequentially). The decision may depend upon what the insurance company will cover. Medicaid rules differ by state, and some cover implant surgery for only one implant at a time. Some insurance companies do the same. Others will allow for simultaneous implants. The team needs to know the type of coverage the patient has prior to making a surgical decision (Klein, 2011, pp. 60–61).

Other Considerations. One major question that always arises is, "When is it the best time to get a cochlear implant?" Recent research by Dr. Anu Sharma and her colleagues at the University of Colorado at Boulder points very clearly to the importance of having an implant by the age of 3.5 years. This research focused explicitly on the brain's ability to respond to sound. Dr. Sharma looked at the length of time it took for the brain to respond and the impact sound deprivation had on these responses. Her team found that children who received cochlear implants by the age of 3.5 years had responses that were like those of a child with normal hearing. Children receiving implants between 3.5 and 7 years had a variety of responses but did not typically demonstrate the same response patterns as the younger recipients. Children who received implants after the age of 7 years demonstrated responses that reflected "cortical reorganization," indicating that the neural pathways for hearing had physically changed and responded in different and less connected ways to sound (Sharma, Nash, & Dorman, 2009).

Chute and Nevins (2006) talk about a Zone of Cochlear Implant Performance with two planes; the physiologic zone encompasses anatomy, physiology, and cognitive development, while the intervention zone encompasses the variety of support services an implant user might receive. Within these zones, Chute and Nevins review each of the areas taken into consideration when determining candidacy for implantation and the impact these have on the potential success or failure of the cochlear implant's performance. Within the physiologic zone, there is little that is within our control; we can only work with what the child has anatomically. Most opportunity for change lies in the intervention zone. The amount and quality of services and support can make a difference for the child along the success continuum. Chute and Nevins believe that "Any progress, no matter how small or how slow, should be indicative of success" (p. 40). Current professional feedback seems to indicate that parents (and educators) have high positive expectations for their children's performance after implantation, and when the expected progress isn't made or isn't made as quickly as expected, the implant is considered a failure. As educators, therapists, and parents, it is crucial to our students' success to view any and all progress made while using a cochlear implant as movement forward.

One of the biggest problems for children who receive cochlear implants appears to be a lack of follow-through after the initial postsurgical period. There is no doubt that families have good intentions. Parents would not put their child through an invasive surgical procedure without hoping to have positive results. Sadly, it is sometimes reported by teachers, therapists, and audiologists that caregiver follow-up is a problem. There are many missed appointments and missed mapping (explained later in this chapter) sessions. There is inconsistency in the use of the equipment. There is little carryover or support of new skills once the therapist or teacher ends a session (Personal communication, M. Barnes, 3/6/13; J. McCoy, 1/ 20/12; A. Thompson, 4/22/10; M. Lewis, 7/9/10; L. Johnston, 8/10/09). The follow-up issue should always be a part of the assessment and candidacy process. Ertmer (2005) notes that "...some parents fail to take full advantage of these programs.... Parental commitment to communication intervention should be assessed prior to making the decision to provide an implant" (p. 177). "The key factor for a child with a cochlear implant to be successful is the family"... Specialists at House Ear Institute note, "We cannot simply provide a child with a cochlear implant without helping the parents to understand their new roles as teacher, language facilitator and advocate" (House Ear Institute, 2010). Thus, lack of follow-up can have a negative impact on the child's use of the implant.

The decision to receive a cochlear implant is a serious one and should not be taken lightly. It is crucially important for parents to understand all that is involved before and especially after the implantation process. It is even more important for the implant team to examine all of the assessment data and then help guide parents in their decision-making process. CIs are still inaccurately viewed by many hopeful individuals as a way to "fix" hearing loss. It is the professional team's responsibility to make sure that everyone understands that a CI is not a fix but just another tool to assist in communication development.

The Surgical Procedure. Ertmer (2005) provides an excellent description of the surgical procedure for cochlear implantation. Prior to surgery, a variety of preparatory activities take place, such as blood tests, hearing tests, and insurance approval. The surgery itself is approximately a two- to three-hour procedure. The child has general anesthesia and is asleep for the entire process. The skin behind the selected ear is shaved and sterilized. An incision is made that will be hidden by the hairline. The flap of skin is pulled back gently and a surgical drilling tool is used to create a depression in the mastoid bone. The size of the depression depends upon the size of the internal receiver unit. A tiny passageway is drilled through the bone into the middle ear cavity. Great care is taken during this process so that the facial nerve is not disturbed in any way. The electrode array is inserted through this tunnel into the middle ear. Another tiny hole is made in the round window or cochlear wall, and the electrode is guided through this hole and along the basilar membrane in the scala tympani until it goes as far into the cochlea as possible. If the child is very young, a tiny loop of electrode cable is coiled near the receiver and allows the implant to remain undisturbed during the child's head growth. Once in place, the implant is activated and tested via inner-operative monitoring. If all parts are working correctly, the internal parts are fixed in place with a biocompatible cement or sutures, and the incision is closed. X-rays or CT scans may also be taken to document the position of the internal parts of the CI.

Children spend the night in the hospital and go home the next day. There might be some pain and stiffness in the neck and numbness on the head behind the implanted ear. Sometimes there is a change in taste that goes away within weeks. The numbness may last a bit longer. The child is given time for the surgical area to begin the healing process before the implant is activated, usually two to six weeks after surgery. Figure 6.16 provides an image of how a cochlear implant looks after implantation.

Figure 6.16. Implanted Cochlear Implant Device

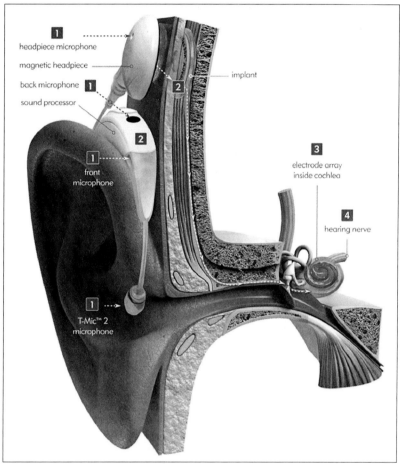

Image provided courtesy of Advanced Bionics, LLC.

Mapping. Mapping is the next step in the process. After the waiting period, the family returns to the audiologist to have the implant activated. This process is called mapping because the audiologist creates a guide, or map, in the electrodes so that they are set to respond at certain voltage levels that are detectable but not uncomfortable for the child. The amount of power that a child requires for each electrode is different, so it is critical that parents, teachers, and audiologists keep a close eye on the child's responses to sound. Cochlear implants are mapped several times until the most appropriate levels are found for the child. The audiologist will use "T-levels" to obtain the threshold levels, or lowest levels at which the child perceives sound and "C-levels" to obtain the levels at which the child indicates sound is comfortable.

To begin the process, the child's external components are fit, and a determination is made regarding the way in which the implant will initially be worn (clipped to the body for a tiny baby or ear level for an older baby and toddler). The magnet attached to the transmitter is adjusted for the correct amount of magnetic force to make contact with the internal receiver. During activation, the CI is worn by the child and connected through a wire to a computer that has mapping software. An audiologist or SLP will watch the child for responses to stimulation while a second audiologist begins using the computer to map the implant. The audiologist selects a stimulating mode for the implant that dictates the size of the area in which nerve cells are stimulated and the amount of electrical current needed to get a hearing response. Next, the audiologist sets the voltage for each electrode. The map controls the minimum and maximum amount of current that flows to each electrode and then is delivered to the auditory nerve fibers. The goal is to have all stimulation above the threshold (T-levels) yet still at a comfortable level (C-levels). The range for this amount of stimulation is called the dynamic range. The initial dynamic range may be small for a first-time CI user. As the child becomes accustomed to listening with the CI, the dynamic range changes and becomes wider so that the child can gain the maximum benefit from the electrical stimulation available for the cochlea. This is why an implant needs to be periodically remapped. As listening skills improve, the map is adjusted to accommodate for that growth, and additional stimulation is provided to facilitate even better listening opportunities.

Figure 6.17. Child Having CI Mapped

Figure 6.17 shows a child having his implant mapped by his audiologist. After mapping is completed, the output of the electrodes is balanced to ensure that voltage ranges are similar across the array. For young children, this is done automatically by the computer (known as neural response telemetry or NRT). Older children and adults can provide their own judgment related to the loudness and pitch of a signal produced by one or more electrodes. Figure 6.18 provides an image of a computer-mapped cochlear implant device.

Figure 6.18. Computer Image of a Completed CI Map

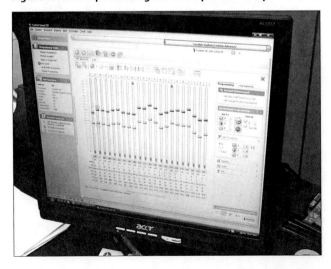

Finally, the moment that the family is waiting for arrives. The implant is turned on (activated), and speech or toy sounds are presented to the child. A child's reaction will vary greatly, and parents need to be informed that the child may respond with anything from a huge smile to tears. It is important that parents are comforting and positive with the child so that the first experiences are as positive as possible. Soft voices and familiar toys are the best initial stimulation. After the child experiences the sounds for the first time, the audiologist provides the parents with information about a wearing schedule to help the child become used to the implant. Ultimately, you want the child to wear the implant during all waking hours. At that point, the activation phase is now complete.

It is particularly important for early intervention services to be established so that they continue immediately after the implant is activated. The child should have the services of a certified teacher of deaf and hard of hearing children (preferably one with some coursework in early intervention), an SLP who has specific training in working with a child who has hearing loss (preferably one who has coursework and experience working with cochlear implants), and other early interventionists who have been identified as part of the child's team (Klein, 2011, pp. 64–65).

Follow-Up. To ensure that the CI is in working order and to facilitate the growth of listening and communication skills, follow-up by parents and a number of professionals is crucial. As noted previously, TODs, SLPs, and audiologists report that there is a significant downturn in performance when there are difficulties with follow-up activities.

The question becomes, "Who is the individual responsible for ensuring the appropriate follow-up takes place?" The answer to that question depends upon when the implant takes place and who the members of the team are at that time. When a baby or toddler receives an implant, social workers and early interventionists (EIs) are part of the team, and typically one of them becomes the case manager for the child and his family. Depending upon the roles and responsibilities outlined by the employer of the case manager, some important follow-ups can fall through the cracks. For example, a newly implanted child should return to the audiologist for remapping frequently during the first year. Each implant center has a schedule that it shares with the parent at the time the implant is activated. It becomes the parents' responsibility to make sure that they return for the scheduled mapping sessions. That being said, parents are extremely busy, often have other children and other concerns to deal with, and can easily forget to make an appointment for a mapping visit. Part of the remapping reminder responsibility should fall to the case manager. This is the person who is coordinating the services for the child and should maintain a master schedule for each child. Reminder conversations and notes can be sent to parents on a regular basis when the case manager utilizes a master schedule.

When a CI recipient is of school age, the case manager often becomes the SLP or the TOD. Even though the parent continues to be the individual ultimately responsible for scheduling remapping appointments, the TOD or SLP should also maintain a mapping schedule and routinely send parents updates and reminders about the remapping appointments.

In addition to the case manager, the audiology department of the implant center should also play a part in helping parents remember their remapping appointment responsibilities. It is not enough for the implant center to complete the surgery and turn on the unit. They should also have outreach personnel who follow up with every child through at least the first year post-implant. It is well documented that inaccurate mapping results in poor outcomes for CI users. Follow-up by the implant center itself could have a major impact in reducing these missed mapping appointments.

A second critical area of follow-up relates to the child's listening skills and communication development. Each of the CI manufacturers indicates on its website that there is no one more important to the development of good listening and communication skills than the parent. The parent is always the child's first teacher in everything, and that is even more so in the case of a child with a CI. Typically, when a child receives a CI, he is also assigned at least an SLP and a teacher of some sort. The teacher may be an early interventionist, or a TOD, or a special education teacher with experience in the birth–3 years population. The important thing is that these professionals must have some knowledge and experience with helping parents to develop good listening skills in their children. In most cases, these professionals each meet at the family's home weekly for a 60–90 minute visit. During this visit, a variety of skills are modeled for the parent, and the parent is asked to use the new skills with his child. The professional provides guidance and support so that the parent feels comfortable using the new skills for the following week. This can be extremely challenging for the parent, and it would help if the teacher or SLP provided mid-week follow-up contacts to ensure that the new skills are being used and to answer any questions the parent might have. That little bit of additional follow-up might be enough to facilitate the ongoing listening skill development needed for a new CI user to become a good CI user.

Focused follow-up in these two areas can make a difference in the child's successful use of a CI. When the map is accurate, and parents and professionals are working together on listening and communication skills, the likelihood of a more positive outcome is probable.

Care and Maintenance. As with any expensive and delicate piece of equipment, the CI must be maintained properly so that it will function correctly for the wearer. The CI is a sealed unit; there are only a few parts that need to be checked routinely. To assure that maintenance becomes a daily routine, just as with hearing aids, the CI should be kept in a dry environment that is readily accessible.

Cochlear implants work on batteries, and several models have optional rechargeable batteries. If using disposable batteries, the battery compartment should be open when the CI is not being worn. If using rechargeable batteries, the unit should be placed in its charger when not being worn. Batteries should be checked daily and replaced as needed.

Using the implant in wet environments has long been a goal for CI manufacturers. Currently, with the exception of the Advanced Bionics Neptune implant, CIs are not typically waterproof (although they may be water-resistant) and can suffer the same fate as hearing aids when exposed to extreme moisture. It is important to note that the waterproof aspects of the Neptune are limited. It is approved for submersion in no more than 3 feet of water for no longer than 30 minutes. In addition, it is not approved for saltwater immersion. In general, it is important to keep CIs dry and to have desiccant materials available should the CI become wet.

All CIs (except for the MED-EL Rondo) have cords that attach the BTE component of the CI with the transmitter. This cord should be checked for kinks or small cracks that can interrupt the travel of the sound signals to the internally implanted device. The wearer should also check all controls daily (whether a switch or remote style) to ensure that each feature on the controls works properly. Any problems with a CI require that the individual return to the audiologist for assistance and repairs.

Surgical and Equipment Concerns. As with any sort of surgery, there are always risks involved and these are discussed prior to making the final surgical decision. The following problems have been reported on rare occasions: (1) injury to the facial nerve during insertion of the array through the middle ear, (2) reactions to general anesthesia, (3) cerebrospinal fluid leakage from the hole created in the inner ear or elsewhere, (4) taste disturbance (the cranial nerve for taste also runs through the middle ear), (5) perilymph fluid leak from the cochlea through the hole created to place the electrode array in the cochlea, (6) reparative granuloma (a mass of granulation tissue) as a result of localized inflammation if the body rejects the implant itself, (7) meningitis—there was one particular type of array that appeared to be related to increased chance of contracting meningitis; that array is no longer used in CI surgery, (8) tinnitus (ringing in the ears), (9) vertigo or dizziness, (10) wound infection, (11) numbness around the ear, (12) blood or fluid collection at the surgery site, and (13) unforeseen complications from surgical procedure (Taormina-Weiss, 2012).

In addition to the surgical risks, as with any piece of technological equipment, medical or otherwise, there is always a possibility of hardware and/or software failure. The audiologist or CI manufacturer can remedy software failures, such as problems with the speech processor program. External hardware problems need to be addressed by the CI manufacturer. A surgeon must address internal hardware problems, those involving the receiver or electrode array, because it will likely involve the removal of the implanted device.

Given that hundreds of thousands of CI surgeries have been completed worldwide to date, the frequency of any of these problems is very low and should not necessarily dissuade a potential CI candidate from investigating having the surgery. A completely informed decision for surgery is always a best practice.

Other Concerns. Taormina-Weiss (2012) provides an excellent summary of the various everyday difficulties one might encounter in the use of a CI. The following information contains excerpts from her discussion.

Any device we use in adjunct to our usual body functions can impact our daily activities. One major impact of the use of a CI includes problems related to specific medical tests or procedures. For instance, one typically cannot have an MRI test done because of the danger to the patient. The CI can become dislodged or the internal magnet can be demagnetized. There are some implants available that are FDA-approved for MRI testing under very controlled conditions and at low levels of magnetism. Other treatments related to electrical stimulation to brain tissues are also dangerous for CI users.

In addition to these medical concerns, there might be issues with the CI wearer's ability to completely understand speech and process spoken language. There are no tests or diagnostic indicators that can predict with any certainty that the CI will allow the wearer to fully and completely access spoken communication and language. For a parent who is expecting his child to sound "like a normally hearing child," the chance of disappointment is great. There are many physiological variables impacting CI performance that are beyond anyone's control. A surgeon and audiologist can recommend the best possible CI with the best possible fit, the surgery can be flawless, and the child can receive regular professional services and have parents who follow through on every single suggestion, but something physiological gets in the way of allowing that child "perfect" communication skills (aside from the fact that there are very few hearing people who exhibit "perfect" communication skills).

Finally, there are just everyday logistics that can become cumbersome. The CI wearer will have a dependency upon batteries, either disposable or rechargeable. Remembering to recharge a battery on a regular basis can add to the burden of everyday chores. The CI wearer might occasionally hear strange sounds that are caused by interactions with other magnetic fields. In addition, skin irritation can become a problem if the magnet is set too tightly to the scalp.

Learn More about Deaf Culture

The best way to learn about Deaf culture is to immerse yourself in the community. We all don't have that option, so the next best thing is to read books that will help you understand the community and its mores. The following books, many of which are classics in the field of Deaf education, can help you understand more about the fascinating world of deafness and Deaf culture.

A Journey into the Deaf World by Harlan Lane

A Place of Their Own: Creating the Deaf Community in America by Jon Vickrey Van Cleve

Deaf in America: Voices from a Culture by Carol Padden

Deaf Like Me by Thomas and James Spradley

Everyone Here Spoke Sign Language: Hereditary Deafness on Martha's Vineyard by Nora Ellen Groce

Inside Deaf Culture by Carol Padden

Train Go Sorry: Inside a Deaf World by Leah Hager Cohen

When the Mind Hears: A History of the Deaf by Harlan Lane

Deaf Culture Concerns

Although this book is not the place for a lengthy discussion on "Deaf Culture and the Deaf community" and its historical response to the use of cochlear implants, it would be remiss for us not to address the issue in a basic way. Members of the Deaf community have a variety of views; however, the general perspective of the Deaf community is that there is absolutely nothing wrong with a person who is deaf. They strongly feel that nothing needs to be fixed because nothing is broken. Therefore, the use of a CI is both unnecessary and a medical risk.

Josh Aronson's award-winning documentary film entitled *Sound and Fury* and his follow-up *Sound and Fury—Six Years Later* brought this argument to the mainstream and stirred a remarkable amount of discussion among the general public, as well as those in the various fields who work with individuals who are D/deaf or hard of hearing. For information about these films and a wonderful Q&A discussion between National Association of the Deaf and Alexander Graham Bell Association for the Deaf and Hard of Hearing representatives regarding this documentary and the issues surrounding cochlear implantation, go to the following website: http://www.pbs.org/wnet/soundandfury/cochlear/debate.html.

Today, members of the Deaf community recognize that hearing parents are likely to be responsive to the idea of cochlear implants. There remains concern that these same parents are not given all possible options when making decisions for their children. Even though it appears the intensity of the anti-CI discussions is reduced, the Deaf community continues to feel strongly that CIs remain unnecessary and are an affront to Deaf culture and its existence.

Therapy Models and Strategies

There are a variety of options available to parents whose children have had cochlear implant surgery. We can assume that the primary reason that parents elect to move forward with cochlear implant surgery is to provide their child with what they consider the best chance for developing spoken language. The intent of the implant is to provide improved hearing sensitivity and speech perceptibility. Speech will not develop on its own; the child needs to learn to listen in order to learn how to make sense of the incoming sounds.

Listening and Spoken Language Approach: Aural-Oral and Auditory-Verbal Therapy Models. There are two speech therapy models whose focus is on developing spoken language through listening. Developing speech through listening is called the Listening and Spoken Language (LSL) approach. The two models of this approach are the **Aural-Oral therapy model** and the **Auditory-Verbal Therapy (AVT) model.** Both of these models have longstanding histories and supporters. Daniel Ling (2002) is most closely associated with the Aural-Oral model, and Warren Estabrooks (2006) is the currently recognized expert in AVT. The two models are similar in their focus on listening as the primary means by which a child should develop spoken communication skills. Neither model promotes the use of any form of sign language or other hand-signal system to promote speech. The major difference between the two models is that the AVT model is strictly unisensory. This means that only hearing is used at all times and that speechreading, or the use of tactile cues, is not endorsed as part of the child's training.

With the increased number of children receiving cochlear implants, the early intervention programs and schools offering oral communication options have also increased. The Oral Deaf Education website (www.oraldeafed.org) provides a current list of the facilities that offer Listening and Spoken Language educational services. The best source for locating certified Listening and Spoken Language Specialists (Auditory-Verbal Therapists) is through the Alexander Graham Bell Association for the Deaf and Hard of Hearing website (www.agbell.org).

Figure 6.19. Cued Speech Handshapes and Hand Positions

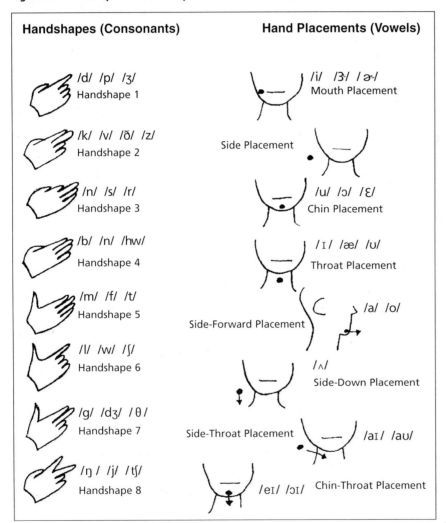

Visually Supported Models. For parents interested in providing additional sensory or linguistic input in their child's spoken communication program, the use of **American Sign Language (ASL)**, English-based sign language systems and **Cued Speech/Language** are available choices. The English-based sign language system programs are often referred to as Total Communication. American Sign Language is used as a basis of language development in **Bi-Bi (Bilingual/Bicultural)** programs that then transition to spoken and written English later in the child's development. Cued Speech/Language programs are not as widely available but are being used with more frequency as the system is being recognized as one that can assist in spoken communication development. Cued Speech/Language consists of eight handshapes that represent all of the consonants in English and four hand positions around the mouth and throat that represent the vowels. Using the handshapes and hand positions provides a visual representation of speech. Figure 6.19 illustrates these handshapes and hand positions.

Proponents of using these modes of communication in addition to listening suggest that the early and immediate development of a visual language provides the linguistic foundation upon which spoken communication can develop. There are EI and school programs that offer sign language options.

With any child who has a hearing loss, the focus of spoken communication development should be to enable the child to use all possible tools at his disposal to communicate effectively and efficiently. The same should be said for children who have cochlear implants. To date, there is no research available that definitively states which child will be "poster-child" perfect in the development of spoken communication skills. As with any population, performance varies widely. It is our responsibility as professionals to help parents understand this point. Their child, may indeed, become a model child for the CI. On the other hand, their child might be limited for unknown or unforeseen circumstances and develop auditory detection or discrimination skills only. She might be able to produce single words or basic sentences with intelligibility. We must remember that these skills do fall within the range of spoken communication and that they are not failures in the system. This latter child needs to use more than one tool to communicate effectively. The question becomes, what do we do from Day 1 to encourage the best possible outcome, given each child's unique situation? The child's team helps to make that decision.

Using Sign Language with a Cochlear Implant. In 2009, the Cochlear Implant Education Center at the Laurent Clerc National Deaf Education Center at Gallaudet University hosted a large national conference, "Cochlear Implants and Sign Language: Building Foundations for Effective Educational Practices." At this conference, the use of ASL with children who have CIs was discussed from a variety of perspectives. The participants in this conference were deaf/Deaf and hearing and represented all levels of education from across the United States. The outcome of this conference resulted in three high impact strategies that focused on networking and collaboration, development and sharing of resources, and encouragement of outreach activities to stimulate and reinforce the use of ASL with students who use CIs. A summary of the proceedings from this conference can be found at: http://www.gallaudet.edu/clerc_center/information_and_resources/cochlear_implant_education_center/cochlear_implants_and_sign_language_building_foundations_for_effective_educational_practices.html.

This conference helped to support the efficacy of using ASL (and in the authors' opinions, other English-based sign language systems or Cued Speech/Language) in addition to spoken language as an appropriate option for any child who has hearing loss. Experience shows that once an individual is able to communicate through spoken communication, other modes fade and are used only when there is difficulty in understanding speech.

Brainstem Implants

As we discussed in the candidacy section, not all children are eligible for cochlear implantation. For example, if a child is born without cochleae, there is no way to provide a cochlear implant. Adults who suffer from neurofibromatosis type II are unable to process sound from the cochlea. The medical profession is now on the cutting edge of another type of implant called a **brainstem implant**. As noted in Shannon (2011):

> The auditory brainstem implant (ABI) is similar in design and function to a CI, except that the electrode is placed on the first auditory relay station in the brainstem, the cochlear nucleus (CN). The ABI electrode array is a small (8 × 3 mm) paddle that contains 21 small electrode contacts. . . . The CN also has multiple cell types that are specialized to extract different types of information from the VIII nerve input. The ABI electrode array is placed along the surface of the CN and each electrode likely activates a variety of neuron types, possibly with different characteristic frequencies. . . .

The House Ear Institute (2013) announced in January 2013 that the FDA has now approved ABI trials for children. In May 2013, three-year-old Grayson Clamp became the first child in the United States to receive an ABI (WRAL.com, 2013). His progress will be monitored closely!

Hearing Assistance Technology (HAT)

Classroom Amplification Systems

In addition to a personal hearing aid, there are systems that allow an individual to receive amplified sound in the general environment. Each of these systems is set up to accommodate a listener's needs in a large group setting. Typically, sound engineers examine the acoustic properties of a facility, such as a stadium or auditorium, to determine what the best system would be for that particular environment. Educational audiologists examine classroom environments and other school environments to determine the best sound input combinations for a child with hearing loss. All of the following systems improve the signal-to-noise ratio (SNR) for the listener. These systems allow a person using **hearing assistance technology (HAT)** to hear individual speakers in a large, noisy, or crowded environment by having the amplified sound sent directly to his own personal hearing aid. The signal (amplified speech) is then louder than the noise (environmental sounds), thus improving the SNR.

Induction Loop System

The **induction loop system** uses the interactive relationship between electricity and magnetism to enable sound to be transmitted to a **telecoil** inside a personal hearing aid. An induction loop is a hardwire system that can be set up in a large area, such as around the periphery of a room, or in a small personal area, such as surrounding a favorite chair. In addition, it is possible to wear a personal loop around the neck, making sound accessible within almost any location. The sound waves within the loop area are converted into electrical current that flows through the wire and into a magnetic field, which is then picked up by the telecoil wire inside the hearing aid. The voltage is amplified and converted back to sound by a receiver. That sound is transmitted to the listener through the telecoil setting of the hearing aid. The signal received through the telecoil sounds as if the speaker is closer to the person wearing the hearing aid than if the microphone were used alone. Induction loops can be set up in classrooms or anywhere in a home environment. As long as a loop system is available, the user can use induction loop technology.

Frequency Modulated Systems

Frequency modulated (FM) systems are a second type of group amplification system; these systems use radio-frequency transmissions. An FM system is a portable system that allows the user to move among many different environments and maintain an excellent SNR with little distortion. The speaker wears a transmitter that sends the speech signal at a particular FM frequency, and the listener wears a receiver that is either a separate listening device or a device coupled to the personal hearing aid. The receiver is set to match the FM frequency of the transmitter. In this way, multiple FM units can be used within the same environment because they are transmitting on different FM frequencies. Therefore, each listener receives only the information sent by his specific FM transmitter. These systems can be used in virtually any environment—from a classroom in a school for deaf children, to a classroom in a neighborhood school, to even to an area completely separate from the school, such as a field trip to the zoo. FM systems are designed so that a transmission degrades after a certain distance from the transmitter; however, FM systems are not usually affected by obstructions in the environment.

The FM systems differ from loop systems in that they do not convert sound to another form of energy. Instead, the transmitter modifies the sound signal, and a receiver picks up the modified signal and produces a voltage that is proportional to the original signal.

The FM transmission systems have some disadvantages. The range of FM signals available for transmission is controlled by regulatory agencies. Each country has specified bands that are licensed to be available for FM uses. In addition, on occasion, an FM user may experience an interfering signal or drop out (the signal is lost).

Infrared System

A third form of group amplification is the **infrared system (IR)** of transmission. Infrared works on the principles of electromagnetic radio energy but at a much higher frequency. This is an electromagnetic signal that is perceived as red light. This signal behaves like light waves, so it can be easily blocked or attenuated (reduced) by items in the environment. The audio signal is modulated as an infrared light signal; the receiver picks up the infrared signal using a headphone, earphone, or coupling device attached to the personal hearing aid, and converts the light signal back to an audio signal. This type of device is often used in public auditoriums and theaters and is popular in classrooms designed explicitly for deaf children. Infrared transmitters are placed strategically throughout the room, and the listener wears a headphone device that allows reception of the performance.

Sound-Field System

A fourth system that has gained recent popularity is the classroom **sound-field amplification system**. This amplification system is based on the use of acoustic gain in the environment; the listener receives acoustic signals through the regular microphone of his personal hearing aid. This system is based on the premise that a general increase in the intensity of the speech signal in the open environment reduces the level of the background sound enhancing the signal-to-noise ratio. This is accomplished by placing speakers strategically around the classroom. The teacher speaks into a microphone and the message is amplified for everyone in the class. The system is wireless, which allows the teacher to move effortlessly around the room. In addition, extra microphones can be ordered and used by all students in the room to amplify their own voices as well.

There are advantages and disadvantages to each system. The major strength of the FM, loop, and infrared systems is the significant increase in the SNR because the sound is transmitted in a nonacoustic form. There is much less opportunity for distortion and reverberation in the signal with these systems. The sound-field amplification system is the most convenient and least expensive. In addition, it has the potential to help *all* of the students in the classroom maintain their focus on the instruction, and it can help reduce vocal strain for the teacher. Major disadvantages of each system, in general, include the drop and interference problems experienced by FM systems, transmission blockage for infrared systems, the limiting spatial nature of the loop systems, and the possibility of less than adequate SNR increases in the sound-field amplification systems.

Digital Modulation (DM) System

As with all technologies, there are always new developments in the pipeline. The latest and greatest amplification strategy being developed presently is the **digital modulation (DM)** technology. Phonak's (2013) **Roger system** is the newest system being introduced in schools across the country. This is a truly remarkable new technology. The Roger system uses the concept of Bluetooth wireless technology (think of Bluetooth headphones, hands-free earpieces for cell phones, and other Bluetooth connective technology you use) to transmit signals that are digitized into tiny units. Here is how it works: a sound source (speech) is digitized and the signal is transmitted in short (microsecond) bursts of code that broadcast repeatedly at different channels at 2.4000 and 2.4835 GHz. The Roger systems constantly monitor to determine which channels are free and "hop" around the channels occupied by other systems. The digital codes let the receivers know which signals are available, and that ensures privacy. The teacher or audiologist does not have to assign specific frequencies to any one student! The point of the system is to significantly reduce problems with transmission, improve the clarity of the signal, and significantly increase the SNR to enable listeners to hear well in noisy environments. With this type of signal, there is virtually no distortion. Recent research (Thibodeau, 2012) demonstrated that the DM signal was far superior to any other signal (particularly in noise). Her research subjects heard the speech signal significantly better with the DM system than with the traditional or adapted FM systems. This improvement was seen for both hearing aid and cochlear implant users. The difference in the sound quality and improved SNR is amazing. Listen for yourself to the difference by visiting the Phonak website: https://www.phonakpro.com/us/b2b/en/products/roger.html

Summary

We covered a plethora of information in this chapter. You were briefly introduced to the history of the hearing aid and provided with the basic principles of how a hearing aid works. We described what a hearing aid can and cannot do in alleviating hearing loss. Different types of hearing aids were discussed, and information was provided about those models most appropriate for use with children. Care and maintenance was reviewed. Next, we provided you with extensive information on cochlear implants, including their design and function. We also discussed candidacy for implantation, the surgical procedure, and the importance of follow-up care and activities, including mapping. The types of therapy services available to develop good listening skills using the CI and the concerns of the Deaf community about cochlear implants were presented. In the final section of this chapter, we reviewed the currently available Hearing Assistance Technologies (HAT), described how each operates, and introduced you to the latest technology to hit the field (digitally modulated amplification systems).

Know that this technology will continue to change and morph over time. What is "great" today will become obsolete tomorrow. One thing can be said to summarize hearing aids, implants, and HAT—expect change.

Chapter 6 Food for Thought

1. Read the opening scenario again. What should be going through Caleigh's mind as she addresses the gentleman in her Urgicare?

2. How do the osseointegrated, middle ear implant, and in-the-mouth hearing aids differ from traditional BTE aids?

3. Explain the concept of maximum output and its importance to the hearing aid wearer.

4. Who are the members of the CI surgical team, and what are their roles in the decision making process?

5. Compare and contrast the five HAT systems described in this chapter.

6. What is your opinion concerning the use of ASL with a child who has a CI?

Chapter 7

Wired Up and Hear We Go: Aural Rehabilitation

Scenario

Grant gradually lost his hearing sometime within the first two years of life. His parents became concerned when he did not understand what was being said to him. They noticed that his cousins of similar ages understood more and said more words as well. At age two, his speech was delayed and he only babbled sounds, no real words. His parents enrolled him in early intervention and he began working with a teacher of the deaf (TOD) and a speech-language pathologist (SLP). Two months later, Grant was diagnosed with severe to profound hearing loss bilaterally. He was fit with hearing aids and after a trial period of several months, it was determined that Grant was a candidate for a cochlear implant. He received a cochlear implant at age three.

Grant continued to receive early intervention services while attending a specialized preschool classroom for children with mixed disabilities. His TOD focused on Grant's ability to wear his implant and hear during classroom story time and classroom instruction. At the same time, his SLP was working on improving his ability to follow directions and make requests. His audiogram showed that with his cochlear implant, Grant was able to hear low and high frequency speech sounds at a conversational level. Grant was making small gains with his speech, but he continued to fall significantly behind his peers in his expressive language and language comprehension skills.

By age five, Grant had had over three years of intervention with a TOD and an SLP, and almost two years of listening experience using his cochlear implant. Yet he started kindergarten with major deficits in his listening, speech, and language skills. He communicated through a combination of gestures, sounds, and a few real words that were difficult to understand. He was unable to follow simple verbal directions without visual and gestural cues.

Formal testing revealed that Grant's cognitive skills were in the average range; however, his speech and language skills were similar to that of a one-year-old child. He was becoming frustrated with his limited ability to communicate.

Grant's parents were confused and upset. They wondered how their smart child who could hear so well still had so much trouble understanding and using speech. They wondered if they had made wrong choices with his educational placement and decision to give him the cochlear implant. And most of all, they worried that Grant would never be able to communicate well and therefore never finish school and become an independent adult.

When you finish reading this chapter, you will be able to assist Grant's parents in continuing to develop his communication skills.

Key Vocabulary		
acoustic highlighting auditory comprehension auditory detection auditory discrimination auditory identification aural habilitation	aural rehabilitation background noise critical period hearing age incidental learning manner of production	parentese place of production features plasticity prosody suprasegmental

It's Not Like Wearing Glasses

Unfortunately, a common misconception about hearing loss is that hearing aids, cochlear implants, and other hearing devices correct hearing loss in the same way that glasses correct vision problems. As stated in Chapter 6, you cannot put a hearing aid or cochlear implant on a child and correct hearing so that it will sound the same as sound heard by an unaffected, undamaged ear. Glasses can restore normal vision, but hearing aids and cochlear implants cannot restore normal hearing. In addition, though the device may enable a child's ears to hear the sound, the brain needs to learn how to process and interpret the new auditory signal that is coming in. A child needs to learn to listen. This is the goal of aural (re)habilitation. For a child who has never developed listening skills, it is more accurately referred to as **aural habilitation**. For a child who has had a period of time with hearing and then has lost hearing, the process is better named **aural rehabilitation**. The ability to hear and listen is a prerequisite to spoken language development.

In our example, Grant was able to hear the speech and environmental sounds well, but his brain had not yet learned how to take that information and make it meaningful. He had not yet learned to listen. Although he received specialized services from knowledgeable individuals, nobody provided Grant with precise and systematic activities to address development of his auditory system. Without a strong foundation of auditory development, he was unable to fully benefit from the therapy provided.

Auditory skills develop over time. They develop by hearing the sounds around us: environmental noises, music, and speech. A child who is born without a hearing loss has already been hearing sounds while in the womb. Research on infants has shown that babies in the first few weeks of life are able to recognize their mother's voice (Université de Montréal, 2010). Researchers have also demonstrated that infants show preference for listening to voices speaking their native language by age six months (Kuhl, Williams, Lacerda, Stevens, & Lindblom, 1992). However, a child's auditory skills are not fully developed at birth. The brain needs time, practice, and repeated exposure to auditory information in order to make sense of what is heard. A vast amount of listening development occurs in the first year of life. Before a child is ready to speak his first words, his brain has been taking in and making sense of the auditory world around him. When a child misses out even on a small amount of listening experience, the effect can be significant and long-lasting if he is not given opportunities to develop the foundational auditory skills that he lacks.

Critical and Sensitive Periods

Research tells us that the human brain is most receptive to learning listening and speaking skills in the early years of life. The first 3½ years of life are considered the most sensitive period for learning because that is when the neural plasticity of the brain is functioning at its maximum level (Sharma, Dorman, & Spahr, 2002; Sharma, Dorman, & Kral, 2005). **Plasticity** refers to the ability of the brain to grow and change based on the stimuli received. Because the first 3½ years have been identified as having the greatest plasticity, the brain is most able to soak up listening and language information at this time. Brain plasticity continues to function at its most elastic and efficient levels in the time period from 0 to 7 years. This is considered the **critical period** for developing listening and spoken language skills. Brain imaging research has clearly identified auditory regions of the brain that are active during listening tasks (Sharma & Nash, 2009). When looking at images of brains that have had less auditory exposure due to deafness, the auditory centers are less active when they are presented with sound. The most interesting feature of this work is that the auditory regions in the auditorily deprived individuals were found to be active when visual information was presented. So what was shown is that the brain reassigned the function of the auditory region since it was not being used. This research shows the plasticity of the brain and confirms what educators have known for many years: stimulating the auditory regions and pathways in the brain in the early years is critical for the development of effective listening and spoken language skills.

Auditory Access Is the Foundation of Auditory Skill Development

The first and most important way to provide auditory access to the brain is to ensure that children have early access to sound. Early diagnosis and intervention are essential to effective aural rehabilitation (Yoshinago-Itano, Sedey, Coulter, & Mehl, 1998).

After a child is diagnosed with hearing loss and fit with a hearing device, it is crucial that he wears his device all the time. Children who do not have hearing loss are hearing whenever they are awake; therefore, they are continually developing their listening skills throughout the day. Children with hearing loss who have already had a period of time without optimal hearing need to listen as much as possible. From the day they are fit with a hearing device, it is recommended that they wear the device whenever they are awake.

Having children wear their hearing devices is often easier said than done. Babies and toddlers do not always easily accept having a foreign object on their ear(s). Preschool-age and older children may not like the way the aid looks or feels and will often take it off. No matter what the age of the child, when a hearing device is newly fit, it will likely sound very different from what the child is accustomed to and he may not like it. Parents, teachers, and other caregivers need to be aware of the importance of keeping the hearing devices on all of the time. The adults are the ones who will have to maintain diligence in putting the hearing devices back on the child every time the devices come off. If the child takes it off 100 times a day, it needs to go back on 101 times (personal communication, Don Goldberg, 2007). Parents may become weary of this and give in. They may feel like two hours in a day is long enough and good enough. If this happens, the child will miss out on a huge amount of auditory input. It can be helpful to give the parents a realistic example of how this limited use of hearing devices will affect their child. Karen Rossi's Learn to Talk Around the Clock curriculum (2003) provides a great example of the effects of limited use of hearing devices in children. This example uses simple calculations to compare the number of hours of listening time for children who wear a hearing device for a limited amount of time to that of a child without hearing loss who hears during all waking hours. At age three, it is estimated that a child who wears his hearing device(s) for only three hours a day will have three years less listening experience than those who are listening whenever they are awake.

Children need to hear as much as possible during the day in order to benefit from incidental learning. Incidental language learning is informal learning that occurs as a result of exposure to language in the environment, without direct teaching. Ears are open 24/7 and so, without even consciously attending to the sounds and speech around them, hearing children collect and often retain the information, vocabulary, and grammatical structures they hear incidentally. It has been estimated that as much as 90 percent of what children learn, including their vocabulary, is learned by listening to speech that is not directed to them, or hearing incidentally (Anderson, 2013). Therefore, as educators and caregivers, we would naturally want to give this same opportunity to children who have hearing loss.

Appropriate Audiological Management

In addition to establishing full-time use of hearing devices, the devices need to be properly maintained to ensure that they are always functioning as they were designed. Full-time use won't matter much if the microphone is clogged or the battery is dead. Parents, teachers, and caregivers need to know how to perform daily listening checks, change batteries, and troubleshoot any problems that may occur with the devices. Frequent audiological appointments are also necessary to be sure that the hearing device is programmed correctly to meet the child's specific listening needs.

Working with Parents/Caregivers

Parents play a key role in any aural rehabilitation program. They will be the constant in their child's life because the child's therapists and teachers may change from year to year. Parents/caregivers are also going to spend more time with their child than any professional. They are also the ones who are able to integrate listening skills with their daily activities. The more the act of listening is part of a child's everyday life, the more he will learn to use his listening skills. Parents who are educated about deafness and aural rehabilitation are able to be more involved in their child's rehabilitation program. Parents who are involved are better able to provide what their child needs to be successful. The level of parental involvement is highly correlated to the amount of a child's success (Calderon, 2000).

Parental Grief

Sometimes parents are not ready to be involved in the way the professionals want and need them to be. Many times, the grief of dealing with having a child with hearing loss prevents them from being able to be productive members of the team. Professionals need to be aware of the possibility that the parents may be having a hard time dealing with the grief. One cannot predict the level of grief and the impact it may have based on the severity of the child's hearing loss or other issues. Each parent responds differently, and it is often the professionals working with the child who encounter parental behaviors and attitudes that are related to the grief they are experiencing. It is best for teachers and therapists to listen without judgment or suggestions. Without knowing all facets of the situation or the scope of emotions the parent is experiencing, suggestions made by teachers or therapists may be misguided or misinterpreted. Parent support groups or programs that match families to other families with similar circumstances can be extremely helpful. Often, families of a child with hearing loss have never met anyone else with hearing loss and do not know any other families of children with hearing loss. This can cause feelings of isolation and uncertainty about the future. Just knowing someone else who has gone through similar problems can be a comfort and a valuable source of information.

Empowering Parents

Frequent parent participation and communication are key to successful rehabilitation at all ages and stages of an aural rehabilitation program. It is important for parents to understand their child's strengths and needs so that they can comfortably address those needs during daily interactions. Children are in school or a therapy session for only a relatively brief period of time. Skills will take much longer to carry over and generalize if they are addressed only during therapy sessions and classroom time. Teachers and therapists should maintain frequent communication with parents and caregivers. Phone calls, communication folders or notebooks, emails, and parent meetings are all good ways to involve parents.

Considering the parent/caregiver as teacher and teacher as coach, which is a hallmark of the Auditory-Verbal approach, can be a great way to empower parents to help their child develop auditory skills. Instead of just telling a parent or caregiver what to practice or sending home a note/activity, the target strategy or skill is modeled for the parent/caregiver in person. Then the parent has an opportunity to practice the strategy with the child while the teacher (coach) watches and provides constructive feedback. The goal is for the parent/caregiver to leave the session with complete understanding and confidence to address the target skill in the home. An empowered parent/caregiver will work better and more often with his child, so naturally the child will demonstrate faster progress. Parents/caregivers are motivated by their child's progress, especially when they know that they played a part in it. Then they are more likely to continue to be involved, which sets up a win-win cycle for parent/caregiver, child, and teacher.

Normal Acquisition of Auditory Skills

In order to look at an undeveloped auditory system and determine appropriate goals and interventions, it is necessary to have a clear picture of the way auditory skills develop. The goal for a child with hearing loss should be to achieve auditory skills that are as close as possible to those of his peers who do not have hearing loss. Auditory skills do not develop in clearly definable, discrete steps. They develop as a part of the overall child, intertwined with the development of his cognitive skills, social skills, emotional maturity, speech skills, and motor development. Figure 7.1 represents a description of Erber's (1982) main stages of auditory development. It can be used to take a broad look at the hierarchical development of auditory skills.

Figure 7.1. Hierarchy of Auditory Development

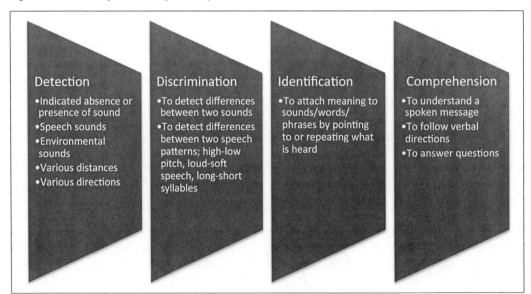

Detection
- Indicated absence or presence of sound
- Speech sounds
- Environmental sounds
- Various distances
- Various directions

Discrimination
- To detect differences between two sounds
- To detect differences between two speech patterns; high-low pitch, loud-soft speech, long-short syllables

Identification
- To attach meaning to sounds/words/ phrases by pointing to or repeating what is heard

Comprehension
- To understand a spoken message
- To follow verbal directions
- To answer questions

When tracking auditory development, it is important to select a detailed curriculum or checklist that follows the natural developmental sequence of auditory skills exhibited in typically developing children who do not have hearing loss. This will serve as a clear roadmap of auditory development that you can use to select appropriate auditory goals and guide your expectations for both short- and long-term education plans. There are a number of published developmental scales, checklists, and curriculums that are available to assist in tracking auditory development. Some especially helpful scales include Listen, Learn and Talk (Cochlear Ltd., 2003), the HELP Strands (Parks, 1992), Auditory Learning Guide: "The ALG" (Walker, 2009), and the Cottage Acquisition Scales for Listening, Language, and Speech (CASLLS) (Wilkes, 1999). The CASLLS is an example of an easy-to-use, comprehensive tool for tracking auditory development that was created for use with children who have hearing loss. It is intended to be used to track child development in the context of what is expected for the child's chronological age. The CASLLS also contains detailed developmental sequences for tracking of cognitive, social, and speech development across age levels. Figure 7.2 is a representative sample of a CASLLS checklist at the preverbal level.

Figure 7.2. Sample Page from the CASLLS Program—Preverbal Level

Cognition/Play

0-3 months	O	A
shows anticipation of the activity when cue is given for familiar routine[1]		
recognizes mother		
aware of/reacts to unfamiliar situations		
attends to or turns head towards bright lights and colors		
lifts head when held at caregivers shoulder and when lying on stomach		
follows moving object with eyes only[2]		

3-6 months	O	A
reaches for objects		
works for toy out of reach		
smiles at/reaches for mirror image		
enjoys being played with[3]		
experiments with cause & effect: shakes rattle		

6-9 months	O	A
moves obstacle to obtain object (5-8 months)		
gives, points, shows		
reacts differently to strangers		
searches for partially hidden object (emerging object permanence)		
imitates arm movements		
drinks from a sippy cup		
pulls ring off peg		
transfers objects from one hand to the other (crosses midline)		
bangs two blocks together		

9-12 months	O	A
repeats pleasurable actions – cause & effect (squeezed doll squeaks)		
begins awareness of in/out (objects/containers)		
problem solves how to pick up multiple objects[4]		
brings one object momentarily above another[5]		
finds hidden objects (object permanence)		
places block after block on table (like counting)		
recognizes inverted object (emerging top/bottom, front/back)[6]		
moves self toward desired object		
looks behind self to find object that circled away		

Listening

0-3 months	O	A
quiets/excites in response to novel sounds[7]		
responds or startles to loud sounds		
shows a preference for primary caregiver's voice		

3-6 months	O	A
cries at an angry tone of voice		
distinguishes emotions by tone of voice (4-7 months)		
begins to respond to parentese		
searches for the speaker		
begins to attach meaning to familiar sounds		

6-9 months	O	A
randomly echoes pitch, duration[8]		
attends to music/singing		
responds to sounds when source is not visible		
stops activity when called		
enjoys listening to a large number of onomatopoeias[9]		
locates sound source		
responds to speech in moderately noisy environment		

9-12 months	O	A
responds physically to music		
responds when name is called		
demonstrates association of onomatopoeias with objects		
responds to simple verbal requests[10]		
responds to questions by searching[11]		
takes first conversational turns		
shows awareness of body parts		
can look for named object that is out of sight (first true word)		
will pick up toy/object on request		
understands (receptively): **hot**		
all gone		
more		
up		
bye-bye		
no-no		
mama or daddy		

Social Interaction

0-3 months	O	A
begins to develop a social smile		
demonstrates turn-taking (cooing noises and vocal play)		
has preference for faces		
quiets/excites in response to caregiver		
attends to speaker's eyes and mouth[12]		

3-6 months	O	A
maintains eye contact appropriately		
takes turns by vocalizing		
shares joint attention[13]		
responds to other people's expression of emotion		

6-9 months	O	A
copies facial expressions		
calls to get attention		
enjoys being played with		
demonstrates attachment		
shows face/acts shy		
reaches/extends arm to request		

9-12 months	O	A
affectionate to familiar people		
begins directing others (pushes, pulls, tugs)		
participates in verbal routines[14]		
repeats actions that are laughed at		
resists removal of toy[15]		
vocalizes with gestures to: **protest, reject**		
request object		
request action		
call		
express feelings		
notice/recognize		
respond to others		
uses play routines: **give & take**		
build & bash		
Responds appropriately to vocal intonation and facial expressions		

Hearing Age/Listening Age

When working with children who are d/hh, it is important to understand the concept of **hearing age**. This is the age, usually stated in both years and months, that a child has been hearing in the speech range. In other words, it indicates how long he has had access to quality amplification that enables him to hear speech. Calculating the hearing age is more black-and-white for some children than it is for others. For example, if a 24-month-old child was born profoundly deaf and received a cochlear implant at 12 months, his hearing age would be 12 months. If a 9-month-old child was diagnosed with hearing loss at birth and received hearing aids that brought his hearing into the speech range at 6 months of age, then his hearing age would be 3 months. It gets a little more complicated for children who are inconsistent users of their devices. If a child has had hearing aids for 9 months but only wears them a few hours each day, you cannot really say that he has been listening for 9 months. In these types of cases, educators who are interested in a child's hearing age need to use their best estimate.

The concept of hearing age is useful for framing expectations of auditory progress and setting goals. If a child has a hearing age of three months, it would be unrealistic to expect him to demonstrate auditory skills that are developmentally at the two- to three-year level, even if his chronological age is between two and three years. Understanding hearing age is helpful when working with families who may be disappointed when their child is not hearing and understanding speech as well as they think he should be for his age. The concept of hearing age is also helpful when interpreting scores on standardized assessments of listening or spoken language abilities. If a seven-year-old child has an auditory comprehension score that is more than two standard deviations below the mean for his age level, we know that he has deficits with his auditory skills. However, if that child has a hearing age of three years, five months, and we compare his performance to other children in that age range, we may find that he is developing auditory skills as expected for his level of listening experience. It is important to understand the value of using the concept of hearing age, but it is equally important to remember not to let a child's hearing age limit your expectations for his progress. The ultimate goal, at all times, should be to develop auditory skills that are equivalent with the child's chronological age.

Evaluation

Any good plan for auditory development will begin with a clear and accurate determination of the child's level of auditory functioning. This is best done using a combination of standardized and nonstandardized assessments. Standardized assessments will provide a good comparison of how the child is functioning compared to other children at the same age level. Nonstandardized measures, which can take the form of checklists, an analysis of a language sample, and specific auditory tasks that do not have an available standardized component, will help to fill in the gaps that the standardized assessments may not provide.

Ling Six-Sound Test. Regardless of what assessment tools are chosen, every assessment should begin with the Ling Six-Sound Test (Ling, 1989). This simple test was developed by Daniel Ling in order to determine if the child with hearing loss was hearing all the sounds across the speech spectrum. A combination of six vowel and consonant sounds were chosen that correspond to the various speech frequencies heard in human speech (/a/, /u/, /i/, /s/, /ʃ/, and /m/). Sometimes, a seventh "sound," silence, is added to the mix. Silence is added to determine if the child is able to detect the absence and presence of sound. If a child is able to hear and discriminate all of the Ling sounds, we know that he is hearing across the speech spectrum. If he is unable to hear or discriminate the sounds, we can be sure that he is not hearing well across the speech spectrum and will have difficulty hearing speech accurately.

In new listeners, as well as children who are under two years of age, it is relatively easy to determine detection of the six Ling sounds. Determining whether a child can discriminate the sounds will be much more difficult. Use of a picture card representing each sound is appropriate if the child is unable or unwilling to repeat back the sounds when they are presented. Figure 7.3 shows a therapist using pictures to complete the Ling Six-Sound Test with her student. Figure 7.4 shows a parent doing a Ling Six-Sound Test with her child. If a child is not able to detect all the Ling sounds, that child's formal auditory, articulation, and language tests, as well as observational data, should be interpreted with caution. Optimal hearing levels need to be established before a true picture of the child's areas of strength and weakness can be determined. If a child is already able to detect and discriminate the Ling six sounds well, but does not perform as expected prior to an evaluation, the evaluation should be postponed until the hearing status is back to normal. The cause of the change should be investigated to determine if it is mechanical, for example, due to a malfunctioning hearing aid, or medical, such as caused

Figure 7.3. Completing the Ling Six-Sound Test

Figure 7.4. Parent Performing the Ling Six-Sound Test

by a bout of otitis media. There is no sense in completing an evaluation on a child who is not hearing the same way he usually hears. You also may want to review the sidebar "How to Administer a Ling Six-Sound Test" to learn how to administer the Ling Six-Sound Test.

How to Administer a Ling Six-Sound Test

1. Stand approximately six feet from the child.
2. Place yourself behind him, or use a listening hoop to block your lip and face movements.
3. Tell the child that you want him to say the sounds that he hears.
4. Present each sound with the same duration, loudness, and intonation pattern. This is very important in order to be sure that the child is hearing the actual acoustic features of the sound and not the suprasegmental qualities.
5. Vary the amount of time between sounds.
6. Vary the order that the sounds are presented each time to avoid memorization of the test.
7. If there are sounds that are not detected or confused with other sounds, move three feet closer and try those sounds again.
8. If there are sounds that are still un detected or in error, try going six inches from the child's hearing device.
9. Make notes regarding which sounds were accurate at which distances.

Standardized Tests That Target Auditory Skills.

There are many available language tests that include features of auditory development, usually termed **auditory comprehension** as a part of the overall test. Some tests will use the term *receptive language*, which when talking about hearing, also refers to auditory comprehension. Tests of receptive vocabulary are targeting auditory identification skills. Some tests also delve a little deeper by including subtests that measure auditory memory or auditory discrimination skills. Table 7.1 lists many of the tests frequently used to assess auditory skills for d/hh children.

However, most standardized tests for children do not thoroughly measure auditory discrimination and auditory memory skills. For this reason, additional measures of auditory function are recommended in order to get a complete picture of a child's overall auditory function. Additional testing can be used to measure a child's ability to discriminate between similar sounding words and syllables, as well as his ability to remember sequences of auditory information. Both of these skills are necessary for the development of auditory comprehension and clear speech production. See Table 7.2 for a list of nonstandardized measures of auditory function.

Audiologists can also assess auditory functioning of children as part of their assessment battery. Data from a child's audiological testing can often help to confirm auditory skill abilities and needs as determined by the educational test battery. Testing done in the soundproof booth at an audiology office offers a controlled environment with a consistent and specific level of sound for test administration. Please refer to Chapter 5 for a detailed description of audiological assessment.

Table 7.1. Standardized Tests Used to Assess Auditory Skills/Receptive Language

Name of Test	Age Range	Skills Assessed	Source
Clinical Evaluation of Language Fundamentals–Preschool 2 (CELF-P:2)	3–6 years	Receptive language, sentence memory, and expressive language	Pearson Assessments https://psychcorp.pearsonassessments.com
Clinical Evaluation of Language Fundamentals– 4th Edition (CELF–4)	6–21 years	Receptive language, sentence memory, and expressive language	Pearson Assessments https://psychcorp.pearsonassessments.com
Listening Comprehension Test –2	6–11 years	Vocabulary and auditory comprehension	Linguasystems www.linguisystems.com
Peabody Picture Vocabulary Test – 4 (PPVT–4)	2.6 years to adult	Receptive vocabulary	Pearson Assessments https://psychcorp.pearsonassessments.com
Preschool Language Scale- 5th Edition (PLS–5)	Birth to 6:11 years	Receptive and expressive language	Pearson Assessments https://psychcorp.pearsonassessments.com
Receptive One-Word Picture Vocabulary Test (ROWPVT)	2–18.11 years	Receptive vocabulary	Pearson Assessments https://psychcorp.pearsonassessments.com
Test of Auditory Processing Skills – 3rd Edition (TAPS–3)	4–18:11 years	Word discrimination, auditory comprehension, word memory, sentence memory	Therapro www.therapro.com
Test for Auditory Comprehension of Language – Third Edition (TACL–3)	3–9.11 years	Vocabulary and receptive language	Pearson Assessments https://psychcorp.pearsonassessments.com
Test of Language Development Primary – 4th Edition (TOLD–P:4)	4–8:11 years	Receptive language, expressive language, and word discrimination	Pro-Ed www.proedinc.com
Test of Language Development Intermediate – 4th Edition (TOLD–I:4)	8–12.11 years	Receptive language and expressive language	Pro-Ed www.proedinc.com

Table 7.2. Additional Criterion-Referenced (Nonstandardized) Measures of Auditory Function

Name of Test	Age Range	Skills Assessed	Source
Auditory Perception Test for the Hearing Impaired	3 years +	Auditory skills from awareness to comprehension	Plural Publishing www.pluralpublishing.com
AuSpLan	Any age	Auditory, speech,and Language	www.advancedbionics.com
Cottage Acquisition Scales of Listening, Language, and Speech (CASLLS)	Birth–8 years	Listening, speech, expressive language , receptive language, social interaction	Sunshine Cottage School for Deaf Children www.sunshinecottage.org
The Compass Test	3 years+	Word level consonant discrimination	Dave Sindrey www.hearingjourney.com
Early Speech Perception Test (ESP)	3 years +	Pattern perception, word discrimination, word identification	Central Institute for the Deaf www.cidedu.com
Hawaii Early Learning Profile (HELP)	Birth–3 years	Overall development including receptive language	Vort Corporation www.vort.com
Phonetic Level Evaluation (PLE)	3 years+	Auditory Identification	Daniel Ling http://firstyears.org/c4/u6/lingeval.pdf
SKI-HI Language Development Scale	Birth–5 years	Receptive and expressive language	The SKI-HI Institute www.hopepubl.com
Speech Perception Instructional Curriculum and Evaluation (SPICE)	3 years +	Sound and word perception to auditory comprehension	Central Institute for the Deaf www.cidedu.com

Listening Strategies

As soon as a child is identified as having a hearing loss, strategies to help him develop auditory skills should be considered and employed. There are a variety of important and helpful strategies that can be categorized into three major groups: (1) strategies that help optimize auditory input, (2) strategies that encourage listening skill development, and (3) strategies that encourage auditory comprehension and learning. These strategies are not listed by age or level of hearing loss. A variety of strategies from each of these categories will be needed regardless of the child's age, degree of hearing loss, or type of hearing device being used. The way in which the strategies are used will vary, depending on the individual characteristics of each child.

Strategies to Optimize Auditory Input

We are going to present five important strategies to enhance auditory input. Each strategy is described and application tasks suggested. First and foremost, the two tenets that apply to all children with hearing loss at all times in their lives are (1) to wear hearing devices during all waking hours and (2) to diligently maintain hearing devices in good working order. This cannot be emphasized enough. Parents and teachers should perform daily listening checks using the Ling Six-Sound Test to ensure that the child is able to hear speech sounds clearly. No other strategy, teaching method, or technique will be of much use if the child is unable to hear. You can have fabulous language input or numerous creative ideas to highlight target sounds and it will all be meaningless if the child cannot hear you well. Similarly, you may have spent hours teaching a family how to call attention to sounds and model appropriate language for their child, but if you haven't taught them the importance of checking the hearing device and maintaining it, you have failed and your work will be useless.

> Strategy #1: Ensure the device works properly and is used at all times.

The second strategy involves noise. Background noise is present to some degree in most situations throughout our daily routines. Adults have learned how to listen in the presence of noise by ignoring the competing noise and focusing on the desired signal. This is a difficult task for children and an even more difficult task for children who have hearing loss. Even a mild level of background noise can impede their ability to attend when someone is speaking to them. Yes, it is important for children with hearing loss to learn how to manage in background noise; however, practice in background noise should not be initiated until more basic levels of auditory skill development are mastered.

Reducing background noise is an important strategy for children who are developing skills along the auditory hierarchy and especially for all new listeners. A strong, consistent auditory sier to listen to and therefore will help children to listen for longer periods of time.

earing or hard of hearing, think of a time that you may have had to communicate

d background noise. Think of a wedding or dinner when a loud band begins play-

d to hear, even for an experienced listener. Often, it may be so difficult that you re-

ttempts to communicate or stop trying to pay attention while in that environment.

with hearing loss, everyday background noise can be this annoying and difficult.

Parents/caregivers should be instructed to critically evaluate their homes and other environments where their child frequently communicates. They should think beyond the obvious sources of background sounds such as televisions and music players to recognize the noise produced by appliances, street activities, and heating/air conditioning units. Parents/caregivers and teachers need to consider modifications in both home and school settings that might include the following: placing carpets or installed carpeting on hard floors, using window treatments such as drapes or shades, and covering ceilings with acoustic tile or other sound-dampening materials. Background noise cannot be eliminated entirely, but it is important to take steps to reduce it, especially in areas where a child will be listening and learning.

> Strategy #2: Control the environment for noise, and only introduce noise after good listening skills are established.

Look at the sidebar "Minimizing Noise in the Classroom Environment" for a list of accommodations that will improve the classroom listening environment.

The third way to provide optimal auditory input is to speak close to the child's hearing device. Keeping within three feet, the length of a yardstick, can dramatically improve the auditory signal going to the child. It is also important to remember that it is easier to hear if the signal is at the same horizontal level as the hearing device. If a speaker is standing up and a child is sitting on the floor, the difference in level creates distance and decreases the strength of the auditory signal.

For parents and caregivers of babies, sitting the child on your lap is much better than standing over him while he crawls on the floor. For an older child, sitting down next to him while helping with homework or reading is preferred to standing beside him while he is sitting.

> Strategy #3: Provide the best possible signal for the child's listening efforts.

Acoustic highlighting is the fourth strategy. It refers to a variety of ways that the speaker can make part of the message easier to hear. This is not just speaking louder, even though that is one simple way to acoustically highlight. You can also highlight a word, sound, or phrase by leaning in closer to the listener, therefore making the signal louder. You can highlight in other ways, such as changing the stress pattern of the sentence. For example, in the following

Minimizing Noise in the Classroom Environment

Inexpensive/easy accommodations:

- Preferential seating for the student close to sound source
- Carpet
- Fabric window coverings
- Fabric on parts of walls
- Keep the door closed
- Close the window
- Go to a room away from external noise
- Rubber mats under electronics
- Tennis balls or rubber on chair and table legs
- Use a portable sound-field amplification system

Expensive/labor-intensive accommodations:

- Use a personal FM system
- Use a built-in sound-field amplification system
- Acoustic tiles on ceiling
- Special acoustic blinds for windows
- Sound dampening in duct work
- External landscape to block sounds
- Thick padding under wall-to-wall carpeting
- Heavier, sound-blocking doors
- Double pane windows

sentences—"I gave it to HER" or "I GAVE it to her"—the speaker highlights the objective pronoun and then the verb by stressing the target word. You can highlight some target sounds by extending them (e.g., "yessss" or "tooooo").

Pausing before the target word or phrase is another way to acoustically highlight (e.g., "I gave it to…her"; "Put the toy…in the box"). Slowing down the speaking rate for part of a message or placing the target word/phrase at the end of the sentence are other ways to make the target easier to hear.

Although it may sound like a contradiction, whispering is another way to acoustically highlight a target sound, word, or phrase. Whispering part of a message calls attention to that part because it is different. Children will often stop and focus their listening when the speaker whispers. Do you remember your elementary years when a particularly angry teacher stopped yelling at the class and started whispering? What happened? The entire class quieted down and listened. You probably already use this technique in your communication repertoire. And, no, this is *not* like muttering under your breath when the boss has given you an assignment that should take at least five hours and says she wants it on her desk in under an hour. That type of whispering is definitely different than whispering as described in this technique! At any rate, whispering is especially effective when trying to highlight voiceless consonants (/s/, /ʃ/, /h/, /f/, and so on). The acoustic energy of vowels is greater than voiceless consonants. As a result, the consonants are more difficult to hear in connected speech. Take the word *shoe* as an example. Try saying *shoe* three times in a quiet, medium, and loud voice. If a child doesn't hear the word and you say it louder, the only thing that is louder is the vowel, which overshadows the /ʃ/ sound. Now try whispering the word *shoe*. When you reduce the volume of the vowel, the voiceless consonant /sh/ is much easier to hear.

> Strategy #4: Use acoustic highlighting to emphasize target speech sounds, words, or phrases.

The fifth and final strategy is using "parentese." **Parentese**, also called motherese, is the special way that adults talk to babies and young children using highly expressive speech and language patterns. The main features of parentese are:

- Singsong intonation patterns
- Higher pitch
- Slower speaking rate
- Shorter sentences
- Child-focused
- Repetitive
- More pausing – wait and listen
- Repeating what the child says
- Expanding child's utterances
- Abundant facial expressions

Parentese conveys warmth and happiness while promoting social interaction for children. Many people and caregivers naturally use parentese when interacting with young children, but some don't and require instruction and practice.

Parentese is helpful for children with hearing loss who are learning to listen for several reasons. First of all, it gains and holds a child's attention better. Research has shown that babies actually prefer hearing parentese and will attend to spoken language longer. You can test this out for yourself if you are in a room with a baby or toddler. Start off by saying a few sentences the way that you would if you were talking to another adult. Then say the same thing again with parentese features, and check the child's facial expression and level of attention. You will undoubtedly see a difference in the child's reaction.

The singsong voice patterns used in parentese highlight the suprasegmental features of speech. **Suprasegmentals** are the components of speech including pitch, loudness, and intonational changes that give tone and rhythm to spoken language. Suprasegmentals are important for development of a natural sounding voice. Children need to hear suprasegmental patterns repeatedly in order to use them in their spontaneous speech.

Parentese introduces the concept of turn-taking in conversation by modeling the back and forth of a conversation. This encourages children to listen for the break in the utterance that signals it is their turn to talk. Parentese also provides the auditory repetition needed to foster children's ability to learn vocabulary and how to construct sentences.

It's easy and natural to use parentese with young children. However, older children who are newer listeners can also benefit from hearing parentese. Although a bit more challenging and awkward at first, it is possible to use features of parentese in a way that is age-appropriate for older children. Lowering your pitch somewhat from what you would use with a baby, but continuing to use exaggerated intonational patterns is one way to extend parentese to older children. Slightly slowing your speaking rate and pausing more frequently during conversations can also be very helpful for children of any age who still need to develop their auditory skills. The goal for older children continues to be acoustic highlighting of the auditory information that facilitates the ability to learn to listen.

> Strategy #5: Use parentese as a form of acoustic highlighting to emphasize speech sound and vocabulary growth as well as to develop conversational skills.

Strategies to Encourage Listening Skill Development: Learning to Listen

In this section, we have nine strategies to share with you. After a child is fit with a hearing aid, cochlear implant, or other hearing device, he may be able to hear, but he does not yet know how to listen. Depending upon how long he went without adequate hearing for processing sounds and speech, he may have developed heightened awareness in vision and may do really well reading visual cues. He may continue to rely on his finely honed visual abilities despite his newly improved hearing levels. Our first strategy points to the importance of simply attending to sound. It is helpful to spend some time early on teaching the child to attend to both environmental sounds and spoken language. You can play the "I hear that!" game

Figure 7.5. Listening for Speech

any time a sound occurs in the child's environment. (See Figure 7.5.) If the dog barks or the phone rings, the adult points to her own ear and says, "I hear that!" You can then tell and/or show the child where the sound is coming from. This will help him improve his auditory identification skills. The "I hear that" game can also be played with speech. This can be done at home as well as at school (e.g., "I heard Daddy. He is calling you"; "I heard Matthew say 'It's my turn.'").

> Strategy #1: Pay attention to the sounds around you.

The second strategy emphasizes listening over seeing as a first avenue of awareness. Using visuals such as objects, pictures, or videos while teaching, enhances the lesson and makes learning more fun. By slightly tweaking the presentation order and presenting the auditory information *before* you present the visual, you are motivating the child to use his listening skills. It teaches the student that there is a value to listening and that he can use listening to obtain information about the world around him. It also teaches the child that he can hear things before he can see them. This is sometimes referred to as a type of auditory imprinting because you are helping imprint the auditory information into the child's developing auditory brain.

Here is an example of how you would use this strategy: In a more traditional interaction, auditory and visual information are presented together. The teacher opens a box and takes out a toy cow. While showing the child the cow, she says, "The cow says, 'Moooo.'" A slight tweak to this interaction provides an excellent opportunity to use this strategy: The teacher holds the closed box and says, "I have a cow in this box. Listen, I hear it. The cow says, 'Moooo.'" Then she pulls the cow out of the box to show the child. The child learns that the auditory message provides information about the experience to come.

> Strategy #2: Provide auditory experiences first, before visual representations, to encourage and enhance focused listening skills.

The third strategy is called the auditory sandwich, often used to describe a simple technique to build auditory comprehension when a child relies on visual and/or tactile supports to gain information. The term refers to the order of presentation: First auditory information, then visual or tactile information, and then auditory information again. The middle of the auditory sandwich can consist of pictures, written words, signs, or gestures. By sandwiching the needed cues between the auditory information, the teacher is able to build auditory skills by bridging from the child's stronger visual skills.

Here is an example of the use of the auditory sandwich in action: The child enters the room and the teacher says, "Sit down." The child does not understand. The teacher then signs "Sit" and gestures toward the chair. As the child sits, the teacher nods and affirms the auditory message by again saying, "Sit down."

> Strategy #3: Create an auditory sandwich by using the child's current strengths (e.g., visual information) between two auditory presentations of the message to stimulate listening and responding to a linguistic utterance.

The fourth strategy, wait time, may not seem like a strategy at all, but it is important just the same. In general, children need longer times to process information when compared with adults. Children who are d/hh need even more processing time. In the quest to give children abundant auditory input, mistakes are often made by not giving the young listener enough wait time. It's easy to say that children need more wait time, but it is not as easy to consistently provide it. In order to provide more wait time, the speaker must slow the pace of his input. Easy ways to do this include: pausing between sentences; chunking longer sentences into shorter, more manageable phrases; and pausing before responding to the child's question or comment.

All of these techniques give the listener more time to process what is being said. All too often, well-intentioned parents, caregivers, or educators will ask a question and when a response is not immediately given, they assume that the child doesn't understand and they rephrase or simplify the question. This creates more auditory noise that the listener needs to work through. It is better to pause after asking the first question. It may seem like a long time, but a newer listener may need up to 10 seconds of pause time before processing and responding to simple questions.

> Strategy #4: Provide adequate wait time to allow the listener to fully process the message and come up with his own response.

The fifth strategy involves repetition. Repetition is very important for auditory learning. Children need to hear a word in context multiple times before the word becomes part of their vocabulary. One of the great things about this strategy is that young children love repetition. They will seek out repetition in games and stories. Think back to the thousands of time you made your own parent read the same bedtime book to you each night. We are guessing if you could, you'd not be averse to having Mom come over tonight and read it to you at least one more time! Repetition makes things predictable and it helps children learn. Repetition provides increased exposure to speech and language forms, helping the listener build language connections. If you continually hear the words *bounce, throw, catch,* and *ball* together in conversation, you will begin to figure out how and why those words go together. The other great thing about repetition is that it is very natural for children, especially early listeners. You can say the same word multiple times when interacting with a child and it will not sound unusual to him. However, adults sometimes feel awkward initially and may need a period of adjustment to use this strategy comfortably and regularly.

Consider the use of repetition in the following example. An adult and child are playing with a ball, and the word *ball* is not one that the child spontaneously uses. While throwing, rolling, and catching a ball the adult may say things like, "You caught it"; "It bounced really high that time"; "my turn"; "get ready"; and "throw it." Now consider the same sentences with the word *ball* deliberately targeted for repetition. "You caught the ball." "The ball bounced really high." "My turn to throw the ball." "Get ready, here comes the ball." "Throw the ball." It's easy to see how this simple tweak to the language input could increase the likelihood of the child acquiring the targeted vocabulary.

> Strategy #5: Repetition facilitates listening and language growth.

Strategy six, using auditory closure, is an activity often played while reading or singing. This is the ability to fill in the missing part of a word or phrase. It is a strategy that encourages listening development because the child needs to listen to the phrase and fill in the missing part. For example, Adult: "Ready, set, …" Child: "Go!" This technique is best used after the targeted word or phrase has been modeled multiple times for the child, using repetition and highlighting strategies. This strategy helps develop understanding of sentence patterns and durational patterns, which are patterns of sounds and syllables that make up a word or phrase. Auditory closure practice also helps to build auditory memory skills. The back and forth of auditory closure encourages the child to take turns speaking. Auditory closure can be used with children from toddler age up through to teens. With very young children, a good amount of wait time and expectant facial expressions will be needed for them to get the idea. Using an older child or another adult to model is also helpful. Young children are often responsive to auditory closure used during singing. For example, Adult: "The wheels on the bus go…" Child: "round and round." For older children, the same idea can be applied to the lines of a poem, a repetitive story, chant, or cheer such as the reprise in "There was an old lady who swallowed a fly…."

> Strategy #6: Stimulate listening skills by playing games that encourage the child's completion of directions, lyrics, poems, and rhymes.

The seventh strategy logically follows number six. Auditory closure often involves the rhythm or musicality of speech. What is better than using songs and music to enhance listening skills? The technology available in current hearing aids and cochlear implants allows the listener to hear and enjoy all types of music. Children who are deaf or hard of hearing can benefit in numerous ways from listening to music, singing along, and playing instruments. We already discussed the need for repetition in development of speech/language and listening skills. Music provides repetition in a fun way. Receptive vocabulary and auditory comprehension skills are easily built in the learning of simple songs.

Music also helps to teach attentive listening. Children can listen to different types of music, and they can learn to identify a variety of auditory features including loud, soft, fast, slow, and patterns of rhythm. The music used does not need to be limited to traditional children's songs. A rich auditory environment can be better achieved using a variety of song types and musical styles.

In addition to the auditory benefits, singing also helps to develop a natural sounding voice. **Prosody** refers to the melody of speech created by the pitch of the voice and the stress and intonation patterns. The longer a child who is deaf or hard of hearing has gone without adequate access to sound in the speech range, the more at risk he is for developing speech that has an unnatural quality, a sound that has been called "deaf speech." Unnatural prosody often affects speech intelligibility and can also interfere with social interactions. Listening to songs and singing along is a great way to practice the prosodic elements of speech, including pitch changes, intonation patterns, and loudness changes, all of which are necessary for a natural-sounding voice.

Singing can also help auditory memory skills. This makes sense if you think about how much easier it is to remember something when it is in a song. As adults, we may forget the exact words that someone said a short time ago but easily call up the lyrics of songs that we haven't heard for 10 years. Songs such as the alphabet song, and the days of the week were designed to capitalize on the auditory memory benefits of song. This strategy can help young children build their auditory memory for simple vocabulary and sentence expansion. It can also help older children remember language rules or even complex language such as history facts that need to be memorized for a test.

Use of the Learning to Listen Sounds strategy became a mainstay in Auditory-Verbal Therapy programs. Teachers and parents found that the use of "Learning to Listen" sounds was helpful in the early stages of developing listening skills (Estabrooks, 2001). These are sounds that are matched with objects; for example, "Ch ch ch" for a train, "woof-woof" for a dog, and "meow" for a cat. For the most part, they are sounds that young children usually make for the corresponding object.

They are helpful in developing auditory skills in the early stages of listening development because they are easier to hear since they differ more than words in duration, loudness, and pitch (Sindrey, 1997). For example, a new listener will have a good deal of difficulty hearing the differences among the words *cow, cat,* and *car.* They are all single syllable words that start with the same sound. They will have a much easier time discriminating the differences among *mooo, meow,* and *brmm-brmm.* Teaching Learning to Listen sounds will help children learn to attach meaning to the sounds and to process differences between vowels and consonants. It is best to start with a small set of sounds that are acoustically different from each other and then gradually increase the number of sounds to which the child is exposed. Start with sounds that have completely different characteristics, contrasting pitches and durations. For example, "moo" and "woof-woof" are good choices because they are different in pitch and duration. The sounds "quack-quack," "woof-woof," and "oink-oink" would not be good choices for a beginning listener because the durational patterns are too similar. This discrimination skill involves small or fine differences, and using this type of more advanced Learning to Listen activity occurs later.

For young children, this strategy works best by using objects that correspond to the sounds you have chosen. Table 7.3 provides a list of suggested sounds and objects perfect for these activities. Even though playing with animal toys and making sound effects may not be age appropriate for a given child, the practice of learning to listen to the differences in the Learning to Listen activity should not be skipped. Flashcards with pictures or written words are sufficient substitutes for older children.

Table 7.3. Learning to Listen Sounds

Airplane	ahhhhhh (rising intonation)
Ambulance	ee-oo ee-oo ee-oo
Boat	puh puh puh (whisper)
Bus	buh buh buh (with voice)
Car	brmmm brmmm brmmm (lip trill)
Fire truck	rrrrrrRRRRRrrrrrr (rising/alling intonation)
Police car	wooo wooo wooo
Train	ch ch ch ch (not choo choo)
Bear	grrrrr
Bird	tweet-tweet
Cat	meow
Chicken	buck-buck-buck
Cow	moooo
Dog	woof-woof
Duck	quack-quack
Horse	click click click (tongue click)
Monkey	oo-oo-oo eee
Mouse	squeak-squeak
Lion	roar
Owl	hoooo
Pig	oink-oink
Rabbit	hop-hop-hop
Rooster	cock-a-doodle-doo
Sheep	baa
Snake	SSsssssss
Baby	shhhhhh; wah wah wah; walk walk walk
Clock	tick tock
Ghost	OOooOOooOOoo (rising/falling intonation)
Phone	brringg brringg
Santa Claus	ho ho ho
Slide	up up up—wheee

The first thing that you want to do when working with Learning to Listen sounds is to teach the child to associate the sound with the picture or object. The goal is that he becomes able to hear the differences in the features of the sounds. He may or may not be able to imitate the differences yet, and that is okay. That will continue to develop over time. Repeated practice with the Learning to Listen sounds is a great way to encourage development of a wider variety of vowel and consonant combinations. After the child is able to identify a small set of sounds, you can start to practice discriminating sounds. Start with a set of two. You can put out two objects or pictures, produce one of the sounds, and encourage the child to show you which one he heard. Playing this as a game or play scenario works well for motivation. For example, if you are using animal sounds, you can tell the child that it is time to feed the animals. Ask the child to listen for which animal to feed next. You can use the same idea for vehicles going down a hill or even simply objects that the child gets to throw into a basket. The more fun the child is having with it, the longer you will be able to practice the auditory skills behind the game. Activities incorporating the Learning to Listen sounds are generally easy for parents and caregivers to implement in the home.

> Strategy #7: Use music and sound imitation in all forms to help a child with auditory memory, developing prosody, increasing vocabulary, improving speech production, and advancing language.

The eighth strategy in this section involves self-monitoring through an auditory feedback loop. Children learn to talk by hearing speech and imitating what they hear. At first, they are not able to exactly imitate the sounds and words they are hearing. The act of babbling is how hearing infants and toddlers begin to develop their auditory feedback loop. They hear a sound and attempt to produce the sound. Then they listen to what they said and determine if it matches what they heard. If not, they will try again. As adults, we are continually using this auditory feedback loop to monitor how our speech output sounds. For adults with well-developed speech abilities, minor disruptions to the loop will often result in difficulty monitoring speaking volume. Think about a time that you may have had water in your ears or an ear infection. For children with developed speech, disruptions to the auditory feedback loop can result in reductions in speech volume, unusual speech prosody, and reduced articulation precision. For children without developed speech, disruptions to the auditory feedback loop can result in significant speech production issues. Figure 7.6 provides a schematic view of the auditory feedback loop.

Figure 7.6. Developing the Auditory Feedback Loop

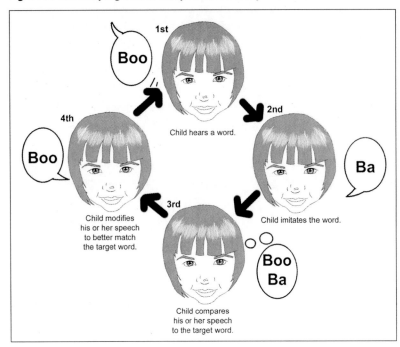

For children who are d/hh, it is essential to develop a strong auditory feedback loop. It will be the backbone for clear speech development. Many of the strategies that have been already described in this chapter will help to develop the auditory feedback loop.

Speech Babble is another important strategy that is used to help develop the auditory feedback loop in children with hearing loss. It is a systematic way to practice auditory discrimination and memory skills by listening and imitating exactly what was heard. Just as when working with Learning to Listen sounds, you begin Speech Babble with sounds that are very different from each other (e.g., /a/ versus /u/) and gradually work up to sounds that are more and more similar (e.g., /s/ versus /z/). Acoustic similarity of consonants varies depending on manner, place, and voice characteristics of each consonant. The **manner** of a consonant sound refers to the way in which it is produced. For example, sounds like /m/ and /n/ are called nasals because they are produced with nasal resonance. Sounds such as /s/ and /f/ are called fricatives because they are produced by airflow coming through the teeth, lips, and tongue. The **place** of a consonant refers to where the consonant is produced. For example, some consonants such as /b/ are produced with the lips, /t/ is produced with the tongue tip in the front of the mouth, and /g/ is produced with tongue movement towards the back of the mouth. The last characteristic, **voicing**, refers to the presence or absence of vocal cord vibration. Voiced consonants, such as /z/, /d/, and /n/, are produced with vocal cord vibration; voiceless consonants, such as /s/, /t/, and /p/ are produced without. You can feel voiced/voiceless contrasts by placing your hand on your throat while saying /s/ and then /z/. Did you notice the vibration when you produced /z/?

When practicing speech babble, it is necessary to begin with sounds that are different and move gradually toward sounds that are acoustically more similar. After vowel contrasts are mastered, it is easiest to discriminate consonants that differ in manner, then consonants that differ in voicing, and lastly, consonants that differ in place.

Figure 7.7 illustrates the key steps of a speech babble hierarchy that was developed by Kathryn Wilson based on information provided by Simser (1993). At each level, you should start at two syllables and move to three and then four syllables before moving on to the next level. For example, if you were working on alternated vowels, you could start with the two-syllable combination "ba-bee," then "ba-ba-bee," and then "ba-bee-ba-bee." By asking the child to repeat back the sequence several times before he hears it again, you are also helping to strengthen his auditory memory skills.

Speech babble tasks enable the listener to fine-tune his listening skills. As a result, the child is better able to break down multisyllabic words when they are heard and then say them with greater ease. As the child moves through the speech babble hierarchy, he builds and strengthens his auditory feedback loop and is better able to monitor his own speech output, improving the rate and automaticity of his speech.

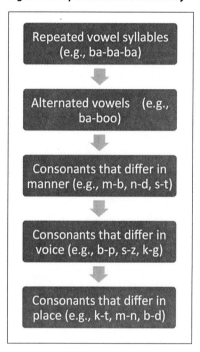

Figure 7.7. Speech Babble Hierarchy

Listening to nonsense syllable sequences and repeating them can be very monotonous work for children of any age. Parents and teachers can easily make it into a fun, age-appropriate activity by interspersing turns with a toy, craft, or game between listening trials. For young children, activities such as stacking blocks to make a tower or throwing beanbags at a target work well. For older children or teens, you can make a craft product such as a necklace or sand art, or take turns with a game such as Connect Four or Battleship.

> Strategy #8: Develop a strong auditory feedback loop to encourage natural self-monitoring skills.

Many people struggle to listen in the presence of background noise. For a child with hearing loss, this struggle can be significant. Therefore, the last strategy that we will address involves practice at this level. The world is a noisy place, and there is only so much that can be done to alter the environment in each listening situation. The difference between the loudness level of the auditory signal and the background noise present in a given environment can be measured. As noted in Chapter 6, this measurement is called the signal to noise ratio or the S/N or SNR. An

S/N ratio of 0 dB (decibels) means that the signal and the background noise are at the same level. This is a challenging listening situation even for an adult. Because children are still developing their language and cognitive skills, they are not good at using context cues of the conversation to fill in the words or sounds that they didn't hear correctly. The amount of difficulty they will have varies depending on a child's hearing age, chronological age, language level, and other individual factors. Therefore, children with normal hearing require an S/N ratio in the +15 to +20 dB range for optimal listening and language learning (Cole & Flexor, 2008).

Unfortunately, children will encounter many listening situations with unfavorable and variable S/N ratios, including most classrooms. So while a child with hearing loss is in the early stages of developing his auditory skills, it is good to keep the S/N ratio high. After a child has developed auditory skills to the comprehension level, it is beneficial to assess her auditory skills in a quiet setting and compare that to her skills in the presence of background noise. If there is a significant difference, direct practice listening in noise is warranted.

Practice listening in background noise is best done systematically with a progressively more challenging S/N ratio. There are inexpensive decibel meters available for computers and mobile devices that can be used to measure both the primary auditory signal (speaker's voice) and the level of background noise. Remember also that the distance from the speaker and the noise source will also affect the S/N ratio. The type of background noise also matters. It is easier to listen to a speech signal with background noise that does not contain speech, such as white noise, environmental noise, or music. Background noise that contains voices is much harder, and background noise containing audible conversation is the most difficult listening situation. If you think about yourself, you probably have experienced all of these listening situations and can remember that it is much more difficult to carry on a conversation when there are competing conversations in the background, especially if one likes to eavesdrop!

Children who practice a variety of auditory skills in background noise will be better prepared to have successful communicative interactions in real-world environments. Recommended skills to practice in background noise include repeating sentences of various lengths, following verbal directions, answering questions, listening to recorded speech, and maintaining a conversation.

> Strategy #9: Practice listening in background noise in order to prepare children to communicate in a variety of environments.

Strategies to Encourage Auditory Comprehension

Detection, discrimination, and identification of sound are all foundational skills needed to build comprehension of the auditory signal. Hearing words, phrases, and sentences in the context of meaningful real-life situations best develops auditory comprehension. Children begin to understand words by associating what they hear with what is happening around them. Consistency and repetition are useful in the early stages of comprehension. If a child hears "uh-oh" every time something falls or spills, he learns that "uh-oh" means that a problem has occurred. If he hears "Bye-bye" every time someone leaves, he learns that "Bye-bye" is something we say to each other right before we part. In this section, we will present several strategies that will assist in the development of auditory comprehension skills.

Self-Talk/Parallel Talk. Self-talk and parallel talk are key strategies that parents and teachers can use to boost auditory comprehension. Self-talk is simple talking about what you are doing while you are doing it. "I'm cleaning the table"; "I'm going to throw the ball"; "I'm putting your socks on." Self-talk is effective only if the child is attending to what the speaker is doing. Accidents and other novel situations are ideal times to use self-talk because the child is already interested and engaged in the activity or situation.

Here are two examples of self-talk: (1) With a young child: The parent spills milk on the table while the child is watching. Parent: "Oh, no! I spilled the milk. What a mess! Let me get some paper towels to wipe this up. Uh-oh, the milk is dripping onto the floor. I better hurry up and wipe it, wipe, wipe, wipe. That's better. Now it's all clean." (2) With an older child: The parent can't find the car keys. Parent: "I can't find my keys anywhere! I thought they were on the counter, but I don't see them. I'm going to check the coffee table. No, they're not there either. Ugh, this is really frustrating! Where did I put those keys?"

Parallel talk is similar to self-talk, but you are talking about what the child is doing or watching. The child is already engaged so the adult is basically adding language to the moment.

Here are some examples of parallel talk:
- "Wow! You have a big bear. You're hugging your bear"
- "You are drinking a lot. You must be thirsty. Mmm, is that milk good?"
- "I like how you are coloring your picture. That's a pretty shade of blue that you're using."

If you think about it, we could call a basic strategy Just Talk! The more a child is exposed to conversation and talking, the better he will be at listening, understanding, and speaking. Parents, teachers, and caregivers should be encouraged to talk with children frequently. They don't have to talk only about what they are doing, but also about what they see, labeling objects and actions, and describing things around them. They can tell stories, talk about how they feel, what happened yesterday, what might happen tomorrow, why something happened, how someone else might feel, or about something that they thought was funny. This list can go on and on. The same rule applies to auditory skills as any other skill that is being learned: The more guided practice you do, the better you will be at that skill.

Modeling and Expansion. Another strategy is called modeling and expansion. It is important for adults to model language to children so that they can develop their auditory skills during daily interactions. Expansion is a technique that parents or teachers often use naturally with children who are developing their speaking and listening skills. Expansion is adding more information to the child's utterance. The parent provides a model of an expanded sentence that the child could use as his language matures. This will look different depending on the child's expressive language level. This expanded information can be in the form of more words, descriptors, or more complex grammatical forms. This helps build auditory comprehension by showing the child what additional words and phrases can go with his existing speech. As with other strategies, modeling and expansion is best used within the context of real-life communicative activities.

Some examples of expansion might look like this:

Child: "Ball"   Parent: "That's a red ball."
Child: "Mommy throw ball"   Parent: "Mommy will throw the ball high."
Child: "Where Grandma?"   Parent: "Where is Grandma?"
                                         or "Where did Grandma go?"

Reading Aloud. Last but not least, reading aloud is an easy and powerful way to build auditory comprehension skills. This can be started with infants using simple board books and continued through each stage of development. Books with flaps, tabs, and pop-ups can help engage the busy toddler. Picture books with vibrant pictures and rhythmic verses are great for preschool children. Elementary and older students can listen to chapter books, magazine articles, and news stories. There are many benefits to reading aloud with children. Written language often contains vocabulary and grammar that are not used in conversational speech. Listening to stories read aloud allows for exposure to, and an understanding of, a wider range of vocabulary and grammatical forms. Research shows that children who are read to regularly in early childhood go on to have better reading skills in elementary school (Trelease, 2006). Reading aloud to children helps to increase their vocabulary, and increased vocabulary leads to improved auditory comprehension as well as improved reading comprehension. Many previously mentioned auditory development strategies such as repetition, parentese, and auditory first can easily be incorporated into read-aloud activities.

Auditory Activities

The final part of this chapter focuses on specific auditory activities to engage all levels of the listening hierarchy. There are many high-quality curriculums available that focus on development of auditory skills. Several that are recommended for your exploration include: Speech Perception Instructional Curriculum and Evaluation (SPICE) (Moog, Biedenstein, & Davidson, 1995), CID SPICE for Life (West & Manley, 2013), Cottage Acquisition Scales of Listening, Language, and Speech (CASLLS) (Wilkes, 1999), and Learn to Talk Around the Clock (Rossi, 2003). However, we believe that the most effective program to develop auditory skills in children is one that is individualized to meet the needs of each specific child and draws from a variety of sources. Expensive material and/or elaborate toys are not necessary. The following sections contain simple ideas for activities that foster development of auditory skills at the four primary auditory development levels of detection, discrimination, identification, and comprehension. They are activities that can be used by parents, teachers, or therapists and that can be modified to work with a wide range of age levels. Most of these activities can be done either in one-on-one situations or in small group settings.

Activities to Develop Auditory Skills at the Detection Level.

- Present a variety of environmental sounds—door slam, telephone, radio, vacuum— out of the child's visual field and watch to see if the child turns his head, changes his facial expression, or stops his activity. After consistent detection of sounds is achieved, vary the distances and locations of the sounds. Older children can be directly asked to verbally or physically indicate that they heard something.

- Present speech at a variety of loudness, pitch, and duration levels, and look for a reaction.

- Vary the distance from the sound to the child's ear and record his responses.

- Conditioned response games: Start by modeling an action that the child is to do each time he hears the target sound. This can be dropping a block into a can, a peg into a board, a ring on a stacker, a ball into a basket, and so on. This activity is typically not appropriate until a child is about two years old. The younger the child, the more likely he may need to have multiple models before he can reliably do this task. Older children and teens can usually indicate verbally or with a raise of their hand, but doing something a little different like making a simple craft project, may make the activity more enjoyable and therefore more successful.

- "Go" games: This is any game that requires the child to wait and listen for the target sound before he acts. It can be a race and he can wait to hear the word "Go!" He can hold a ball and wait to hear the word "throw." He can be sitting and waiting to hear the word "stand" or walking around the room and waiting to hear the word "stop."

- Sleep/Wake-up game: This game is a favorite of younger children. Have the child pretend to sleep and only wake up when he hears someone say, "Wake up."

- Play music that is popular for the child's age level. Have him listen for the stop and start of the music.

Activities to Develop Auditory Skills at the Discrimination Level. Remember that auditory discrimination means that the child can determine that sounds are different from each other. The child's response indicates if the sounds are the same or different.

- Present sounds, words, and phrases that differ in durational patterns; e.g., "Mooo" vs. "Quack-quack-quack"; "Hi" vs. "Hello"; "Sit down" vs. "Give me the book."

- Present speech at two different volumes or two different pitches and have the child listen for the change.

- Ask the child to listen for the difference between the speech pattern of a statement versus the rising intonation pattern of a question; e.g., "I want to go home" vs. "Can I go home?"

- Present a series of sounds or words to the child. Tell him that he needs to listen for a sound that is different. Randomly present a different sound. Make it fun by having the child do a physical action such as jump or clap when he hears the different sound. This can be done using Learning to Listen sounds, syllables, or real words.

- Ask an older child to indicate whether something is the same or different by saying "same" or "different" or by placing chips or markers next to the printed words *same* and *different*.

- Present recorded music or voice to the child. Practice listening for a change in song or a change in voice (e.g., a woman's voice, a child's voice, or a man's voice).

Activities to Develop Auditory Skills at the Identification Level. At this stage, the child is able to attach meaning to sounds. Increasing or decreasing the set size can adjust the difficulty level of identification activities. The three types of sets that can be used are closed set, limited set, and open set. Closed set refers to any set that has a clearly defined number of items. An example of a closed set would be a group of five animals: a dog, a cat, a pig, a cow, and a snake. A limited set is a set that is defined by a given situational or contextual cue (Tye-Murray, 2004). Examples of limited sets include categories such as animals, things in the kitchen, or words related to a baseball game. The listener has some idea of what might be heard, based on his knowledge of the given set. Because an open set is not limited to a given category or number of items, it represents the most difficult listening set.

Some additional activities to develop auditory skills at the identification level include:

- Hide and Seek: This is the traditional game with a listening twist. Each child hides and then comes out when his or her name is heard.

- Listening Match: Place a set of objects or pictures in front of the child. Have the child match the presented sound to the correct picture or object. Make this more fun by having the child do something with each object when it is identified. For example, if the objects are animals, the child can pretend to feed or bathe each animal. If using picture cards, the child can color the pictures, glue them to a poster, or smack them with a (clean!) flyswatter.

- You Say, I Say: Take turns imitating what the other person is saying. For younger or more impulsive children, an auditory hoop or hand gesture can be used to indicate whose turn it is to speak. Recording and playing back the voices can add another level of fun to this activity.

- Packing a Bag: Pick the type of bag that you will pack (grocery bag, vacation suitcase, school backpack, sports duffle, and so on). Then listen for items from that set to place into the bag. If real items are not available, pictures of the items can also be used.

- Family Photographs: Children of all ages love to look at family photographs. They can practice identifying names of family members, activities, actions, or objects in the photos.

- Play "Go Fish" with a set of cards containing the target listening set.

- Can You Find? Ask the child to find objects that are in the room.

Activities to Develop Auditory Skills at the Comprehension Level. Auditory comprehension is a broad term that refers to the ability to understand spoken messages including conversation, questions, verbal directions, and sequence of information. Task difficulty will vary depending on size and type of the set, the length and complexity of the message, and the level of familiarity of the message.

- Simon Says: This old-time favorite requires comprehension of verbal directions and can easily be used in a group setting. Have children stand back-to-back if you want to reduce the use of visual cues.

- Perform an action with a toy, e.g., "Can you make the bear jump off the table? Can the doll go to sleep?"

- Barrier Games: Put up a small visual divider. Place the listener on one side of the divider and the speaker on the other. Have two identical sets of materials. The speaker gives specific verbal directions to the listener while doing the same thing on his side of the barrier; for example, "Draw a red circle at the top of the paper." After several turns, remove the barrier and compare the results.

- Listen to a read-aloud story and answer questions about the story. Magazine and newspaper articles can also be used for older children.

- Can You Find? Use pictures or photographs that represent the sentences that will be practiced; for example, "Can you find 'The boy is swimming in the lake'?"

- Build a Structure: Give the child step-by-step verbal directions to build, for example, a house or a car, from blocks.

- Family Photographs: Using family photographs to generate practice answering questions and having conversation is motivating for most children.

Language Experiences. The final activity presented in this section is a tried-and-true strategy used in teaching d/hh children for decades. Recording a language experience is an overall language development strategy that can be used to reinforce and review language that occurred during an activity (Roberston, 2000). It can take the form of a journal entry, a photo with a caption, a chart, or an illustration with some written explanation. It's a great way to engage children because they are writing and talking about their own interests and experiences. And we all love to talk about ourselves. so kids might as well start early! It's also a good auditory comprehension strategy because it gives the child an additional opportunity to review the words and sentences that go with a particular a real-life experience. By putting multiple language experience pages into a book, you can create a language development tool that applies many auditory development strategies at the same time, including repetition, self-talk/parallel talk, expansion, and reading aloud. The language experience book is a flexible tool that is naturally customized to each child based on his age, interests, and personal style. Added benefits of using a language experience book include practice with written language, practice with handwriting, and increased exposure to new and/or more complex language structures. Children with limited language skills often use their language experience books as conversation helpers when interacting with family members, classmates, and other less familiar adults.

Summary

Auditory development is the necessary first step in development of spoken language skills. It is very important to remember that after a child receives a hearing device, he does not automatically become a listener. Parents, caregivers, and teachers need to provide aural (re)habilitation in order to foster the developing auditory skills of the d/hh child. This chapter presented numerous strategies and activities that can be used to develop listening skills at all levels of the auditory hierarchy. The most successful course of action will employ activities that develop skills in the context of real, everyday communicative interactions.

Chapter 7 Food for Thought

1. Reflecting on the opening scenario of this chapter, what additional steps could have been taken with Grant's therapy that could have resulted in more successful outcomes?

2. Why might a parent display some resistance to having his or her child wear a hearing device? What would you do to lessen this reaction and get that hearing device on that child during all waking hours?

3. What can be done to help a parent provide optimal auditory input to his or her child?

4. Explain the significance of developing a child's auditory feedback loop.

5. What is the best way to measure auditory skills in children?

In Conclusion…

You made it! We hope that you had a successful journey along the way. We know that you can answer all of those questions that relate back to our opening scenarios, right?

You now know the important laws and regulations that impact children and adults with hearing loss, and you know who the people are that work with those individuals. You know that a child with a hearing loss is entitled to services that ensure accessibility to the same things that all hearing people have access to, such as teacher's lectures, movies, theaters, and working audiological equipment. You also learned that the professionals who work with d/hh children should be knowledgeable and experienced in working with this population and that teamwork is one key to success.

We bet you never realized how incredibly complicated and cool sound is! Now you know how sound is made, how it is measured, and why the components of sound have such an important impact on speech—both understanding and producing it. And, now you are also in a unique position to think about sound in a different way when working with d/hh children. You will always think, "How well is this child hearing the sounds around him, and what can I do to make it better?"

You learned that the hearing mechanism is one amazing machine! The astounding speed and agility with which we hear and make sense of the sounds we hear is nothing short of miraculous. You learned the names and functions of all the anatomical parts involved, and that there is a sequence that involves a number of types of energy exchange along the way to the brain, and that the brain is where sound is actually heard and interpreted.

As with anything else in our world, the hearing process is one that can be impacted by genetics and the environment. You learned about the major causes of hearing loss and how that can impact a person's ability to interact with the world around him. You understand that sometimes there is nothing you can do about a hearing loss, and sometimes there are all sorts of things you can do.

As an individual who may work in a school or clinic setting, you have a more salient view of the need for accurate hearing testing and testing results. You now understand that a single hearing test is not the way to provide the most appropriate diagnosis of type and degree of hearing loss. You understand that a hearing screening is just that, a screening, and if a child is found to have a hearing loss, then a fully licensed and certified audiologist is the only person equipped to evaluate the loss and make appropriate recommendations.. You are now familiar with a range of hearing assessments that are administered when determining hearing loss, and you can read the resulting reports and comprehend the language that is used to describe the hearing loss.

One of the best things you can do now is to thoroughly explain to the layperson why hearing aids, cochlear implants, and other hearing assistive technologies do *not* fix hearing when there is a permanent hearing loss! You understand the capabilities of the finest digital hearing aids. You learned about the serious nature of cochlear implantation and that cochlear implants don't work anything like a hearing aid. You learned that when using either a hearing aid or a cochlear implant, maximum benefit from the technology is dependent on quality training, frequent use, and practice. You also recognize the importance of getting sound to a child diagnosed with hearing loss as soon as possible. Happily, there are many ways to provide an additional signal to a person wearing a hearing aid or cochlear implant when in a movie theater or on a stroll at the zoo. The various hearing assistive technology products can literally bring the sounds directly to the person's ear.

And, last, but certainly not least, you learned a multitude of strategies that are effective in the habilitation and rehabilitation phases of working with individuals with hearing loss. Babies and toddlers are habilitated because they learn their listening skills from scratch. Those who have progressive hearing losses or acquired their losses later receive rehabilitation services to refresh and relearn their listening behaviors. In addition to the many professionals who work on a team to encourage successful acquisition of listening and speaking skills, the parents are perhaps the most important factor in the child's success. You have learned how to encourage parent involvement and keep the momentum moving forward in the development of over-all communication skills, regardless of the mode of communication: spoken language, cued speech/language, ASL, or a Signed English system.

Wow! You have learned a great deal of useful information in a relatively short period of time. Well done! Remember that your learning should not stop here. We cannot begin to predict the future for hearing aids, implants, hair cell regeneration, gene splicing, new evaluation tools, new strategies and instructional best practices, new technologies, or new laws that will help individuals with hearing loss continue to access the world around them. But we can encourage you to be on the lookout for all the new things that will, most certainly, come down the pike. It is your job to be as informed as you can be so that you are an effective member of the child's team. We congratulate you on your achievements thus far and wish you well in your future learning endeavors.

Kate Reynolds, Ph.D.
Cynthia Richburg, Ph.D., CCC-A
Diane Klein, Ph.D.
Michelle Parfitt, M.S., CCC-SLP, LSLS Cert. AVEd

References

Introduction

Berk, R. (2002). *Humor as an instructional defibrillator*. Sterling, VA: Stylus Publishing.

Chapter 1

Administrators—Legal rights. Educational Interpreter Performance Assessment (EIPA). Retrieved from http://www.classroominterpreting.org/Admin/legal_rights.asp

American Speech-Language-Hearing Association. (2004). *Roles of speech-language pathologists and teachers of children who are deaf and hard of hearing in the development of communicative and linguistic competence* [Guidelines]. Available from www.asha.org/policy

Americans with Disabilities Act of 1990, Public Law 101-336, 42, U.S.C. 12101 *et seq.: U.S. Statues at Large, 104,* 327–378 (1991).

Americans with Disabilities Act of 2008. Amendments Act of 2008, Public Law 110-325. Statute 122. Volume 154. Sept. 25, 2008. p. 3553-3559.

Argenyi v. Creighton University, 703 F.3d 441 (8th Cir. 2013).

ASHA Certification Standards. Retrieved July 16, 2013, from http://www.asha.org/Certification/Certification Standards-for-SLP--Clinical-Practicum/

Assistance to States for the Education of Children with Disabilities. CFR Title 34, Subtitle B. Chapter III, Part 300, Subpart A,§ 300.12(b), Educational Service Agency. Retrieved from http://www.gpo.gov/fdsys/pkg/CFR-2013-title34-vol2/xml/CFR-2013-title34-vol2-sec300-12.xml

Building the legacy: IDEA 2004. U.S. Department of Education. Retrieved from http://idea.ed.gov/explore/home

Bullard, C. and Luckner, J. (2013). *The itinerant teacher's handbook* (2nd ed.). Hillsboro, OR: Butte Publications.

California State University – East Bay, Campus Directory, Faculty Profiles, Amy Rowley. Retrieved from http://www20.csueastbay.edu/directory/profiles/mll/rowleyamy-june.html

Court decision supports CART in the classroom for students who are deaf and hard of hearing. Listening and Spoken Language Knowledge Center. Alexander Graham Bell Association for the Deaf and Hard of Hearing. Retrieved from http://www.hearingloss.org/sites/default/files/docs/CourtDecision_CARTinClassroom.pdf

D. H. v. Poway Unified School District, Dist. Court, SD California, 2012. Retrieved from http://scholar.google.com/scholar_case?case=2914260550982143447&hl=en&assdt=&as_vis=1&oi=scholarr

Education for All Handicapped Children Act of 1975, Public Law 94-142, 20, U.S.C. 1401-1461: *U.S. Statutes at Large, 89,* 773–779 (1975).

Hendrich Hudson School District Board of Education v. Rowley. (1982). 102 S. Ct. 3034.

Hoenig v. Doe. The United States Supreme Court, 484 U. S. 305, HOENIG, California Superintendent of Public Instruction v. DOE, et al., No. 86-728, January 20, 1988.

K.M. ex rel. Bright v. Tustin Unified School Dist., 725 F.3d 1088 (9th Cir.2013).

Indiana Protection & Advocacy Services. Retrieved from http://www.in.gov/ipas/2411.htm

Individuals with Disabilities Education Act Amendments of 1991, Public Law 102-119. Volume 105, Statute 105, p 587-608. Congressional Record, Vol. 137 (October 7, 1991). Retrieved from http://www.gpo.gov/fdsys/granule/STATUTE-105/STATUTE-105-Pg587/content-detail.html

Individuals with Disabilities Education Act Amendments of 1997. Pub. L. No. 105-17, 111, Stat. 38 (1997). Codified as amended at 20 U.S.C Section 1400-1485.

Individuals with Disabilities Education Act of 1990 (IDEA), Pub. L No. 101-476, 20. U.S.C. 1400 *et seq.: U.S. Statutes at Large, 104*, 1103–1151 (1990).

Individuals with Disabilities Education Improvement Act of 2004, Pub. L. No. 108-446, 20 U.S.C. §1400 et seq. (2004).

Johnson, C. D., & Seaton, J. (2012). *Educational audiology handbook.* (2nd ed.). Clifton Park, NY: Delmar-Cengage Learning.

Kreisman, B. M., & John, A. B. (2010). A case law review of the Individuals with Disabilities Education Act for children with hearing loss or auditory processing disorders. *Journal of the American Academy of Audiology, 21*, 426–440.

Luckner, J. L., Slike, S. B., & Johnson, H. (2012). Helping students who are deaf or hard of hearing succeed. *Teaching Exceptional Children, 44*(4), 58.

Martin, E., Martin, R., & Terman, D. (1996). The legislative and litigation history of special education. *The Future of Children, 6*, 25–39.

Model Secondary School for the Deaf at Gallaudet College. Public Law 89-694. Oct. 15,1966. Statute 80, p.1027-1028, Retrieved from www.gpo.gov/fdsys/pkg/STATUTE-80/pdf/STATUTE-80-Pg1027.pdf

Montgomery, J. (1990). Building administrative support for collaboration. In W. A. Secord & E. H. Wigg (Eds.), *Best Practices in School Speech-Language Pathology* (pp. 49–56). San Antonio, TX: Psychological Corporation.

National Technical Institute for the Deaf. *Public Law* 89-36. June 8, 1965. Statute 79. p. 125–127. Retrieved from www.gpo.gov/fdsys/pkg/STATUTE-79/pdf/STATUTE-79-Pg125.pdf

Rehabilitation Act of 1973, Section 504, 29, U.S.C. 794: *U.S. Statutes at Large, 87*, 335–394 (1973).

Richburg, C. M., & Smiley, D. F. (2012). *School-based audiology.* San Diego, CA: Plural Publishing.

Roeser, R. J., & Downs, M. P. (2004). *Auditory disorders in school children: The law, identification, remediation* (4th ed.). New York, NY: Thieme.

Seaton, J. B., & Johnson, C. D. (2010). Educational policy influences on educational audiology: A review of the past decade. *Journal of Educational Audiology, 16,* 20–29.

Supreme Court denies schools' appeal. Listening and Spoken Language Knowledge Center. Alexander Graham Bell Association for the Deaf and Hard of Hearing. Retrieved August 28, 2013, from http://www. listeningandspokenlanguage.org/Document.aspx?id=2029

Teachers of the Deaf Act of 1961, Public Law 87-276, Statute 75, Sept. 22, 1961. p. 575-576. Retrieved from www.gpo.gov/fdsys/pkg/STATUTE-75/pdf/STATUTE-75-Pg575.pdf

Chapter 2

DeBonis, D. A., & Donohue, C. L. (2008). *Survey of audiology: Fundamentals for audiologists and health professionals* (2nd ed.). Boston, MA: Pearson Education.

Deutsch, L. J., & Richards, A. M. (1979). *Elementary hearing science.* Baltimore, MD: University Park Press.

Fletcher, H., & Munson, W. A. (1933). Loudness, its definition, measurement, and calculation. *Journal of the Acoustical Society of America, 5,* 82–105.

Hall, J. W. (2014). *Introduction to audiology today.* Boston, MA. Pearson Education.

Hoff, E. (2014). *Language development* (5th ed.). Belmont, CA: Cengage Learning.

Martin, F. N., & Clark, J. G. (2012). *Introduction to audiology.* Boston, MA: Pearson Education.

Nicolosi, L., Harryman, E., & Kresheck, J. (2004). *Terminology of communication disorders: Speech-language-hearing* (5th ed.). Baltimore, MD: Lippincott Williams & Wilkins.

Speaks, C. E. (1999). *Introduction to sound.* San Francisco, CA: Cengage Learning.

Chapter 3

Bailey, R. Anatomical directional terms and body planes. About.com Guide. Retrieved from http://biology. about.com/od/anatomy/a/aa072007a.htm

Boys Town National Research Hospital. My baby's hearing. Retrieved from http://www.babyhearing.org/Audiologists/verification/probemicrophone.asp

Christensen, V. What is the stapedius? Retrieved 2013 from http://www.wisegeek.com/what-is-the-stapedius.htm

Gelfand, S. (2009). *Essentials of audiology* (3rd ed.). New York, NY: Thieme Medical Publishers.

Hill, M. A. (2013). Hearing—Middle ear development. Retrieved July 22, 2013, from http://embryology.med. unsw.edu.au/embryology/index.php?title=Hearing_-_Middle_Ear_Development

Kemp, D. T. The OAE story. The Institute of Laryngology & Otology, the UCL Centre for Auditory Research and the Royal National TNE Hospital. Retrieved March 29, 2014, from http://www.oae-ilo.co.uk/downloads/advisories/the%20oae%20story.pdf

Martin, F., & Clark, J. (2012). *Introduction to audiology* (11th ed). Upper Saddle River, NJ: Pearson Education.

Peterson, M., & Bell, T. (2008). *Foundations of audiology: A practical approach.* Upper Saddle River, NJ: Pearson Education.

Pinna. Merriam-Webster Online Dictionary. Retrieved from http://www.merriam-webster.com/dictionary/pinna

Valsalva maneuver. Merriam-Webster Online Dictionary. Retrieved from http://www.merriam-webster.com/dictionary/valsalva%20maneuver

Van De Water, T., & Staecker, H. (2005). *Otolaryngology: Basic science and clinical review.* New York, NY: Thieme Medical Publishers.

Chapter 4

Arnos, K. S. (2002). Ethical issues in genetic counseling and testing for deafness. In V. Gutman (Ed.), *Ethics in mental health and deafness* (pp. 149–161). Washington, DC: Gallaudet University Press.

Bacterial meningitis. Centers for Disease Control and Prevention. Retrieved from http://www.cdc.gov/meningitis/bacterial.html

Bakhshaee, M., Hassanzadeh, M., Nourizadeh, N., Karimi, E., Moghiman, T., & Shakeri, M. (2008). Hearing impairment in pregnancy toxemia. *Otolaryngology Head Neck Surgery, 139*(2), 298–300.

Beck, D. L. (Web content editor for the American Academy of Audiology). Interview with Charles Berlin, PhD: Auditory Neuropathy Spectrum Disorder, OAEs, ABR, and more. Retrieved January 2, 2014, from http://www.audiology.org/news/Pages/20120809.aspx

Bernabei, D. Testing for Connexin 26: One family's story. Hands & Voices. Retrieved from http://www.handsandvoices.org/articles/fam_perspectives/connexin.html

Bluestone, C. D., Stool, S. E., Alper, C. M., & Arjmand, E. M. (2002). *Pediatric Otolaryngology* (4th ed., Vol. 1). Philadelphia, PA: Elsevier Health Sciences.

Branchiootorenal spectrum disorders. U.S. National Library of Medicine, National Institutes of Health, Medline Plus website. Retrieved from http://www.ncbi.nlm.nih.gov/books/NBK1380/

Brooks, A. C. (1994). Middle ear infections in children. *Science News, 146,* 332–333.

Causes of hearing loss. My Baby's Hearing website. Boys Town National Research Hospital and The National Institute on Deafness and Other Communication Disorders. Retrieved from http://www.babyhearing.org/hearing-amplification/causes/genetics.asp

Chandran, A., Herbert, H., Misurski, D., & Santosham, M. (2011). Long-term sequelae of childhood bacterial meningitis: An underappreciated problem. *The Pediatric Infectious Disease Journal, 30*(1):3–6.

Cone, B., Dorn, P., Konrad-Martin, D., Lister, J., Ortiz, C., & Schairer, K. (2011). Ototoxic medications (medication effects). The American Speech and Hearing Association's Audiology Information Series. Retrieved from http://www.asha.org/public/hearing/Ototoxic-Medications/

Fact sheet: Genes and hearing loss. The American Academy of Otolaryngology – Head and Neck Surgery. Retrieved from http://www.entnet.org/healthinformation/genes-and-hearing-loss.cfm

Fetal alcohol syndrome. Children's Hospital of Philadelphia (CHOP). Retrieved from http://www.chop.edu/healthinfo/fetal-alcohol-syndrome-fas.html

Graven, S. N., & Browne, J. V. (2008). Auditory development in the fetus and infant. *Newborn and Infant Nursing Reviews, 8*(4), 187–193.

Harrington, D. O. (2007). From bench to barstool. *SUNY Upstate Outlook,* 6:3, 14–15.

Herpes Simplex II. American Social Health Association (ASHA). Retrieved from http://www.ashasexualhealth.org/std-sti/Herpes.html

Hilgert, N., Smith, R. J. H., & Van Camp, G. (2009). Forty-six genes causing non-syndrome X hearing impairment: Which should be analyzed in DNA diagnostics? *Mutation Research, 681,* 189–196.

History of the name CHARGE. The CHARGE Syndrome Foundation. Retrieved from http://www.chargesyndrome.org/about-charge.asp

How many babies are affected by congenital CMV infection? Centers for Disease Control. Retrieved April 1, 2014, from http://www.cdc.gov/cmv/trends-stats.html#affected

Keats, B. J. B., & Corey, D. P. (1999). The Usher syndromes. American Journal of Medical Genetics, 89, 158–166.

Keats, B. J. B., & Lentz J. Usher Syndrome Type I. (1999, December 10 [Updated 2013, June 20]). In R. A. Pagon, M. P. Adam, T. D. Bird, et al. (Eds.), *GeneReviews*® [Internet]. Seattle, WA: University of Washington. Available from http://www.ncbi.nlm.nih.gov/books/NBK1265/

Martin, F. N., & Clark, J. G. (2012). *Introduction to audiology* (11th ed). New York, NY: Pearson.

Meningitis and septicaemia: After effects—What happens next? The Meningitis Centre, Australia. Retrieved from http://www.meningitis.com.au/images/meningitis---iojoo.pdf

Moores, D. (2000). *Educating the deaf: Psychology, principles, and practices* (5th ed.). Boston, MA: Cengage Learning/Houghton Mifflin.

Otitis media. American Speech and Hearing Association (ASHA). Retrieved from http://www.asha.org/aud/articles/otitismedia/

Otitis media. Kids MD Health Topics, Boston Children's Hospital. Retrieved April 1, 2014, from http://www.childrenshospital.org/health-topics/conditions/otitis-media

Pregnancy week by week. Mayo Clinic. Retrieved from http://www.mayoclinic.com/health/prenatal-care/PR00112/NSECTIONGROUP=2

Reid, M. E., & Lomas-Francis, C. (1997). *The blood group antigen facts book.* New York, NY: Academic Press.

Rh incompatibility. Medscape. Retrieved April 1, 2014, from http://emedicine.medscape.com/article/797150-overview#a0199_

Rubella (German measles) during pregnancy. (2012). Baby Center Medical Advisory Board. Retrieved from http://www.babycenter.com/0_rubella-german-measles-during-pregnancy_9527.bc

Sex-linked recessive. Medline Plus, U.S. National Library of Medicine, National Institutes of Health. Retrieved March 30, 2014, from http://www.nlm.nih.gov/medlineplus/ency/article/002051.htm

Shemesh, R. (2010). Hearing impairment: Definitions, assessment and management. In J. H. Stone and M. Blouin (Eds.), *International encyclopedia of rehabilitation*. Available from http://cirrie.buffalo.edu/encyclopedia/en/article/272/

Shott, S. R., Joseph, A., & Heithaus, D. (2001). Hearing loss in children with Down syndrome. *International Journal of Pediatric Otorhinolaryngology, 201*:6, 199–205.

Signing, Alexander Graham Bell and the NAD. Through deaf eyes. PBS series. Retrieved from http://www.pbs.org/weta/throughdeafeyes/deaflife/bell_nad.html

Smith, R. J. H., Shearer, A. E., Hildebrand, M. S., & Van Camp. G. (1999, February 14 [updated 2013, January 3]). Deafness and hereditary hearing loss overview. In R. A. Pagon, M. P. Adam, T. D. Bird, et al. (Eds.), *GeneReviews®* [Internet]. Seattle, WA: University of Washington. Retrieved from http://www.ncbi.nlm.nih.gov/books/NBK1434/

Smith, R. J. H., Sheffield, A. M., & Van Camp, G. (1998, September 28 [Updated 2012, April 19]). Nonsyndromic Hearing Loss and Deafness, DFNA3. In R. A. Pagon, M. P. Adam, T. D. Bird, et al. (Eds.), *GeneReviews®* [Internet]. Seattle, WA: University of Washington. Retrieved from http://www.ncbi.nlm.nih.gov/books/NBK1536/

Stapedectomy. *Encyclopedia of Surgery*. Retrieved from http://www.surgeryencyclopedia.com/Pa-St/Stapedectomy.html

The Human Genome Project completion: Frequently asked questions. National Human Genome Research Institute. Retrieved March 30, 2014, from http://www.genome.gov/11006943

Thigpen, M. C., Whitney, C. G., Messonnier, N. E., Zell, E. R., Lynfield, R., Hadler, J. L., . . . Schuchat, A. (2011). Bacterial meningitis in the United States, 1998–2007. Emerging Infections Programs Network. *The New England Journal of Medicine, 364*:2016–2025. Retrieved from http://www.nejm.org/doi/full/10.1056/NEJMoa1005384#t=articleTop

Tympanostomy tubes: Eustachian tube bypass with imperfections. (2002). *Infectious Diseases in Children*, Healio Pediatrics. Retrieved from http://www.healio.com/pediatrics/respiratory-infections/news/print/infectious-diseases-in-children/%7B506b942c-059a-445a-98cd-6ab36428cf77%7D/tympanostomy-tubes-eustachian-tube-bypass-with-imperfections

Vincent, R., Oates, J., & Sperling, N. M. (2002, November 23). Stapedotomy for tympanosclerotic stapes fixation: Is it safe and efficient? A review of 68 cases. *Otology and Neurotology 6*: 866–872.

What causes preeclampsia? Preeclampsia Foundation. Retrieved from http://www.preeclampsia.org/health-information/faq#prezero

What is Waardenburg syndrome? Genetics Home References. Retrieved April 2, 2014, from http://ghr.nlm.nih.gov/condition/waardenburg-syndrome

When is an employer required to provide hearing protectors? (2002). *Hearing conservation*. Occupational Safety & Health Administration, U.S. Department of Labor. Retrieved April 1, 2014, from https://www.osha.gov/Publications/OSHA3074/osha3074.html

Willacy, H. Alport syndrome. (2011). Patient.co,UK. Retrieved from http://www.patient.co.uk/doctor/Alport%27s-Syndrome.htm

Chapter 5

American National Standards Institute. (1991). Maximum permissible ambient noise levels for audiometric test rooms (ANSI S3.1-1991). New York, NY: Acoustical Society of America.

American Speech-Language-Hearing Association. (1997). Guidelines for audiologic screening [Guidelines]. Available from www.asha.org/policy

American Speech-Language-Hearing Association. (2005). Guidelines for manual pure-tone audiometry [Guidelines]. Available from www.asha.org/policy

American Speech-Language-Hearing Association. (1988).Guidelines for determining threshold level for speech [Guidelines]. Available from www.asha.org/policy/GL1988-00008.htm

Cunningham, M., & Cox, E. O. (2003). Hearing assessment in infants and children: Recommendations beyond neonatal screening. *Pediatrics, 111*(2), 436–440.

Kemper, A. R., & Downs, S. M. (2000). A cost-effective analysis of newborn hearing screening strategies. *Archives of Pediatric and Adolescent Medicine, 154*(5), 484–488.

Killion, M., Niquette, P., Gudmundsen, G., Revit, L., & Banerjee, S. (2004). Development of a quick speech-in-noise test for measuring signal-to-noise ratio loss in normal hearing and hearing impaired listeners. *Journal of the Acoustical Society of America, 116*(4), 2395–2405.

Newborn hearing screening; Early childhood hearing screening. National Center for Hearing Assessment and Management, Utah State University. Retrieved April 3, 2014, from http://www.infanthearing.org/screening/index.htm

Nillson, M., Soli, S., & Sullivan, J. (1994). Development of the Hearing in Noise Test for the measurement of speech reception thresholds in quiet and in noise. *Journal of the Acoustical Society of America, 95*, 1085–1099.

Niskar, A., Kieszak, S., Holmes, A., Esteban, E., Rubin, C., & Brody, D. (2001). Estimated prevalence of noise-induced hearing threshold shifts among children 6 to 19 years of age: The Third National Health and Nutrition Survey, 1988–1994, United States. *Pediatrics, 108*(1), 40–43.

Northern, J. L., & Downs, M. P. (2001). *Hearing in children* (5th ed.). Philadelphia, PA: Lippincott Williams & Wilkins.

Payne, K. B., Langbauer, W. R., & Thomas, E. M. (1986). Infrasonic calls of the Asian elephant (*Elephas maximus*). *Behavioral Ecology and Sociobiology, 18*(4), 297–301.

Roeser, R. J., & Downs, M. P. (2004). *Auditory disorders in school children: The law, identification, remediation* (4th ed.). New York, NY: Thieme.

Sales, G. D., & Pye, D. (1974). *Ultrasonic communication by animals.* London, England: Chapman and Hall.

Yost, W. A. (2000). *Fundamentals of hearing* (4th ed.). San Diego, CA: Academic Press.

Chapter 6

ASHA. (2013). Hearing aids and cell phones. Retrieved July 19, 2012, from http://www.asha.org/public/hearing/Hearing-Aids-and-Cell-Phones/

Chute, P., & Nevins, M. E. (2006). *School professionals working with children with cochlear implants.* San Diego, CA: Plural Publishing.

DeBonis, D. A., & Donohue, C. L. (2008*). Survey of audiology: Fundamentals for audiologists and health professionals* (2nd ed.). Boston, MA: Allyn & Bacon.

Ertmer, D. (2005). *The source for children with cochlear implants.* East Moline, IL: LinguiSystems.

Estabrooks, W. (2006). *Auditory-verbal therapy and practice.* Washington, DC: Alexander Graham Bell Association for the Deaf and Hard of Hearing.

House Ear Institute. (2010). 30th anniversary of first pediatric cochlear implant. Retrieved August 24, 2010, from http://newsroom.hei.org/pr/hei/30th-anniversary-of-first-pediatric-164364.aspx

House Ear Institute. (2013). FDA approves clinical trial of auditory brainstem implant procedure for children in the U.S. Retrieved September 2, 2013, from http://www.houseearclinic.com/about/research/pediatricabi/press-02

Kates, J. M. (2008). Digital hearing aids. San Diego, CA: Plural Publishing.

Klein, D. H. (2011). *Spoken communication for students who are deaf or hard of hearing: A multidisciplinary approach* (2nd ed.). Hillsboro, OR: Butte Publications.

Ling, D. (2002). *Speech and the hearing-impaired child: Theory and practice.* Washington, DC: Alexander Graham Bell Association for the Deaf.

Niparko, J. K. (2009). *Cochlear implants: Principles and practices* (2nd ed.). Philadelphia, PA: Wolters Kluwer/Lippincott Williams & Wilkins.

Papsin, B. C., & Gordon, K. A. (2008). Bilateral cochlear implants should be the standard for children with bilateral sensorineural deafness. *Current Opinion in Otolaryngology & Head & Neck Surgery, 16*(1), 69–74.

Phonak. (2013). Roger—Bridging the understanding gap. Retrieved September 1, 2013, from https://www.phonakpro.com/us/b2b/en/products/roger.html

Shannon, R. V. (2011, March 15). Auditory brainstem implants. *The ASHA Leader.*

Sharma, A., Nash, A. A., & Dorman, M. (2009). Cortical development, plasticity and re-organization in children with cochlear implants. *Journal of Communication Disorders, 42,* 272–279.

Sonitus Medical (2013). SoundBite™, retrieved July 19, 2013, from http://www.sonitusmedical.com/

Sound and fury. Retrieved September 1, 2013, from http://www.pbs.org/wnet/soundandfury/index.html

Stach, B. (1997). *Comprehensive dictionary of audiology illustrated.* Baltimore, MD: Lippincott Williams & Wilkins.

Taormina-Weiss, W. (2012, September 21). Cochlear implants—Facts, benefits, and risks. Retrieved August 28, 2013, from http://www.disabled-world.com/disability/types/hearing/communication/cochlear.php

Thibodeau, L. (2012). Results with devices that utilize DM technology. Advances in Audiology Conference, Las Vegas, NV. Retrieved from /https://www.phonakpro.com/content/dam/phonak/gc_hq/b2b/en/events/2012/dec_las_vegas/Proceedings/Wednesday/Thibodeau_L_Results_with_devices_that_utilize_DM_technology.pdf

Washington University School of Medicine. (2009). Bernard Becker Medical Library. Deafness in disguise. Retrieved September 30, 2013, from http://beckerexhibits.wustl.edu/did/index.htm

WRAL.com. (2013). New implant helps child with rare hearing disorder. Retrieved September 2, 2013, from http://www.wral.com/new-implant-helps-child-with-rare-hearing-disorder/12493782

Chapter 7

Anderson, K. (2013). Does he have to wear his hearing aids? Really? He seems to hear okay. Retrieved September 6, 2013, from https://successforkidswithhearingloss.com

Calderon, R. (2000). Parent involvement in deaf children's programs as a predictor of child's language, early reading, and social-emotional development. *Journal of Deaf Studies and Deaf Education, 5,* 140–155.

Cochlear Ltd. (2003). Listen, Learn, and Talk.

Cole, E., & Flexor, C. (2008). *Children with hearing loss: Developing listening and talking, birth to six.* San Diego, CA: Plural Publishing.

Estabrooks, W. (Ed.). (2001). *50 FAQs about AVT.* Toronto, Canada: Learning to Listen Foundation.

Erber, N. (1982). *Auditory training.* Washington, DC: Alexander Graham Bell Association for the Deaf.

Kuhl, P. K., Williams, K. A., Lacerda, F., Stevens, K. N., & Lindblom, B. (1992). Linguistic experience alters phonetic perception in infants by 6 months of age. *Science, 255*(5044), 606–608.

Ling, D. (1989). *Foundations of spoken language for the hearing-impaired child.* Washington, DC: Alexander Graham Bell Association for the Deaf.

Moog, J., Biedenstein, J., & Davidson, L. (1995). *Speech perception instructional curriculum and evaluation.* St. Louis, MO: Central Institute for the Deaf.

Parks, S. (1992). *HELP Strands: Curriculum-based developmental assessment birth to three years.* Palo Alto, CA: Vort Corporation.

Robertson, L. (2000). *Literacy learning for children who are deaf or hard of hearing.* Washington, DC: Alexander Graham Bell Association for the Deaf.

Rossi, K. (2003). *Learn to talk around the clock: A professional's early intervention toolbox.* Washington, DC: Alexander Graham Bell Association for the Deaf.

Sharma, A., Dorman, M. F., & Kral, A. (2005). The influence of a sensitive period on central auditory development in children with unilateral and bilateral cochlear implants. *Hearing Research, (1)*203, 134–143.

Sharma, A., Dorman, M. F., & Spahr, A. J. (2002). A sensitive period for the development of the central auditory system in children with cochlear implants: Implications for age of implantation. *Ear and Hearing, 23*(6), 532–539.

Sharma, A., & Nash, A. (2009, April 14). Brain maturation in children with cochlear implants. *The ASHA Leader.* Retrieved from http://www.asha.org/Publications/leader/2009/090414/f090414b.htm

Simser, J. I. (1993). Auditory-verbal intervention: Infants and toddlers. *Volta Review, 95,* 271–229.

Sindrey, D. (1997). *Listening games for littles* (2nd ed. with CD). Wordplay Publications.

Tye-Murray, N. (2004). *Foundations of aural rehabilitation: Children, adults, and their family members* (2nd ed.). Clifton Park, NY: Thomson Delmar Learning.

Trelease, J. (2006). *The read-aloud handbook* (6th ed). New York, NY: Penguin Books.

Université de Montréal. (2010, December 17). Mom's voice plays a special role in activating newborn's brain. *Science Daily.* Retrieved March 24, 2011, from http:www.sciencedaily.com/releases/2010/12/101215195234.htm

Walker, B. (2009). Auditory learning guide: "The ALG." Retrieved from http://www.firstyears.org/c4/alg/alg.pdf

West, J., & Manley, J. (2013). *CID SPICE for Life.* St. Louis, MO: Central Institute for the Deaf.

Wilkes, E. (1999). *Cottage acquistion scales for listening, language, and speech.* San Antonio, TX: Sunshine Cottage School for the Deaf.

Yoshinaga-Itano, C., Sedey, A., Coulter, D., & Mehl, A. (1998). Language of early- and later-identified children with hearing loss. *Pediatrics 102*(5), 1161–1171.

Glossary

acoustic immittance: a coined term used by audiologists to refer to either acoustic impedance or acoustic admittance; referring to middle ear measures used to assess middle ear function, including tympanometry and acoustic reflex assessments

acoustic immittance bridge: the electronic device used to test either impedance (stiffness) or admittance (compliance) of the ossicular chain in the middle ear system (aka. tympanometry) and the reflex contraction of the tensor tympani and stapedius muscles in response to intense sounds (aka. acoustic reflexes)

acoustic neuroma: generic term, also known as an acoustic tumor or acoustic Schwannoma, referring to a growth on the auditory nerve

acoustic reflex arch: referring to acoustic reflex pathway from the outer ear to the lower brainstem and back again. An intense stimulus (loud sound) travels from the outer ear up to the lower brainstem and then back down the facial nerve to activate the stapius muscle contraction on both sides of the head, therefore allowing the acoustic immittance bridge to record the contractions.

acoustic reflex decay: refers to the decrease in the magnitude of the stapedius reflex that occurs with a 10-second acoustic stimulus; indicative of a retrocochlear disorder

acoustic reflex threshold: the lowest intensity at which the stapedial muscle contracts to an intense stimulus (loud sound)

acoustics: the study and science of sound and its perception

acute otitis media: inflammation of the middle ear, lasting no more than 21 days

adventitious hearing loss: a hearing loss occurring after birth, often a result of accident or illness; also known as an acquired hearing loss

aided threshold: the point at which a listener can first determine that a sound is becoming audible when an amplifier (usually a hearing aid) is used

air conduction: transmission of sound to the inner ear through the outer and middle ear structures

air-conduction testing (AC): refers to the presentation of a pure tone or speech stimulus through an earphone or speaker to determine the threshold of hearing sensitivity

air-conduction threshold: the lowest level at which a pure tone or speech stimulus is heard through an earphone or speaker

allele: a single gene of a gene pair that accounts for one half of the genetic code for a trait

American Board of Audiology (ABA): a certifying board for audiologists

American Sign Language (ASL): a visual-gestural language created by deaf people, based on a system of hand shapes, hand positions, and hand movements that is used for communication

American Speech-Language-Hearing Association (ASHA): a national organization for primarily speech-language pathologists and audiologists to establish guidelines and protocol of practice. In addition, this association certifies these professionals with the Certificate of Clinical Competence (CCC).

Americans with Disabilities Act (ADA): a United States public law (PL 101-336) enacted in 1990 with the intent of providing equal opportunities for persons with disabilities

amplification: the process of making sounds louder or more intense

amplification device: any object that is used to make sounds louder for a listener. Ear horns made from actual animal horns were an early form of device; digital electronic battery-operated devices are used at the current time.

amplitude: a term used to describe the displacement of a vibration (the size of a sound wave) that results in the intensity of a sound

ampulla (sing.)/ampullae (pl.): the bulbous part at the end of each of the semicircular canals leading to the utricle

annular ring/annulus: a ring-shaped ligament that holds the tympanic membrane in place

anoxia: absence or loss of oxygen in body tissues

anterior: anatomical direction referring to structures located to the front or forward

anterior/superior semicircular canal: topmost and forward-facing semicircular canal

antihelix: ridge of cartilage anterior and parallel to helix

antitragus: projection on the ridge of cartilage opposite the tragus

aperiodic: relating to sound waves; the motion is unpredictable and nonrepetitive and is typically referred to as noise

apical end/apex: referring to the tip or uppermost point of the cochlea

asymmetrical hearing loss: referring to hearing loss characterized by different thresholds or different recognition/discrimination abilities between ears (one ear hears better than the other)

attenuator dial: referring to the mechanism by which the intensity of the stimuli being presented through an audiometer is varied up or down (volume control)

audiogram: graphical representation of the threshold of sensitivity of hearing measured at several different frequencies

audiometer: a device for measuring hearing in which changes in the frequency and the intensity of sounds/speech are manipulated for hearing testing purposes

audiometry: technique of measuring the sense of hearing by means of an audiometer

auditory brainstem response test (ABR): referring to the electrical activity evoked by very brief sounds that originate within the auditory nerve and/or auditory portions of the brainstem and used in testing the hearing of infants and in the detection of auditory abnormalities in older children and adults

auditory comprehension: a broad term that refers to the ability to understand spoken messages, including conversation, questions, verbal directions, and sequence of information

auditory cortex: an area in the temporal lobe of the brain where sound is perceived and cognitive processes allow that sound to be recognized and understood

auditory detection: the ability to react to the presence or absence of sound

auditory discrimination: referring to the processes of distinguishing among stimuli and responding appropriately; recognizing that sounds differ from one another

auditory evoked potential (AEP): electrical activity evoked by sounds within the auditory portions of the peripheral or central nervous system and recorded with electrodes placed on the head

auditory identification: referring to the level of auditory skill development in which meaning is attached to sounds and sound is able to be labeled; the third level of auditory skill development, following discrimination and preceding comprehension

auditory nerve: see "eighth cranial nerve" entry

auditory steady-state response test (ASSR): a form of auditory evoked potential, similar to the auditory brainstem response (ABR) test, but utilizing slightly different equipment and algorithms to evoke the response

Auditory-Verbal Therapy (AVT): a model of speech therapy used to develop Listening and Spoken Language (LSL). This model focuses explicitly on the use of auditory skills without the use of visual or tactile cues or prompts.

aural habilitation: referring to the intervention methodologies for children initially learning to develop their listening skills

Aural-Oral therapy: a model of speech therapy used to develop Listening and Spoken Language (LSL) that focuses on the use of listening skills and allows for the use of visual or tactile supports (not sign language)

aural rehabilitation: referring to the intervention methodologies for persons who are relearning listening skills

auricle: also known as pinna; referring to the cartilaginous portion of the outer ear

autosomal dominant: referring to genetic inheritance; when a single dominant gene from a parent causes the display of an inherited trait

autosomal recessive: referring to genetic inheritance; when both parents passing along a recessive gene causes the display of an inherited trait

background noise: sounds that occur in the environment that can impede a listener's ability to clearly hear a message

basilar end/base: referring to the bottom or lowermost point of the cochlea

behind-the-ear aid (BTE): a type of hearing aid that has a small case that sits behind the ear structure and uses tubing connected to an ear mold or ear bud to channel amplified sound to the external ear canal

bilateral hearing loss: hearing loss that occurs in both ears: sometimes used synonymously with binaural hearing loss

Bilingual/Bicultural (Bi-Bi): a model of instruction that utilizes American Sign Language as the primary language for teaching the content areas (math, science, reading, social studies); components of Deaf culture are woven throughout instruction as well; ASL is used to bridge language skills to written and spoken English.

binaural: referring to both ears (e.g., a binaural hearing loss is loss in both ears); opposite of *monaural*

bone-anchored hearing aid (Baha): an osseointegrated type of hearing aid that is used when there are physical anomalies in the outer or middle ear structures that prohibit the use of any air conduction-style amplification device

bone-conduction testing: refers to the presentation of a pure tone or speech stimulus through a bone oscillator placed on the skull, usually the mastoid process, to determine the threshold of hearing sensitivity

bone-conduction threshold (BC): the lowest intensity level at which tonal or speech stimuli can be recognized through a bone oscillator placed on the skull

bone oscillator: a vibratory device that transmits sound and is used for bone-conduction testing

brainstem: also referring to auditory brainstem; the portion of the brain between the spinal cord and cerebrum through with the auditory nerve passes

brainstem implant: an implanted surgical device that is designed to take sound, digitize it, and then send the digitized electric signal to the brain via the placement of an electrode on the first auditory relay station in the brainstem, the cochlear nucleus (CN); the neural stimulation at this level then travels the auditory nerve to the brain, where it is interpreted as sound

broadband noise: sound containing a wide range of frequencies

calibration: electronic determination that an electrical device (such as an amplifier) or an acoustic transducer (such as an audiometer) is functioning according to defined characteristics. The term usually also implies correction of the device, if necessary.

cancellation: a process that occurs when sounds or sound waves that are in exact opposite phase to each other come together and cancel each other out, thereby producing no sound

carrier: referring to a person whose genetic makeup passes on an inherited trait

(central) auditory processing testing ([C]AP): testing that identifies characteristics of a processing problem contained within the central auditory nervous system. A central auditory processing disorder is characterized by difficulties with attention, detection, identification of a signal, long- and short-term memory, retrieving previously learned information (regarding language), sequencing and organizing capabilities, listening to speech in noise, and localizing sounds. Tests are varied but include binaural or dichotic listening tasks, listening in background noise, and temporal auditory tasks.

central masking: a change in hearing threshold in one ear associated with the presentation of masking noise to the opposite ear

Certificate of Clinical Competence (CCC): the certificate issued to audiologists and speech-language pathologists by the American Speech-Language-Hearing Association

cerumen: earwax

chromosome: the basic unit of genes

chronic otitis media: persistent inflammation of the middle ear having a duration of longer than eight weeks

Clinical Fellowship Year (CFY): following college graduation, a period of supervised clinical practice under the direction of a certified SLP

cochlea: snail-shaped organ of hearing

cochlear duct: also known as the scala media; the membranous portion of the cochlea containing the organ of Corti, between the scala vestibuli and scala tympani

cochlear implant: a surgically implanted device that is designed to take sound, digitize it, and then send the digitized electric signal to the brain via the placement of an electrode array in the scala tympani in the cochlea; the neural stimulation then travels the auditory nerve to the brain where it is interpreted as sound

coloboma: a hole in a part of the eye

Communication Access Real-Time Translation (CART): a form of transcription that utilizes two computers (one for the CART operator and one for the student) to provide a real-time, verbatim script of everything said during a classroom lecture

completely-in-the-canal hearing aid (CIC): a style of hearing aid in which the casing fits entirely in the ear canal so much so that it is difficult to see, thus being cosmetically appealing to persons being fit for amplification

complex signal: sounds that are made up of more than one vibrating source or sound wave

compression: referring to sound propagation; the area in which air molecules are condensed from a pressure exerting a force (opposite of *rarefaction*)

compression limiting: a method for manipulating sound in which an outgoing signal is compacted into a person's dynamic listening range

concha: the bowl-like structure of the outer ear contained within the pinna

conditioned play audiometry: a technique for hearing testing in young children that trains the patient to perform a game-type activity (such as dropping blocks into a bucket or putting pegs into holes) every time a sound is heard; also referred to as Play Audiometry

conductive hearing loss: hearing loss created by a blockage or other problem occurring in the outer or middle ear systems

cone of light: the reflection of light bouncing off the tympanic membrane from the otoscope

congenital hearing loss: hearing loss that is present at birth

cookie-bite audiogram: referring to a configuration of hearing loss in which the lowest frequencies and the highest frequencies are better than the middle frequencies. The audiometric configuration gets its name because it appears as if someone has taken a bite out of the audiogram.

critical period: referring to the optimal time frame in which listening, speech, and language skills are developed at an early age; ages birth to seven years

cross hearing: occurs when the stimulus presented to the test ear exceeds the interaural attention (insulation) provided by the head for air- or bone-conduction testing. In this situation, the stimulus crosses over to the nontest ear and is heard in that ear.

crus: referring to any anatomical structure resembling a leg. In the auditory system, the outer ear's concha area has a crus. The middle ear contains two ossicles that have crura (plural for *crus*).

cycles per second (cps): refers to how many complete waveforms occur over a one-second period of time; also referred to as hertz (Hz)

dampened: when sounds are made softer; also known as attenuated

dB hearing level (dBHL): the intensity level (in decibels) of a signal as it relates to human hearing; often used with audiometers and audiograms

dB sensation level (dBSL): the intensity level (in decibels) of a signal presentation or a response above a specified threshold; often used when testing speech recognition abilities on the audiogram

dB sound pressure level (dBSPL): the intensity level (in decibels) of a signal as it is measured by equipment, such as a sound level meter; often used for measuring sound from an environment

decibel (dB): a measure of sound pressure; the term used to measure the intensity of a sound

digital noise reduction: Noise reduction is the process of removing noise from a signal. Newer digital hearing aids have the ability to filter out noise from the incoming signal using specific algorithms in the electronics.

digitally modulated (DM): a form of amplification technology that is based on digitizing the signals and transmitting them through Bluetooth technology; research indicates it is a better transmitter of amplified sound signals than the FM, infrared, or loop technologies.

directional microphone: a microphone that is designed to receive sound from a particular direction (i.e., from the front or back of a hearing aid user). This type of microphone may help hearing aid users hear better.

distortion product otoacoustic emissions: sounds recorded in the external ear canal associated with activation and movements of the outer hair cells in the cochlea in response to stimulation with two closely spaced pure tones.

dominant genetic transmission: referring to the key concept of Mendelian inheritance; it is a relationship between alleles of a single gene, in which one allele (the dominant allele) masks the shown characteristics of a second allele (the recessive allele) at the same gene locus.

due process: the legal requirement that the state must respect all of the rights owed to a person; notice (usually written) must be given to inform an individual of the decision or activity that will have an effect on his rights. The individual then has the right to grieve and appeal any legal decisions. Due process is meant to protect individuals from governmental harm.

dynamic range: an individual's dynamic range is found by subtracting the speech reception threshold (SRT) from the threshold of discomfort (TD) or uncomfortable loudness level (UCL), the level at which speech becomes uncomfortably loud. The dynamic range is calculated for the purpose of fitting amplification properly.

early intervention (EI): referring to early childhood intervention, which is a support and educational system for very young children (birth to six years) who have been identified with a special need or are at risk for developmental delays

ear mold: a device that connects a hearing aid to the patient's external ear canal. Ear molds are often custom-made for a particular patient, using a cast and mold technique.

educational benefit: a term that applies to IDEIA, which states that schools are required only to provide the services that would allow a student to receive benefit from an academic program; they do not have to provide services above and beyond that which enables the child to perform at a passing level.

Educational Interpreter Performance Assessment (EIPA): Established in 1999, the Educational Interpreter Performance Assessment (EIPA) Diagnostic Center is the only program of its kind in the world. The program focuses on supporting the unique skills required for sign interpretation in the educational setting.

eighth cranial nerve (8th CN or CN VIII): referring to the acoustic or auditory nerve, also known as the vestibulocochlear nerve; the eighth cranial nerve of the twelve cerebral nerves arising in the brain

elasticity: the capacity of an object that has been deformed to return to its natural shape

electrode array: referring to the configuration of electrodes placed into the cochlea during a cochlear implantation; the array emits an electric current or voltage to stimulate the regions of the cochlea that are damaged or destroyed.

electroencephalogram (EEG): the tracing made by an electroencephalograph showing changes in the electrical potentials in the brain; also known as an electrogram

electrophysiology: referring to the audiological tests and equipment used to measure the electrical activity of neurons, and particularly action potential activity in the brain in response to auditory stimuli

endolymph: a fluid in the auditory and vestibular portions of the inner ear, specifically within the scala media

endolymphatic hydrops: also known as Ménière's disease; the malfunction of hearing and balance caused by the imbalance of excessive inner ear fluids

energy source (force): referring to the source exerting power on an object capable of vibrating, thereby setting up the motion responsible for sound

epitympanic recess: the "attic" or upper portion of the middle ear cavity

equal loudness contours: curved lines that indicate the sound pressures necessary at each frequency to produce the sensation of equal loudness (volume) for normally hearing listeners

etiology: the study of the factors that cause an abnormal condition or disease

eustachian tube: a passageway that permits communication between the middle ear space and the posterior region of the mouth. The opening and closing of this tube equalizes the pressure in the middle ear with the pressure in the person's environment. The tube is lined with a mucous membrane and normally remains closed until it is opened with swallowing and chewing.

external auditory meatus: also known as the external auditory canal; the passageway or channel in the outer ear leading from the pinna's concha to the tympanic membrane (eardrum)

first formant (F_1): the formant with the lowest frequency

formant: frequency regions for vowels and resonant consonants that have high amounts of acoustic energy; reflected by black bars on a spectrogram

free appropriate public education (FAPE): an educational right of children with disabilities in the United States that is guaranteed by the Rehabilitation Act of 1973 and the Individuals with Disabilities Education Act (IDEA)

frequency: a property of sound defined as the number of cycles or oscillations of a vibrating body within a specified unit of time (usually a second). The unit for frequency is Hz (for hertz).

frequency modulation (FM): variations in the frequency of a radio carrier wave in accordance with an audio or other signal; used in hearing aid terminology and in audiometric testing terminology

frontal lobe: one of the paired lobes of the brain lying immediately behind the forehead. The frontal lobes are responsible for behavior, learning, personality, and voluntary movement.

gain: increase in the amplitude or energy of an electrical signal with amplification. Gain is the difference between the input signal and the output signal.

gene: ultramicroscopic, self-reproducing, protein particle in the chromosome that transmits hereditary characteristics

gene mapping: the creation of a genetic map assigning DNA fragments to chromosomes

general education: colloquially known as "gen-ed"; generalized instructional content, materials, resources, and processes for evaluating the attainment of educational objectives; referring to the courses required by all students within a school or school district

genetics: the science that deals with hereditary characteristics transmitted by genes

genetic transmission: the transfer of genetic information from genes of one generation to the genes of another generation; almost synonymous with heredity

genotype: the typical hereditary characteristics of an individual, transmitted by genes

gestational age: the time in weeks after conception. A full-term birth is 40 weeks. Premature infants with a gestational age of as little as 26 to 27 weeks can now survive with intensive care.

hair cell motility: the motion of the outer hair cells created by sound entering the cochlea and moving the anatomical structures; the movement of the outer hair cells is primarily caused by the cell's ability to change in length and shape. In addition, the cell's stereocilia are embedded in the tectorial membrane while the cell rests on the basilar membrane. A sheering of the stereocilia is created as sound travels along the basilar membrane, enhancing the motility of the hair cells.

hearing age: refers to the ability of a congenitally hearing impaired child to understand speech when compared with the chronological age of a child hearing normally from birth. A child's hearing age is largely governed by the period of time that the child has had access to adequate personal amplification and aural habilitation.

hearing aids: electrical devices that amplify sound to improve hearing and communication

hearing assistance technology (HAT): referring to a group of electrical devices consisting of a microphone worn by a talker and earphones on, or loudspeakers near, a listener; also referred to as hearing assistive technology and assistive listening devices (ALD). These devices improve the signal-to-noise ratio within a listening environment (classroom, theater, church) with the goal of improving speech perception.

Hearing-in-Noise Test (HINT): a test of speech perception that involves repeating sentences in the presence of speech spectrum noise. Testing is conducted at different speech-to-noise ratios. This test was developed by Nilsson, Soli, and Sullivan in 1994 and is extensively used for determining appropriate amplification options.

hearing mechanism: There are three main components of the human ear: the outer ear, the middle ear, and the inner ear.

hearing screening: an abbreviated form of hearing test that assesses the ability of an individual to hear only in the range of speech frequencies (500Hz, 1000Hz, 2000Hz, and 4000Hz). A screening is used to identify individuals who are at risk for a hearing loss.

hearing threshold: the minimal level of intensity at which sound pressure will produce the sensation of hearing

helicotrema: the opening at the apex of the cochlea that allows a wave to be transmitted through the perilymph of the scala vestibule to the scala tympani

helix: the inwardly curved ridge at the edge of the pinna (outer ear)

hertz (Hz): the unit of frequency indicating cycles per second; named in honor of the German physicist Heinrich Hertz

in-the-canal hearing aid (ITC): a style of small hearing aid that fits entirely within the external auditory canal

in-the-ear hearing aid (ITE): a style of hearing aid that fits entirely within the concha of the pinna and extends into the external auditory canal

incidental learning: a form of learning that is not immediately expressed in an overt response; learning that occurs without any obvious reinforcement of a behavior or associations that are learned.

Children with normal hearing experience incidental learning through their auditory systems on a daily basis, while children with hearing loss miss out on incidental learning due to the absence of auditory cues, including speech and language.

inclusion: referring to the practice of integrating all students (with and without hearing loss) into the classroom and daily activities of the general education classroom

incus: the second ossicle within the ossicular chain; the ossicle that is connected laterally to the malleus and medially to the stapes

Individualized Education Plan (IEP): a federally mandated educational plan meant to provide special services to school-age children with disabilities. It is meant to be reviewed and updated once a year.

Individualized Family Service Plan (IFSP): a federally mandated educational plan meant to provide special services to preschool children with disabilities or developmental delays and their families

Individuals with Disabilities Education Act (IDEA): a United States Federal Law PL 94-142 and 99-457) that governs how states and public agencies provide early intervention, special education, and related services to children with disabilities. It mandated free and appropriate education for children over three years of age.

Individuals with Disabilities Education Improvement Act (IDEIA): the latest (2004) reauthorization of IDEA; referred to as PL 108-446

induction loop system: a hearing assistance technology using a continuous wire carrying electrical energy from an amplifier around the circumference of a room or table, thereby creating a magnetic field. The magnetic field can be picked up by the telecoil in wearable hearing aids, thus transmitting amplified signals to the hearing aid wearer. This system enhances the signal-to-noise ratio.

inertia: the resistance of any object to change its shape or its state of motion; the tendency of an object to remain in motion once it is set in motion or remain at rest if left alone

infrared system: a hearing assistance technology consisting of a microphone/transmitter placed near the sound source of interest that transmits the signal through infrared light waves to a receiver/amplifier, often found in a room-mounted, desk-mounted, or ear-level device; used to enhance the signal-to-noise ratio

infrasound: sound waves with frequencies below the lower limit of human audibility

inner ear: portion of the ear bounded laterally by the oval and round windows and medially by the internal auditory canal. It contains the cochlea and semicircular canals.

inner hair cells: the single row of cells within the organ of Corti that communicates with auditory nerve fibers to transmit signals to the brain. There are approximately 3,500 inner hair cells in the human cochlea.

input compression: a form of sound manipulation in which the incoming signal is compressed into the dynamic range and the volume control impacts the gain

intensity: a term referring to the magnitude of sound energy per unit area; used to describe sound levels used in measuring sounds or testing hearing

interaural attenuation: the decrease in a signal presented to one ear before it crosses over to the other ear; created by the head

interdisciplinary collaboration: a cooperative endeavor that applies the methods and approaches of several disciplines

International Phonetic Alphabet (IPA): the system of symbols for speech sounds adopted by the International Phonetic Association. Each speech sound is represented by a distinctive symbol.

kneepoint: the point, in sound decibels, at which a compression circuit begins to reduce the gain; also called compression threshold when referring to hearing aid technology

lateral: referring to the side of a body or anatomical structure

least restrictive environment (LRE): identified in the U.S. Individuals with Disabilities Education Act (PL 94-142) as one of the six principles that govern the education of students with disabilities and other special needs. By law, schools are required to provide a free appropriate public education (FAPE) in an environment that is the least limiting and appropriate to the individual student's needs.

linear scale: a scale in which the change between two values is perceived on the basis of the *difference* between the values. Thus, a change from 1 to 2 is perceived as the same amount of increase as from 4 to 5. Human hearing is not measured on a linear scale (see "logarithmic scale").

lobule: the fleshy portion of skin at the base of the pinna; also known as the ear lobe

logarithmic scale: a scale in which the change between two values is perceived on the basis of the *ratio* of two values. Thus, a change from 1 to 2 (ratio of 1:2) is perceived as the same amount of increase as the change from 4 to 8 (also a ratio of 1:2). Human hearing is measured on a logarithmic scale.

longitudinal wave: referring to a sound wave that vibrates in the direction of propagation. A wave propagating along the length of a stretched Slinky™ toy, where the distance between coils increases and decreases, is a good visualization of longitudinal waves. Sound waves in air are longitudinal, pressure waves.

loudness: the psychological correlate to sound intensity. Increases in sound intensity are perceived as increased loudness. The relationship between intensity and loudness is not one-to-one but, rather, logarithmic.

malingerer: a person who falsifies or exaggerates hearing loss

malleus: the first of the three tiny bones (ossicles) within the ossicular chain. The manubrium of the malleus rests against the inner surface of the tympanic membrane and can usually be seen with otoscopic examination of the ear.

manner of production: referring to a segmental component of speech production that relates to the type of air flow used to create a sound, such as plosive (an exploded puff of air) or fricative (air flow that is squeezed between two surfaces causing turbulence)

manubrium: the handle, or lower process, of the malleus (ossicle)

mapping: the process of establishing a map in a cochlear implant; the process of establishing thresholds and suprathresholds, as well as the frequency range, in the speech processor of a cochlear implant

masking: refers to an audiological testing procedure used to prevent an inaccurate response from the nontest ear that could occur if a test signal crossed over the head from the test ear; the process of presenting narrowband noise to the better (nontest) ear when the possibility of crossover is present in a testing situation

masking noise: a mixture of frequencies made up of various ranges (e.g., broadband or narrow broadband). For audiometric testing purposes, narrowband and speech noise are commonly used as maskers.

mastoid bone: rounded hard protrusion at the lower end of the skull behind the external ear. It is honeycombed with air-filled cells.

maximum output: In hearing aids, this term is usually used to express the average of the saturation output pressures at 500, 1000, and 2000 Hz. It is more often referred to as the output of the hearing aid.

medial: referring to the midline of a body or anatomical structure

medium: any material through which sound pressure waves may pass (examples include air, wood, steel, and water)

mel: a subjective unit describing tone-pitch relationships. Researchers often use the mel scale (instead of Hz and the frequency scale) as a means for asking people to judge the relationship between two or more pitches. The name *mel* comes from the word *melody* to indicate that the scale is based on pitch comparisons.

Mendelian inheritance: the study of inheritance, or the passing of genetic traits from one generation to the next. Derived from the work of Gregor Mendel, this term refers to the laws of inheritance and defines the basic rules of genetics.

microphone: the device in a hearing aid, cochlear implant, or hearing assistance technology that converts sound waves into electrical energy variations, which may then be amplified or transmitted

middle ear: portion of the ear bound laterally by the tympanic membrane and medially by the oval window. It contains the ossicular chain, tensor tympani and stapedius muscles, eustachian tube, epitympanic recess, and multiple tendons and ligaments. The healthy middle ear cavity is air-filled.

midline: a medial line, especially the medial line or plane of a body or anatomical structure

mixed hearing loss: hearing loss created by both sensorineural loss (damage to the cochlea and/or eighth cranial nerve) and conductive loss (a blockage in the outer or middle ear systems)

monaural: referring to only one ear (e.g., a monaural hearing loss is loss in only one ear); opposite of *binaural*

multidisciplinary collaboration: a cooperative endeavor that applies the methods and approaches of several disciplines

myringoplasty: the surgical closure of a perforation (hole) in the tympanic membrane

narrowband noise: a signal generally produced by filtering broadband, or white, noise (e.g., one-third octave band filtering). For audiological testing, narrowband noise is used when masking pure-tone thresholds.

nasopharynx: the upper part of the pharynx, connecting with the nasal cavity above the soft palate

noise: sound produced by inconsistent or irregular vibrations; sound that is loud or unpleasant or that causes disturbance

noise-induced hearing loss (NIHL): damage to the cochlea caused by high-intensity sound that is either consistent and steady over time (such as industrial noise in a work environment) or sudden and instantaneous (such as a gunshot or explosion); a form of sensorineural hearing loss

noise-notch audiogram: the description of an audiogram on which a drop or notch in the 2000 to 4000 Hz range is identified. This notch indicates that a person has a noise-induced hearing loss due to damage in the basal region of the cochlea.

nonlinear system: often used to describe the auditory system and refer to the logarithmic scaling of the basilar membrane; a physics term referring to a system in which the output of the system is not directly proportional to the input. A nonlinear system does not operate on a linear scale.

nonsyndromic hearing loss: a genetically transmitted disorder whose only trait is hearing loss

nontest ear: usually referring to the "better" ear during audiometric testing. It is the ear that is not being tested and should, therefore, not be contributing to the responses (hearing thresholds) of the test ear.

omnidirectional microphone: a microphone that has the same sensitivity to sound regardless of the direction of the incoming signal

open fitting: on a hearing aid, a type of ear piece that is similar to an ear mold but is very small and does not occlude the entire ear canal; allows environmental sounds to be easily channeled in a natural way to the ear

organ of Corti: on the basilar membrane in the cochlear duct, a membrane that contains the sensory and supporting hair cells for hearing

osseointegrated hearing aid: a type of hearing aid that has components implanted in the mastoid process of the temporal bone behind the ear; it relays sound to the cochlea through vibrations from a bone oscillator attached to the implanted component (refer to Baha)

ossicles: the three middle ear bones: malleus, incus, and stapes

ossicular chain: refers to the connected sequence of the ossicles in the middle ear cavity; the malleus is the most laterally located in the chain (closest to outer ear), while the stapes is most medially located in the chain (closest to cochlea). The incus connects these two ossicles to complete the chain.

ossiculoplasty: surgical repair of the ossicles

otoacoustic emissions (OAE): sounds recorded in the external ear canal associated with activation and movements of the outer hair cells in the cochlea in response to stimulation from acoustic stimuli. Otoacoustic emissions are evidence of essentially normal outer hair cell function.

otoscope: an instrument used to view the ear canal and the tympanic membrane

ototoxic: a substance that has a poisonous effect on the ear, especially the hair cells of the cochlea

outer ear: the outermost part of the hearing mechanism, containing the auricle, external auditory meatus, and ending at the tympanic membrane

outer hair cells: the three to four rows of cells within the organ of Corti that appear to be responsible for fine-tuning frequency resolution and providing sensitivity to the inner hair cells. There are approximately 12,000 outer hair cells in the human cochlea.

output compression: a form of sound manipulation that flattens the sound signal after the volume control, which allows for an expanded dynamic range for low gain settings and lower kneepoints for high gain settings

oval window: the entry to the cochlea; the footplate of the stapes fits into the oval window and initiates the fluid wave within the cochlear duct

parentese: a distinct form of speech and language that parents use with babies, characterized by a higher pitched voice with more inflection and reduced sentence length in spoken language

pars flaccida: also called Shrapnell's membrane, the flaccid layer of the tympanic membrane, containing two layers of tissue

pars tensa: stiffer portion of tympanic membrane, containing four layers of tissue

PE tubes: abbreviation for pressure equalization tubes; refer to "tympanostomy tube"

peak clipping: a type of sound manipulation that limits the maximum output intensity of an amplifier by removing alternate current amplitude peaks at a certain level

perception: awareness, recognition, and interpretation of stimuli received at the brain

perforated TM: a tear or other opening in the tympanic membrane

perilymph: cochlear fluid found in the scala vestibuli and scala tympani

perinatal: time period around the time of birth from 28 weeks to 7 days past birth

periodic: sound waves that are predictable and repetitive, such as pure tones

permanent threshold shift: irreversible loss of hearing due to excessive exposure to loud noise

personal amplification device: any device that a single person can use to amplify sound signals, such as a hearing aid or a personal FM hearing assistance technology unit

phase: a characteristic of sound, the timing of a pure tone that is described in degrees

phenotype: the traits or characteristics that an individual displays

Phonak Roger system: a digitally modulated (DM) amplification technology that utilizes Bluetooth technology

phonetically balanced word list: monosyllabic words that are equal in stress and are used during hearing testing to determine speech discrimination scores

phons: a term to measure loudness, used by hearing scientists

physical concepts: the terms used when discussing the production of sound that relate to the tangible components of sound and its measurement, such as intensity and frequency

pinna: see "auricle"

pitch: term used to describe the perception of the tone/frequency of a sound; sounds with a higher frequency have a high pitch, sounds with a lower frequency have a low pitch

PL 94-142: a federal public law first passed in 1975, also known as the Education for All Handicapped Children Act, and renamed Individuals with Disabilities Education Act, mandating free appropriate public education for all children with handicaps; refer to "Individuals with Disabilities Education Act (IDEA)"

place of production features: referring to components of speech production that relate to the location in the mouth where articulators make contact in order to produce speech sounds

plasticity: referring to the brain's ability to grow neural networks or connections; during a child's early years, the brain has more plasticity to develop neural connections when stimulated by sensory stimulation

posterior: anatomical position relating to structures to the back or behind

posterior/inferior semicircular canal: the semicircular canal located below and behind the anterior canal

postlingual: hearing loss occurring after the development of speech and language, typically considered at the age of three years

postnatal: after birth

pre-auricular tags: anomaly characterized by a small cartilaginous appendage anterior to the auricle

prelingual: hearing loss occurring prior to the development of speech and language skills, typically three years of age

prenatal loss: hearing loss occurring prior to birth

presbycusis: progressive loss of hearing sensitivity related to age

pressure (dynes/cm2): force exerted per unit area, expressed in dynes per square centimeter

progressive loss: a hearing loss that deteriorates over time

promontory: an anatomical feature in the labyrinthine wall of the middle ear; a bony prominence that separates the oval and round windows

prosody: also referred to as suprasegmentals; rhythmic features of speech production that include stress, intonation, duration, and juncture

psychoacoustics: refers to the measurements of the psychological correlates of the physical characteristics of sound

psychophysical: the manner by which we cognitively perceive sound; the physical characteristic of frequency is perceived as pitch and intensity is perceived as loudness

pullout: a model of speech therapy where the child leaves the regular classroom and works with an SLP in a separate instructional space in the school

Punnett square: chart used to describe genotype inheritance possibilities

pure-tone average (PTA): average of hearing sensitivity to pure-tone signals at 500Hz, 1000Hz, and 2000Hz; this score is used to help identify the degree of hearing loss in each ear

pure-tone threshold: the lowest level of intensity at which a sound stimulus is audible

pure tones: simple, periodic sound waves; referring to a single frequency of sound

purulent: a type of otitis media with effusion that contain pus

push-in: a model of speech therapy in which the SLP works with the child within the regular classroom setting

rarefaction: referring to sound propagation, sound waves cause air molecules to compress (become compact) and then expand (become less compact); the second half of the cycle of a sound wave

receiver: the component in an amplification system that converts electrical energy into acoustic energy

receptor: sensory nerve endings

reflected: when sound is made softer by bouncing off of surfaces in the environment

refracted: the deflection of a sound wave as it moves from one medium to another

Registery of Interpreters for the Deaf (RID): organization that tests and certifies individuals using sign language in a professional capacity, such as educational, medical, legal, and so on

reinforcement: a form of acoustic enhancement used to augment direct, reflected, or reverberant sound

Reissner's membrane: membrane that separates the scala vestibuli and the cochlear duct

related service: Under the federal IDEIA law, individuals identified as having handicapping conditions are eligible to receive a variety of support services in addition to the basic educational services dictated by the handicapping condition; these additional services are classified as related services.

residual hearing: the hearing that an individual is able to use that is not affected by hearing loss

resource room: a model of educational service delivery that involves small group or individual instruction in a separate classroom designated for children with specifically identified educational needs; children attend only part of their school day in the resource room

retrocochlear pathways: referring to the neural pathways beyond the cochlea, specifically CN VIII and the auditory portions of the brainstem

reverberated: prolongation of a sound due to multiple reflections

round window: located at the basal end of the cochlea at the scala tympani; a membrane that provides pressure release for the fluid traveling through the cochlea; it is also the location through which a cochlear implant electrode array is inserted

saccule: the smaller of the two vestibular sacs

sagittal/median plane: vertical plane that divides a body into right and left parts

scala media: middle of the three canals of the cochlear duct, bordered by the basilar and Reissner's membranes and containing the organ of Corti; also contains endolymph

scala tympani: lowermost of the three canals of the cochlear duct terminating at the helicotrema and the round window; contains perilymph

scala vestibuli: uppermost of the three canals in the cochlear duct terminating at the helicotrema and the oval window; contains perilymph

second formant (F_2): the second frequency region of prominent energy in the acoustic spectrum of speech sounds; provides the most important cues for discrimination of vowel sounds

self-contained classroom: a model of educational delivery in which a student spends the entire day with a special education teacher and special education peers

semicircular canals: three canals in the osseous labyrinth of the vestibular system that respond to angular motion; helps control balance

sensorineural: a type of hearing loss that results from damage to the cochlea

Shrapnell's membrane: pars flaccida portion of the tympanic membrane

sign language: Means of communication for the deaf in which formalized gestures perform the function of words; includes sign, pidgin sign English, and Sign or Manual English

signal-to-noise ratio (S/N or SNR): difference in decibels between a sound of interest to the background noise; you want the signal to be louder than the noise

simple harmonic motion (SHM): continuous, symmetric, periodic back-and-forth movement of an object set into motion

sound booth: a specially designed sound-treated room used for formal diagnostic hearing testing; built to conform to American National Standards Institute (ANSI) standards

sound level meter: an electronic device that measures sound intensity (in sound pressure level and other weighting scales, such as dBA and dBC)

sound pressure level: magnitude or quantity of sound energy relative to a reference pressure

sound propagation: referring to the steps involved in the production of a sound; includes energy source, object, vibration, medium, and receptor

sound waves: energy generated by a vibrating body that causes compressions and rarefactions in a flexible medium

SoundBite™ in-the-mouth aid: a type of amplification device that transmits amplified sound using a biteplate device through the jaw and bones of the head to the cochlea

Soundbridge Vibrating Ossicle Prosthesis system (VORP): a type of amplification device that utilizes a small vibrating mechanism attached to the ossicles, which then transmits sounds to the cochlea; a middle ear implant

speech audiometry: audiological tests that utilize speech signals to determine a person's speech detection, speech reception threshold, and speech recognition skills

speech discrimination score: see "speech recognition score"

speech-in-noise test (SIN): a test where a monosyllabic, phonetically balanced word list is presented to a listener at the same time competing noise is presented in the same ear

speech processor: component of a cochlear implant device that digitizes an incoming speech signal and modifies it based upon a special coding program transforming the speech into electrical impulses that are sent to the electrode array in the cochlea

speech reception threshold: see "speech recognition threshold (SRT)"

speech recognition score: also known as word recognition score or speech discrimination score; measurement obtained from speech recognition testing and expressed in a percentage score

speech recognition testing: referring to the speech test used by an audiologist to determine a listener's ability to perceive and identify a word; also known as speech discrimination or word recognition testing. A carrier phrase of "Say the word___" is used prior to saying a one-syllable, phonetically balanced word, such as *hit* or *pass*. The listener is expected to repeat that word back to the audiologist.

speech recognition threshold (SRT): the lowest intensity level at which 50 percent of spondaic words can be identified during speech reception threshold testing; also known as speech reception threshold

speech-spectrum noise: used as a form of masking noise, this noise contains only the frequencies contained within speech (approximately 500 Hz to 4000 Hz); also known as babble or speech noise

spiral ganglion: cell bodies of the auditory nerve fibers clustered in the modiolus

spondee words: two-syllable words with equal stress on each syllable; used for speech reception threshold testing

stapedectomy: surgical removal of the stapes footplate with a prosthetic replacement; treatment for stapes fixation such as otosclerosis

stapedial footplate: the base of the stapes that fits into the oval window of the cochlea

stapedial muscle/stapedius: along with the tensor tympani, one of two striated muscles of the middle ear; innervated by the facial nerve

stapes: the third bone in the ossicular chain, located medially to the incus; the stirrup-shaped ossicle

stenosis: narrowing in the opening of a canal

stereocilia: the hairlike structures located on top of the outer and inner hair cells within the cochlea

superior: anatomical direction referring to structures that are toward the top or upper surface

suppurative otitis media: inflammation of the middle ear with effusion containing pus

suprasegmental: prosodic (rhythmic) features of language including stress, intonation, duration, and juncture

suprathreshold: an intensity level that is above the threshold level

syndromic hearing loss: a genetically transmitted disorder that has traits in addition to hearing loss

tectorial membrane: membrane within the scala media overlying the organ of Corti where the cilia of the outer hair cells are embedded

telecoil: an induction coil in a hearing aid that allows reception of electromagnetic signals from a telephone or loop amplification system

temporary threshold shift: a reversible hearing loss due to auditory fatigue following excessive exposure to loud noise

tensor tympani: one of two striated muscles in the middle ear

threshold: referring to the lowest intensity level at which a signal is perceived at least 50 percent of the time

tinnitus: a sensation of ringing or other sounds in the ear or head

titer: a measurement of the concentration of a substance in a solution

tragus: landmark in the auricle; small cartilaginous flap on the anterior wall of the external meatus

transdisciplinary collaboration: the act of professionals committing to providing integrated services across several disciplines

transducer: device that converts energy from one form to another, such as electrical energy to sound

transient-evoked otoacoustic emissions: sounds recorded in the external ear canal associated with activation and movements of the outer hair cells in the cochlea in response to stimulation with very brief (transient) auditory stimuli

transliterator: a professional who is trained and certified to translate spoken speech into Cued Speech / Language or vice versa

transverse plane: a slice in the horizontal plane dividing into upper and lower sections

transverse waves: a wave whose medium particles travel in right angles to the wave motion

tunnel of Corti: triangular space formed by the inner and outer walls of the organ of Corti

tympanic membrane: a thin membranous vibrating tissue at the end of the ear canal and forming the wall to the middle ear cavity; also known as eardrum

tympanometry: procedure used in assessing middle ear function where the immittance of the middle ear and tympanic membrane are measured as air pressure delivered to the ear canal is varied

tympanoplasty: reconstructive surgery of a perforation in the tympanic membrane

tympanostomy tube: a small tube inserted into the eardrum in order to keep the middle ear air-filled for a prolonged period of time; also known as a grommet, pressure equalization tube, PE tube, or myringotomy tube. These tubes are used to prevent the accumulation of fluid in the middle ear cavity.

ultrasound: sound with a frequency above the range of human hearing, 20,000 Hz+

umbo: the end of the cone of the tympanic membrane; the location on the tympanic membrane where the tip of the manubrium of the malleus attaches to the medial side of the tympanic membrane

unaided threshold: the softest sound or speech signal that can be heard without the use of a hearing aid

unilateral: on one side only

unilateral hearing loss: hearing loss in one ear only

utricle: the larger of the two vestibular sacs

vestibular nerve: see "eighth cranial nerve"

vestibular system: superior to the cochlea, sharing the same nerve innervation (vestibulocochlear nerve/ CN VIII); helps to control balance

vibrations: oscillation of an object between two points; action that repeats itself and travels in a straight line

visual reinforcement audiometry (VRA): a form of pediatric hearing assessment in which the correct response to an auditory stimulus is reinforced with the activation of a lighted toy contained in a smoked-glass box within the test booth

vocal folds: membranous tissue in the larynx that vibrates when air is pushed through the closed folds, producing a voice

vocal tract: the part of the speech mechanism above the vocal folds that include the pharynx and the oral and nasal cavities

voicing: action of the vocal cords during speech sound production; when the cords vibrate, the sound is voiced

vowels: voiced speech sound that results from air moving through the vocal cavity without friction or stoppage; tongue and lip position dictate the vowel produced

wide dynamic range compression: a form of sound manipulation, designed to deliver signals to the listener that are between the threshold of sensitivity and the discomfort level in a way that matches loudness growth

word recognition score (WRS): see "speech recognition score"

X-linked transmission: genetically transmitted disorders that are associated with the female (X) chromosome

About the Authors

Kate Reynolds, Ph.D., has been the coordinator of the graduate level program in deaf education at the University of New Orleans (UNO) since 2000. She pioneered the use of videoconferencing and other distance learning technologies at UNO and created an online program where students see one another and all classes offer interpreters and real-time captioning. Kate received her undergraduate degree from the University of Maryland with a major in speech and hearing sciences and a minor in dance. She earned her M.Ed. at McDaniel College (formerly Western Maryland College), focusing in deafness and multiple disabilities. After teaching for several years in pre-K–12 and university classrooms, and working as a special education district director, Kate completed her doctorate in special education at the University of Southern Mississippi. Kate presents papers internationally and serves on the executive board of the Association of College Educators–Deaf and Hard of Hearing.

Cynthia McCormick Richburg, Ph.D., is currently a professor at Indiana University of Pennsylvania (IUP) in the Speech-Language Pathology and Audiology Program in the Department of Special Education and Clinical Services. Dr. Richburg has 14 peer-reviewed articles, 3 book chapters, and 47 international and national presentations. She is co-author of the textbook *School-Based Audiology* (Plural Publishing). She was the 2009–2011 editor for the *Journal of Educational Audiology,* and has served 4 years as an associate editor for the journal. She continues to teach, see clients in the IUP clinic, and present on the topic of central auditory processing disorder at state and national conferences.

Diane Heller Klein, Ph.D., earned a degree in Speech and Language Pathology from Ohio University, and degrees in Deaf Education and Special Education with an emphasis in Deafness from the University of Pittsburgh. Dr. Klein is Professor Emeritus of the Indiana University of Pennsylvania (IUP) Deaf Education Program. Retired in 2010, she was the program director for 12 years and coordinated and supervised all student teaching placements for 17 years. Dr. Klein has worked with individuals of all ages who have hearing loss for over 38 years in a variety of capacities. In addition to her work at IUP, for six years Dr. Klein served as an adjunct assistant professor for the University of New Orleans in their online Deaf Education Program.

She is the author of the textbook *Spoken Communication for Students Who Are Deaf or Hard of Hearing: A Multidisciplinary Approach,* 2nd edition. Dr. Klein currently provides consultative services and workshops in the areas of Common Core Standards applications to services for d/hh students, and communication and literacy development for students with cochlear implants in public schools.

Michelle Parfitt, MA, CCC-SLP, LSLS Cert. AVEd, is the Speech and Auditory-Verbal Therapy Coordinator at DePaul School for Hearing and Speech in Pittsburgh, PA. She is a certified Auditory Verbal Educator who has been working as a pediatric speech/language pathologist for more than 20 years. She has presented to numerous professional and parent groups regarding listening and spoken language development strategies for children with hearing loss.

Paul Malbrough, Jr., is a freelance digital illustrator from New Orleans, LA. He graduated from the University of New Orleans with a degree in Fine Arts Studio–Digital Media in 2011, and was voted one of the top 50 young artists in New York during the 2011 Curate NYC competition. Although very different from the album covers and movie posters that Paul usually does, he looks forward to doing more scientific-based illustrations and textbook work in the future.

Index